The Most Popular Search Tools on the Web

Name of Tool	URL
AltaVista	Altavista.digital.com
Excite	www.excite.com
HotBot	www.hotbot.com
Infoseek	www.infoseek.com
LookSmart	www.looksmart.com
Lycos	www.lycos.com
NorthernLight	www.northernlight.com
WebCrawler	www.webcrawler.com
Yahoo!	www.yahoo.com

People-Finding Services on the Web

Name	URL	Description
Switchboard	www.switchboard.com	Contains listings for millions of personal and business phone numbers, as well as mailing addresses. You can also find Web sites and email addresses.
Four11	www.four11.com	This service, which recently merged with Yahoo!, has separate listings for email addresses. Also found here are telephone numbers for individuals, Yellow Page listings, and AT&T toll-free numbers. You can also find links to email and mailing addresses for various celebrities.
Big Foot	www.bigfoot.com	Featuring an Advanced Directory Search, free personal email, and other "feetures," Big Foot is more like a community than a directory.
Internet Address Finder	www.iaf.com	Contains almost 7 million email addresses. Users add their listings to the database. The service is available in five languages other than English.
Who Where	www.whowhere.com	Use this site to find not only people, but apartments, cars, and jobs. Choose whether you want to find an email address or phone number and address.

Great Sources for News on the Web

Site Name	URL	Description
ABC News	abcnews.com	Updated headlines, news, and weather. Local news and audio clips are available.
CBS	www.cbs.com	Enter your zip code to get news, sports scores, and weather presented from your local CBS television affiliate's perspective.
MSNBC	www.msnbc.com	Microsoft and NBC team up to provide you with the latest news. Click the link to Quick News if you're in a hurry.
CNN Interactive	www.cnn.com	The news is broken into categories—such as World, U.S., Local, Showbiz, and Books—making it easy to find what you want to know. You can also view the site in Spanish.
USA Today	www.usatoday.com	The online version of the popular newspaper is easy to read and move through. Click a headline to read the full story.
Wall Street Journal	www.wsj.com	The Wall Street Journal Interactive online packs as much financial clout as its print version. Subscriptions cost around $49 per year, but you can preview the site free of charge for two weeks before you decide to subscribe.
The New York Times	www.thenewyorktimes.com	The New York Times online is free, but you'll need to register first. The online version retains the look of the print version.
Washington Post	www.washingtonpost.com	For what's happening in Washington, the Washington Post can't be beat. Political stories and the paper's Style section are its strong points.
The Times	www.the-times.co.uk	How about the news from a British perspective? You'll find international news at the site, along with the latest cricket scores and standings.

Unusual Sites for Kids

Kid's Site	URL	Description
Berit's Best Sites for Kids	db.cochran.com/li_toc:theoPage.db	This site features links to rated sites with excellent descriptions. Many of the links point to unusual links that you won't see anywhere else.
Yuckiest Site on the Internet	www.nj.com/yucky/index.html	Although this site is actually designed as a resource for science facts, kids forget the site is educational! Meet people who eat cockroaches or who grow worms for fun.
Crayola	www.crayola.com	Visit a virtual museum or color an interactive card. This site changes often to match the season, so check back often.
Just for Kids	scholastic.com/kids/index.htm	Kids can visit the Magic School Bus, a Goosebumps page, or join the Baby Sitters Club at this site designed by Scholastic Magazine.
Sports Illustrated for Kids	pathfinder.com/SIFK	Similar to the magazine of the same name, this site features sports with a kids' slant.
Solaria	www.solariagames.com/	Designed for older children or teens, this site features interactive games. Additionally, you'll find a contests and a chat area.
Teens (sites.com)	www.sites.com/teens/	Links to a variety of sites just for teens, including sites that contain movie reviews, advice on dating, and even a page for new teen drivers.

Great Software Sites

Site Name	URL	Description
Tucows	www.tucows.com	Links to the most popular shareware on the Web.
Download.com	www.download.com	Reviews of programs, along with the most popular software titles. Search for the program you want, or locate it in a category.
File Mine	www.filemine.com	You prospect File Mine for the files you want. You can select multiple files and download them at the same time or download individual files as you see them.
Softseek	www.softseek.com	Organized by categories. Additionally, the newest releases, editor's picks, and top downloads are listed.
Jumbo! The Download Network	www.jumbo.com	With 250,000 titles, you're sure to find the program you want. In addition to downloading software, visit Jumbo to play games or Jumbo Lotto.
SquareOne Technology-Shareware Downloads	www.squareonetech.com/sharware.html	Only a handful of programs are available here. You can download individual programs or purchase a mega-CD-ROM that contains most of the programs for under $40.
Microsoft	www.microsoft.com/msdownload	Free software that can be used with Internet Explorer and other Microsoft products.
Netscape	home.netscape.com/download/su2.html	Software obtained here is designed for use in the Netscape Communicator suite.

Using the Internet

Fourth Edition

Barbara Kasser

A Division of Macmillan Computer Publishing, USA
201 W. 103rd Street
Indianapolis, Indiana 46290

Contents at a Glance

Using the Internet, Fourth Edition

Library of Congress Catalog No.: 97-80935

ISBN: 0-7897-1584-8

00 99 98   6 5 4 3 2

Interpretation of the printing code: the rightmost double-digit number is the year of the book's printing; the rightmost single-digit number, the number of the book's printing. For example, a printing code of 98-1 shows that the first printing of the book occurred in 1998.

Credits

Executive Editor
Karen Reinisch

Acquisitions Editor
Don Essig

Development Editor
Melanie Palaisa

Technical Editor
Bill Bruns

Managing Editor
Thomas F. Hayes

Project Editor
Karen A. Walsh

Copy Editor
Molly Schaller

Indexer
Tim Tate

Production Team
Carol Bowers
Mona Brown
Ayanna Lacey
Gene Redding

Graphics Image Specialists
Sadie Crawford
Wil Cruz

Cover Designers
Dan Armstrong
Ruth Harvey

Book Designers
Nathan Clement
Ruth Harvey

Contents

About the Author

Barbara Kasser is a computer/Internet trainer, a "self-proclaimed Internet junkie." She has taught people how to use computers for 20 years, and currently teaches weekend Internet classes. Barbara has written training manuals on exploring the Internet and the World Wide Web, searching on the Internet, electronic mail, newsgroups, Internet conferencing, and creating Web sites. Barbara authored *Netscape Navigator 4.0, Browsing and Beyond*, and co-authored *Internet Explorer 4.0, One Step at a Time*.

About the Technical Editor

Bill Bruns is the Manager of System Services for the College of Medicine at the University of Illinois. He originally wanted to work in television production, but got interested in computers while working on an undergraduate internship at *Square One TV*, a children's mathematics show produced by the Children's Television Workshop. Bill has been a technical editor for Que for almost three years and has worked on such titles as *Platinum HTML 4, Java 1.1 and Javascript 1.2, Running a Perfect Netscape Site*, several editions of *Using the Internet*, and several editions of *Special Edition Using the Internet*. Previously, he has built and operated networks and information systems departments at the University of Illinois' Illini Student Union and at New York University's Tisch School of the Arts. Bill holds bachelor degrees in Telecommunications and English Literature from Indiana University, a Masters of Public Administration from New York University. He is also a Certified Netware Engineer. You can find him on the web at http://www.staff.uiuc.edu/~bruns1 or via email at bruns1@prairienet.org.

Dedication

To Bill Kasser, my husband, who endured bad dinners and lonely nights and weekends while I worked on the book. Bill, thanks for your love and support. Without them, I could never write a single word.

Acknowledgments

So many people work tirelessly behind the scenes at Macmillan to create a finished product. I have been blessed with the best of teams and I thank each and every one of the people who worked on the project. My deepest gratitude to Melanie Palaisa, quite possibly the best Development Editor in the world, who oversaw each chapter with humor, patience, and grace. Special thanks to Don Essig, Karen Walsh and Molly Schaller for their efforts. Also, thanks to Bill Bruns, the technical editor, for doing a bang-up job and making me laugh.

My friends deserve a big hug too. My appreciation to David Fugate of Waterside Productions. To Bea Ensign and Leslye Webb, my loyal readers and helpers, thanks for everything. To Ken Shenkman, my pal and fellow Internet junkie, who stayed on the phone with me in the middle of the night, created special sites and helped out in so many other ways, I say thank you from the bottom of my heart.

Finally, to each and every person who has worked to put a site out there on the Web, my heartfelt gratitude. You make the Web the wondrous place it is for all of us.

We'd Like to Hear from You!

Que Corporation has a long-standing reputation for high-quality books and products. To ensure your continued satisfaction, we also understand the importance of customer service and support.

Orders, Catalogs, and Customer Service

To order other Que or Macmillan Computer Publishing books, catalogs, or products, please contact our Customer Service Department:

Phone: 1-800-428-5331
Fax: 1-800-835-3202
International Fax: 1-317-228-4400
Or visit our online bookstore: http://www.mcp.com/

Introduction

Who Should Read This Book?

Anyone who wants to learn more about the Internet should grab a copy of *Using the Internet, Fourth Edition* and read it straight through! Seriously, the book is designed for anyone who wants to know more about that vast cyber-wonderland called the Internet. If you're a seasoned Internet user, you'll find clear, concise explanations of things with which you might have already worked. If you're tired of feeling left out because everyone's talking about or using the Internet, you'll discover all the information you need to get started in this book. Internet veteran or novice, you'll find exactly what you need to take control of your Internet sessions and make the Internet work to your advantage.

You should be a Windows 95, NT, or 98 user who is familiar with simple Windows concepts, such as dialog boxes and menus, and how to work with your mouse. You should also have a basic understanding of how the files and folders are arranged inside your computer.

If you haven't signed up with an Internet Service Provider yet, you'll be able to select one that's right for you based on the information that's provided. If you don't have the programs you need to work with the Internet, or you're using an older version of Internet Explorer or Netscape Navigator, you'll learn how to download and install the latest and greatest versions of the software.

What Makes This Book Different?

With so many books available about the Internet, why should you select *Using the Internet, Fourth Edition*? Well, for one thing, this book speaks to you. I understand your excitement at being part of the Internet community, your concerns about security, and your fears that the whole thing will be over your head. I wrote this book to get you up and running on the Internet as quickly as possible.

As a software trainer, I understand both Internet Explorer and Netscape Communicator and know how to help my students learn to use each program to its fullest capacity. Both software products are tools to help you accomplish your Internet objectives—such as looking at pages on the World Wide Web, sending and receiving email, and communicating in real-time. In addition to explanations about Internet concepts, I've also included step-by-step instructions for both Internet Explorer and Netscape Communicator. No matter which program you're using, you'll find the steps you need to get the job done.

Also included in this book are listings of Web sites that pertain to the topic that's being discussed. I've done lots of research to find Web sites that you might like to visit or that illustrate a particular section in the book. The lists generally include site titles, Web addresses (URLs), and descriptions. That way, when you read about a topic, you can visit a related site immediately. Use the listed sites as the starting point of your Web experience.

Everyone has different reasons for using the Internet. Some people use it for research and others to have fun. Many businesses use the Internet as a way to transact business and communicate with customers and employees. The beauty of the Internet is that it provides so much information and so many opportunities for communication.

My job is to tell you about many of these opportunities and show you the fastest way to take advantage of them. I take that job seriously. When you're finished reading this book, I want you to be able to take control of the Internet. Most of all, I want you to love using the Internet as much as I do.

How to Use This Book

You can start at page 1 and read straight through. You can also page through the Table of Contents to find the topic for which you're looking. You'll find the information you need whichever method you choose.

Although you don't need to start with the first chapter, each chapter is designed to build on the knowledge you gained in previous chapters. If you're an Internet "newbie," begin with Chapter 1 and work through each successive chapter.

The step-by-step exercises in the book walk you through exactly what you need to know to accomplish a task. I'll tell you if you need to be connected to the Internet to perform the steps. I'll also let you know if you need anything else, such as a pad and paper to jot down a Web address.

When you're finished with the book, don't tuck it away on a shelf. Instead, keep it handy so that you can refer to it whenever you need a little help. Of course, you can use the book as a directory to many Web sites.

How This Book Is Organized

I've broken down the book into seven parts that are designed to give you the most knowledge in the shortest time.

Part I: Internet Basics

This is the place to learn what the Internet is, who owns the Internet, and who makes the rules. You'll find a section about how to get connected, with lots of advice to help you choose the service that's right for you. Information about commercial service providers, such as America Online, CompuServe and Prodigy, is contained in this section. You'll also learn about the most popular browsers, Microsoft Internet Explorer and Netscape Navigator. When your browser is set up, you'll take a brief trip out onto the World Wide Web.

Part II: Taking Control of the Internet

Now that you've gotten a basic understanding of the Internet, it's time to learn how to navigate through Web pages. You'll learn about Web addresses, called URLs, and how to move from page to page. You'll jump to new pages with hyperlinks and learn what to do if a link doesn't work. You'll also learn how to search for the Web documents you want to find with site directories and search engines. Because setting up effective queries is the best way to find specific documents, you'll get lots of tips to help you design your queries. The Internet is a great place to obtain new software for your computer; you'll learn how to download and install new programs. You'll also learn where to go to get new software.

Part III: Contacting the World with Email and Newsgroups

Reach out to the world through the Internet. You'll learn how to set up your browser's mail program to send and receive email. You'll find out how to create messages to one person or to a group. If you want to attach files from your computer to an outgoing mail message or tackle the files you receive from someone else, you'll learn how in Part III. Because filing your messages in your own filing system helps you to keep track of your mail, you'll learn how to manage your mail with folders. If you want to use a third-party mail program, such as Juno or Eudora Light, I'll show you how. After you're a mail ace, you'll enter the world of newsgroups. You'll learn how to participate in newsgroup discussions and learn some netiquette (newsgroup manners.)

Part IV: Turning to the Internet for Information

Harness the information on the Internet to your own computer. You'll explore several places to obtain information. You'll find sites for all ages—toddlers through teens. Additionally, you'll learn how to implement measures to keep your kids safe. This part explores the various options on the Internet available for research. Whether you're writing a research paper, a thesis, or just need to find out information, you'll discover how to use the World Wide Web as an educational resource. If you're looking for a new job, you'll learn how the Internet can play a role in changing careers. You'll also create an electronic résumé and visit a few job banks. Shopping on the Web is fun and easy. You'll find links to the best cybermalls. If you find something you want to buy, you'll learn how to make sure your purchases are secure. Finally, you'll discover the best news sources on the Web. You'll learn how to have the latest information automatically transferred to your computer so that you can view it when you're not connected to the Internet.

Part V: Communicating in Real-time

In this part, you'll discover the excitement of using the Internet for real-time communication. You'll learn how to use your browser to visit a chat site on the Web. You'll also learn how to use Microsoft Chat to talk to your friends and colleagues. If your computer is equipped with a sound card, speakers, and a microphone, you'll learn how to participate in a conference—the Internet equivalent of a long-distance call but without the expensive long-distance charges.

Part VI: Putting Yourself on the Internet

After you've learned what the Internet offers, it's time to put your own information out there for the world to see. You'll learn to create some dynamite-looking Web pages without knowing HTML, the language in which pages are written. If you're a small-business owner, you'll learn how to post your company's Web site to the Web. You'll also learn how to create a virtual office on the Web. If you're concerned about your company's important data, you'll learn how to use the Internet to back up the files and protect them.

Part VII: Glossary and Appendixes

Using the Internet, Fourth Edition contains a glossary and three appendixes. Use the Glossary to find words that are highlighted in the chapters. Appendix A, "Background Information About the Internet," gives you an in-depth look at the origins of the Internet and the World Wide Web. Appendix B, "Employer Sites from A to Z," provides a listing of some of the Web's best sources for employment. Appendix C, "Shopper's Guide," is a shopper's delight on the Web. From familiar merchants such as Eddie Bauer to unusual ones such as NetGrocer, you're sure to find the products for which you're looking.

Special Book Elements

Throughout *Using the Internet, Fourth Edition* you'll find special elements designed to help you find information quickly.

- *Menu and dialog box commands and options.* You can easily find the onscreen menu and dialog box commands by looking for bold text like you see in this direction: Open the **File** menu and click **Save**.
- *Hotkeys for commands.* The underlined keys onscreen that activate commands and options are also underlined in the book as shown in the previous example.

- *Combination and shortcut keystrokes.* Text that directs you to hold down several keys simultaneously is connected with a plus sign (+), such as Ctrl+P.

- *Graphical icons with the commands they execute.* Look for icons like this in text and steps. These indicate buttons onscreen that you can click to accomplish the procedure.

- *Cross references.* If there's a related topic that is prerequisite to the section or steps you are reading, or a topic that builds further on what you are reading, you'll find the cross reference to it after the steps or at the end of the section like this:

SEE ALSO

➤ *You'll find information on Java applets on page 19.*

- *Glossary terms.* For all the terms that appear in the glossary, you'll find the first appearance of that term in the text in *italic* along with its definition.

- *Sidebars.* Information related to the task at hand, or "inside" information from the author is offset in sidebars as not to interfere with the task at hand and to make it easy to find this valuable information. Each of these sidebars has a short title to help you quickly identify the information you'll find there. You'll find the same kind of information in these that you might find in notes, tips, or warnings in other books but here, the titles should be more informative.

From Here

You're ready to begin your journey onto the Internet. Be prepared for a wonderful experience. The Internet's blend of information, communication tools, and fun stuff ensures there's something for everyone. Have a great time!

Internet Basics

What Is the Internet?

The Internet is the name given to a vast and wonderful system that connects people and information through computers. By using the Internet, you can look up information on any subject you might imagine or send and receive messages through email. If you have a hobby, favorite television show, or special interest, you can join a newsgroup and share your views with common-minded people. One of the newest advances enables you to participate in a real-time conversation across the Internet—without incurring a penny in long distance charges. Even more exciting advances are waiting on the horizon.

The best way to approach the Internet is to choose something you want to find. Chances are, whatever you want to find is out there. Airline prices, current events, career information, recipes, and menus all vie for your attention. One of the hardest decisions you'll need to make on the Internet is when to stop your journey. Even the shortest visit can turn into an hours-long trip.

Most people connect to the Internet from their homes or offices. Many public libraries and universities offer Internet access—sometimes free of charge. Traditionally, you have needed a computer and a telephone line to access the Internet. However, the newest technology enables you to use your television set to get connected. After you are connected, you can switch back and forth between your favorite television show and the Internet.

The most exciting aspect of today's Internet is the empowerment it offers. Knowledge is power. By finding information about topics that you feel are important, you gain the upper hand in many situations. Here are a few examples:

My good friend's 10-year-old daughter, Roxanne, suffers from epilepsy. Last year, her doctors agreed that Roxanne would grow out of it and provided little support for the family. When it seemed like Roxanne's condition was growing worse, my friend, Virginia, logged on to the Internet. Within a few days, Virginia discovered an online support group for parents of epileptic children. She found pages and pages of medical information. Best of all, she discovered information about a doctor who had successfully treated cases that sounded like Roxanne's. Virginia sent the doctor an email message and received an answer the next day. Although the doctor was located on the other side of the world, he sent Virginia a list of his colleagues in the United States. Roxanne got a new doctor, and her condition improved dramatically. The Internet played a major role in helping a young girl live a normal, happy life.

Rob, another friend of mine, lost his job when the company where he had worked for 15 years went through a downsizing phase. Rob was shattered. He had kids in college and a mortgage. Unemployment hadn't been part of his plans. After exhausting all the usual job search techniques, Rob concentrated on finding a job through the Internet. User groups pointed him to the best Internet job listings. Rob found a listing that matched his qualifications and sent a message to the prospective employer. In a short time he was asked to first email his résumé, and then email a list of references. The next day a message appeared in Rob's email Inbox, asking when he would be available for an interview. Happily, Rob got the job, and the Internet scored another success.

Today's Internet enables people from all over the world to share ideas and knowledge. The Internet has established itself as a permanent member of our society and economy. It won't take long for you to make the Internet part of your daily life!

SEE ALSO

➤ *You can find more information about WebTV on page 43. WebTV Combines the Internet and Your Television.*

➤ *If you're interested in making a career or job change, see page 285.*

Who Owns the Internet?

No one owns the Internet.

Even the provider that you or your company pays for access doesn't own the Internet. Instead, the access provider functions like a gatekeeper—they let you in, and then let you out. However, the access providers don't own the road you use to get there.

Your local phone company owns the telephone lines you use to connect to the Internet. The regional Bell operating companies and long-distance carriers own the leased lines that connect most of the network. These phone lines are tied into several high-speed links, each called a backbone. Major communications companies—most notably, Sprint—own or rent the backbone links.

The Internet is simply too big to be owned by a single person or a conglomerate. Whether you're part of a company who owns the equipment or a user who posts a page to the World Wide Web, you're a partial owner of the Internet.

A few years ago, the phrase "Information Superhighway" could be heard everywhere. The Information Superhighway is considered the Internet backbone because it's responsible for transporting masses of data back and forth across long distances by way of fiber-optic cable that criss-crosses countries around the globe.

Seven major companies are involved in the backbone business. They range from Bolt, Beranek, & Newman (BBN), one of the original architects of the old ARPA network, to Apex Global Information Services (AGIS), which was founded in 1994 to provide Internet-related services. America Online (AOL) owns Advanced Network Services (ANS), which operates more than 12,000 miles of fiber-optic pathways. Sprint and MCI both operate major portions of the fiber-optic cable. UUNet Technologies, now owned by MFS Communications, manages the largest number of national and international connections. Finally, PSINet leases lines from a number of regional telephone companies, but purchases all their own routing and switching gear.

You're probably wondering who runs the Internet. Read on.

Who Makes the Rules?

Just like Internet ownership, you won't find a specific group or person who governs the Internet. This lack of rules and regulations makes the Internet more interesting, but occasionally results in strange or unusual content. Right now, what appears on the Internet is determined by the person who puts it there. So, valuable information co-exists with pornography and instructions (usually bogus) on how to build a bomb. Fortunately, you can spend your whole life on the Internet and never encounter items you feel are objectionable or in bad taste.

Although no board of directors or fat-cat bosses make the rules, several organizations share Internet administration responsibilities.

The Internet Society

The *Internet Society* (*ISOC*), located in Reston, Virginia is a non-profit, non-governmental organization that brings users of the Internet community together. During its conferences and meetings, the ISOC attempts to address the issues of how to generate progress and growth for the Internet. The ISOC currently has more than 7,000 individual members from more than 150 countries and more than 100 organizational members. In fact, the membership list reads like a who's who of the Internet community.

Internet Engineering Task Force

The Internet Engineering Task Force, or IETF, is the main standards organization for the Internet. The IETF is an open, large international community of network designers, operators, vendors, and researchers concerned with the evolution of the Internet architecture and the continued smooth operation of the Internet. Involvement in the IETF is available to any interested individual.

Internet Architecture Board

The IAB, short for *Internet Architecture Board*, is an important arm of the IETF and is responsible for setting and overseeing Internet technical standards. These standards are important to you, other Internet users, and me because they enable the combination of products from different manufacturers to create one customized system. Without standards, Internet users from all over the world would have a hard time accessing and using the Internet.

SEE ALSO

➤ *Learn more about Internet domain names on page 91.*

Council of Registrars

CORE oversees the registrars of Internet domain names. On November 4, 1997, CORE signed a contract with Emergent Corporation to build and operate a new Internet Domain Name Shared Registry Systems (SRS). CORE works closely with the InterNIC.

InterNIC

The *InterNIC*, shortened from Network Information Center, is a collaborative project between AT&T and Network Solutions, Inc. (NSI) and is supported by the National Science Foundation. InterNIC provides these important services:

- *Registration Services*. Domain name and IP addressing assignment.
- *Support Services*. Outreach, education, and information services for the Internet community.
- *Net Scout Services*. Online publications that summarize recent happenings of interest to Internet users.

Who Pays for the Internet?

Remember the old song that went something like, "The music goes round and round...?" Well, understanding who pays for the Internet is something like understanding the song. The National Science Foundation currently subsidizes a portion of the costs. The users, such as you or your company, pay Internet Service Providers (ISPs) or Commercial Online Services like America Online or CompuServe for Internet access. In turn, these providers pay inter-network providers for connection to their servers.

Although commercialization is relatively new, advertisers pay a huge chunk of money to support the Internet. Their money pays for better equipment and lines. Like television, the fees that advertisers pay to hawk their products across the Internet underwrite many of the costs that you would have to pay otherwise. Of course, the flip side of Internet commercialization is that you're barraged with non-stop advertising at many Web sites.

Who Uses the Internet?

It seems like everyone uses the Internet these days. Actually, Internet users come from every age and income bracket. Users connect from home, school, and work. Ask your friends and colleagues if they've used the Internet. You'll probably be surprised at how many people you know are happily using the Internet right now.

The Internet is the fastest growing market in the world. Although it's hard to get an exact count, it's safe to say that 30-40 million users currently exist, and about 1 million new users are added each month. More than 95,000 companies are currently conducting business on the Internet. At least 73 new Web sites are added to the World Wide Web, a portion of the Internet, each day.

What Can You Do on the Internet?

For starters, the first thing you can expect to find on the Internet is information. In fact, information is still the Internet's main product. Information is available in many formats. Most of the information you see is contained on the World Wide Web, although it still can be obtained from other, older sources traditionally used for educational purposes.

The type of information you find is largely dependent on what you're looking for. If you're a student and need to do research on a topic, the Internet is a great place to start. If you're using the Internet to track your investments and investigate new financial opportunities, you're at the right place. Want to buy a new

Patronize Internet merchants

Think about supporting Internet advertisers by buying their products. At the least, take the time to view some of the ads you come across. The ads are usually entertaining and informative, and help to defray some of the costs that you would have to pay otherwise.

computer or appliance? How about finding the phone number of an old friend whom you haven't seen in years? You could find recipes for leftover turkey or low-fat fried chicken. Want to read your hometown newspaper right from your computer? All these, and more, await you on the Internet.

Second only to information are the opportunities for communication provided by the Internet. Electronic mail—or email, for short—offers you the opportunity to exchange messages with people all over the world. You can attach computer files, like letters and memos, to messages that you send. If you'd like to find a group of people who share your interests, you can join a newsgroup. Messages posted to a newsgroup, unlike email, are posted to an electronic bulletin board so that all the users can read and reply.

If you prefer communication in real-time, you can visit a Chat server. Even though the discussion in chat rooms is textual—you need to type your comments and then send them—the conversation moves along so quickly that you can easily forget that you're typing. (My sister likened it to watching a foreign movie with subtitles.) And of course, if your computer is equipped with a sound card and a microphone, you can engage in a long-distance conversation with anyone, anywhere, without paying a penny in long-distance charges.

After you've become comfortable with the Internet, you might decide to create your own presence by creating a page that will be placed on the World Wide Web. You can design your page to display photos and other graphic images about you, your family, and your interests, or you can just use unadorned text. You can add sounds, music and, of course, links to other Web sites you like.

The page you design can be fun or it can serve an important purpose. Grade school classes are creating their own Web pages. This year, instead of a traditional birthday gift, my son is giving his friends their own Web pages. On a more serious side, many people are putting résumés and other job-search related material on the Web.

Pages on the Internet are designed in a special language called *Hypertext Markup Language*, or *HTML*. Just a few years ago, you needed to know HTML if you wanted to create content for the Web. Now, however, many programs enable you to type text and drag and drop images while the programs create the underlying code for you. Using one of these programs, you can create an exciting Web page without knowing a drop of HTML.

The Internet is so vast and its options are so varied that before long you'll wonder how you ever lived without it. In fact, you'll find yourself preaching information about the Internet to your friends. Just wait!

SEE ALSO

➤ *Learn more about how to create Web pages on page 409.*

➤ *Learn how to create a resume with Netscape Composer on page 421.*

Putting Your Business on the Internet

If you are the owner or operator of a small business, have you considered putting your business on the Internet? Whether you have a product to sell or want to be able to communicate with your employees who are scattered in several locations, the Internet is a great way to get quick results.

A Web site for your company instantly makes your business a global presence. Your page is accessible to anyone who's using the Internet anywhere in the world. International exposure, which used to cost thousands of dollars, is yours at a very small price.

You can use the Internet to tell people about your company and what it has to offer. With one page or a collection of linked pages, you can show your company's hours, product line, location, and contact information. You can even use your site to offer other information or advice. For example, one janitorial supply company with which I work includes floor care tips on their site.

If you are selling a product, think about selling it over the Internet. People can visit your site and order your product. With a minimal investment on your part, you can reap the benefits of having a global business that never closes. If you're concerned about security issues for your customers, you can take steps to make your site more secure.

Setting up an Intranet is another way to use the Internet for your small business. An Intranet is a site to which only your employees have access. An Intranet is beneficial to companies that have employees in many different locations. The site can work as an employee bulletin board. You can post memos, letters, spreadsheets, or other pertinent facts your employees need to see.

SEE ALSO

➤ *Learn about setting up a small business on the Web on page 437.*

➤ *Learn about intranets on page 45.*

Looking at Standard Internet Components

Fortunately, the Internet is broken into distinct segments to help you get around. One segment, the World Wide Web, is the fastest growing area on the Internet. Your tour of the Web involves visiting Web sites. (Touring the Web is sometimes called "surfing.") Email and newsgroups are other commonly used Internet factions.

The World Wide Web

The World Wide Web is where you'll spend much of your Internet time. (The Web is the nickname most people use for the World Wide Web.) The Web is one of the newest and most popular Internet services. Prior to the development of the Web, you had to type a series of complicated commands to navigate through the maze of information on the Internet. If you didn't know what you were looking for, it was very easy to get lost or hung up.

Clients and servers make it work

At this point, you're probably wondering how the Internet works. What element enables all the computers, not to mention the thousands of miles of telephone cabling, to work together to bring you the Internet? The answer is simple—clients and servers.

Servers are the programs that provide resources. Clients, on the other hand, are the programs that you use on your computer to tap into the resources. The purpose of the computers, cabling, and all the other equipment is to let the servers and clients talk among each other.

The Web was developed by CERN (the European Laboratory for Particle Physics) to enable anyone to access and view documents that were stored on servers anywhere on the Internet. Although the World Wide Web originated as a program for use by only CERN researchers, its appeal quickly overwhelmed the Internet community. Special client applications, called browsers, were developed to take advantage of the Web's amazing capabilities.

Web sites are the pages you visit as you travel around on the World Wide Web. Every Web site consists of one or more documents, called pages. A *home page* is the first page of a Web site that serves as a cover or index by introducing and organizing the material at the site. Even if a site has only one page, the first page is called the home page. Figure 1.1 shows the home page for Macmillan Computer Publishing.

They mean the Web

When people talk about looking at sites on the Internet, most of the time they're talking about the World Wide Web.

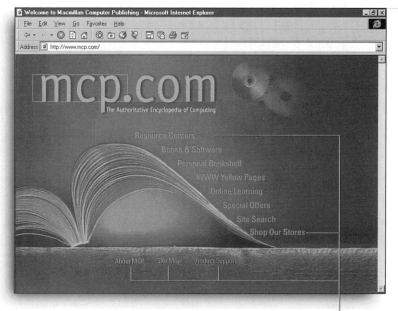

FIGURE 1.1

The Macmillan home page has links to other pages.

1 Click one of the links to move to another page

Pages on the World Wide Web are different from the pages you find in books. For one thing, a Web page doesn't have a set page size and can be short or long. When you print one Web page, you could end up with several sheets of printed material. Also, instead of page numbers, every page on the Web has its own address, called a *URL* (pronouned either *U-R-L* or *earl*).

The Web pages you visit might be simple, with only a few lines of text, or they can be elaborate documents, filled with colors, different typefaces, and graphic images. Some of the images might move or change when you pass your mouse over them. In addition, Web pages can contain sound and other multimedia effects. Some pages are so well-designed that they look like something out of a Hollywood studio.

Although looking at a visual feast is exciting, what makes Web pages so special is their capability to contain *hyperlinks*. A hyperlink is a link to another page or location on the Web. Either text or graphics can be set up as a hyperlink. When you click the link with your mouse, you're whisked to another related site that might actually be located on a server halfway around the world. By using hyperlinks, you can move quickly from site to site.

The value of hyperlinks can't be overstated. For example, let's say you go to your local public library to do some research for a science project. After you get the volumes you need and start making notes, the book refers you to another book for more information. Now you have to find the other book (hopefully, it's there in the library) and find the page that's referenced in the first book. And, of course, the second book refers you to a third book and the whole process starts again. Hyperlinks bypass most of this painful process. When you click a hyperlink, you're moved to the new site in a few seconds. If the new page contains links to other related sites, you can click these links to move rapidly through the material.

SEE ALSO

➤ *Learn about URLs on page 90.*

➤ *Learn to travel through the World Wide Web with hyperlinks on page 83.*

Viewing Internet Channels

Channels represent the latest and greatest advance on the Internet. Channels enable you to view up-to-the-moment information that's moved to your computer. Many companies now feature channels as part of the Internet service they offer. So many channels are available that you can choose the one you want from one of many categories (see Figure 1.2). What can you expect when you view a channel? The best way to describe it is a cross between a television show and a Web page.

FIGURE 1.2

The Microsoft Channel Guide has several categories from which to choose.

Many channels enable you to specify when you want the channel information transferred to your computer. For example, you can schedule a news delivery for first thing in the morning. Some programs that use channels can actually dial the content provider and obtain the desired information, even if you're not connected to the Internet.

The technology that enables information to be delivered to your computer at pre-selected times is called *push technology*. *Webcasters*, also called push applications, deliver the information you select to your computer. By using channels that provide streams of information from Web sources, Webcasting programs send headlines or complete articles directly to your computer. After the text copies to your computer, you can view the channel content whenever you want.

Push technology employs cutting-edge techniques and is rapidly becoming an important way to provide news and other information. Currently, rival companies have different formats for their channels. However, Microsoft developed a standard called Channel Definition Format, or CDF for short. CDF promises to standardize the way channel content is delivered. In the next few years, expect to see hundreds, or maybe even thousands, of new push channels.

SEE ALSO

➤ *For a more in-depth look at Internet channels, see page 333.*

Electronic Mail (Email)

Email is everywhere! You might already have an email address at work or at school. If you already have Internet access, you probably have an email address from your provider. It's funny to think that email was invented as a diversion for the original users of the ARPAnet. Now, instead of a diversion, email plays an important part in how you communicate.

The mechanics of email are similar to sending regular mail, called "snail mail." You type a message using your email client (see Figure 1.3) and then post the message in your Outbox. The message is then transmitted across the Internet by means of various gateways and ends up in the addressee's Inbox. If the addressee is unavailable when the message is delivered, the message remains as an unopened piece of mail until it has been read. Because email follows a standard format, it doesn't matter if you and the addressee are using the same mail client program.

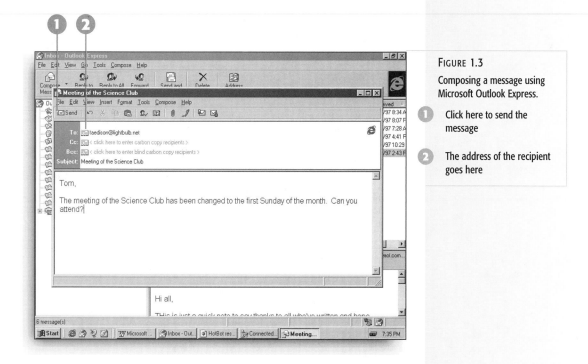

FIGURE 1.3

Composing a message using Microsoft Outlook Express.

1 Click here to send the message

2 The address of the recipient goes here

The major differences between email and snail mail are obvious. For one, you don't need to turn over couch cushions looking for a stamp before you can send your email. The second difference is even more exciting—email is usually delivered in a matter of minutes, rather than days. This means that you can exchange several messages over the course of a day without racking up postage charges.

Email is rapidly becoming a business standard. Because you can attach computer files to the messages you send, email is an excellent way to share information with your business associates and colleagues. However, such rapid delivery also has a down side. Because email deliveries generally take minutes, the turnaround time on a project speeds up. (When I was writing this book, I'd submit my manuscript files in the morning and have corrections back by lunchtime!)

Although email is a great business tool, it can also be used for more pedestrian reasons. My family is scattered all over the world, but we regularly keep in touch via email. Friends who hadn't spoken for years are now exchanging family gossip by email.

Newsgroups

Internet newsgroups conduct online discussion on just about any topic you can imagine. These discussions work like the bulletin boards that you see at the supermarket or the library—someone posts a message or question and then anyone who wants to posts a comment or reply below the original message (see Figure 1.4). The original message is called a *thread*.

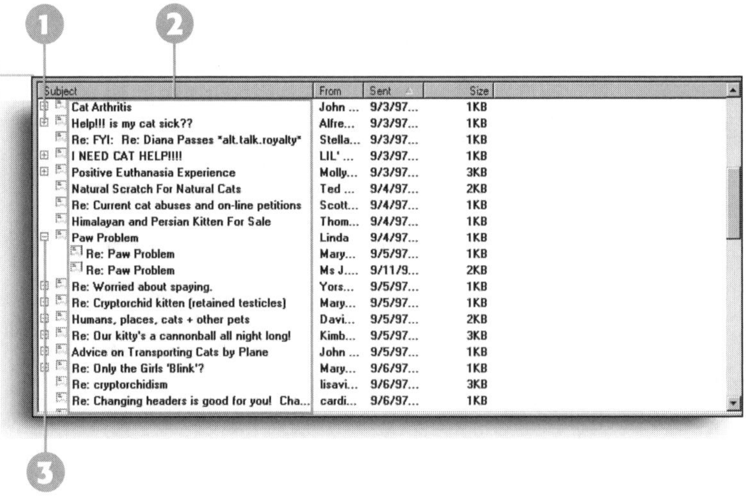

FIGURE 1.4

Messages have been posted to a newsgroup about cats.

1 The plus sign indicates that more messages pertaining to this subject have been posted but are not currently displayed

2 Message headers (subjects) are shown here

3 The minus sign indicates that additional messages pertaining to the original subject are visible

Subject	From	Sent	Size
Cat Arthritis	John ...	9/3/97...	1KB
Help!!! is my cat sick??	Alfre...	9/3/97...	1KB
Re: FYI: Re: Diana Passes "alt.talk.royalty"	Stella...	9/3/97...	1KB
I NEED CAT HELP!!!!	LIL' ...	9/3/97...	1KB
Positive Euthanasia Experience	Molly...	9/3/97...	3KB
Natural Scratch For Natural Cats	Ted ...	9/4/97...	2KB
Re: Current cat abuses and on-line petitions	Scott...	9/4/97...	1KB
Himalayan and Persian Kitten For Sale	Thom...	9/4/97...	1KB
Paw Problem	Linda	9/4/97...	1KB
Re: Paw Problem	Mary...	9/5/97...	1KB
Re: Paw Problem	Ms J...	9/11/9...	2KB
Re: Worried about spaying.	Yors...	9/5/97...	1KB
Re: Cryptorchid kitten (retained testicles)	Mary...	9/5/97...	1KB
Humans, places, cats + other pets	Davi...	9/5/97...	2KB
Re: Our kitty's a cannonball all night long!	Kimb...	9/5/97...	3KB
Advice on Transporting Cats by Plane	John ...	9/5/97...	1KB
Re: Only the Girls 'Blink'?	Mary...	9/5/97...	3KB
Re: cryptorchidism	lisavi...	9/6/97...	3KB
Re: Changing headers is good for you! Cha...	cardi...	9/6/97...	1KB

Most of the Internet newsgroups are part of a network called Usenet (short for User's Network). More than 30,000 Usenet groups exist on the Internet. Your Internet provider may have its own groups as well. Additionally, you might be able to participate in regional discussions or discussions that concern only employees of your company or students at your school.

Internet discussions can be moderated or unmoderated. Moderated discussions are usually more serious because the moderator has the right to refuse to post any message that doesn't conform to the rules of the group. Unmoderated discussions often get heated and exciting.

Online discussions are very popular. A discussion group that talks about a popular Tuesday-night police show receives almost 300 postings every day. You can follow the postings of the groups that interest you without ever posting your own comments, or you can become an active participant.

Because newsgroup postings look and act very similar to email messages, your news client (the program you use to view newsgroups) might be integrated into your email program.

SEE ALSO

➤ *Learn all about newsgroups on page 219.*

How About Some Java?

If you've read any recent computer publications, you've probably come across the term "Java" once or twice. If you're wondering what Java does, you're among the majority of Internet users. It seems that everyone's heard of Java, but few people know what it's used for.

Actually, Java is a programming platform invented by the folks at Sun Microsystems. A platform is the base on which software program designers can build computer applications. By using Java, developers can design programs, like word processing or spreadsheet applications, that will run on any computer running just about any operating system. For example, if you're running Windows 95 and your neighbor uses a Mac, you each have to use very different programs to create a memo that looks the same. Theoretically, one word processing program based on Java would be able to run on both computers.

When Java is added to Web pages, the results can be both entertaining and business-oriented. If you visit a Web page with a scrolling stock ticker or a twisting clock, chances are good that Java is working behind the scenes. Java can also be used to create sophisticated online ordering systems. (My husband's company is implementing a Java-based order system on a Web page. The customer fills out an online order form, and a Java program contacts the warehouse, sets up shipping, and makes the appropriate entries to the accounts receivable system.)

Simple forms of Java programming, called Java applets, are springing up everywhere on the Web. A Java applet can change the color of a button or add text to the bottom of the screen when your mouse passes over a pre-set trigger. Java applets can play music or add flashing, psychedelic effects to a page.

The best information about Java is that you don't have to do anything to get it! If you're using one of the newest versions of your Web browser, the Java programming that's built into the page will be apparent to you. Sit back and enjoy it.

Getting Connected

Now that you've gotten a feel for what the Internet is all about, you're ready to get connected. How do you do it? What hardware do you need? Relax! When you're done with this chapter, you'll know everything you need to connect to the Internet and begin your journey.

Basic Equipment You Need

First off, you need a computer to connect to the Internet. Minimum system requirements generally state that a computer has a 486/DX processor with 8 megabytes of Random Access Memory (RAM). Your monitor should support VGA (Video Graphics Array) or SuperVGA. If you're connecting to the Internet through a phone line, you need a modem. (You learn all about modems later in this chapter). The information in this book assumes you're running one of the later versions of Windows—95 or NT.

Your computer also needs several megabytes of free space to install helper applications and the plug-ins needed to bring you movies, graphics, and sounds. Although neither are mandatory, a sound card and speakers help you to take advantage of the sound effects and music added to many Internet sites. You also need a mouse or other pointing device.

Keep in mind that the minimum requirements are exactly that— the barebones minimum you need to get connected. If you have a faster processor, preferably a Pentium or higher, and more RAM, your computer will provide a smoother ride to the Internet. If you have an older computer and plan to spend a lot of time on the Internet, think seriously about upgrading your hardware. After all, would you want to drive the Autobahn in an old Model A Ford?

Modems Make It Happen

After you determine that your computer has the horsepower to take you to the Internet, you need to consider your modem. Unless you're connecting to the Internet from your office or school network, your modem is a key player in getting you connected.

Why is it so important? Your *modem*, an acronym for MOdulator-DEModulator, is a device that your computer needs to connect to other computers through the phone lines. Your modem performs two important functions:

- Converts your outgoing computer data into digital signals which can be transmitted via a phone line
- Transforms incoming analog signals into their digital equivalents so they can be read by your computer

Inside or Outside?

Modems come in two "flavors"—external or internal. Internal modems are built on a card that plugs into a PCI or ISA expansion slot and uses one of your serial ports to communicate with the computer. (Don't worry if you're not sure what these technical terms mean; an internal modem is already connected when you buy the computer.) Because an internal modem is part of your computer, it utilizes your computer's power supply.

External modems are generally contained in their own casing and attach through a serial port located in the back of your computer. External modems need to have their own power supply.

The following table provides a little information about each type of modem.

TABLE 2.1 Comparison of internal and external modems

	Interior Modem	Exterior Modem
Cost	Less expensive because they don't need as many components	More expensive because they need their own power supply
Ease of installation	Not for novices	Simple; plugs into a port in the back of your computer

continues...

TABLE 2.1   **Continued**

	Interior Modem	Exterior Modem
Portable	Cannot easily be moved from computer to computer	Easy to move
Advantages	No external cables to accidentally disconnect. Standard equipment in most newer computers.	Flashing lights, called LEDs and LCDs, which provide information about your online session
Reliability	Excellent	Excellent

Speed Is the Rage

Speed is the primary consideration in today's modems. If you're buying a new one, the slowest modem you should consider is one that is capable of transmitting data at 28,000 kilobits per second. A 28.8 modem, and its faster cousin, the 33.6, are the speeds commonly found on most modems for sale. Even if you have a modem capable of high-speed transmissions, the phone lines in your area might not support such fast rates, and you might find that you connect at slower speeds.

The newest modems manufactured by Rockwell and U.S. Robotics boast transmission rates of 56,600 kilobits per second. Before you rush out and buy one these high-speed modems, it's important to know that both modems use different technologies to achieve their speed. Because this technology doesn't have a current standard, a major battle is brewing to determine which modem captures the market share. Many Internet Service Providers are installing equipment that supports both technologies to keep old customers and attract new ones.

Waiting in the wings are even faster Internet connections. Many television cable companies presently offer high-speed cable connection with speeds that make 56.6 modems seem like they're crawling. (Call your cable company to see if the service is available in your area.) Although the cable service is generally expensive, the cost is expected to come down fast.

Right now, if you have a 28.8 modem or higher, wait for a while before you buy a new one. Let the market determine the industry standard before you plunk down your hard-earned dollars.

Which Modem Should You Buy?

If you've purchased your computer within the past two years or so, your computer probably has a modem installed. If it doesn't, or you plan to upgrade and are unsure about which modem to buy, you're not alone. Most people don't hesitate to pay more than $1000 or more for a new computer, but shy away from purchasing a new modem. The following advice will help you get the modem that's right for you.

- *Buy your modem from a reputable retail store or mail-order outlet.* If you buy your modem from a reputable place, you'll probably be able to return it if it doesn't function properly.

- *Don't buy a bargain basement modem.* The old saying, "You get what you pay for," definitely applies to modems. Even though you might be able to buy a cheaper modem from a computer trade show or from a friend of a friend, you don't know what you're getting. Worse, most really cheap modems don't provide written documentation.

- *Check the installation instructions to make sure you understand them.* After you've made sure that you modem comes with instructions, make sure you can follow them! If the instructions are written in techno-babble that you don't understand, you'll have an awful time installing the modem.

- *Make sure that the modem manufacturer offers technical support.* Even the most experienced user runs into some unexpected installation or use problems sometimes. It's nice to know that a live person can walk you through the difficult times.

- *Check with your Internet Service Provider to find out what brand and type of modems they use.* Similar modems often communicate at higher speeds (more reliably) than dissimilar ones.

What is baud?

When people talk about modem speeds, they often incorrectly use the term baud in reference to the transmission speed of data. The term "baud," named after the 19th century French inventor Baudot, originally referred to the speed a telegrapher could send Morse code. When people use the word baud, they're really referring to bits per second (bps).

Checking Your Modem Configuration

Most of the time you don't need to know what's going on under the case of your computer. However, after your modem is installed, it's a good idea to check out the modem configuration. Make a note of the settings you find; you might need to know the information when you set up an account with an Internet Service Provider.

If you're using Windows 95, perform the following steps to check the configuration of your modem:

Modem configuration

1. Double-click the My Computer icon on your Windows desktop.

2. Double-click the **Control Panel** folder. The Control Panel opens and displays several icons.

3. Double-click the Modem icon, which looks like a telephone. (If you don't see the Modem icon when you first open the Control Panel, use the scrollbars to move down through the rows of icons that appear in the Control Panel.) The Modems Properties dialog box appears, as shown in Figure 2.1.

FIGURE 2.1

The Modems Properties dialog box contains information about your modem.

 Your modem appears here

4. Click the modem name that's shown in the box one time to select it and then click **Properties**.

5. A new Modems Properties dialog box that displays the name of your modem appears, layered over the original Modems Properties dialog box. The new box contains detailed information about your modem.

6. If it's not already selected, click the **General** tab (see Figure 2.2).

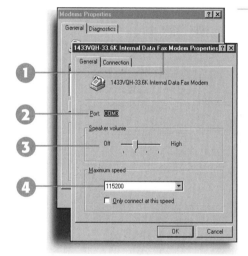

FIGURE 2.2

Specific information about your modem appears.

1 Name of your modem

2 Com Port to which your modem is connected

3 Modem speaker volume setting

4 Maximum connection speed

7. Click **OK** to close the Modems Properties dialog box that contains specific information about your modem. When that box closes, click **OK** to close the Modems Properties dialog box and return to the Control Panel.

8. Click the **Close** button (the X) on the Control Panel title bar.

Additional settings about your modem are contained within the Modems Properties dialog box. Although it's unlikely that you'll be asked about those settings, you can access the information by clicking the **Dialing Properties** button and the **Connection** tab.

More Hardware Can Optimize Your Internet Experience

A few extra or upgraded pieces of equipment can turn your Internet experience into an extra-special time. Keep in mind that everything on the list is optional; for example, you don't need a larger monitor or a microphone to have a great time on the Internet. Unless you have loads of extra money, pick and choose the pieces that fit in with the way you plan to use the Internet. You can always wait and buy additional hardware whenever you feel you need it. The following list shows items you might consider adding to your system later on.

- *19-inch monitor.* The larger the monitor, the more you see! (However, make sure your desk or computer cart can accommodate a larger monitor before you bring it home.) Prices on 19-inch monitors have never been cheaper. If you're buying a new computer, you can generally upgrade to a 19-inch monitor for a few hundred dollars more. If you really want to splurge, get a 21-inch monitor.

- *32-bit sound card.* The newest cards are 32-bit models with wavetable synthesis and are fully duplexed. Most sound cards produce sound by a process called FM synthesis. Wavetable synthesis is superior to FM because it uses actual recorded samples of the sound which are manipulated by MIDI commands. (Even if you don't understand how this works, take my word that the sound produced by a card with wavetable synthesis sounds live, not tinny or machine-like!)

- *The best computer speakers.* The best speakers utilize a sub-woofer system and produce rich bass tones and symphonic sound. The very best speakers are capable of surround sound. Make sure you use computer speakers. Never attach your home stereo speakers to your computer. For one thing, the sound will be awful because stereo speakers need more power than your computer's sound card amplifier can produce. Also, home stereo speakers aren't magnetically shielded. If you use stereo speakers with your computer, you run the risk of warping your monitor as well as damaging the data on your hard drive or floppies.

- *Color printer.* It's great to be able to produce a hard copy of a Web site that looks as good on paper as it did on your monitor. Color laser printers are expensive. Color inkjet printers are reasonable in price and produce dynamite looking output.

- *Computer microphone.* If you plan to participate in an Internet conference, get a computer microphone. The mike plugs into the sound card and enables you to talk over the Internet. (Make sure you have a sound card before you buy a microphone.) Internet microphones are inexpensive.

Whenever you have some free time, cruise down to your local computer store or flip to the back portion of a computer magazine and look at the ads. The equipment shown here, and other hardware additions, such as cameras and scanners, can pay for themselves in enjoyment.

SEE ALSO

➤ *You learn about Internet conferencing on page 377.*

Accessing the Internet

You have the right computer and the right modem. You've set up your computer microphone. Before you finally make the move to get connected, take a few minutes to understand how the pieces fit together.

Using TCP/IP

TCP/IP stands for Transmission Control Protocol/Internet Protocol and is the protocol responsible for making sure that your computer can communicate with all the other computers it encounters on the Internet. TCP/IP and its companion, an IP address, go hand-in-hand in getting you connected to the Internet. Although you needn't trouble yourself with all the technical details of TCP/IP, use the following analogy to understand how it works.

Let's say that you meet up with a long-lost cousin who lives across the world. Even though you look alike and share a lot of the same genetic makeup, you can't communicate because you both speak different languages. Can you imagine how happy you would be if a simple language enabled you to speak like cousins who had grown up together? In computerese, TCP/IP is that universal language. TCP/IP enables computers, no matter which brand or type, to communicate with one another.

Understanding IP Addressing

The whole concept and use of IP numbers can be incredibly technical, but you need to understand only a small bit of information.

To connect to the Internet, every computer, including yours, must be identified by a unique number, called an *IP address*. IP addresses are written as a series of four numbers, separated by periods. For example, the following is an example of an IP address:

159.97.6.175

The URL (Web address) of a page on the World Wide Web or an email address is translated into an IP address, so the computer can read it. For example, when you want to see the Web page at http://www.mcp.com, or send an email to your buddy, freddy@freeloader.com, your computer breaks down the Web or email address into an IP address.

This all happens through an amazing process called *name resolution*, which occurs behinds the scenes most of the time that you're on the Internet. When you type a Web address or an email address, the necessary portion of text is translated into an IP address and sent along. It's much easier for you to remember an email address like kingarthur@camelot.com than kingarthur@159.62.172.12!

In the following exercise, you obtain the IP address that's assigned to your computer. Unless you have a direct Internet connection, you need to be already connected to the Internet for the steps to work. Additionally, you must be using Windows 95.

Finding your IP number

1. Click the **Start** button and choose **Run** from the **Start** menu. The Run dialog box appears.

2. Type `winipcfg` in the **Open** text box and click **OK**.

3. In a moment, the IP configuration dialog box appears, displaying your IP number, as shown in Figure 2.3. If you were planning to use a program such as Microsoft NetMeeting for Internet conferencing, you would need to know this number to continue.

FIGURE 2.3

The IP Configuration dialog box displays information about your Internet connection.

1 The IP number assigned to your computer

4. Click **OK** to close the IP Configuration dialog box.

SEE ALSO

➤ *You learn more about Web addresses on page 90.*

Making the Connection

Now that you have all the theory behind you, it's time to actually make the connection and jump onto the Internet with both feet. You can access the Internet in a few different ways.

If your office or school has an Internet connection, it's likely that you can get access without having to pay a dime. Check with the folks who run the computer department, usually called Information Services. Of course, if you visit the Internet from your desk at work, you'll probably be subject to some restrictions, such as the types of sites you can visit and what kind of messages you can send. Additionally, the places you access from your work computer might be monitored.

Connecting to the backbone

To connect to the Internet, you need to attach to the Internet "backbone," a superhighway of cabling that enables massive amounts of voice, data, and video to be combined and transmitted at extremely high speeds. Very few computers have direct access to the backbone. Your Internet Service Provider leases a high-speed line, called a T1 or T3 connection, and then, for a fee, provides you with a gateway (or bandwidth) to the Internet backbone.

A good solution for the home user is to connect to the Internet through an *Internet Service Provider*, or ISP for short. Depending on your geographic area, you can probably open a phone directory and find listings for several Internet providers. Most ISPs grant you Internet access and include an email address and the capability to connect to Usenet (newsgroups). Additionally, some ISPs enable you to store personal Web pages on their server.

Another route to the Internet is offered by several commercial online services. America Online is the best known of this type of service. Commercial online services, sometimes called COSs, provide email, news, electronic shopping, chat, and original content, as well as access to the Internet. Unfortunately, Internet access is generally secondary to the list of other services provided by an online service.

How Do I Choose a Provider?

Choosing the right ISP is a primary step in getting connected. Every day more and more new providers are competing for your business. Both local and national ISPs exist, each with different service options and payment schedules.

Before you select an ISP, be sure you know what you need:

- If you travel frequently and need to be able to connect to the Internet from hotels and conference rooms far from your local area code, you need a provider that offers national or even international access as part of the package.
- How many hours a month do you intend to be connected?
- Do you need just one account or multiple accounts for other family or your staff members?

After you've jotted down your conditions, you can match them to the services offered by an ISP.

Start your search by asking your friends and colleagues which service providers they use. Take advantage of their experience. Most people who are already connected will be happy to share their provider's name. Check the business section of your local newspaper and look in the *Yellow Pages*. Speak to the people in the computer department at your company.

When you've decided on a provider, call and ask a few questions before you commit. Don't feel strange or shy about calling first. After all, your ISP is going to be your lifeline to the Internet. If the service fails, you're left with a computer, modem, and no place to go. If you're using the Internet for business, downtime can mean lost money to you.

Use the questions shown here as a springboard. If you can think of additional questions, ask them, too!

1. How long have you been providing access to the Internet and how many subscribers do you have?

2. How many of those subscribers can be connected to the Internet at one time?

3. What services and software will I receive if I subscribe to your service?

4. What is the cost of your service? Are there any hidden costs like a setup fee, a charge for calling technical support, or extra costs if I have my own Web site? Do you offer different service options or pricing plans?

5. Do you give discounts to groups such as students or employees of a company? If so, am I entitled to the discount?

6. Do you charge monthly, quarterly, or annually? Is it less expensive if I choose to subscribe for a longer time period?

7. Can I call Tech Support if I have a problem with your service? What are Tech Support's hours?

8. Do you provide outside training or give me detailed instructions on setting up the connection?

9. Do you have local access numbers for my calling area?

10. During the past three months, how many hours was the service unavailable? What caused the outages and what was done to correct the problem and prevent it from occurring in the future?

Every Business Needs a Good ISP

If you're setting up your business on the Internet, your choice of ISPs becomes much more important. Your ISP is your lifeline to the Internet. As a casual home user, changing ISPs generally means giving out your new email address and maybe missing a few messages. As a business user, changing ISPs can result in a loss of valuable time and revenue.

Connecting your small business to the Internet is more than simply plugging a couple of cables together. You need to consider several factors in your search for an ISP. Make sure that the ISP has an unblemished record of connection time. If the ISP has had more than one or two outages in the past three months, think seriously before you make a commitment. After all, every time someone can't find your Web page or send you email, you could be losing money.

Select an ISP that can provide your company with business-oriented features. For example, if you need to develop a Web site, choose an ISP that offers both expert Web page design and hosting services. You might need to interface your inventory to an Internet information browser. Or, perhaps you plan to create an intranet, a "mini" Internet that is accessible only to your employees. Setting up these types of services demands an ISP with an in-depth knowledge of both Internet technology and computer systems integration. Be sure that the provider you select for your business service has knowledge in all these areas and can help you to make your company's "Net presence" profitable and productive.

SEE ALSO

➤ *You learn more about intranets on page 45.*

National or Local ISP?

Open your local phone directory to "Internet" and, most likely, you'll see ads for several local ISPs. When it's time to choose a provider, you can opt to connect via a local ISP or choose a big, well-known national provider. Which should you choose?

Depending on the geographic area in which you live, the choice might be simple. One or the other provider might not offer a local telephone number for you to call. (If you're going to have to make a long-distance call every time you access the Internet, you can rack up huge phone charges in a hurry.)

Choosing a national ISP makes good sense if you travel or if you're new to the Internet. Many of the long-distance services offer national Internet access, in addition to their telephone services. Generally, these companies offer their Internet service separately from their long distance service. You can sign up with Sprint or AT&T to provide your Internet access, even if you don't use the company as your long-distance carrier.

Because most national ISPs are backed by big networks with extensive resources, you can expect reliable service. Sometimes, national ISPs are a bit more expensive than local ISPs. Some national ISPs might not have local access numbers, resulting in long-distance charges every time you connect.

Local ISPs, on the other hand, might offer more personalized service. If something goes wrong, you might find it's easier to get through quickly to the tech support people to resolve the problem. If you're setting up your business on the Internet, your local ISP might have a representative who can meet you personally. The differences between local and national ISPs can be compared to shopping in a big brand-name supermarket or buying your groceries from the small market across from your house. Both have distinct advantages; it's up to you to decide which provider best meets your needs.

Connecting with Sprint Internet Passport

Sprint Internet Passport, the Internet access service provided by Sprint, is a great way to get connected. You can enjoy the benefits of Sprint's ultra-sophisticated equipment and expertise. Additionally, Sprint Internet Passport offers a "Get Connected" guarantee, promising you'll get a free week of Internet access for each time you can't connect when you dial in to their service. When you install Sprint Internet Passport, you also install Internet Explorer 4.

Sprint provides 24-hour-a-day, seven-day-a-week customer service and technical support. Internet access is provided for more than 200 local points and a national access number. Sprint

Internet Passport gives you your first month of service free of charge. After that, you can choose from several pricing plans and options.

In addition to the existing free technical support and customer service resources offered by Sprint Internet Passport, subscribers have access to Sprint Personal Trainers. The Personal Trainers answer questions and provide help on a wide range of Internet topics, not just those relating to connectivity issues. Sprint Internet Passport is a great service for individuals and businesses.

Setting Up Sprint Internet Passport

Setting up your Sprint account is easy. Allow yourself about 30 minutes to install the software and complete the registration process. You'll need your credit card number and expiration date, as well as the Registration Code number provided on the back of the CD.

Sprint can help

If you need help during the installation, Sprint Internet Passport has a staff of people waiting to assist you. Feel free to call them at 1-800-786-1400.

The installation package is provided on one CD-ROM that includes the Microsoft Internet Explorer 4 browser. As part of the installation procedure, you install the browser software on the CD before you can access the Internet. The Install Wizard provided by Sprint walks you through the installation process. When the browser software is installed, the Install Wizard closes and you're stepped through a series of registration screens in which you provide your personal information. In no time at all, you're connected and ready to experience the Internet firsthand.

What Are Commercial Service Providers?

America Online, CompuServe, and the Microsoft Network are popular commercial service providers. Although these providers grant you Internet access, the type of service they offer is different from a standard ISP. Instead of giving you the means to connect to the Internet, email, and newsgroup accounts—and possibly a browser—commercial service providers offer a graphical interface that's packed with the provider's own content.

They put you in a point-and-click world where you don't need to know about operating systems or the pros and cons of different Web browsers.

Although these services do possess an appeal for novices and Internet beginners, many people quickly grow tired of the graphical interface that attracted them at first. Becoming Internet savvy doesn't take all that long. After you've got a little Internet experience under your belt, you might not appreciate all the coddling that commercial online services have to offer. Instead, you might choose to go to the Web with a sophisticated browser, like Internet Explorer or Navigator, and search for your own information.

SEE ALSO

➤ *You find out about the function of a browser on page 52.*

Looking at America Online

The America Online service, often called AOL, is the world's most popular Internet online service, with more than 10 million subscribers worldwide. The service provides subscribers with a variety of interactive features, including email, news, sports, weather, financial information and transactions, electronic shopping, and more. Additionally, AOL provides World Wide Web access.

Many new users are introduced to the Internet as AOL subscribers. AOL aggressively markets their service and sends out thousands upon thousands of America Online setup CDs and disks. With a whopping 50 or so free hours the first month you install the service, AOL may be a good way for you to start your Internet journey.

AOL catalogues its various services under channel headings, as shown in Figure 2.4. When you click one of the channel headings, you're presented with another set of choices that relate to the channel you selected. Each time you click a new choice, a window with related information appears layered on top of the windows on the America Online screen. If you find a spot on AOL to which you would like to return, you can simply click the

red heart on the title bar to add the spot to AOL's favorite
places. If you don't want to move through a series of menus to
find a specific topic, you can use a keyword search. AOL looks
through its network and presents links to all the references to
the keyword you entered.

FIGURE 2.4

America Online provides many
different channels.

1 Click a channel to open a
   menu with links to related
   topics

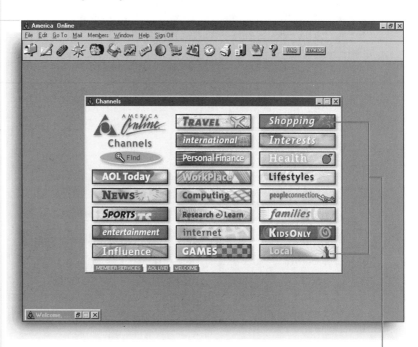

Although AOL has a wealth of information in its own database,
the service offers some standard Internet components, such as
access to the World Wide Web and email. By clicking on the
Internet channel or typing the keywords World Wide Web, you are
taken to the AOL version of a Web browser. AOL also offers
email; your new mail is placed in your mailbox and held until
you read it (see Figures 2.5 and 2.6).

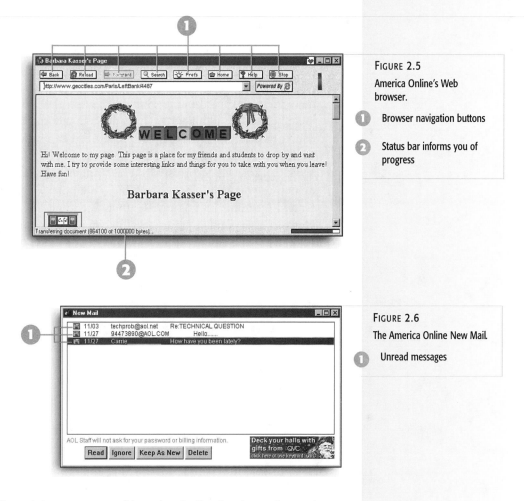

FIGURE 2.5

America Online's Web browser.

1 Browser navigation buttons

2 Status bar informs you of progress

FIGURE 2.6

The America Online New Mail.

1 Unread messages

The pricing structure of America Online has been changed to make the service more competitive with most ISPs. America Online now offers unique "tiered" pricing, which is structured to appeal to a broad range of consumers with different interests, needs, and budgets. You can choose between unlimited use for a flat monthly rate or pay by the hour. If you already have an account with an ISP, you can access AOL for unlimited hours for a small amount per month, using AOL's TCP/IP pricing option.

Looking at the Microsoft Network

The Microsoft Network, or MSN, offers integrated Internet access including an email account, full World Wide Web access with many links to popular Web sites, and thousands of Internet newsgroups. MSN also offers hundreds of special-interest bulletin boards and unique multimedia content. You can find encyclopedias, dictionaries, home-repair and car-buying guides, as well as up-to-date news and information from the MSN's news package, MSN News. MSN has content relationships with numerous companies including NBC, Paramount, USA Today, United Airlines, and Starwave Corporation. The Microsoft Network is available in more than 50 countries, with access software in 26 languages.

The MSN is organized into channels of Shows and what Microsoft calls Essentials. The Essentials contain some of the following selections:

- *Internet Gaming Zone*. A site that contains several games for kids and adults
- *Investor*. A service that provides investment tips and enables you to track your investments
- *Computing On MSN*. A friendly and helpful technical resource for computer users
- *Expedia*. A great travel guide with information on the best hotels, cheapest airfares, and car rentals
- *Encarta*. Access to the Microsoft's huge multimedia library

Additionally, MSN offers subscribers links to sites that cover shopping, care car, a wine guide, and a huge virtual music store. Microsoft adds new services to MSN on a regular basis, such as a Communications channel that contains chat rooms for MSN members and a Find channel that offers a huge online repository of telephone directories and email addresses.

It's easy to subscribe to the Microsoft Network. If you purchase a new Microsoft software product or even a new computer that's running Windows, you'll be provided with a Microsoft Network CD or a Setup MSN icon on your desktop. Pop the CD-ROM into your CD-ROM drive and you're on your way.

The Setup procedure for the MSN is so much fun, you might forget that you're actually subscribing. An interactive movie provides an entertaining look at a preview of the services offered by MSN (see Figure 2.7). Follow the prompts to view all the preview screens and learn about the services.

Free installation CDs

Microsoft offers free MSN installation CDs. Call 1-800-FREE-MSN if you want a CD to install the Microsoft Network.

FIGURE 2.7

The MSN preview has the look and feel of a interactive movie.

1 Click a person or a channel number to continue

When you're done viewing the preview, click **Join MSN** to begin the setup process. The installation process for MSN takes around 25 minutes and requires about 30 megabytes of space on your hard drive. You should close all open programs before you begin the installation.

When all the files have been copied to your computer, you are asked to provide personal and billing information. An icon to the MSN Network is installed on your desktop and to your **Start** menu, as shown in Figure 2.8 After you restart your computer, you'll be ready to connect to the Internet through the MSN.

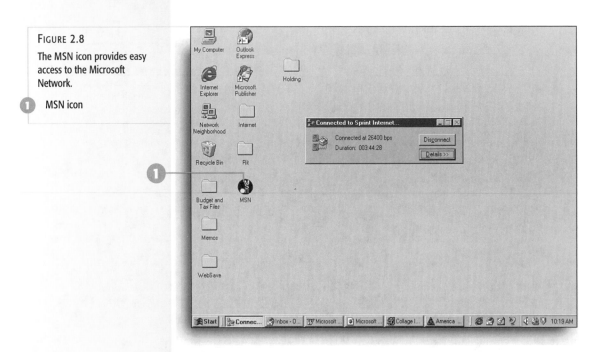

FIGURE 2.8

The MSN icon provides easy
access to the Microsoft
Network.

1   MSN icon

The Microsoft Network has a few different fee schedules. Your
first 30 days are free. After that period, you can choose one flat
fee for unlimited Internet access, or you can decide to pay
a nominal fee for using MSN five hours a month. If you select
the latter plan, you pay an additional per-hour charge if you
exceed your five hours. Of course, you can switch your service
plan at any time.

Looking at CompuServe

CompuServe, another commercial service provider, used to be
considered the best online service for computer professionals
and others in the technical field. Recently, CompuServe has
added many new services and features aimed at the home-based
Internet user. CompuServe has a vast library of organized business and educational information.

If you select CompuServe as your commercial service provider,
you'll get the standard Internet components, including Web
browsing and email. You'll also have access to CompuServe
Forums, which are set up to provide information on a wide

variety of topics. Most Forums consist of three parts: Message Boards, Library Files, and Conference Rooms. It's easy to move around in CompuServe; click the **Go** button (a green stoplight icon) to move directly to a service.

CompuServe is easy to install. You'll need to install the CompuServe software from disks or CDs provided by CompuServe. You can choose between a Typical installation (recommended for most users) or a Custom installation (an option for users who already have connections to the Internet). As part of the CompuServe installation process, the Microsoft Internet Explorer browser is installed on your computer.

Payment plans for CompuServe include both a standard unlimited service and an hourly rate. CompuServe subscribers are given the first month of service free of charge.

Comparing Online Providers

With so many providers and so many different service options, you might feel unsure about which one to choose. Use Table 2.2 to contrast and compare the options provided by each provider.

WebTV Combines the Internet and Your Television

WebTV is one of the latest Internet technologies. If you don't have a computer, or you just enjoy watching television, WebTV brings the Internet directly to your TV screen. Using a special receiver or terminal, you use your TV remote to switch back and forth between the Internet and your favorite TV programs.

The combination of broadcast television and the Internet started in September 1996 when WebTV Networks, Inc. offered the first Internet terminal to consumers. These WebTV Internet terminals utilize the existing technologies of both television and the telephone to enable you to switch between television and the Internet. Although at first many people were skeptical, the combination proved to be a runaway success.

TABLE 2.2   Comparison of service providers

Name/Type	Level of Internet Access	Web Browser	Allow Personal Web Page	Provide Installation Software	Offer Technical Support	First Month Free	Comments
Local or National	Full Internet access	Depends on ISP	Usually	Usually	Optional	Depends	Each ISP offers different service options—check carefully before you sign up!
America Online (COS)	Full Internet access	AOL's own browser powered by Internet Explorer	Yes	Yes	Yes	Yes	More subscribers than connections—may be hard to connect.
Microsoft Network (COS)	Full Internet access	Internet Explorer	No	Yes	Yes	Yes	Heavy graphics require lots of extra hard drive service. May revamp service in the future.
Compu-Serve	Full Internet access	Internet Explorer	Yes	Yes	Yes (excellent support options)	Yes	Provides unwieldy email address, such as arthur@ 752410, 5434.

Setting up WebTV is simple. You need to get either a WebTV Internet Terminal or a WebTV Plus Receiver and a monthly subscription to the WebTV Network Service. WebTV Networks, Inc. offers two levels of service: the WebTV Network (which requires the WebTV Internet Terminal), and the WebTV Plus Network (which uses the WebTV Plus Receiver). Choose the first option, the WebTV Network, if all you want is to enhance your television with Internet access. If you want to completely integrate your television with the Internet, choose WebTV Plus.

WebTV is making its way to all areas of the United States. The WebTV headquarters is located in Palo Alto, California. You can contact them at (415) 326-3240 for more information on getting connected.

Many people think that the WebTV concept might be the future of both the Internet and television. You can be part of the new generation!

Connecting to the Internet from Work

Millions of people now have Internet access from the workplace. If you have a connection to the Internet at your desk, chances are that the sites you visit can be tracked by the person in charge of maintaining Internet security. (Forewarned is forearmed—don't go anywhere you might be ashamed of later!)

Many companies provide Internet access to their employees in conjunction with a corporate *intranet*. Unlike the Internet, which covers the world, an intranet is designed to be viewed by the employees of a particular company or group. However, similar to the Internet, it doesn't matter if the employees are located in the same building or scattered across the globe.

What Is an Intranet?

An intranet uses the same tools and techniques as the global Internet to provide information and services, but within a company or organization. An intranet can work equally well within the confines of a small company with a few employees scattered in different locations or within a large, global corporation. If you have an intranet at your office or school, you view documents that look just like the ones on the Web. An intranet can be up and running without any connection to the outside world. An intranet has three basic uses:

- *Internal bulletin board*. Delivers corporate information, such as telephone and email directories, human resources databases, forms, meeting schedules, and discussion threads.
- *Communications delivery*. A cost-effective mechanism for transporting information. Employees send email instead of sending a fax or making expensive telephone calls for interoffice communications. Additionally, file transfer protocol (FTP) replaces expensive express mail or overnight delivery, whether at the same location or your company's other locations.
- *Day-to-day business functions*. Functions might include order processing sales tracking, inventory control, and delivery status. By placing documents such as company policy manuals and employee phone listings on the intranet, a company can save thousands of dollars in both printing and distribution costs.

A sample of an intranet page is shown in Figure 2.9.

The benefits of intranets are being discovered every day as more companies integrate them into their workplaces. One of the most significant and noticeable benefits is the increased productivity that results from quick company-wide communications and data sharing.

The cost of an intranet is inexpensive compared to the resulting long-term savings. Most companies already have most of the hardware resources required, such as computers, modems, and phone lines. The other equipment needed is readily available and relatively cheap compared to putting together, and then maintaining, a straight local or wide area network.

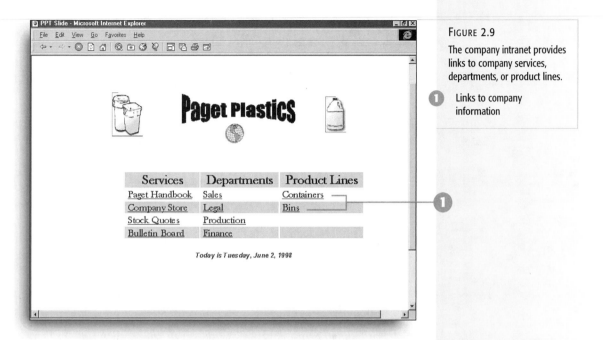

FIGURE 2.9

The company intranet provides links to company services, departments, or product lines.

1 Links to company information

Employees usually have rights to view most of the documents on an intranet. However, the network administrator can set up a *firewall*, which prevents employees from using their browsers to access documents on the World Wide Web. Some intranets require employees to log in with a name and password, and others pass employees through to the intranet opening page.

If you work for a company with more than a few employees, don't be surprised if your employer sets up an intranet in the near future.

Extending the Intranet to an Extranet

Now that you know all about intranets, the next logical step to explore is an *extranet*. In its simplest form, an extranet is an expanded intranet that can include customers, clients, suppliers, and almost anyone else who has contact with your business on a daily basis. You actually give people outside your company (who relate to your business) access to your intranet using Internet technology. Extranets help businesses improve customer service, increase revenue, and save time, money, and resources.

A firewall keeps your company safe

Firewalls use a combination of software and hardware to prevent unauthorized users from sneaking into your company through the Internet and having access to files stored on the computer system. The firewall also prevents users inside the wall (the employees of your company) from accessing some sites that might be considered security risks.

Even though your corporate firewall might prevent you from using the Internet at work as you would at home, be grateful. The firewall protects you from potential security risks that could result in lost data.

A company that supplies janitorial supplies to other companies, for example, might allow its customers to browse its catalog and place orders online, eliminating the need for sales representatives. Or a travel agent could link up with several cruise lines and others in the vacation field. Other uses for an extranet include

- Providing training programs or other educational material
- Having discussion groups in which to share ideas and experiences among colleagues and clients
- Furnishing schedules of company hours and holidays

An extranet can allow access to all the sites on the intranet, or it can restrict users to only certain areas. For example, a travel agent that books group tours might be allowed to see different pages from an individual who's looking for a weekend getaway for his family. The login method to an extranet needs to be set up carefully to ensure that external visitors to the intranet stay only in the pages to which they have access.

Building an extranet is hard work—even harder than building an intranet! Many issues—compatibility, access, and security—need to be worked out before the external users are provided access. An extranet requires more planning than an intranet and costs more, too. Costs need to be built in for training, security, additional firewalls, and ID/password controls.

What Is a Freenet?

A *Freenet* provides free, public-access to the Internet. Freenets are often sponsored or supported by local library systems. Although they don't usually offer all the tools provided by an ISP, Freenets give email services and limited access to the World Wide Web. Additionally, some Freenets provide access to community and government databases. Many Freenets exist around the world, but each one is tailored to meet the needs of the local community. No two Freenets are identical.

You can compare a Freenet to a large online encyclopedia that contains information about a metropolitan area. The information is placed on a large, dedicated computer, hooked up to the phone system, and made available to the general public, free of charge. Most Freenets can support hundreds of users simultaneously, but the number of local users who can use the Freenet at one location depends on the number of phone lines purchased and dedicated to Freenet use.

Volunteers, local government, and corporations provide the information you view on a Freenet. These information providers are the Freenet's lifeblood. They work together to keep the information on the Freenet current, and they ensure that the information keeps pace with the community's information needs. (No one wants to read about the Fourth of July parade at Christmastime.) Freenets invite information providers from all sectors of the community to supply information for placement on the system. See Figure 2.10 for an example of a Freenet page.

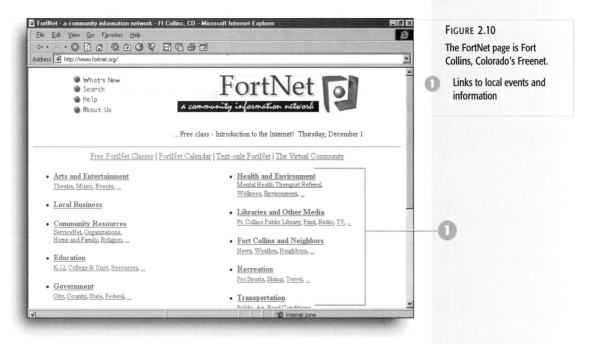

FIGURE 2.10

The FortNet page is Fort Collins, Colorado's Freenet.

1 Links to local events and information

Many Freenets have Usage Policies that spell out what a user can do and where he can go on the network. Even though Freenet users have access to the Internet, Web usage is not intended to be recreational. For example, a Freenet user isn't supposed to use the service as a way to find the latest gossip about her favorite television star. Instead, Freenet users are expected to look at only the documents on the Web that deal with educational or community issues.

Freenets usually provide free email accounts to their users. The mail system of most Freenets isn't very sophisticated, and only allows short text messages. You can't attach a document or include graphics images in a Freenet mail message. Still, Freenet mail services make email available to many people who otherwise wouldn't have access to an electronic mailbox.

A few years ago, Freenets could only be accessed with programs such as Telnet and other older Internet programs. Now, with the explosion of the World Wide Web and the popularity of browser programs such as Internet Explorer or Netscape, most Freenet sites offer a Web version with color and pictures in addition to the text-only version.

If you're planning to become an Internet "power" user, a Freenet isn't for you. However, if you don't have a way of getting Internet access (for example, you don't own a computer), check with your local library to see if you can get a Freenet account.

SEE ALSO

➤ *Read about other ways to get free email on page 216.*

Choosing and Using a Browser

Understanding what a browser does

Looking at the components of Netscape Communicator and Internet Explorer

Installing your browser

Working with the Internet Explorer Active Desktop

Traveling the Web with links

HotJava browser

Another Web browser is on the horizon. Sun Microsystems claims HotJava, their new browser, is the future of the Web. Although the early release of HotJava doesn't contain as many features as Communicator or Internet Explorer, Sun promises to improve it soon.

After you've established your connection to the Internet, you need a client program called a *browser* to bring the pages of the World Wide Web to your computer. The name "browser" is descriptive, because the program lets you browse through all the pages on the Web. Think of the browser as your passport to visit the Web. Although older browsers exist, such as text-based Lynx that's used by many vision-impaired computer users, we'll concentrate on the latest versions of the most popular browsers available to you. Currently, the two most common and powerful browsers are Netscape Navigator and Microsoft Internet Explorer.

What Does a Browser Do?

Browsers perform many functions. The first and most important thing your browser does is communicate with the server that stores the page you want to see. To understand why this job is so important, you need to first understand that the World Wide Web provides the global environment for the information you want to access. This information is stored on Web pages that contain many different elements, such as text, image, audio, and video. A Web page can be located on a server anywhere in the world. When you request a page, your browser first needs to determine on which server the page is stored, ask the server for permission to fetch it, and then load the page on your computer. All this is truly amazing when you realize that the entire process takes seconds, instead of minutes or hours!

The responsibility doesn't stop after the page is loaded. Your browser works to manage your entire Web experience. Navigation aids are provided, such as the capability to move back and forth between pages you've viewed during the current session. A history of the pages to which you've navigated is maintained. Your browser also lets you keep a record of the pages to which you want to return later on, so you can return with one simple click. The correct display of fonts, colors, and images is another task for the browser. Want to print a page or save it to the hard drive of your computer? Your browser handles these jobs, too.

Which Browser Is Right for You?

Unfortunately, no set formula can determine which browser is better. Both Netscape Navigator and Microsoft Internet Explorer perform most of the same Web functions on your computer. (I use both of them interchangeably.) Both offer online technical support. Each browser claims to be the biggest and best. How do you decide?

Many times the choice is easy. If you're accessing the Internet from your home or school, the folks that handle the computer network have already made that decision for you, and one of the programs is already installed for your use. If you're using an ISP to connect, the provider probably furnished one to you when you signed up. For example, Sprint Internet Passport provides Internet Explorer as part of their service.

One or the other browser might not run on your computer. Usually, the instructions for installation are very specific about types of computers that can be used with the browser. However, if you're not sure whether a particular browser will work on your computer, read the requirements on the CD cover or the browser's Web site before you go through an installation process. If your ISP offers technical support, call the "hot line" and ask for advice.

You might already have an older version of either Navigator or Internet Explorer installed on your computer and decide you would like to upgrade to the latest and greatest version. Or, you might be just getting started with the Internet and need to obtain a browser. If a browser isn't already installed on your computer, furnished to you by your ISP, or you decide you want to change, both Netscape Navigator and Internet Explorer are easy to obtain. You'll find Netscape at www.netscape.com and Microsoft at www.microsoft.com. Follow the instructions shown on the Netscape or Microsoft page to download the programs. You can also obtain the browsers from one of these sources:

- Copies of Netscape Communicator, the complete suite that includes many Internet features including the Navigator browser and the standalone version of Navigator, are available at your local software store for a nominal price. Or, you can contact the Netscape Sales Center at 1-800-278-1015 to order the suite free of charge.

- Microsoft Internet Explorer's suite of Web-related programs can be ordered free of charge on CD by calling the

It's a GUI world

Both popular browsers feature a graphical user interface, or *GUI* (pronounced goo-ey), that sets up a colorful onscreen way for you to interact with a software program on your computer. In addition to using your keyboard, you can use a mouse or other pointing device to make choices from drop-down menus and buttons.

Using betas

Beta software is a pre-release of a program that's distributed prior to its final, commercial release. Beta software is often incomplete and can cause errors or even crash your computer.

Both Netscape and Microsoft usually make available several versions of their newest browsers in beta format as the final products are being developed.

If you decide to use a beta browser, back up your important files so that, if the beta crashes your system, you'll be able to restore your computer.

Microsoft Sales Department at 1-800-426-9400. (If you download the product, Internet Explorer is free.) A CD that contains the Internet Explorer suite and many other related programs designed to enhance your Internet experience is available at your local software store for under $30.

It's important to understand that both Web-browsing software programs are part of a suite of products in which each separate program performs another Internet-related function. Table 3.1 shows the main components of both Netscape Communicator and Internet Explorer. Because both Microsoft and Netscape periodically release upgraded versions, additional features might be available when you set up your browser software.

TABLE 3.1 Components of the Internet Explorer and Netscape Communicator Suites

	Microsoft Internet Explorer	Netscape Communicator 4
Browser	Internet Explorer	Navigator
Desktop Integration	Active Desktop	None
Channels	Active Channels	Netcaster
Electronic Mail	Outlook Express	Messenger
Newsgroups	Outlook Express	Collabra
Internet Collaboration	NetMeeting	Conference
Chatting	Chat	AOL Instant Messenger (Communicator Version 4 and higher)
HTML Authoring	Front Page Express	Composer
Security	Security Zones	Certificate Management

SEE ALSO

➤ *You can find more information about Internet Service Providers on page 32.*

➤ *You'll learn about downloading files on page 145.*

Upgrading Your Browser

If an older version of Navigator or Internet Explorer is installed on your computer, you can upgrade without too many problems. If you're computer savvy, you might want to uninstall the older browser before you install the new one. If you're not sure how to handle the uninstall process, simply install the browser according to the directions provided with the documentation that comes with your browser or from your ISP. When the procedure is complete, you'll have the latest and greatest version.

As a rule, installing one version over another goes off without a hitch. If you're using Netscape Mail or Microsoft Internet Mail, the installation procedure should incorporate any of your saved messages and your address book into the new program. Additionally, your Bookmarks or Favorites should be visible in the new browser.

Be aware that strange things sometimes happen when you install a newer program over an older one. Depending on the other software that you have installed on your computer, the installation process might not recognize your mail or your bookmark (favorites) files. Protect yourself. Print out the mail messages you want to save, or save each of them to a file. Make a note of the bookmarks you really want to keep. Most importantly, back up your computer before you begin, including the Windows Registry.

If the worst happens and the installation doesn't go quite as smoothly as you planned, just restore your computer files from your backup. Even if you don't have a backup, you won't lose all browser settings if you've taken a few minutes before the installation to jot them down. Don't worry too much though; usually, installing the newest versions of Netscape and Internet Explorer doesn't cause problems.

Looking at Netscape Navigator

Netscape Navigator is the most widely used Web browser. Because Netscape offers versions of Navigator for most types of computers, such as Macintosh, UNIX, and Sun workstations, many corporations and schools choose it for large, cross-platform networks. Additionally, Netscape is free to educational institutions. Your ISP might include Netscape Communicator or Navigator as part of your installation package.

Although the instructions in this book are designed for users working on a personal computer that's running Windows 95 or NT, Netscape Communicator has versions for many types of computers. Table 3.2 shows the system requirements that Netscape Communicator requires for three computer platforms. Although the table lists the minimum system requirements, Navigator and any other Communicator components will run much faster and more efficiently if your computer has a Pentium processor or additional RAM.

The right name

When most people refer to Netscape Navigator, they incorrectly call the browser "Netscape." This is not correct, because Netscape Communications Corporation makes many software programs in addition to the Navigator browser.

TABLE 3.2 **Netscape Communicator platforms and system requirements**

Type of Computer	Processor	Operating System	Required Memory
IBM PC-compatible	486 minimum, preferably a Pentium	Windows 3.x Windows 95 Windows NT	16 megabytes
Apple	68030 minimum or Power PC	Macintosh System 7.5 or later	16 megabytes
Sun	SPARC	Solaris 2.4, 2.5 or SUN OS 4.1.3	64 megabytes

In addition to supporting different computer platforms, Netscape provides a few versions of software to fit the features of the Internet that you will use most.

Netscape Communicator, Standard Edition, is your best bet if you're using a newer computer and want to take advantage of all Netscape's bells and whistles. If you're accessing the Internet from a network of linked computers in your workplace or from school, the network administrator may select Netscape Communicator, Professional Edition, which contains all of the components from the Standard Edition, plus three additional elements. If you only want to use the Navigator browser, or you're short on hard drive space, Netscape Navigator, Stand Alone, will work best for you. Table 3.3 shows what's provided in each version of the Netscape software.

TABLE 3.3 **Netscape versions**

Program	Description	Communicator Standard Edition	Communicator Professional Edition	Navigator Stand Alone
Navigator	Web browser	Y	Y	Y
Netcaster	Uses push technology to bring you channels	Y	Y	Y
Messenger	Mail client that enables you to send and receive email	Y	Y	
Collabra	News client that enables you to read and send postings to newsgroups	Y	Y	
Composer	Web page designer that enables you to create Web pages without knowing HTML	Y	Y	
AOL Instant Messenger	Enables you to exchange private real-time messages with other people connected to the Internet	Y	Y	
Conference	Enables you to have a real-time conference with a friend or colleague across the Internet in either voice or text mode	Y	Y	

continues…

Some now, some later

Even though the Communicator suite contains several programs, you needn't install them all. You can always come back and install the other programs later.

TABLE 3.3 **Continued**

Program	Description	Communicator Standard Edition	Communicator Professional Edition	Navigator Stand Alone
Calendar	Enables co-workers to share calendars and time schedules		Y	
AutoAdmin	Allows Communicator to be centrally managed		Y	
IBM Host On-Demand	Provides a 3270 emulator for access to mainframes		Y	

Installing Netscape Communicator on Your Computer

Before you can take advantage of all Navigator's advanced features, you need to install it onto the hard drive of your computer. (If your ISP provided Netscape software as part of your package and you already have Netscape installed, check with your ISP before you install the browser software again.)

The installation procedure is painless and relatively easy. Your computer needs to be started and running Windows, but you don't need to be connected to the Internet during the installation process.

Take it slow

Always allow yourself ample time to complete an installation. It's too hard to get everything done properly if you're watching the clock. Schedule yourself more time than you think you'll need.

Depending on where you've obtained your Netscape software, the installation instructions might vary. For example, your ISP may have an installation procedure that steps you through placing the Netscape software in a special folder. Therefore, it's very important to follow the instructions that have been provided for you with the software.

Keep your ISP's phone number handy, and don't feel the least bit shy or strange about calling for assistance. If you need additional help with getting your version of Netscape software installed or if you're upgrading from an older version, you can always contact Netscape Tech Support at 1-800-639-0939 for installation assistance. The Netscape line offers both a fax service and a human representative to help you through the installation.

Because Navigator is part of the Communicator suite, the installation process generally covers installing the other Communicator programs at the same time. Therefore, you need to install Communicator even if you're installing only the Navigator browser portion. Installing Netscape Communicator from the CD is handled like the installation of other Windows programs. Fortunately, the Communicator install program does most of the work during the installation; all you need to do is read each screen and click **Next** to step through it.

Make sure that you've closed all the open programs on your computer before you begin the installation. Place the CD-ROM in the CD-ROM drive and follow the onscreen prompts. In a few short minutes, the installation of files will be complete. The installation process finishes with a registration process that you complete in Navigator after you've connected to the Internet.

Now that you have Navigator installed, you're ready to jump into the Web with both feet. Before you can start looking around, you need to first create a system *profile* and then get registered to access the NetCenter channels. Don't worry—you'll be on your way to the Web in a very short time.

In this exercise, you set up your profile and register to access the NetCenter channels. The whole process takes only a few minutes and, best of all, you'll need to do this only one time. If you can, make a note of the information your ISP provided to you about your account, including your email address and the names of your mail and news servers. If you don't have the information handy, you can always add it to your profile at another time.

What are profiles?

Profiles hold the settings, preferences, bookmarks, and stored messages for each user. Even if you're the only Navigator user on your computer, you still need to create a profile.

Setting up your profile

  1. Click the **Start** button on the Windows taskbar to open the **Start** menu.

2. Click **Programs**. Choose Netscape Communicator and then slide across to Netscape Navigator. The **Netscape Communicator** submenu appears, as shown in Figure 3.1.

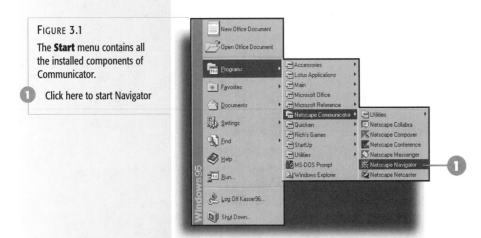

3. Click the **Netscape Navigator** menu selection. In a few seconds, the New Profile Setup dialog box appears. Read the information and click **Next** to continue.

4. The next dialog box asks for your name and email address. Type the information in the appropriate boxes and click **Next** to continue.

5. The third dialog box displays your profile name (which is based on your username) and the folder in which your Netscape settings will be stored. Click Finish to continue.

6. The fourth and fifth dialog boxes ask for information about the names of the incoming and outgoing mail servers. In each box, fill in the names provided by your ISP and click **Next** to continue. If you don't know the information now, leave the boxes blank and click **Next**.

7. The final dialog box asks for information about the name of your ISP's news server. If you know the correct name, enter it; if not, leave the box blank. Click **Finish**. In a moment, Navigator launches and displays the Netscape Registration page, as shown in Figure 3.2.

FIGURE 3.2
Netscape welcomes you!

8. Although you can choose from any one of the options available on the Netscape Registration page, click **Register Now** to be able to receive channel content through Communicator's NetCenter.

9. When the Product Registration page appears, click the underlined, colored text that reads **Sign Me Up**.

10. Although you can fill in all the fields, you only need to complete the fields marked with an asterisk (*). Fill in the information on the Registration page and click the **Next** button.

11. The next page to appear contains a Membership Survey. Although it's not mandatory for you to provide any of the information requested on the form, the information you provide helps Netscape develop better software based on a composite of its users. Click the down arrow next to the fields you want to complete, and choose the information from the list that best describes you. When you're through, click the **Next** button to continue.

12. A new page appears, congratulating you and advising that you're a registered NetCenter member.

13. Click the underlined text that reads **Go to Netcenter**.

14. Read the information on the NetCenter page, using your Page Down key to move down.

Good work! You're ready to move on to your first real visit to the World Wide Web.

SEE ALSO

➤ *Not sure about your news server? You'll be able to update the information and learn about news on page 224.*

Looking at the Navigator Screen

The Navigator screen contains many elements. Figure 3.3 shows a Web page and illustrates Navigator's individual components.

The following describes each element on the Navigator screen:

- *Title bar.* The title bar displays the title of the page that's displayed.

- *Navigation toolbar.* The Navigation toolbar enables you to access the most common commands.

- *Location/Netsite box.* The URL or address of the Web page that's on the screen appears here. You can type a different address to move to another page.

- *Page Proxy icon.* Information about the page that's on the screen, such as the URL, is stored in the Page Proxy icon. You can drag the Page Proxy icon on top of the Bookmarks icon so you'll be able to return to the page later on.

- *Hyperlinks.* Click a hyperlink to move to the place referenced by the link, either on the same page or a new Web location.

- *Menu bar.* Similar to other Windows programs, Navigator features a menu from which you can select commands.

- *Location toolbar.* The Location toolbar displays the Web address of the page that's displayed on the screen and provides you with quick access to your bookmarks.

- *Personal toolbar.* The Personal toolbar features folders and icons for sites to which you want to return.

FIGURE 3.3

The Computer Coach home page is displayed on the Netscape screen.

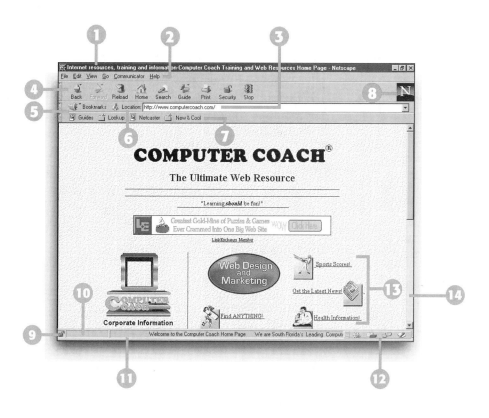

① Title bar	⑧ Page Proxy icon
② Menu bar	⑨ Security information
③ Location/Netsite box	⑩ Status bar
④ Navigation toolbar	⑪ Scrolling ticker
⑤ Location toolbar	⑫ Component bar
⑥ Page Proxy icon	⑬ Hyperlinks
⑦ Personal toolbar	⑭ Scrollbar

- *Link icon.* When you're viewing a page you want to revisit, drag the link icon into the bookmark folder or the Personal Toolbar to set a bookmark.

- *Netscape icon.* The icon that displays the logo of Netscape Communications Corporation serves two purposes. First, the icon shows a fireworks display when Navigator is fetching a page you requested. Second, you can move to the Netscape home page when you click the Netscape icon.

- *Security information.* The lock icon represents the security of the page that's onscreen. When the lock handle is closed, the page is secure.

- *Component bar.* This bar offers speedy access to some of the other programs in Netscape Communicator. In Figure 3.3, the bar is docked, or anchored, at the bottom-right corner of the screen. The bar can also "float" on top of the Navigator screen so you can move it around.

- *Status bar.* Information about the current page is displayed here.

- *Scrolling ticker.* This scrolling ticker is a Java applet and is not standard to every page on the Web.

- *Scrollbar.* The vertical bar that appears on the right side of the window and contains arrows at either end, a gray or colored area in the middle, and a scroll box that reflects your vertical position on the page. Drag the scroll box up or down within the scrollbar to move through the page.

Moving Around in Navigator

Navigator makes it easy to navigate through the page that's on the screen. In this exercise, you use some of Navigator's special tools as you move through the Web and look at different Web pages.

Use Navigator's tools to move around the Web

1. Navigator should be open from the last exercise. If it's not already open, open Navigator by clicking the **Start** button and choose Netscape Communicator and then Netscape Navigator. In a few seconds, a Web page appears on the Navigator screen.

2. The Component bar, a bar that contains shortcuts to other Communicator programs, appears on the screen. Click the **Communicator** menu and choose **Dock Component Bar**. The bar becomes smaller and anchors to the right-bottom corner of the Navigator window.

3. Position your mouse arrow in the Netscape icon (the big "N") and click once. Stars and comets flare and a planet revolves around the Netscape "N" as Navigator moves you to the Netscape home page. Additionally, as the page is accessed, several messages flash across the Status bar. In a moment, Netscape's home page appears.

4. Locate the words **Document:Done** on the Status bar, and click in the Location box. The Web address that's currently displayed in the box appears highlighted, as shown in Figure 3.4.

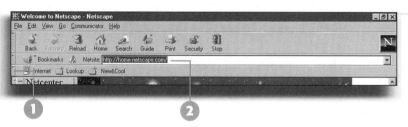

FIGURE 3.4

The Web address in the Location box appears highlighted when you click inside the box.

① Click this arrow to close the Personal Toolbar

② Web address for current page

5. Type the following Web address carefully in the box: www.computercoach.com/. (It's not necessary to delete the text that's already on the box, because the new text will overwrite the old text.) After you've made sure you haven't made any typos, press Enter.

6. The stars and comets flash in the Netscape icon as Navigator accesses the Computer Coach page. When the Computer Coach page is finished loading, the words **Document:Done** appear in the Status bar. (If you have a sound card and speakers, you hear a catchy tune!) Place your mouse pointer over each of the buttons on the Navigation toolbar.

After a second, a ScreenTip appears in a yellow balloon, showing you the button's name and what it does. Figure 3.5 shows the Navigation toolbar displaying a ScreenTip.

FIGURE 3.5

Screen tips are a great way to learn the function of each button.

7. Currently, the Personal toolbar is displayed on the screen. At the very left of the toolbar is a riveted tab icon with an arrow pointing downward. Click the downward arrow to close the Personal Toolbar, as shown in Figure 3.5.

The toolbar closes, and a small arrow that's pointing to the right appears. When you want to redisplay the toolbar, click the right arrow. You can close and then redisplay any of Navigator's toolbars by following this procedure.

8. Move your mouse arrow around the text and graphics on the Computer Coach page. The mouse arrow changes to the shape of a hand as it passes over underlined and different colored text, called hyperlinks, on the page.

9. The Computer Coach page is too long to fit on your computer screen. Drag the right scroll box down slowly to view the lower portions of the page.

Use the Page Up and Page Down keys

Although you can use the vertical scroll box to move up and down in a Web page, you can also use the Page Up and Page Down keys on your keyboard. Press the Page Up key. The view of the page changes as you see more of the top portion of the page.

Reload the page

Whenever you click the Reload button, Navigator contacts the Web server that stores the page, obtains any new information that's been added to it, and redisplays the page for you to view.

10. Click the Reload button on the Navigation toolbar. The Computer Coach Web page is redrawn on the screen and, if your computer has a sound card and speakers, you hear a different tune.

11. Click inside the Location/Netsite box. When the current URL appears highlighted, type www.mrshowbiz.com and press Enter. When the Mr. ShowBiz page appears, take a moment to explore the page.

12. Click the Back button on the Navigation toolbar. The Computer Coach page reappears. Each time you click the Back button you move backward through one previously viewed site.

13. Click the Forward button on the Navigation toolbar. After a brief moment, the Mr. Showbiz page appears again on your

screen. You click the Forward button to move ahead after you've used the Back button. You know that you've moved to the beginning or end of the sites you've already seen when either the Back or Forward button is dimmed.

14. Click the Home button to return to the first page you see when Navigator is launched.

15. Because Navigator is a Windows program, you close it as you would any other Windows program. Click the Close box (the box with the X on the Navigator title bar). The program closes and you're returned to your Windows desktop.

SEE ALSO

➤ *You learn more about hyperlinks on page 83.*

➤ *You'll learn how to change the opening page in Navigator on page 114.*

Looking at Internet Explorer

Microsoft introduced Internet Explorer 4.0 in the late summer of 1997. This version features many exciting new components and includes the option to change the way you work with your Windows files and folders. Although Netscape Navigator is still the most popular browser, Internet Explorer is quickly gaining percentages of users.

If you use mostly Microsoft software, such as the Microsoft Office suite of products, making Internet Explorer your Web browser makes good sense. The browser is tightly integrated with other Microsoft software. For example, if you need online help with Word or Excel while you're connected to the Internet, you can click **Help**, **Microsoft on the Web** to launch Internet Explorer and move to the appropriate technical support site. (If you're a Netscape user, the technical support page will appear in Navigator but some of the site's features may not be available.)

Internet Explorer has some exciting features. An *Autosearch* function enables you to search for documents through Yahoo!, a popular navigational guide, without first accessing the Yahoo! page. You can increase the size of the viewing area by using the

---

A shortcut for the Back and Forward buttons

Click the right mouse button on the Back or Forward button to view the page titles of sites you've seen during the present session. Now you won't have to cycle back through each individual page you visited during your online session because you can move to it immediately by clicking the page title.

full screen option. In addition to its great browser, Internet Explorer's components bring the rest of the Internet to you.

One of Internet Explorer's newest features is its capability to integrate the Web with your Windows desktop. You can turn the *Active Desktop* feature on or off when you install Internet Explorer. If you turn it on, the Active Desktop changes the way Windows looks and works; Internet Explorer becomes the Windows Explorer, making working with the files and folders on your hard drive just like navigating the Web. You also have the option of changing the way you open programs, folders, and files to single-clicking instead of double-clicking. (If you're an established Windows user, you can turn off the single-click feature if you can't get used to it.) The Active Desktop streamlines working with the Web and your computer into one process, but it might take some getting used to.

The version of Internet Explorer we're referencing in this book is designed to work in Windows 95 or NT. The computer "horsepower" shown here is the very minimum you'll need. If you can afford a Pentium processor, additional RAM, or a bigger hard drive (or more free space), your Internet experience will be a lot more pleasant. The very minimum your computer needs to run Internet Explorer is

- 486 DX/66 MHz or higher processor
- 8MB of RAM without Active Desktop, 16MB RAM with Active Desktop for Windows 95 computers
- 16MB of RAM without Active Desktop, 24MB RAM with Active Desktop for computers running Windows NT 4
- 66MB free space
- Mouse or other pointing device
- VGA or higher resolution monitor

If you're not using Windows 95 or NT 4, you need to contact Microsoft or visit their Web page and find out if Internet Explorer can successfully run on your computer. The Microsoft technicians will also be able to tell you where you can obtain the version that's right for you.

Like Netscape Communicator, you can obtain Internet Explorer in several ways. Internet Explorer might be a part of the software you're given from your ISP, such as Sprint Internet Passport. You can order an Internet Explorer CD from Microsoft or download it from their Web page. Or you can purchase Internet Explorer Plus, which contains the Internet Explorer suite and many other Internet-related software programs, from your local software store. The Plus pack is a great way to obtain a bundle of good software programs, including McAfeeWebScanX, Cyber Patrol, and Net.Medic, for a small fee.

SEE ALSO

➤ *You'll learn about searching the Web on page 121.*

Internet Explorer, Standard Installation

If you have limited space on your computer or just want to try out the Internet Explorer, installing the Internet Explorer, Standard Edition is a great way to get started. Of course, you can always install any Internet Explorer component after your basic installation is completed.

During the installation of Internet Explorer, you have the option of installing the *Active Desktop*, which allows you to deal with the files, folders, and programs on your computer in the same manner you deal with Web pages.

The following components make up the Internet Explorer, Standard Edition:

- *Internet Explorer.* The Web browser. New features and a selection of different bars make it an exciting way to tour the Web.

- *Outlook Express.* Integrates your email and newsgroups into one easy-to-use package.

- *Active Channels.* Enables you to pick and choose channels from many categories.

Internet Explorer, Full Installation

Install the full installation of Internet Explorer to take advantage of all the related programs in the suite. When you complete a full installation of Internet Explorer, you get the components in the Standard Installation plus the following:

- *Front Page Express.* Makes it possible for you to create Web pages without prior knowledge of HTML.

- *NetMeeting.* Enables you to participate in an Internet conference with up to 32 other participants (although only two members of the conference can engage in voice communication at a time).

- *Chat.* Formerly called Comic Chat, enables you to connect to chat servers and participate in a text conversation with other people across the Internet. The conversations are presented in comic strip-like panes. You can assume the identity of several comic strip characters.

- *NetShow.* Uses compression and streaming technologies to play live or recorded audio, video, and multimedia as it's delivered to the computer, without waiting for the entire file to download and play.

- *Microsoft Wallet.* Includes an electronic wallet where you can securely store and access private information such as credit card numbers, digital certificates, and digital keys for use when you buy something on the Web.

Internet Explorer, Minimum Installation

Choose the minimum installation to install only the Internet Explorer browser.

Installing Internet Explorer from the CD

In this exercise, you install Internet Explorer from the CD provided by Microsoft. Make sure to disconnect from the Internet before you begin the installation procedure.

Installing Internet Explorer 4.0, Standard Edition

1. Begin the installation by closing any open programs on your computer.

2. Place the Internet Explorer CD-ROM in the CD-ROM drive of your computer. If AutoRun is active on your computer, the CD-ROM will automatically open and you can skip steps 3, 4, and 5. If AutoRun is not active, continue with steps 3, 4, and 5, as shown.

3. Click the **Start** Button.

4. Click **Run**; the Run dialog box opens.

5. Type D:\SETUP.EXE (assuming that D is your CD-ROM drive) in the **Open** text box and then click OK.

6. When the Microsoft Internet Explorer 4.0 CD dialog box appears, as illustrated in Figure 3.6, choose **Install Internet Explorer 4.0** from the menu selections at the right side of the screen.

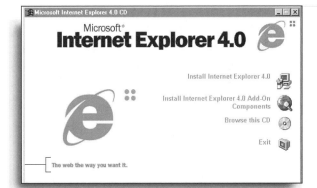

FIGURE 3.6

Begin the installation by clicking **Install Internet Explorer 4.0**.

7. The second Internet Explorer 4.0 Active Setup dialog box appears. Click **Next** to continue.

8. The License Agreement dialog box appears with a portion of the license agreement visible. Read the agreement, using the Page Down key to move to the lower portion of the agreement. When you're finished reading, click the option button next to **I accept the agreement** and then click **Next** to continue.

Follow your ISP's instructions!

Keep in mind that if your ISP furnished you with the Internet Explorer software, the installation procedure shown here might be unnecessary because it might already be set up. If you think Internet Explorer is already installed, or you're unsure about how to proceed, call your ISP for instructions.

9. The Installation Option dialog box is the fourth box to appear and is illustrated in Figure 3.7. The Standard Installation is currently shown in the box. If you want to change to another option, such as the Full Installation, click the down arrow next to Standard Installation and choose the option you want from the list. Then click **Next** to continue.

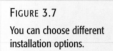

FIGURE 3.7

You can choose different installation options.

1 Click this arrow to display the list of installation types

Installing the Active Desktop

Even if you're not sure if you're going to use the Active Desktop, install it now. You can always turn the feature off from within Windows.

10. The fifth dialog box you see is the Windows Desktop Update. If you want to install the Active Desktop feature, just click **Next**. (**Yes** is already selected for you.) If you don't want to install the Active Desktop feature, click the option button next to **No** and then click **Next**.

11. The Active Channel Selection dialog box appears next. Select the region that most closely matches your geographic location, scrolling the list if necessary, and click **Next** to continue.

12. The seventh box to appear is the Destination folder. Unless you have a good reason for changing the folder, accept the assigned folder location and click **Next**.

13. The Preparing Setup dialog box appears. As the installation proceeds on your computer, you'll be informed of the progress in the status area. When the installation is complete, a small box appears, letting you know that the Setup program will close any open programs and advising you to disconnect from the Internet, if necessary. Click **OK** to continue.

14. After all programs are closed, another dialog box appears, advising that Setup must restart your computer. Click **OK** to allow Setup to restart the computer. When your computer restarts, it will take a short while for Internet Explorer to finish the installation process.

When the installation is completed, your Windows desktop re-appears with a Welcome dialog box, as shown in Figure 3.8, displayed in the center. The box contains three numbered buttons: **Take a Quick Tour**, **Explore Channels**, **Register Online,** and one other button: **Close**. If you have the time, click each of the buttons and follow the instructions to learn more about Internet Explorer.

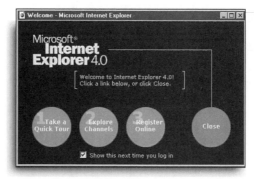

FIGURE 3.8
The Welcome dialog box intro-duces you to some of Internet Explorer's features.

Make sure that, even if you don't step through the brief tours provided by clicking the first two buttons, you click the third but-ton to register your copy of Internet Explorer. You'll be asked to connect to the Internet, and then be presented with some basic information such as your name, address, and the email address you've been given by your ISP. Registration is short, free, and very important. As a registered user, you are entitled to access some Microsoft technical support sites and receive any new updates to the program. When you've completed the registration process, click the fourth button, **Close**, to close the dialog box.

The Welcome box

Don't be surprised if you see the Welcome box the next time you start Windows. Unless you uncheck the box next to **Show this the next time you log in**, displaying the Welcome box will become a part of Windows startup process.

Looking at the Internet Explorer Browser Screen

The Internet Explorer browser screen is made up of many ele-ments. Figure 3.9 shows a Web page and illustrates Navigator's individual components.

FIGURE 3.9

The Computer Coach home page is displayed on the Netscape screen.

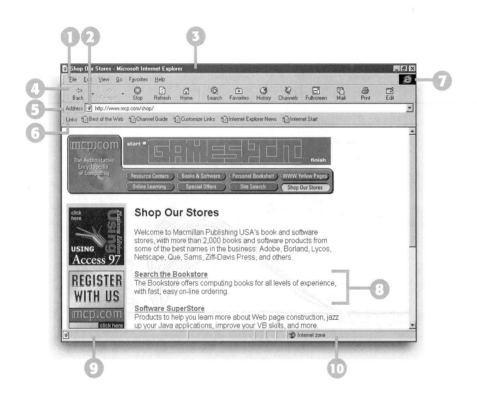

1 Menu bar

2 Page icon

3 Title bar

4 Standard Buttons toolbar

5 Address bar

6 Links toolbar

7 Internet Explorer icon

8 Hyperlinks

9 Status bar

10 Security zone information

The following describes each element shown in Figure 3.9:

- *Menu bar.* Similar to other Windows programs, Internet Explorer features a menu from which you can select commands.

- *Standard Buttons toolbar.* The Standard Buttons toolbar contains commands you'll use as you tour the Web.

- *Address bar.* The Address bar shows the Web address of the page that's displayed on the screen. You can also use the Address bar to search for another site.

- *Links toolbar.* Links on this bar provide a quick way to move to the site. The Links toolbar can be customized to add the links to sites you like.

- *Page icon.* When you're viewing a page you want to revisit, drag the Link icon into the Favorites folder.

- *Internet Explorer icon.* The box that displays the Internet Explorer icon performs two important functions. First, the icon turns, alternately displaying a globe and the Internet Explorer "e" when Internet Explorer accesses a page you requested. Second, you can move to the Microsoft Internet Explorer home page when you click the Internet Explorer icon.

- *Hyperlinks.* Click a hyperlink to move to the place referenced by the link, either on the same page or a new Web location.

- *Security zone.* The security zone displays the level of security of the Web site that appears onscreen. You can set the security zone levels for the pages you view.

- *Status bar.* Information about the current page is displayed here.

- *Title bar.* The title bar displays the title of the page that's displayed.

Getting Started with Internet Explorer

Now that you've had the opportunity to look at a picture of the components that make up the Internet Explorer browser screen, you're ready to do some of your own exploring. In this exercise,

Similar features

You might notice that Netscape Navigator and Internet Explorer look very similar. Both browsers share many common components and features. In fact, both browsers do a great job of bringing Web pages to your computer screen.

you launch the Internet Explorer browser and take a look at some of its unique features as you visit some Web pages. Make sure you're connected to the Internet before you begin the first step.

Taking a tour of the Web with Internet Explorer

1. Starting Internet Explorer is easy! As part of the installation process, Internet Explorer places a Quick Launch toolbar next to your Windows **Start** button (see Figure 3.10). Click the icon that looks like a lowercase E with a ring around it.

FIGURE 3.10

The Quick Launch toolbar holds shortcuts for Internet Explorer programs and features.

① Click here to launch the browser

2. The first Web page to appear could be the Welcome Internet Start page or your ISP's home page. Unless you change it, this page will appear each time you launch Internet Explorer. Read the text on the page. When you're finished reading, click the Internet Explorer icon located on the top-right corner of the Internet Explorer screen.

3. The Microsoft Internet Start page appears. Move your mouse pointer slowly across the buttons on the Standard Buttons toolbar, noticing that each button appears in color and becomes raised when the pointer passes over it.

4. Move your mouse arrow around the text and graphics on the Start Page. The mouse arrow changes to the shape of a hand as it passes over hyperlinks on the page. (You'll learn more about hyperlinks later in this chapter.)

5. Any toolbar that's displayed on the browser screen can be hidden when you're not using it. For now, hide the Links toolbar by positioning your mouse pointer to the right of the buttons on the Links toolbar (so it's in a blank spot) and clicking the right mouse button. A shortcut menu, shown in Figure 3.11, appears.

FIGURE 3.11
A check mark means the toolbar is visible.

6. Click the **Links** item on the shortcut menu. The menu closes and the Links toolbar is removed from the screen. Any time you want to redisplay a toolbar you've hidden, click the **View** menu and choose **Toolbars** and then the name of the toolbar you want to show (in this case, **Links**).

7. Click inside the **Address** box and type the following Web address carefully in the box: www.mcp.com. (You needn't delete the text that's already in the box first because the new text will overwrite the old text.) After you've made sure that you've typed the address correctly, press Enter.

8. The Internet Explorer icon becomes animated and looks, alternately, like a globe and an e with a ring around it as the server that stores the Macmillan home page is contacted. In a moment, the Macmillan page appears on your screen.

9. Click the **Fullscreen** button on the Standard Buttons tool-bar. The Macmillan page fills the screen and the Windows taskbar, the title, menu, and Address bar disappear. At the top of the screen, the Standard Buttons toolbar appears as a row of small buttons without text.

10. The **Fullscreen** button appears depressed on the toolbar that appears at the top of the screen. Click the **Fullscreen** button. The screen is restored to its previous view, with the Windows taskbar redisplayed.

11. Click inside the **Address** box. The current URL appears highlighted. Type www.usatoday.com and press Enter. In a moment or two, the USA Today Web page appears on your screen. Take a moment and read the latest news.

12. Click inside the **Address** box and type www.tvguide.com and press Enter. Now you're looking at the television news! After you've looked around, click the **Back** button on the Standard buttons toolbar to open the page you were viewing previously.

13. Click the **Back** button again. You're stepped back one more page that you've visited.

14. The **Forward** button on the Standard buttons toolbar contains an arrow pointing to the right. Click the arrow to display a list of sites you've seen in the current session and select one from the list to return to that site.

Each time you click the **Back** or **Forward** buttons, you're returned to the site you viewed previously during your current browsing session. If you want to get back to a site that you visited a while ago, clicking the arrow on the button to display the list of sites helps you get back to where you want to go without having to revisit many sites.

15. Click the **Home** button on the Standard button toolbar. The page you saw when you first opened Internet Explorer appears onscreen. You've come full-circle; you're back home again.

16. Close the Internet Explorer browser in the same way that you close any other Windows program. Click the Close box (the box with the X on the Navigator title bar) one time. The program closes and you're returned to your new Windows Active Desktop.

SEE ALSO

➤ *Information on changing your Internet Explorer Start page is shown on page 114.*

Working with the Active Desktop

If you included the Active Desktop component when you installed Internet Explorer, you probably noticed that your Windows desktop looks and acts differently than it did before. One of the main purposes of the Active Desktop is to integrate Windows 95 and Internet Explorer. Instead of double-clicking to open a file or folder, the Active Desktop lets you single-click it, the way you would open a Web page.

The Active Desktop changes the way your desktop looks. You might see a Channel bar, with links to many of Microsoft's new Active Channels. The Active Desktop is customizable in many ways. You can add live desktop items, such as a weather map, scrolling stock ticker, or a clock. You can even add a Web page as a background.

Just for now

The browsing history stored in the **Back** and **Forward** buttons is erased when you close Internet Explorer. You'll find out how to view your browsing history for a chronological period in Chapter 4, "Moving On Through the Web."

Of course you must pay a price for all this visual excitement. Unless you have lots of RAM installed inside your computer, you might notice that the system seems slow or unresponsive. Additionally, without meaning to, you might be using a lot of hard drive space by adding the live content.

You're not locked in to the new desktop; you can change the wallpaper, add a moving item, and even restore the old settings. Because your desktop is where all the action in Windows begins, set up your desktop just the way you want it.

Changing the look and feel of the Active Desktop

1. Although the default Active Desktop wallpaper contains a great link to a tutorial about the Active Desktop (click the words **Tell me about Active Desktop**), most people quickly grow tired of the dark background. To begin the process of changing it, right-click on a blank area of the desktop. A shortcut menu appears.

2. Slide the mouse over to **A**ctive **Desktop** and then **C**ustomize my Desktop, as shown in Figure 3.12.

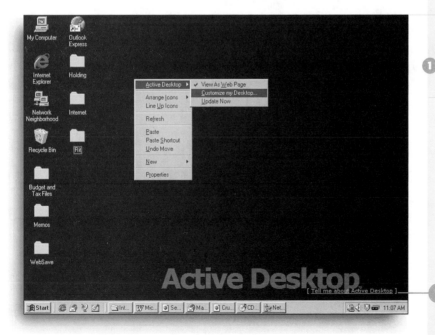

FIGURE 3.12
The Windows Active Desktop.

1 Click here for information on the Active Desktop feature

3. When the Display Properties dialog box appears, choose the **Background** tab (see Figure 3.13).

4. Choose another wallpaper from the list. Notice that when you select one of the names on the list, an example of the wallpaper is displayed in the sample monitor.

5. When you find the wallpaper you like, click **Apply**. The wallpaper you selected replaces the one that was displayed previously.

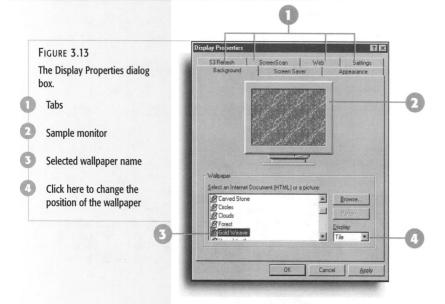

FIGURE 3.13

The Display Properties dialog box.

1 Tabs

2 Sample monitor

3 Selected wallpaper name

4 Click here to change the position of the wallpaper

6. Click the **Web** tab of the Display Properties dialog box.

7. Click the **New** button. The New Active Desktop Item dialog box appears, asking if you would like to close Display Properties and connect to the Microsoft Active Gallery (see Figure 3.14).

8. Click **Yes**. The Internet Explorer browser launches and displays the Microsoft Desktop Gallery.

9. Use the vertical scroll box to move down the page to **Cool Utilities.**

10. Select a desktop item to install, such as the 3D Java Clock chosen in this task. (You're clicking a hyperlink so your mouse takes the shape of a hand.)

FIGURE 3.14
The New Active Desktop Item dialog box will take you to the Web.

11. An example of the Java Clock appears on the new page. Click the **Add to Desktop** button.

12. Click **Y**es in response in the question, **Do you want to add a desktop item to your active desktop?** The Add item to your Active Desktop dialog box appears.

13. Click **OK**. The Downloading Subscriptions dialog box displays briefly as the components needed to display the clock are copied to the hard drive of your computer.

14. Minimize all your open programs to view the Windows desktop. The clock is displayed on your desktop in its own window.

15. The clock can be moved anywhere on your desktop by dragging its title bar. Place your mouse pointer on a blank area on the clock's title bar and click and drag the window to another area of the desktop.

16. Repeat steps 6 through 13 to add more items to your desktop.

SEE ALSO
➤ *You'll learn about Active Channels on page 334.*
➤ *You'll learn more about hyperlinks on page 83.*

Changing Your Active Desktop Settings

When the Active Desktop is installed, you open files and folders with one mouse click. If you're used to opening files and folders by double-clicking them, this new way can make you feel like a Windows novice again (not to mention a clumsy oaf). Wait a few days and see if you get used to the new style of clicking. If not, change it back to the way you like.

Desktop items can slow down your computer

After you install an item to the Active Desktop, open a few of the programs that you normally use. Active Desktop items use a lot of your computer's resources and can slow down your computer. To restore your desktop to its original look, click the Windows **Start** button and select **Settings**, **Active Desktop**, and choose **Customize my Desktop**. Click the **Reset All** button.

If you really don't like the Active Desktop, simply turn it off. Just like a light switch, you can turn the Active Desktop feature on and off when you want to.

Restoring the double-click functionality

1. Click the Windows **Start** button and choose **Settings** and then **Folders & Icons.** The Folder Options dialog box appears with the **General** tab displayed.

2. Click the option button next to **Custom, based on settings you choose,** and then click the **Settings** button. The Custom Settings dialog box appears, layered on top of the Folder Options box.

3. The Custom Settings dialog box is divided into four sections. In the fourth section, labeled **Click items as follows**, click the option button next to **Double-click to open an item (single-click to select)**, as shown in Figure 3.15.

FIGURE 3.15

The Custom Settings dialog box controls many of your Active Desktop settings.

1 Choose this option to restore double-click functionality

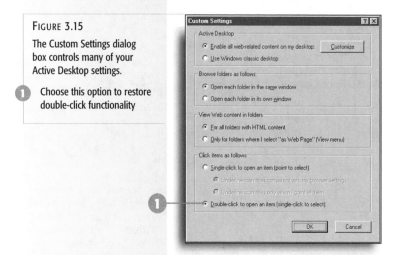

4. Click **OK** to close the Custom Settings dialog box and return to the Folder Options dialog box.

5. Click **OK** to close the Folder Options dialog box. Anytime you want to open a file or folder, double-click it.

Turning off the Active Desktop

1. Turning off the Active Desktop after you've installed it is no problem. Close or minimize all open programs so that your desktop is visible onscreen.

2. Click the Windows **Start** button and select **Settings, Active Desktop,** and then **View as <u>W</u>eb Page**. A check mark next to **View as Web Page** indicates that it's turned on.

3. Click **View as <u>W</u>eb Page** to remove the check mark and turn off the Active Desktop feature. When the desktop appears, all Active Desktop items are removed.

4. Anytime you want to turn on the Active Desktop, perform steps 1 through 3.

Working with Hyperlinks

No matter which browser you use, you'll spend a lot of time moving around the Web with hyperlinks. Think of hyperlinks as the glue that connects Web pages. Your mouse pointer takes the shape of a hand when it passes over a hyperlink. Most of the time, hyperlinks, or links for short, appear in Web pages as underlined, colored text, or graphics. Links are easy to follow; click one and you're whisked to the linked site.

Links work the same way on every browser. Most text links are displayed in blue before you click them. As soon as you click a link, its color changes to purple, letting you know that you've already visited the linked site. Why is this important? When you've looked at one Web site after another as you search for a particular piece if information, it's helpful to know if the site is one you've already visited. (Sometimes, you can visit hundreds of sites in one Web session.) However, using the color method to track where've you been isn't always effective. Many Web designers override this feature and make sure that the color of visited links does not change from their original color.

Touring the Web with hyperlinks

1. If you're not on the Internet, connect now and open your browser by clicking the **<u>S</u>tart** button and opening it from the Windows Start menu.

2. When the browser is launched and displaying a Web site, click inside the box near the top of the screen that contains a

Find out where you're going

If you want to know where a link will take you, point to the link with your mouse and note the address of the Web site in the Status bar at the bottom of the screen.

Web address (it will start with http://). The text in the box appears highlighted.

3. Type the following Web address in the box and press Enter:
http://www.computercoach.com/

4. Watch the Status bar at the bottom left of the screen as the page is accessed. In a short time, the Status bar displays a message indicating that the page is loaded onscreen.

5. Place your mouse pointer in the top-right corner of the browser window and slowly move the pointer around the screen. As you move the pointer down, notice that its shape changes to a hand, which signifies a link, as it passes over different parts of the screen.

6. Position the mouse over one of the graphics images on the page. The pointer assumes the shape of a hand, telling you that the image is a hyperlink. Additionally, a ScreenTip that describes the link appears, as shown in Figure 3.16.

7. Place the mouse pointer over some colored, underlined text on the page so that the mouse pointer's shape changes to a hand.

FIGURE **3.16**

Links can be text or graphics.

1 The hand indicates that the image is a link

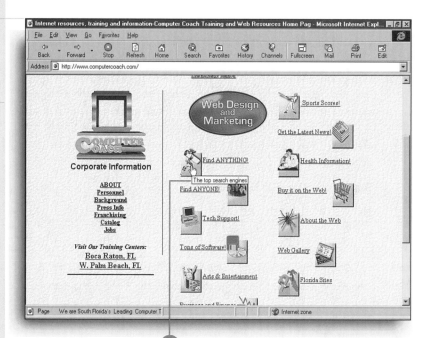

8. Click the underlined text and, in a moment, a new page appears onscreen.

SEE ALSO

➤ *To learn more about Web addresses, see page 90.*

Clicking a Non-working Link

It happens to everyone who spends any time on the Web. You click a link (generally to a site that really looks exciting) and, instead of seeing the new page on the screen, you see an error message. If you're like most people, you back up and try the link again, assuming that you've done something wrong.

Actually, invalid links are the closest thing to a Web epidemic. There are many reasons why clicking a link fails to bring up the expected page. The most common reason is that the page the link refers to has been taken off the Web or it has been moved to a new location. Sadly, it happens all the time. If you click a link and see an error message instead of the linked page, don't be alarmed. It wasn't your fault. The Web needs to find a way to clean up after itself.

Table 3.4 contains a list of common error messages associated with invalid or failed links, what they mean, and what you can do.

TABLE 3.4 Failed links

Error Message	What It Means	Possible Solutions
Error 404 or File not Found	The page has moved to a new location or has been removed from the Web.	You can't do much when you see this type of message. The link you clicked refers to a page that's been removed or relocated.
A connection to the server could not be established or Server not responding	The problem can be at your end or on the server that hosts the linked page.	Check to see if you've accidentally been disconnected from the Internet. If not, try clicking the link again. If you receive the same message, you know that the host server isn't available right now. Try the page later.

continues…

Link anchor

Hyperlinks connect locations on the Web. The portion of the link that causes the mouse arrow to change shape is called a link anchor.

TABLE 3.4 Continued

Error Message	What It Means	Possible Solutions
`Unauthorized entry refused`	You don't have permission to view the page.	Not all pages are open to all; maybe the page requires a username and password. If you're accessing the Internet from your office, the network administrator might have declared the site off-limits.
`Too many users, try again later` or `Connection refused by host`	Too many people are simultaneously trying to access the site.	Wait a bit and try again later.
`Document contains no data` or `Protocol in this address is invalid`	The address you clicked is incorrect.	If the address has a specific page listed, remove the reference to that page and try again. For example, if the address in the address box is something like `http://www.barbara.com/books.htm`, delete the `books.htm` portion and try to connect.

Taking Control of the Internet

Moving On Through the Web

The Address Is Everything

It seems like everyone has a Web site these days. Most major companies have a presence on the Web. Your favorite television news show or soap opera might have a site. Even your friends and relatives can have Web sites. Every site on the Web is identified by its own unique name.

The Web address of each site is called a *URL*, short for Uniform Resource Locator. A URL (sometimes pronounced "earl") is broken up by periods, called dots, and contains letters, slashes, and other punctuation. Although the characters in a URL might look like they've been placed in a hit-and-miss fashion, each symbol, group of letters, and number has its own functions.

The first page of a Web site is called its home page. A site can have just one page called the home page, or it can have many pages that are linked to the main (home) page. Think of a home page as a front door to the rest of the site.

When you're typing a URL, it's important to type it with every dot, slash, and colon in place. If one of the characters is typed incorrectly when you're entering a Web address in the address box of your browser, you'll see an error message instead of the page you expected.

Breaking Down a URL

When you break down a URL into parts, it's easy to understand. Take the following URL:

`http://www.mcp.com`

The `http://` portion is called the protocol type and identifies the document as a Web site. (You probably haven't come across any yet, but other protocols on the Internet include `ftp://` or `telnet://`). Protocol types define the ways computers communicate with one another. Fortunately, your Web browser does all the work of setting up the appropriate method of communication after it reads the protocol type. In fact, when you're typing a URL, you can omit the `http://` portion, as you'll find later in this chapter.

The www portion of the name indicates that this is the Web managing portion of the computer called mcp.com (the http:// portion of the name already identified it as a Web page), which is the actual computer that exists at the domain.

The dot (.) character joins each element of the address. The dot character is pronounced "dot."

The mcp portion of the name is unique and can be defined by the group or person who selected it. In the case of mcp, the letters stand for Macmillan Computer Publishing. The name can be short and abbreviated, or long and descriptive. For example, a friend of mine opened a Web business and used candylandware-house in this portion of the name. Depending on where the domain name is obtained, you might not be able to choose this portion. For example, if your ISP allows you to set up a personal Web page, your URL will probably be something like www.myisp.com~yourname.

The com portion of the name is probably the most familiar; you've heard the phrase "dot com" before. Com, the three letter extension called the top-level *domain*, indicates that the page is registered to a commercial user, or that the Web host that stores the page is a commercial institution.

When you put all the elements together, the URL http://www.mcp.com makes sense!

Domain Names

In the example of Macmillan Computer Publishing's URL, the www, mcp, and com portions combine to form a *domain name*. Customized names, like Macmillan's, need to be registered with a special Internet agency after they've been researched to make sure that the name is unique. After they're registered, these names need to be paid for every year to keep them active.

Domain names are spoken just the way they're read. For example, because the letters www or mcp don't form a word that someone could say, the names of the letters are used instead. However, in my friend's case, the portion of the virtual domain name that reads candylandwarehouse is spoken as one long word.

If you want to tell someone a URL, follow a few simples rule to say it correctly. Whenever you see a period (.), say the word "dot." A forward slash (/) is referred to as slash, a colon character (:) as colon. If the letters in the name form a word that can't be pronounced, pronounce each letter name.

Com Is Only One of Many

Although you're familiar with the domain name com, there are actually six domain names. Table 4.1 lists each domain name and provides a little information about them.

TABLE 4.1   Common domain names

Name	What It Means
com	The site or the host of the site is a commercial enterprise.
net	Net sites are part of a network. Your ISP may use a net domain name.
gov	The site is owned by a U.S. governmental agency.
edu	Educational institutions use edu as their domain name.
mil	mil is a tip that the site is owned by the U.S. military.
org	Non-profit organizations use org.

The three letters of the domain name can be followed by another dot (period) and then a two letter country code. If you don't see a country code, the domain is probably located somewhere in the United States.

New Domain Names

Although there are six domain names, com is drastically overloaded. Because com denotes that either the owner of the name or the Web server that stores the Web page is a commercial enterprise, it's impossible to determine who owns a page that uses a com domain. (For example, a service called GeoCities provides free space for personal home pages to more than one million users. Each of those pages uses the URL www.geocities.com as part of its address, as you'll see in a few minutes.) Additionally, there just aren't enough com names to accommodate all the requests for registration. Fortunately, seven new domain names are in the works (and may already be in effect when you read this book).

The new top-level domain names will be as follows:

- *web*. Web related
- *firm*. Business
- *arts*. Art and culture related
- *info*. Information services
- *rec*. Recreation and entertainment related
- *store*. A business offering goods for sale
- *nom*. Of personal or individual nature

In fact, Emergent Corporation is working to build a new Internet name registration system. In the future, the addition of domain names should mean that domain names will more greatly reflect the type of site they represent. Additionally, because more names will be available, most users will be able to register the exact domain name they want.

Entering URLs

1. Connect to the Internet and open your browser.
2. When your **Start** page appears, click inside the box at the top of the screen that displays a Web address. (The text will begin with http://.) The address appears highlighted.
3. Type www.art4sale.com, or another URL you know, and press Enter. Your browser contacts the server that stores the page and, in a moment, a new Web page appears onscreen.
4. Look carefully at the URL in the **Address** box. Even though you didn't type the http:// portion, your browser filled it in for you.

5. You can use menu commands to move to a new site. (You might want to use the menu method if the toolbar that displays Web addresses is hidden from view.) If you're using Internet Explorer, click **File** and choose **Open**. Navigator's command reads **Open File**.

6. An Open dialog box appears, similar to the one shown in Figure 4.1. (If you're using Navigator, your dialog box looks slightly different, but contains the same basic components.) Type another URL in the **Open** text box. If you want, type www.geocities.com/Paris/LeftBank/4487.

FIGURE 4.1
The Open dialog box.

If the URL contains mixed case (upper- and lowercase) letters, type it exactly as it appears. Depending on where the page is stored, you might not be able to access it otherwise.

7. If you're using the Internet Explorer browser, click **OK**. If you're using Navigator, click **Open**. The dialog box closes and, in a moment, a new Web page appears.

8. Both Internet Explorer and Navigator enable you to type a portion of the URL and let the browser search the Web for the page you want. Click inside the **Address** box and highlight the URL that's shown in the box.

9. Type mcp and press Enter. Although it takes a few seconds longer than if you had typed the complete URL, your browser displays the Macmillan Computer Publishing page.

Keep in mind that this feature, although handy, can't always find the page for which you're looking. Sometimes too many pages match the letters you typed and the wrong one is accessed. If you know the complete URL, type it to be assured of opening the exact page you want.

Using the Stop button

If you change your mind after your browser begins to access the new page, or if you realize you've made a typo, click the Stop button on the toolbar to stop the transfer.

10. When the Macmillan Computer Publishing page is finished loading, click inside the **Address** box. When the URL in the box appears highlighted, type about six characters of one of the URLs you typed previously—for example, `www.art`—and wait a few seconds. Your browser remembers a site you visited previously that matched the portion of the URL you've just entered and fills in the remainder of the URL for you, as shown in Figure 4.2.

FIGURE 4.2

Your browser anticipates where you want to go.

1 The highlighted portion is filled in by your browser

As you type the URL, your browser fills in the rest of the line with a URL that matches what you've typed so far. If the portion filled in by the browser isn't correct, continue typing the URL letter by letter until your browser fills in the rest of the line correctly, or you finish typing.

11. Press Enter to return to the Web page that matches the URL shown in the box.

12. If the new page on your screen contains links, click one and see where it takes you. After you've clicked a link, use your Back button to move back to the previous page.

13. Click the Home button on your browser's toolbar to return to your starting page.

Using Your Browser's History

Until now, you've moved around the Web by clicking links and typing URLs. In the last exercise, you visited several Web sites by typing their URLs. If you were asked to repeat the URLs you typed, you probably couldn't remember each one. Chances are, though, that you remember something about one of the sites that makes you want to go back and take a second look.

As you learned in the previous chapter, you can use the Back and Forward buttons on the toolbar to return to sites you've visited during the current Web session. However, after you quit the browser, the history stored in the Back and Forward buttons is cleared. Unless you remember the specific URL or the location of the link you clicked to find it the first time, a visited Web site is difficult to return to.

Fortunately, both Navigator and Internet Explorer store your browsing history for you. You can use the history to quickly find and revisit sites that you've seen before. Navigator provides a flat text history that opens in a separate window. Internet Explorer displays your history in an Explorer Bar that has a more graphical look. The following exercises show how to use the History feature in Internet Explorer and Navigator, respectively.

Viewing a History of Links and Sites in Internet Explorer

The Internet Explorer Bars provide a way for you to look through a page of links on the left side of the screen, like your History, while displaying the links to which the pages refer on the right. You see an Explorer Bar when you click the History, Search, Channels, or Favorites button on the Standard Buttons toolbar.

By creating a hierarchical structure of weeks, days, and URLs of the home pages you visited, and then each individual page or graphic you saw, you can find your way back to a site. In the following exercise you use the Internet Explorer History Bar to revisit some sites.

Going back with Internet Explorer's History Bar

1. Click the History button on the Internet Explorer Standard Buttons toolbar. An Explorer Bar labeled History appears on the left side of the Internet Explorer browser window.

   Folders for each of your Internet Explorer browsing sessions are displayed in the Bar, as shown in Figure 4.3. The folders are stacked chronologically, first by weeks and then by days.

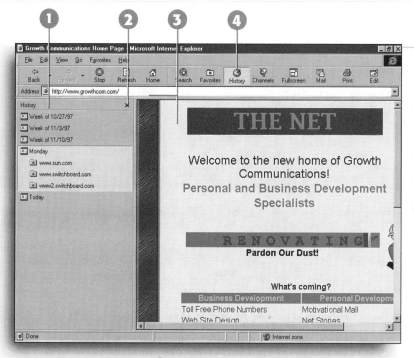

FIGURE 4.3

The Explorer History Bar keeps track of where you've been.

1. Explorer History Bar displays on the left side of the screen

2. Close button

3. Current Web page

4. History button is pressed

2. Click one of the days of the week folders. Each shows the URL of the home page of a site you visited on the date the first folder represents.

3. Click **Today**. When the listing of the sites you visited today appears, click one of the folders. The folder opens and displays the titles of all the pages and graphics you visited at that site, as shown in Figure 4.4.

4. If you want to know more about your previous visit, such as the time you accessed the page or graphics image, right-click it on the Explorer History Bar.

5. Choose **Properties** from the resulting shortcut menu. The Properties dialog box appears and displays the time and date the page was last accessed.

6. When you're finished looking at the Properties dialog box, click **OK** to close it and return to the Explorer History Bar.

FIGURE 4.4

Each site folder holds a record of the pages visited at that site.

1 Site folder displays the URL of the home page

2 Pages and images within the site

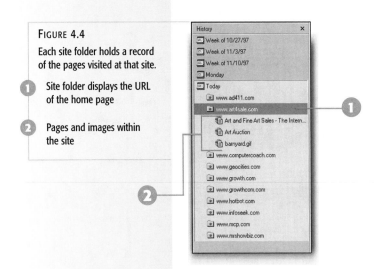

7. Click the title of a page on the History list to which you want to return. The page you requested opens in the browser window on the right side of the screen.

8. Close the Explorer History Bar by clicking the Close button (the **X**) on the right side of the Bar.

Using Navigator's History Feature

When you access your Navigator History window, you're presented with the title, location (URL), dates visited, and other information about Web sites you've visited. Additionally, the Navigator History window enables you to search for a particular keyword or portion of a URL. The search function is especially helpful if your history is lengthy. If you set up profiles for more than one Navigator user on your computer, you'll see only the history that matches your username.

Although you do not need to be connected to the Internet to view your Navigator history, you should be connected if you want to return to the site. Navigator should be open onscreen before you begin to work through the numbered steps.

Exploring the Navigator History List

1. Click **Communicator** and then **History**. Your Navigator History list appears in a small window that's layered over the Navigator screen, as shown in Figure 4.5. Notice that in addition to opening onscreen, a **History** button appears on the Windows taskbar.

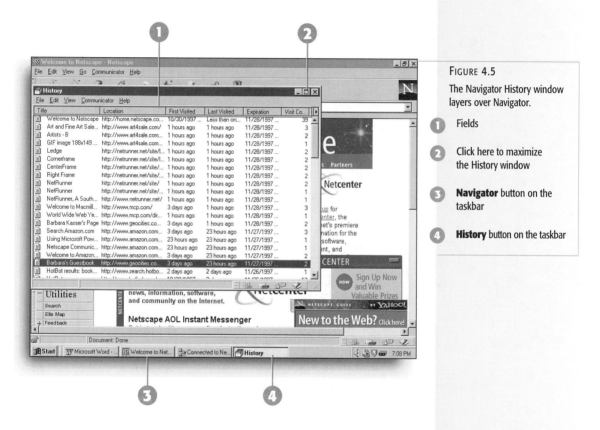

FIGURE 4.5
The Navigator History window layers over Navigator.

1 Fields

2 Click here to maximize the History window

3 **Navigator** button on the taskbar

4 **History** button on the taskbar

2. The small size of the Navigator History window makes it hard to read. Maximize the window by clicking the **Maximize** button. The History window fills the screen.

3. The titles of the sites you've visited might appear truncated. If you can't read all the information in a field, hold your mouse pointer over the truncated information. In a moment, a *ScreenTip* appears that displays all the information in the field.

4. If you can remember a word in its title or a portion of its URL, you can search for a site on the History list. Click **Edit** and then choose **Search History List**. The Search History List dialog box appears, as shown in Figure 4.6.

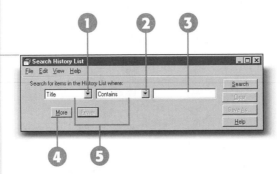

5. The box currently reads **Search for items in the History List where Title Contains**. **Title** is the default field to be searched and the default operator is **Contains**. If you want to search for another field or use another operator, like **Doesn't contain**, **Is**, or **Isn't**, click the down arrow next to the item you wish to change and choose a new one from the drop-down list.

6. Type the keyword, such as a word you remember from the Web page title or a portion of the URL, in the empty text box next to the operator.

7. If you want to add a field to look through, click **More**. Repeat steps 5 and 6 and then click **Search**.

8. Navigator looks through the History List and displays the Web sites that match the criteria you specified.

9. When you've located the entry for the site you want to revisit, double-click its name or location. The corresponding page opens in a new Navigator window. Notice that two **Navigator** buttons now appear on the Windows taskbar.

10. Close the History window by clicking the Close button at the right of the History window title bar.

Computer slow-down

If Navigator is running in more than one window on your computer, such as when you open a site from the History List, you might notice that your system seems sluggish and non-responsive. Close one of the Navigator windows to conserve valuable system resources.

Keeping a List of Your Favorite Sites

You can visit personal favorites—such as cafes, shops, and resorts—again and again. As you visit sites on the Web, you're sure to find some favorite places on the Web too. Internet Explorer calls them *Favorites*. Navigator calls them *Bookmarks*. Both browsers enable you to group these favorite Web sites in a list so you can return to them again and again. After you've set up your list, the sites you like are never more than a few mouse clicks away.

Before too long, your list of Favorites (Bookmarks) grows so long that it becomes difficult to find the one you want. (My sister, an Internet novice, bookmarked more than 250 sites in less than three months!) Fortunately, you can create folders to organize and store your Favorites (Bookmarks). That way, if you're looking for the link to the Mr. Showbiz site, for example, you can find it easily in your Show Business folder.

Although Internet Explorer Favorites and Navigator Bookmarks do roughly the same thing, each browser works a bit differently. Follow the exercises that correspond with the browser you're using. Be sure you are connected to the Internet and your browser is open before beginning the following step by step.

Creating Favorites with Internet Explorer

1. Click inside the **Address** Bar and type a URL, for example www.ad411.com, and press Enter.

2. When the new site appears, right-click on a blank spot on the page (not on a hyperlink) and select **Add to Favorites** from the resulting shortcut menu. The Add Favorite dialog box shown in Figure 4.7 appears onscreen.

3. If it's not already chosen, click the option button next to **No, just add the page to my favorites** and then click **OK**. The page on your screen is now added to your list of Favorites.

4. Verify that your Favorite is set up by clicking **Favorites** on the menu bar. The title of the onscreen page, shown on the Internet Explorer title bar, appears on the list.

Find it fast

Both popular browsers store a record of the last 15 or so URLs you typed (including URLs typed with errors). To return to one of these URLs, click the down arrow next to the address box and click the URL you want to revisit.

Web page or site?

The terms Web page and Web site are synonymous. Each means a document on the World Wide Web.

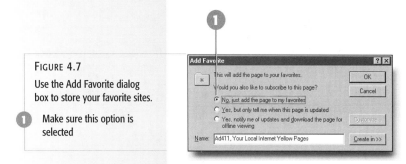

FIGURE 4.7

FIGURE 4.7

Use the Add Favorite dialog box to store your favorite sites.

1 Make sure this option is selected

Organizing your Favorites into folders

1. Click **Favorites** on the menu bar and then **Organize Favorites**. The Organize Favorites dialog box appears, as shown in Figure 4.8. Since I've been using Internet Explorer for a long time, my Favorites probably look different than yours.

FIGURE 4.8

The Organize Favorites dialog box.

1 Create New Folder button

2 Favorite not stored in a folder

3 Folders hold related Favorites

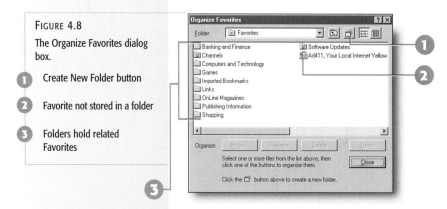

Where did those other folders come from?

Don't be surprised if you see several folders in your Favorites list that you didn't create. Internet Explorer sets up a few folders filled with Favorites for you during the installation process. You can visit any of these sites by choosing **Favorites** on the Internet Explorer menu bar, then opening the folder and clicking the URL of the page you want to visit.

2. Click the Create New Folder button. A closed folder icon appears at the bottom of the Favorites list with the words **New Folder** selected.

3. Type a name for the folder. (The text you type will overwrite the **New Folder** text.) A folder can be called anything you like, as long as the title does not exceed 256 characters.

4. When you're finished typing the folder name, click outside the **Folder** name box.

5. Hold down the left mouse button and drag a Favorite on top of the new folder. As you drag, a shadow copy of the Favorite's icon appears.

6. Release the left mouse button. The Favorite is now placed in a folder.

7. Click the **C**lose button to close the Organize Favorites dialog box.

8. Whenever you want to return to the site to which a Favorite points, click **Fa**vorites, click the proper folder, and then click the Favorite.

Bookmarking sites with Navigator

1. Click in the **Location/Netsite** box (now reading **Go to**). When the present URL in the box appears highlighted, type a URL, such as www.georgemag.com, as demonstrated in Figure 4.9, and press Enter.

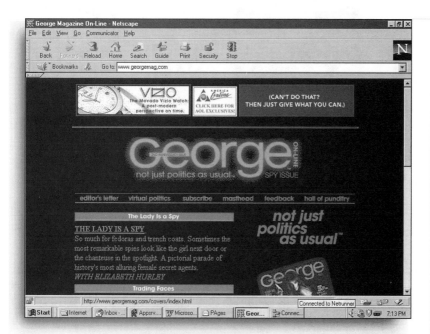

Using folders for Favorites

Your filing system for Favorites can be as simple or elaborate as you like. If you are super-organized, you even create folders within folders, just as you do with the folders that store files on your computer.

Displaying the Favorites list

Similar to how Internet Explorer displays the History list, if you click the Favorites button on the Standard Buttons toolbar, the Favorites list opens in an Explorer Bar on the left side of the screen. If you click a Favorite on the list, the site opens on the right side of the screen.

FIGURE 4.9
A new URL is typed in the **Go to** box.

2. When the new page appears, click the Bookmarks QuickFile icon, located at the side of Location toolbar. A list of folders and bookmarks appears, with commands at the top of the list.

3. Choose **Add Bookmark**, as shown in Figure 4.10. (I've been using Navigator for ages, so my Bookmarks list is probably much more extensive than yours.) The list closes and the bookmark to the Web page is added to the bottom of the list.

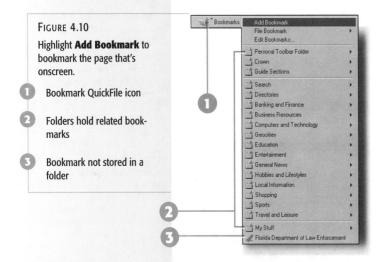

FIGURE 4.10

Highlight **Add Bookmark** to bookmark the page that's onscreen.

1 Bookmark QuickFile icon

2 Folders hold related bookmarks

3 Bookmark not stored in a folder

4. Type another URL, such as www.usta-fl.com, in the **Location/Netsite** box and press Enter. The new page appears onscreen.

5. To bookmark this site, place the mouse pointer on the Page Proxy icon located next to the **Location/Netsite** box. As shown in Figure 4.11, the page icon changes to look like a page with a bookmark on top of it, and the mouse pointer assumes the shape of a hand. Additionally, a ScreenTip and information on the Status bar tell you to how to create the bookmark.

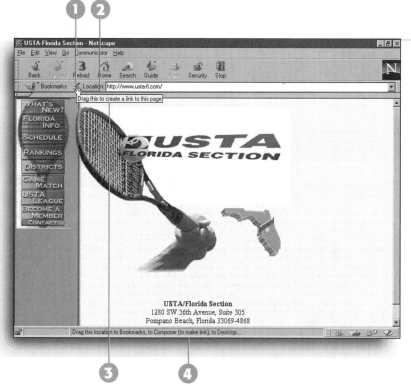

FIGURE 4.11

Drag the Page Proxy icon to create a bookmark.

1 Page Proxy icon

2 Mouse pointer takes the shape of a hand

3 ScreenTip

4 Status bar provides instruction

6. Without releasing the mouse button, drag the Page Proxy icon left to the **Bookmarks**. As it drags, the mouse pointer has a link icon with a small cross above attached.

7. Release the mouse button so that the tip of the mouse pointer is located in any portion of the word **Bookmarks**.

Good work! You've added two bookmarks. Practice adding bookmarks to sites you like.

Arranging your Bookmarks

1. Open the Bookmarks list by clicking the Bookmark QuickFile icon on the Location toolbar. Your Bookmark folders appear with the commands **Add Bookmark**, **File Bookmarks,** and **Edit Bookmarks** at the top.

Create a shortcut to your favorite page

In addition to the two methods you've learned to set bookmarks, Navigator takes advantage of the Windows 95 shortcut menu to provide you with yet another way to navigate when you're viewing a Web site. Right-click the mouse pointer on an empty spot on the Web page. When the shortcut menu appears, click **Add Bookmark**. Take care not to position the mouse pointer on a link or graphics image when you access the shortcut menu.

2. Choose **Edit Bookmarks**. The Bookmarks list appears on top of the Web page that's onscreen.

A plus sign (+) next to a folder indicates that the folder is collapsed or closed. A minus sign (-) next to a folder indicates that the folder is expanded or open; you can see the bookmarks in the folder. (See Figure 4.12.)

FIGURE 4.12

The Bookmarks list shows open and closed folders and bookmarks.

① These folders are collapsed

② This folder is expanded and you can see the bookmarks inside

③ Bookmarks not in a folder

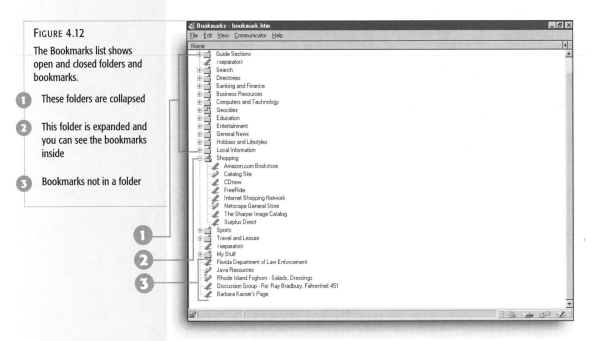

3. Move a bookmark into an existing folder by clicking the bookmark next to the bookmark title and dragging it on top of the folder you want to move it to. When you release the mouse button, the bookmark drops into the folder.

4. To create a new folder to store bookmarks, right-click on the spot on the list where you want the folder to appear. Choose **New Folder** from the shortcut menu.

5. The new folder is displayed on the list and the Bookmark Properties dialog box appears, as shown in Figure 4.13.

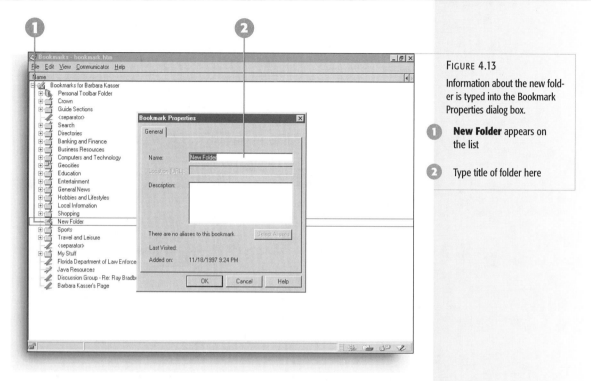

FIGURE 4.13

Information about the new folder is typed into the Bookmark Properties dialog box.

1 **New Folder** appears on the list

2 Type title of folder here

6. Type the name of the new folder in the **Name** text box and click **OK**. The dialog box closes and the folder on the list displays the new name.

7. Repeat step 3 to drag a bookmark into the new folder.

Dealing with Frames

As you tool around the Web visiting pages, you're bound to come across a page that contains *frames*. In fact, some of the pages you visited in this chapter utilize them. Frames enable a Web designer to split a page into multiple rectangular sections, each with its own function and look.

Both browsers support the use of frames. Frames can be used as menu bars, as a way to add visual excitement to a page, and as a means for making a lot of different information available on one page. Because each frame is actually a separate Web page, you can move up and down in one frame while the other frames stay still.

Look at the example of a page with frames shown in Figure 4.14. Two Web pages, each with its own scrolling capability, are combined into one page. If you move through one of the frames with the vertical scrollbar, the other frame remains constant. In this case, frames enable you to actually see two pages on one screen.

FIGURE 4.14

Growthcom's Quote Site is made up of two frames.

1 First Web page

2 Second Web page

3 Vertical scrollbar

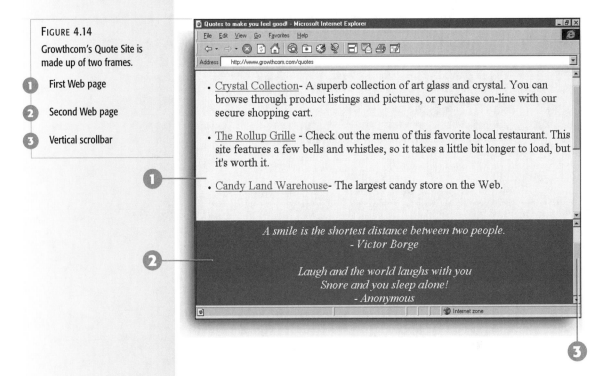

Sometimes frames aren't obvious. In Figure 4.15, one frame holds a menu bar that provides links to related pages at the Palace Bleu Hotel's site, such as **Reservation** or **Amenities**. When you click one of the links on the frame at the left, the larger frame to the right displays the content you requested.

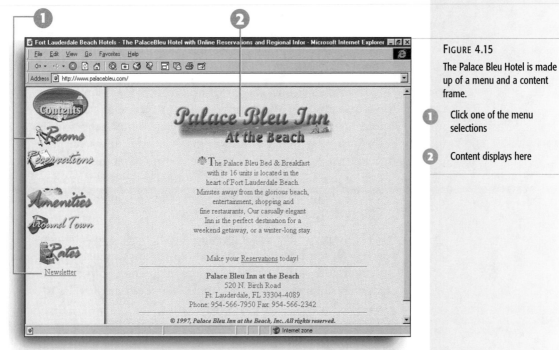

Frame navigation can be tricky. Because each frame on a page acts as its own page, clicking the Back and Forward buttons might not take you out of the page that's onscreen. Instead, you cycle through the frames that make up the page.

If you feel like you can't get out of a page that contains frames, don't get frustrated. Position the mouse pointer in your browser's Back button and click the right mouse button to display a list of page titles you've visited. Choose the title of the page you want to revisit from the list.

Completing Forms

Many pages on the Web require you to complete a form. Forms are fill-in-the-blanks tools that help make the Web interactive by providing a method of communication between you and other points on the Internet. Just like a paper form, a Web form is completed and then sent to another site for processing. If you think about it, you're probably used to filling out forms for many different things. Your income tax, a personal check, and even a lottery card are all examples of different forms with which you may be familiar.

Similar to a personal check that has an area for the amount, the payee, and so on, Web forms contain distinct fields that ask for information. You are required to complete some of the fields on the form to submit it for processing, but often, forms include fields that are optional. After you complete the form, you click a button to transmit it across the Internet. At the receiving end, the information you submitted is processed and, if necessary, information is transmitted back to you.

The forms you encounter on the Web enable you to communicate with someone at the other end to request or transmit information. Although each form provides a different outcome, forms all share common characteristics. Follow these simple rules to navigate through all types of Web forms.

- Click or press Tab to move from field to field. Don't press Enter.

- Complete all required fields, generally identified by an asterisk character. If you don't, the form will be kicked back to you or, worse, discarded at the other end.

- When you've filled in the form, click the appropriate button necessary to transmit it (generally labeled **Send** or **Transmit**). Otherwise, the information you filled in will go nowhere.

Forms that require you to fill in information are common on the Web. You'll encounter this type of form if you request information from a business or buy something online. Like the form shown in Figure 4.16, an information form you submit generally contains required and optional fields. Type the information in each field carefully, because after the form is transmitted you can't correct any typos.

FIGURE 4.16

This form provides information to a business.

1 Required fields

Another Web form is the most common; it enables you to request information. For example, let's say you're looking for Web sites that contain the phrase "browsing the Web." Using a navigational guide such as Yahoo!, you submit the phrase and Yahoo! provides links to Web sites that contain it. Or, you might ask for information on particular type of digital camera on the Kodak Web page. In either case, the form you submit triggers a response from another site on the Web.

SEE ALSO

➤ *You learn all about searching for Web sites on page 121.*

➤ *For a more in-depth look at Internet security, see page 320.*

Security and Forms

You might notice that a box, similar to the one shown in Figure 4.17, appears when you submit a Web form. The box lets you know that the information you're sending might be read by other people. Does it mean you shouldn't proceed?

FIGURE 4.17
The Security Alert dialog box.

To determine whether you should continue, you need to understand what happens when you submit a form. The information you've entered, whether it's your name, a search request or your credit card number, is transmitted across the phone line to another computer. Although your data is in the phone line, it can be intercepted and read by someone else.

Before you panic, please keep in mind that although theoretically the information can be intercepted, in all likelihood, it's probably not. Intercepting a telephone transmission and reading the information is a very difficult and complex task. The conversation you have on the telephone could be "tapped," or listened to by an unauthorized person. So could your Internet data. In either situation, it's highly unlikely that anyone else is listening or looking.

Still, it's best to play it safe. Protect your privacy. Apply the same rules to your Web usage that you apply to telephone transactions. You wouldn't provide detailed personal information to a stranger on the phone, so don't provide it to a stranger on the Web. Although it's the exception rather than the rule, some Web businesses sell your name or other information to mailing lists or other Web merchants. Do business with Web businesses that you know are reputable or have been recommended by a friend or colleague. Don't submit your credit card number or information unless you're sure the sight is secure. It's okay to request information from a search service or search engine.

If you observe these simple rules, you won't have anything to worry about. Actually, many people and businesses on the Web are very concerned about Web security. The data you transmit can be encrypted or scrambled to prevent anyone from observing what you send. Additionally, many Web vendors provide a "secure buy" service that works with a secret personal identification number (PIN). Other companies provide certificates that lock the information you submit from prying eyes.

SEE ALSO

➤ *You'll learn more about buying on the Internet on page 307.*

Recognizing Web Tables

Tables are placed in many Web pages as a means to present information in an easy-to-read manner. Tables don't require any action from you because they're simply navigational tools. Tables can be displayed with borders or lines around them, or they can appear without lines.

Tables are arranged in rows and columns, similar to a word-processing table or spreadsheet. Many Web designers use tables as a way of organizing links to other, related sites. Still other tables are used to present information in a clear and concise way.

An example of a simple Web table appears in Figure 4.18.

Have It Your Way: Configuring Your Browser

Now that you've been using the Web for a bit, you would probably like to be able to change a few things. For one, you might want to change the first page that appears when you open your browser. Additionally, you might want to change the appearance of a page when it's displayed onscreen. The Web and your browser team up to make it easy for you to have it your way.

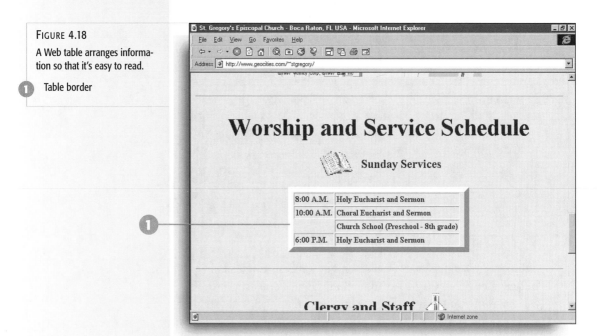

Changing the Start Page

Your Start page appears each time you open your browser. The browser might be the opening pages at Netscape or Microsoft, or it might be the home page of your ISP. Although those pages might be interesting, you're free to change the opening page to any page you want. You also see your Start page when you click the Home button on the toolbar.

Changing your Start page is a snap! Make sure that you know the URL of the page you want to open before you begin the process of changing it.

Changing the Start page in Internet Explorer

1. From within Internet Explorer, click the **View** menu and choose **Internet Options**.

2. When the Internet Options dialog box appears, click the **General** tab and find the first section of the page entitled **Home Page**.

3. Set your page in one of the following ways:

- Click inside the **Add_ress** text box and type the URL of the new opening page. (Type carefully!)

- If the page that's onscreen is the page you want to use, click the **U_se Current** button.

- If you don't want any page to appear when you open Internet Explorer, click the **Use _Blank** button.

4. When you're finished, click **OK**.

Changing the Start page in Netscape Navigator

1. Navigator users should click **_Edit** and then **Pr_eferences** to display the Preferences dialog box.

2. Under the **_Category** section on the left side of the page, click **Navigator**. Information about settings in Navigator appears, as shown in Figure 4.19.

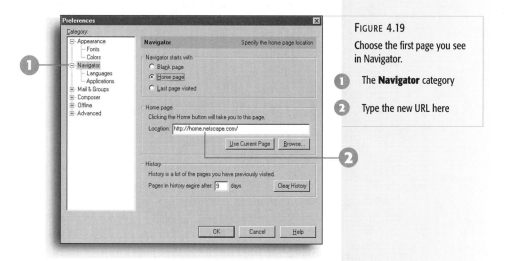

FIGURE 4.19

Choose the first page you see in Navigator.

1 The **Navigator** category

2 Type the new URL here

3. Verify that the option button next to **_Home page** is selected in the **Navigator starts with** section.

4. Move down to the middle section, called **Home page**, and choose one of the following options:

- Click **Use Current Page** if you've moved to the new page you plan to use.

- Click inside the **Location** text box and replace the URL that's currently displayed with the one you want. Check to make sure that the URL you typed has no typos.

5. Click **OK** to close the Preferences dialog box and return to the Navigator screen.

That's it! The next time your browser starts, you'll see the page you just entered.

Switching Fonts

You can change the appearance of the Web page that's displayed onscreen with a few simple mouse clicks. Why would you want to? Perhaps, the font, or typeface, of a page is hard to look at. Or, if you've been staring at your computer for a long time, you might want to blow up the size of the letters to make them easier to read. Using your browser's tools, you can change the appearance of any displayed page to suit your needs. The new font size is in effect until you change it again during the current session or close your browser.

For Internet Explorer users, click the **View** menu and choose **Fonts**. A check mark appears next to the font size that's currently in effect. Click the new size you want to use. If you're not sure, try one level up or down from the font size that's in use now. When the menu closes, the page is redrawn.

For Navigator users, click the **View** menu and then choose **Increase Font** or **Decrease Font**. If the font size still isn't the size you wanted, repeat the step until the font size matches what you wanted.

Printing a Web Page

When the exact page for which you're looking appears onscreen, you might want to print it. After all, what good is a recipe for ceviche with onions, pepper flakes, and cilantro if it's displayed on your computer screen and not in your kitchen? Fortunately, if your computer is connected to a printer, you can print any Web page you see.

Sometimes printing one Web page results in your printer spitting out sheet after sheet. That's because Web "pages" are not really pages, like the ones you create with your favorite word processing program. Instead, Web pages have no logical bottom. Remember how you've had to use your scrollbar to move to the bottom of a Web page? That page, and others like it, might translate to several printed sheets.

Your browser's Print function runs through Windows. If you're familiar with printing from other programs within Windows, you'll find that the procedure for printing from your browser is very similar. Before you begin this exercise, your browser should be visible onscreen.

Sending a page to print

If you're an Internet Explorer user, clicking the Print button on the toolbar sends the onscreen page to the printer. For a bit more control, use the Print command under the **File** menu instead.

Print what you want

1. Click the **File** menu and choose **Print**. The Print dialog box appears, similar to the one shown in Figure 4.20.

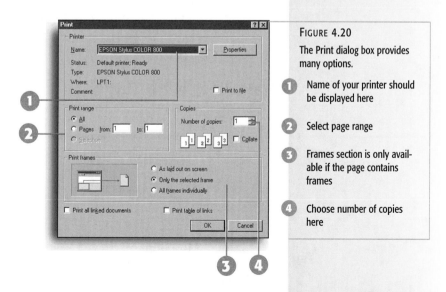

FIGURE 4.20

The Print dialog box provides many options.

❶ Name of your printer should be displayed here

❷ Select page range

❸ Frames section is only available if the page contains frames

❹ Choose number of copies here

2. If the current page contains Frames, Internet Explorer provides a **Print Frames** section in the Print dialog box that enables you to control which frames are printed. Click the option button next to the selection that best describes the way you want the frames to appear: **As laid out on screen**, **Only the selected frame,** or **All frames individually**.

For Navigator users, click inside the frame you want to print, and choose **Print Frame** from the **File** menu. (The Print option will not be available.)

3. Verify that the correct printer is selected in the **Name** box. If not, click the down arrow to open the list of installed printers and select the correct printer.

4. If you want more than one copy, use the spin controls to change the number of copies.

5. If you're printing more than one copy of a lengthy page, check the **Collate** button to ensure that you'll get each set of copies in numbered page order. (Otherwise, you'll print all the copies of page one, then all the copies of page two, and so on.)

6. Depending on what you want to print, click the option button next to **All**, or **Pages**. If you choose the **Pages** option, fill in a starting and ending page number in the corresponding **from** and **to** boxes.

7. Click **OK**. The Print dialog box closes and, in a moment, you have a printed version of the page onscreen.

Saving a Web Page

Both browsers enable you to save any Web page to the hard drive of your computer or to a disk. After you've saved a page, you can open your browser and view the page while you're *not* connected to the Internet. Because a saved page is just like any other Windows document, you can move it, delete it, or store it indefinitely.

You need to understand how a page is constructed before you save it. Most of the pages you look at consist of text and graphics images, or pictures. Some pages might even have other elements, like sound clips. To reconstruct the page after you've saved it, you need to save not only the text portion of the page, but each other element as well.

Saving Web documents

1. Connect to the Internet and open your browser. Find a Web page that you want to save.

2. With the page you want to save visible onscreen, click the **File** menu and choose **Save As**. (If you're viewing a page with frames in Navigator, select **Save Frame As** instead.) The Save HTML Document dialog box appears, as shown in Figure 4.21.

Creating a folder for saved pages

Create a folder on your desktop by right-clicking in a blank area of the desktop and choosing **New**, then **Folder** from the shortcut menu that appears. The name box for the folder is highlighted. Type a new name to replace the words **New Folder,** then click on the desktop or press Enter.

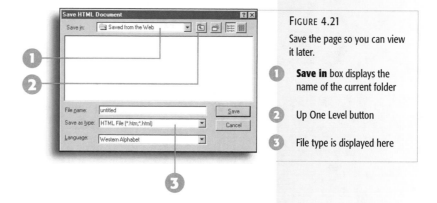

FIGURE 4.21

Save the page so you can view it later.

1 **Save in** box displays the name of the current folder

2 Up One Level button

3 File type is displayed here

3. Navigate to the folder in which you want to store your saved documents. (If you're using a folder on the desktop, click the Up One Level button on the Save HTML Document dialog box toolbar until **Desktop** is visible in the **Save in** box. Find the folder you want, and double-click it to open it.)

4. Click in the **File name** box and type a descriptive name for the Web page.

5. Make sure that the letters **HTML** appear in the **Save as type** box. If they don't, click the down arrow next to the file type that's currently showing and choose **HTML** from the list.

6. Click **Save**. You've saved the text portion of the Web page.

7. Now you need to save each graphics image. Position your mouse pointer on the first graphics image and right-click. Choose **Save Picture As** (Internet Explorer) **or Save Image As** (Navigator).

8. The folder in which you saved the text portion of the page should appear. If it doesn't, navigate to the folder by following the directions in step 3.

9. Because your browser identifies the file name and type, don't change the filename and file type. Click **Save**. The image is saved to your computer.

10. Repeat steps 7, 8, and 9 to save each graphics image on the page.

Opening a saved Web page

1. If it's not already open, launch your browser. (If you're not connected to the Internet, click the **Stop** button to prevent your browser from trying to access your home page.)

2. Click the **File** menu and choose **Open** (**Open Page** in Navigator). The Open (Open Page in Navigator) dialog box appears.

3. Navigate to the folder where you saved the Web page and related graphics with the **Browse** button and choose the file. Alternatively, type the path to the file, such as C:\WINDOWS\DESKTOP\SAVED FROM THE WEB\ and then type the filename. When you're through, the box that contains the filename and folder location should look similar to the one shown in Figure 4.22.

FIGURE 4.22

Use the Open dialog box to open a saved Web page.

1 File name and folder location appear here

4. If you're using Internet Explorer, click **OK**. If you're using Navigator, click **Open**. In a moment, the saved page appears onscreen.

Searching for Information on the Web

Exploring Internet search tools

Harnessing the power of many search tools

Learning effective search techniques

Using your browser's special search features

Beginning Your Search

The World Wide Web is the home to every kind of information you might imagine. The combination of existing Web sites plus all the new pages that appear daily make the Web a giant library. Whether you're searching for one particular fact, or information on a broad topic, looking through millions of Web pages can be a daunting task.

You can't go to a catalogue and look up references to all the Web sites that match your requirements. For one thing, such an index doesn't exist. Even if a master index could be obtained, the sheer volume of the pages that appear, move, and disappear daily on the Web would render the index obsolete in a very short time.

Before you throw your hands up in frustration, take heart! Indexing tools to help you find the pages you want abound on the Web. The tools all work roughly the same way; you form a *search query* made up of a keyword or phrase, and the search tool looks through its database of documents on the Internet. When the search tool has looked through its entire database, it returns a list of documents that match, as shown in Figure 5.1. Each match is called a *hit*.

Document or Web site?

After you conduct a search, some search tools refer to the matching Web pages as documents. Don't get confused; "document" is just another name for a Web site or page.

Different Tools Help You Search

Knowing that search tools exist to help you makes the Internet seem a little smaller and easier to manage. Although several types of search tools exist, you'll use these the most:

- *Site directories.* These sort Web sites into categories. Each category, such as Government, might be further broken down by subcategories like Military, Politics, Law, and Taxes. To move around in a site directory, you generally click the links to each category and subcategory until you find what you're looking for. Or, you can use a keyword search to find specific sites. Most times, the sites listed in a site directory have been registered by their site designers or Webmasters.

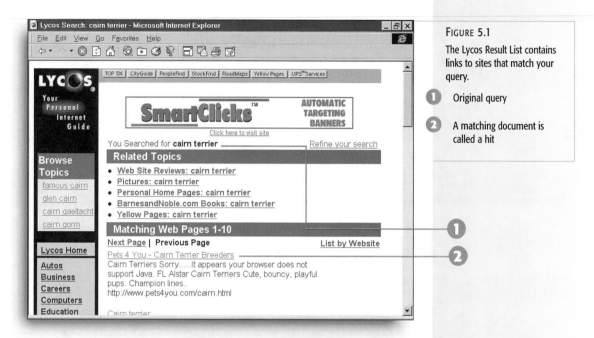

FIGURE 5.1
The Lycos Result List contains links to sites that match your query.

1 Original query

2 A matching document is called a hit

- *Search engines.* These send electronic *crawlers* (called spiders, worms, or robots) through the Web looking for pages to add to their databases of existing Web pages. When the crawler finds a site that hasn't been indexed yet, it adds a new entry to the database with the page title, the URL of the current page and any linked pages, and a portion of the text. (Different search engines use different sections of the text.) Even though crawlers work constantly, the fact that there are so many pages through which to look means that it might take years to find a new site. Consequently, Web-masters can provide the URLs of their sites to the search engines and ask the crawler to add the pages to the index.

Other popular search tools are used as well. Meta-search engines, which simultaneously look through the databases of other search tools, are valuable for pinpointing the pages you need. Webrings, one of the latest tools, enable Web sites with similar interest to form "rings" of sites, providing you with a fast and efficient way to find content. Finally, your browser comes with some special tools to help you find what you need.

All search tools work in a similar way; you enter a search query, and the search tool looks through its index to produce matching sites.

Tips for Setting Up Your Query

When you look for something on the Web, you need to communicate exactly what you want to find. The search tool looks for different documents, based on what you ask for. For example, a query that reads `"restaurants in Italy"` will produce far different results from the query `"Italian restaurants."` Setting up your search is very important.

Use the following hints to help you find what you want on the Web and other Internet locations.

- *Form your query without articles.* Words like *the* and *an* in your search query could produce skewed results. Unless you're looking for something very specific, such as references to a title or book like *The BookShop: A Novel*, exclude articles from your query.

- *Check your spelling.* Type carefully and recheck your typing. Because your search is based on what you type and not, necessarily, what you mean, correct spelling is essential. For example, typing `"Strawberry Fiellds"` won't produce the right documents.

- *Be specific.* Take a few moments and think about your query. Are you looking for the Beatles or only references to the song "Strawberry Fields?" Phrase your query based on what you're looking for.

- *Try a few different word combinations.* Getting the hang of Internet searches takes a little getting used to. If your first search doesn't produce the results you expected, change the query and run the search again.

Let a Search Tool Find What You Want

Take advantage of help

Almost every search tool on the Web has a help system that provides information about how the tool works and the best way to set up your query. Click the **Help** link, read and follow the advice when you compose your query. That way, you'll be sure you're using the tool to its best advantage.

Think of the search tools on the Web as your virtual research assistants. When you have something to find, you tell your assistants exactly what you're looking for and let them do all the digging. If you told five human assistants to find something out for you, each would approach the problem in their own personal way. The search tools, like people, each look through the Internet in slightly different ways and, correspondingly, might come up with different results.

For the most part, the search tools you use provide more than just the capability to look for documents. Many of the tools enable you to look through Usenet or other sources, in addition to the Web. Most offer extra services, such as links to shopping, daily news, or classifieds. Some search tools offer regional guides, stock quotes, or chat rooms.

From all the available search tools, I've chosen the ones that I find most effective. Read the next section to learn some brief information about each of those tools.

SEE ALSO

➤ *You'll enter the world of Usenet on page 220.*

AltaVista

AltaVista, at `altavista.digital.com`, is a search engine that has been a Web fixture for a long time. You can conduct a simple or complex search and limit your results to documents found on the Web or in Usenet. Additionally, you can limit your results to documents found in a particular language. (It's always frustrating when your Results List contains links to documents in languages you can't read.)

AltaVista offers lots of ways to define your search. You can limit the search to a Web page title or URL. You can use wildcards, phrases, and exclude keywords. Although the page doesn't have much of a graphical interface, such as pull-down menus or lists, you can click the **Help** link to find out how to formulate your query.

Excite

Excite is a good search engine to begin your search. Find Excite at www.excite.com. Because the Excite spiders index the full text of a Web page, rather than just the title or special pointers called meta tags, your query will produce many hits. Additionally, the Excite Result List offers links to More Like This sites that match the listed hits. Excite features both a Simple and Power Search.

In addition to searching, Excite offers channels with links to topics like Business and Investing, People and Chat, and Shopping. New channels are added frequently. Links on the Excite site whisk you to stock quotes, a site that books airline flights, and your daily horoscope.

SEE ALSO

➤ *Check out more information about meta tags on page 446.*

➤ *What's a channel? Find out on page 15.*

HotBot

HotBot, at www.hotbot.com, (see Figure 5.2) is one of the best search engines on the Web. You can ask HotBot to look through the Web, or several other Internet locations, including Usenet, Top News Sites, Business, People, Email Addresses, and Classifieds. Within each location, you can add filters that limit your search. For example, in the Top News Sites, you could set a query to search for "contract negotiations" in Sports News. HotBot's SuperSearch feature narrows your results even more.

Top ranking

Hits are ranked by their relevance to the original query. The higher the percentage, the closer the match.

HotBot excels at searching through current news. Using the *NewsBot* database, which is refreshed at regular intervals during the day, you can search through more than 200 sites, including both the Associated Press and Reuters newswires. The NewsBot also scans national and international publications.

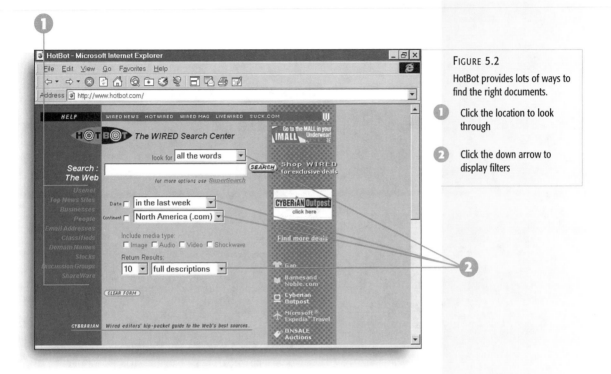

FIGURE 5.2

HotBot provides lots of ways to find the right documents.

① Click the location to look through

② Click the down arrow to display filters

After you've run a search in HotBot, your results are presented in a clear, easy-to-read way, as shown in Figure 5.3. Each hit shows the title, relevancy ranking, a summary, and the date the page was indexed by the HotBot spider (not the date of the page). Also displayed is the page URL and alternate pages, if any are found.

HotBot offers some additional destinations. You can click links to People Finders, which include several online directories. Best of all, you can use the Cybrarian, a directory with links to high-quality reference, media, and technology sites.

Finding documents with HotBot

1. If it's not already open and visible on the screen, open your browser. When your starting page appears, click inside the **Address** box, type www.hotbot.com and press Enter. The HotBot page appears.

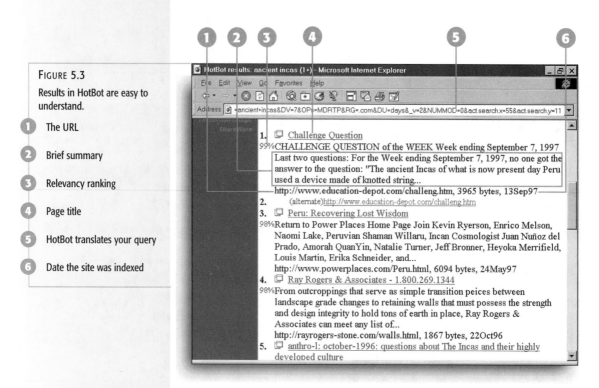

FIGURE 5.3

Results in HotBot are easy to understand.

1 The URL

2 Brief summary

3 Relevancy ranking

4 Page title

5 HotBot translates your query

6 Date the site was indexed

2. Click inside the **Search** box and type a two or three word phrase. (If you can't think of anything, type stock market.) When you're done typing, click **Search**.

3. HotBot searches its index and displays a page of links to Web sites that match the words you typed. Notice that the URL in the **Address** box changes to match HotBot's special query language. (Jot down the total number of hits if you want to compare them against other searches.)

4. By default, HotBot is set up to search the Web for all the words you type. Alter the way the search is performed by clicking the down arrow next to the phrase **all the words** and choosing **the exact phrase**. Click **Search**. When the results appear, the number of hits may decrease.

More or less

Structuring your query to look for **any of the words** generally produces more hits, but might not find the documents that contain the information you want. Using the search filter **the exact phrase** narrows your query and helps find specific documents.

5. Click **Revise Search**. The HotBot search page reappears, with your phrase in the **Search** box. Add one or more filters to your search by selecting one of these options:

   - Click a different location such as **Usenet**, **Top News Sites**.

   - Check the box next to **Date**. Click the down arrow next to **in the last week** and choose a different date range from the list.

   - Check the box next to **Continent**. Click the down arrow next to **North America (.com)** and choose a different location from the list. (**North America** is shown with different top-level domain names.)

6. When you're done, click **Search** again. When the results appear, notice how the number of hits change as you narrow your search query and filter out potential matches.

SEE ALSO

➤ *Review what you know about top-level domain names on page 90.*

Infoseek

Infoseek, at www.infoseek.com, is a search engine that performs best with simple keyword and phrase searches. Choose to look through the Web, Usenet, Companies, or the Infoseek news database. After Infoseek produces a **Result List**, you can narrow the hits even further by refining your search and looking through only the **Result List**. Or, you can type in a completely new query and run another search.

In addition to its searching, Infoseek offers some unusual extras, including email news delivery, foreign language searching, and personalized financial portfolios. You can also search through several daily news services, including Business Wire, the New York Times, USA Today, and CNN.

LookSmart

LookSmart is one of the newer site indexes on the Web. Located at www.looksmart.com, the site directory is designed for "clean" searches. The LookSmart service provides links to high-quality sites that do not contain pornography. A staff of researchers reviews each site before it can be included in the LookSmart database.

LookSmart is easy to use. You can type a keyword in the **Search** text box, or you can click a category on the left side of the page. Each category is displayed with an arrow pointing to the right. Just like your Windows Start menu, clicking a category with a right arrow opens a new menu of related categories, as shown in Figure 5.4. When there are no longer related categories, a document icon indicates you'll see a list of sites, like the list shown in Figure 5.5. Click one of the links on the list or type a keyword in the **Search** text box and click **Go**.

FIGURE 5.4

LookSmart categories work like your Windows **Start** menu.

1 Right arrow indicates more related categories

2 Document indicates links to specific sites will appear

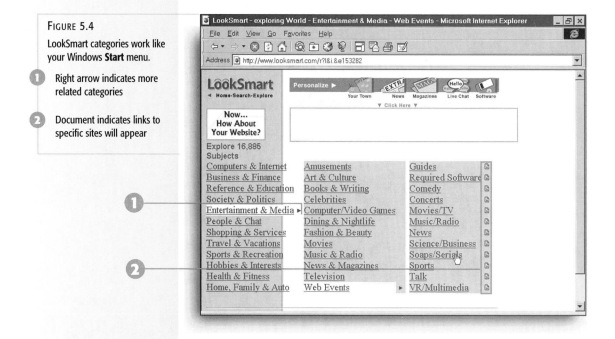

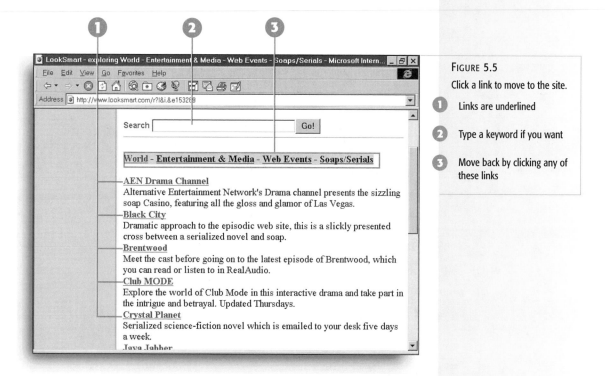

FIGURE 5.5

Click a link to move to the site.

1 Links are underlined

2 Type a keyword if you want

3 Move back by clicking any of these links

Buttons to sites with links to news, magazines, shopping, and software sites are located at the top of every page. You can customize the sites that appear from a long list. You can also create a city guide of regional links to sites in your geographic area.

Setting up a personal LookSmart city guide

1. Type www.looksmart.com in the **Address** box of your browser and press Enter to open the LookSmart home page.

2. Click the **Your Town** button at the top of the page.

3. When the LookSmart Town Selection page appears, click the down arrow and choose a city from the list. (Cities in the U.S. and other countries are listed, so you'll probably be able to find one close to where you live.) After you've selected a city, click the **Save Personalization** button.

4. A new page appears (see Figure 5.6), which contains links to sites such as Television Listings, Local Weather, and other information pertinent to your region. You're going to

choose as many of the listed sites as you want to appear on your personal version of the city guide. If you're ready to set up your personal guide now, click the link that's marked **Click here to choose the (*your city name*) sites for this page** and skip down to step 6.

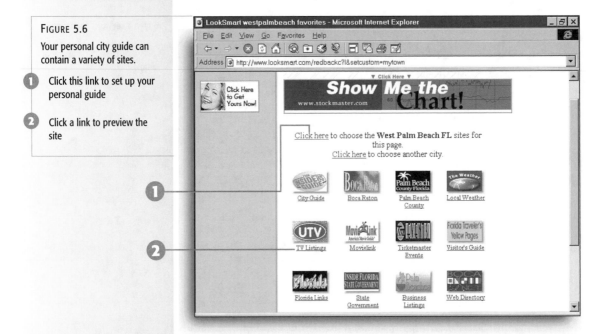

5. (Optional) If you want to preview a regional site before you select it, click its link. When you're finished looking at the regional site, click the Back button on your browser toolbar to move back. Preview as many of the regional sites as you would like. Then click the link marked **Click here to choose the (*your city name*) sites for this page**.

6. When the LookSmart Personalize page appears, check the box next to each of the sites you want for your personal city guide. When you're done, click the **Save Personalization** button at the bottom of the page.

7. In a moment, your regional page appears, displaying the links you selected. The words **Personalization Accepted** appear at the bottom of the page. The next time you visit LookSmart and click the **Your Town** button, your personal guide will appear.

Lycos

Lycos (www.lycos.com) was one of the first search engines to gain national prominence. If you're putting together a simple search, Lycos will prove adequate for the task of finding what you need. However, one of Lycos' greatest strengths is its capability to locate unusual items, such as sounds, graphics files (pictures), recipes, books, or information about a particular stock.

Lycos' page is filled with links to other sites. Use a Lycos Web guide to find links to a wide range of listed categories. One of Lycos' most popular features is the capability to create a map to anywhere you specify. Click the **Road Maps** link on the Lycos home page and follow the simple instructions to create your own map.

Northern Light

Northern Light, located at www.northernlight.com, is a new addition to the Web and works as a search engine and a site index. The service, named after a radically new type of clipper ship built in 1851, is committed to bringing the best technology to its customers. You can search the World Wide Web with the search engine portion or use the site index to look through Northern Light's Special Collection of one million documents not on the Web. (Although the article descriptions are free, you must pay a charge for reading articles from the Special Collection.)

Search results in Northern Light are presented differently from other Web search tools. The results are displayed with Custom Search Folders on the left and the most relevant documents on the right. The Custom Search Folders are unique to each search. To view the documents in each folder, click the folder to open it. The source of each document, such as Personal page or Educational site, is listed with other information about each document.

WebCrawler

The WebCrawler (www.webcrawler.com) search engine is often called the stepchild of the search engine Excite. Like Excite,

WebCrawler features channels and links to people finders, horoscopes, and chat. If you want, you can set up a custom WebCrawler channel (actually a page) with links to sites you choose. WebCrawler also features a commercial section with links to products and services available on the Web.

Simple searches work best with WebCrawler. Even though WebCrawler is an Excite product, a different search technology is used in WebCrawler searches. The **Result List** displays the relevancy ranking and page title of each hit. However, you can customize the presentation of results to include more detail or change the number of hits per page.

Yahoo!

Most people who connect to the Internet have heard of Yahoo! Located at www.yahoo.com, Yahoo!, the most commonly used site index, helps you find just about anything. Yahoo! is organized into top-level categories with layers of subcategories. It generally takes a few clicks to drill down through the subcategory layers and find what you're looking for. Or, you can enter your query in the **Search** text box and let Yahoo! find the matching sites. As an alternative, you can combine the two search techniques and click down into a subcategory before you type your search criteria.

In addition to its categories, Yahoo! features links to all the hot sites on the Web. You'll find links to people, email, sports, news, weather, and more on Yahoo!'s home page. If you have a few minutes, click the buttons to **New** or **Cool** to find some unusual sites. The **Today's News** button provides links to headlines and full news stories in a wide range of categories.

Checking out your favorite company

1. Type www.yahoo.com in the **Address** box of your browser and press Enter to move to the Yahoo! home page.

2. Click the link to the Business and Economy category. When the page of links to the related subcategories appears, click the **Companies** link. (The number of sites grouped under the category appears in parentheses beside the index title.

Note how many company sites are contained in the Yahoo! database.) Do one of the following:

- If you know the name of the company for which you're looking, type the company name in the Search text box and click **Search**. After you've viewed the hits on the **Result List**, click a link to a site that contains interesting information about the company. Read the information, clicking any links on the page.

- Click a subcategory such as **Energy** or **Publishing**. When the next page appears, click a subcategory link to move down further in the index. Or, scroll down past the list of subcategories to the companies shown in the current subcategory. Continue working your way through the subcategories until you find information about the company for which you're looking.

3. After you've viewed the information about the company (and clicked any related links), click the Back button on the browser toolbar as many times as necessary to move back to the Yahoo! home page.

4. Click the **Stock Quote** link on the Yahoo! home page. The Yahoo! Finance Page appears.

5. Type the stock symbol of the company whose information you've been viewing in the **Get Quotes** text box.

6. Currently the quote search is set to return a basic stock quote. For a more detailed quote, click the down arrow next to **basic** and choose another quote type from the list, as shown in Figure 5.7.

7. Click **Get Quotes**. The current stock quote, generally delayed by 20 minutes, appears on the screen.

8. (Optional) If you want to create a free portfolio with Yahoo!, click the **Register/Log In** link and follow the onscreen instructions to create a new account and set up your portfolio. In future visits, you'll be able to access your portfolio by entering your name and password.

Company not found?

Check for spelling errors in the company name you entered. If the search found more than your company, enter the full company name. After you've made adjustments to the query, run the search again.

Find that symbol

If you don't know the company's stock symbol, click the **symbol lookup** link and follow the instructions on the Symbol Ticker Page to find out the correct symbol. Click the Back button as many times as necessary to return to the Yahoo! **Finance** link.

FIGURE 5.7

Find the current stock quote.

1 Company stock symbol

2 Choose a quote type

3 Links to other financial information

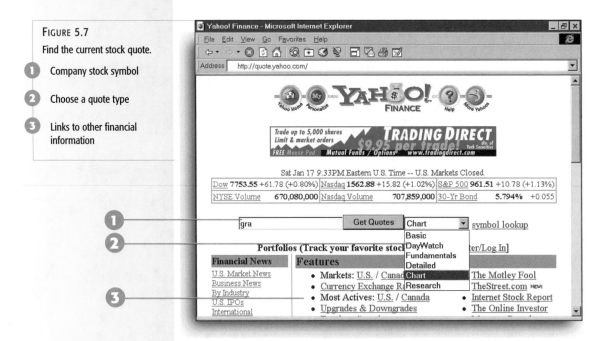

Form Effective Queries

Designing effective search queries is a skill that takes practice. Don't be discouraged if you don't find what you're looking for on the first try. Rephrase the query and try again. Take a look at the online help provided by most search tools, and then tailor your query to take advantage of each search tool's unique way of looking through the Internet.

Use these general rules to help you find what you're looking for:

- *Keep your query short and use keywords.* Remember, it's a computer, not a person, that will be looking at what you've typed. Long, rambling queries such as I'd like to find a recipe for lemon chicken will confuse the search tool and produce poor results. A more effective query would be lemon chicken recipe.

- *Enclose each phrase in double quotes.* Some search tools require quotes and some don't. Play it safe by placing double quotes around each phrase. For example, the query "vegetarian lasagna recipe" will find sites that show the exact phrase, rather than every site with the words vegetarian or lasagna or recipe.

- *Search with a broad query first, and then narrow it down.* With all the millions of documents out there, you run the risk of missing some if you zero in on a specific search early in the game. For example, if you're thinking of planting a butterfly garden, try the search `"flowers that attract butterflies"` before you search for `pentas`.

- *Use logical operators to string your query together.* Here's how these operators work:

  * *OR.* If your query contains more than one word, the search tool automatically assumes that you're looking for any of the words you typed. Using `OR` is the opposite of using double quotes around words and produces the most hits. For example, the query `"using search tools"` finds documents that contain any of those three words.

  * *AND.* The use of `AND` means that the documents found by the search tool must contain each of the words in the query. However, the words don't need to be together to be counted. `AND`, sometimes represented by the & character, limits the number of documents found in the search.

  * *NOT.* When you want to exclude a specific word, use `NOT`. For example, the query `"pasta meal"` `NOT fusili` tells the search tool to eliminate any sites that contain the word fusili, but to display the links to sites that contain the phrase "pasta meal." (Note the double quotes around pasta meal.) The `NOT` character is often represented by a - (hyphen) character.

  * ** (Asterisk).* A wildcard that works as a root expander. Place an `*` at the end of a word to find all words that begin with the letters you typed. For example, searching for `spider*` produces hits to documents with the word "spider" or "spiders."

Meta-search Engines Harness the Power of the Web

With all the search tools available, choosing the right one can sometimes be intimidating. Instead of using several search tools in your quest for the right document, you can use a new type of search tool, called a *meta-engine*. Meta-engines work by simultaneously scanning the databases of multiple search tools, and presenting you with the results. Although meta-engines can't utilize all the controls that a single search engine such as HotBot offers, they help you look quickly through the indexed databases of many sources.

Table 5.1 shows some of the Web's best meta-engines and provides a brief description and information about the results.

TABLE 5.1   **Popular meta-engines**

Engine Name	URL	Description	Results
Meta-Crawler	www.metacrawler.com	Feeds your search query to six search tools and collates the results.	Collated into one easy-to-read sheet.
SavvySearch	guaraldi.cs. colostate.edu:2000/	Set up as an experiment at Colorado State University. Your query can be sent to as many as 19 Internet search tools, including search engines and people finders. Offers searching in many foreign languages.	Easy-to-read results listed by search engine. However, because the computer is often busy, search results might take a long time to appear.
All-4-One	www.all4one.com	Searches Alta-Vista, Lycos, Yahoo!, and Web-Crawler at the same time.	Presents the search results in four separate frames.

Engine Name	URL	Description	Results
Internet Sleuth	www.isleuth.com	Lets you choose which search tools through which to look.	Displays the hits beneath each search tool that found them.
Super Search	www.robtex.com/ search/frameit .htm	Choose to look through the databases of search engines (listed as crawlers) or an extensive list of other categories. Search is powered entirely by Java.	Displays a separate frame for each tool in which a hit was found.

Webrings: An Alternative Way to Search

A *Webring* is a community of related Web pages that are organized into a circular ring. Each page in a ring has links that enable visitors to move to an adjacent site on the ring, access a ring index, or jump to a random site. Web sites are added voluntarily to Webrings. Each ring is managed from one of the sites.

Webrings are fun to visit, but don't contain the volume of information of the other search tools. Still, try a search or two through the Webrings are available to see if you find something new or exceptional. Currently, Webrings are available on many topics, including acrobatics, quilting, mermaids, the macabre, religion, Spanish hotels, the Chevrolet, Dixieland, medieval studies, native American sites, and Winnie the Pooh. Most Webrings are devoted to games.

Visit the Webring home page at www.webring.org. You'll find more information on Webrings and information on how to search. Another site devoted to Webrings is the Ringsurf site, located at www.ringsurf.com.

Getting Search Help from Your Browser

Both Internet Explorer and Navigator are committed to helping you find the documents you want:

- In Internet Explorer, click the **Search** button to open an Explorer bar on the left side of the browser window that enables you to select a Web search engine or site directory, like Infoseek or Yahoo!. In addition, Internet Explorer uses Autosearch, a quick search trick that enables you to search right from the Address bar.

- In Navigator, the Search button launches the Netscape Net Page.

Using Internet Explorer's Explorer bar

1. Click the Search button on the Standard Buttons toolbar from within Internet Explorer. The Search Explorer bar opens in a separate frame on the left side of the browser window, with a popular Web search tool displayed.

2. Type a keyword or phrase in the empty text box on the Search Explorer bar and click the appropriate button to begin the search. (Depending on the Search tool that's displayed, the button might say something like **Search**, **Go Get It**, or **Go**.)

3. The results of your search appear as links on the Search Explorer bar, below your original query. To find out more information about each result link, position the mouse pointer over the link until a ScreenTip appears that shows both the URL and a description of the linked site. The ScreenTip might give you a better idea of whether the information on the Web page meets your needs.

4. Click one of the links on the **Result List**. The Search Explorer bar remains on the left side of the screen and the right side of the frame is filled by the Web page associated with the link, as shown in Figure 5.8.

Your search results are limited

Although accessing a search tool from the Search Explorer bar is convenient, it does have a drawback. You won't have full use of the custom search features usually provided on each search tool's home page.

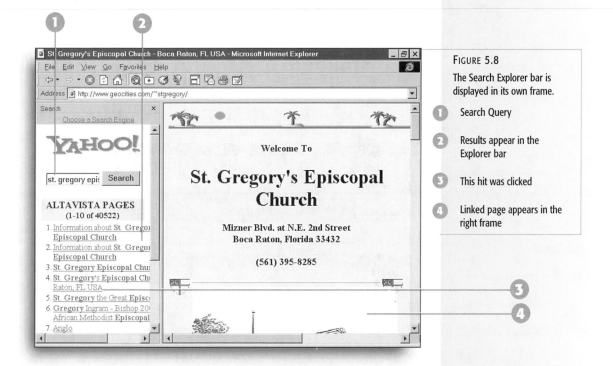

5. The search tool that appears in the Search Explorer bar changes daily. To change the search tool that's currently displayed, click the link labeled **Choose a Search Engine**. The Pick a Search Engine page is displayed in the frame on the right side of the screen.

6. Scroll down the list of available search tools and click a link to the one you would like to use. The search tool you selected appears in the Explorer bar frame.

7. Run the same search again with the new search tool. Repeat steps 6 and 7 any time you want to change the search tool that's currently displayed.

8. Close the Search Explorer bar by clicking the Search button on the Standard Buttons toolbar. Or click the Close button (the X) on the Explorer bar.

Resize the Search Explorer bar

You can resize the Search Explorer bar so that you can see more of the Web page. Place the mouse pointer on the border between the Explorer bar and the browser frame. When the mouse pointer shape changes to a double-headed arrow, hold down the left mouse button and drag the border to the left. Release the mouse button when the frames are sized to your liking.

Using Navigator's Net Search

1. Click the Search button on the Navigation toolbar from within Netscape Navigator. The Netscape Net Search page appears, as shown in Figure 5.9.

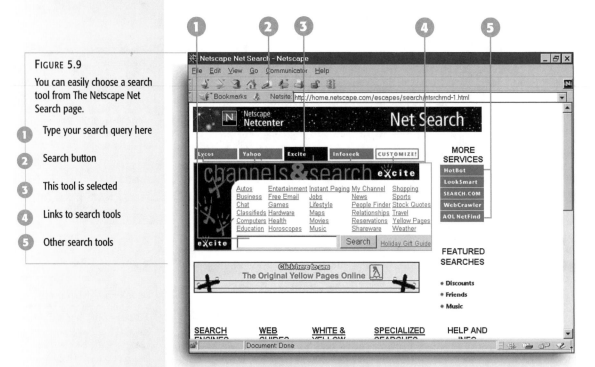

FIGURE 5.9

You can easily choose a search tool from The Netscape Net Search page.

1   Type your search query here

2   Search button

3   This tool is selected

4   Links to search tools

5   Other search tools

2. Across the top is a row of links to popular search tools, with one already selected. Click a link to change to that tool.

3. Type your search query in the text box and click the **Search** button to begin the search. In a moment, the Net Search page disappears as the **Result List** is displayed.

4. When you're done looking at the results, click the Back button on the Navigation toolbar as many times as necessary to return to the Net Search page.

5. If you have a favorite search tool, you can add it to the row of links at the top of the page. Begin the process by clicking the **Customize!** button. A small Customize window containing two questions appears on the screen.

6. Click the down arrow next to the first question, **Which search service would you like to appear on the fifth tab**, and choose your favorite search tool from the list.

7. (Optional) The second question asks which tool you would like to appear whenever you click the Search button. If you would like to select one, click the down arrow next to the default choice—**~ no preference ~**—and choose another tool from the list.

8. When you've made your choices, click **Submit**. A box appears, asking if you're sure that you want these settings. Click **OK**. The next time you access the Netscape Net Search page, the choices you made will appear.

SEE ALSO

➤ *Review information about Explorer bars on on page 96.*

➤ *Review how to use the **Navigator Back** button on page 64.*

Using Internet Explorer's Autosearch

Autosearch is an exclusive Internet Explorer feature that enables you to perform a search directly from the Address bar. Instead of having to open the Search Explorer bar or move to the page of a search tool, you enter your search criteria directly into the Address bar. Autosearch finds the matching documents and displays the hyperlinks.

Use Autosearch to check facts quickly. Because Autosearch only looks through Yahoo! to find matches, your search results might be limited.

Find it fast with Autosearch

1. Click inside the Address bar to highlight the URL that's currently displayed in the box.

2. Type a ? (question mark) or the words Go or Find followed by a space, and then your search criteria, as shown in Figure 5.10, and press Enter. (You don't need to delete the existing text before you type, because the text you type will overwrite the highlighted text.)

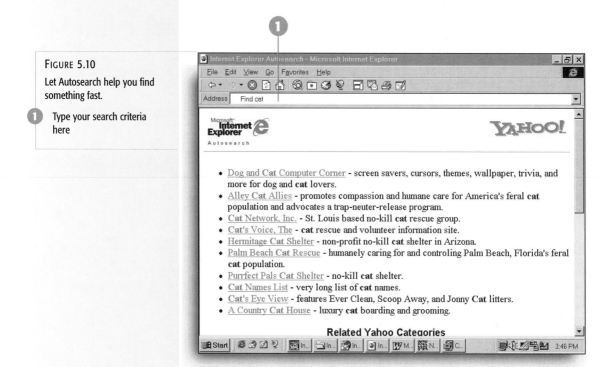

FIGURE 5.10

Let Autosearch help you find something fast.

1 Type your search criteria here

3. In a moment, Yahoo! returns a page of search results that shows links to matching Web sites and brief descriptions of the information available at the site. The words you used as your search query are shown in bold text inside the description.

Getting Software and Files Off the Web

Files for Your Computer

Your browser is more than just a tool that brings Web pages to your computer. Among its many other uses, your browser can be used to obtain files from the Internet for you to use later on. Some of the files you *download* install programs, such as games or programs that help you work with graphics. Some of the other downloadable files extend the capability of your browser. Graphics files can be used in Web pages you design. If you're using the Active Desktop feature of Internet Explorer, some of the files you download can be used as Windows wallpaper or as screensavers.

The files you obtain from the Web come from many different sources. You can find files at sites such as TUCOWS that are designed for downloading. The Macmillan Computer Publishing site has a page devoted to available downloads of files for books you already own. Or, as long as you have the permission of the Web page's author, you can save graphics from Web pages you visit.

They mean the same thing

When you download a file from the Web, you're actually saving it to your computer. The terms "download" and "save" mean the same thing.

Downloading Is Part of a Process

When you download a file to your computer, you're actually transferring information from a remote computer to yours. After the file is located on your computer, you might need to perform a few steps before you can use it. Files that are *compressed* to make them smaller and quicker to download need to be *decompressed* before you can use them. If the file you downloaded is designed to install a program, you need to run the file to set up the program. Some programs are easy to set up. When you select one of these types of files, the download, decompression, and installation procedure is sometimes handled by your browser and requires little intervention from you.

Different Types of Programs Are Available

Software programs are the tools that enable you to use your computer for a specific purpose. For example, your browser is a program that enables you to look at Web pages. You can download thousands of programs from the Web. Both Internet Explorer and Netscape Communicator can be downloaded free of charge. You can find simple children's puzzles or elaborate war games with graphics, sound, and movie effects. How about a program that tracks your expenses or sets up a schedule for routine maintenance on your car? Software like these and other programs is readily available on the Web.

The software you download generally fits into the following four categories.

- *Commercial.* Some well-known programs that you usually purchase from a retail store or catalogue can be obtained from the Web. If a commercial program is available for download, most times you'll find it on the vendor's Web site. Depending on the program, you might need to pay the vendor before you install the program. Sometimes, commercial programs that you download are working demos of the actual program and don't have all the bells and whistles of the full-featured product.

- *Patches, upgrades, and drivers.* Commercial software vendors and hardware manufacturers often offer upgrades or patches to existing files on your computer. For example, Microsoft offered a *patch* to the Office 97 suite of programs several months after the original set of programs was released. Printer manufacturers, such as Hewlett-Packard, offer *drivers* for most of their printers. Most patches and upgrades are obtained from the vendor's Web page and need to be installed like regular programs.

- *Shareware.* Most *shareware* is downloaded and installed on an evaluation basis. Many programs can be used for a limited period of time or number of logins. If you like the program after you've worked with it for a while, you pay a fee and register the program. Registered users often get documentation or technical support that isn't available to unregistered users. Some shareware programs keep track of how many days have elapsed since you installed the program or how often you've used it and don't allow you to open the program when the evaluation period is over.

Rev up your older printer

If you're working with an older printer, visit the Web page of the printer's manufacturer. Look for links to printer drivers and download the latest driver for your printer. (The driver is the way your computer and your printer communicate.) After you install the driver, you'll probably notice that your printer seems to work better.

- *Freeware*. Programs that you can download and use free of charge. Some *freeware* programs are sophisticated, such as Internet Explorer or the Netscape Communicator suite. However, most freeware is written by a single author and is not very complex. Many freeware vendors ask you to register your freeware program.

Each time you download and install a program to your computer, you're using up valuable hard drive space. Additionally, some programs can use up a lot of your computer's resources. Some seemingly-small programs take up a surprising amount of hard drive space and memory. Even if you've got a hard drive with lots of free space, before you download a program, find out how much space it requires and what other system requirements are necessary. Download programs judiciously. Uninstall the programs that you don't care for or ones that seem to interfere with your system's performance.

Where Can I Get a New Program?

Programs can be obtained from many places on the Web. Table 6.1 shows the names and locations of some of the best places to find software on the Web.

TABLE 6.1 **Great software sites**

Site Name	URL	Description
Tucows	www.tucows.com	Links to the most popular shareware on the Web.
Download.com	www.download.com	Reviews of programs, along with the most popular software titles. Search for the program you want or locate it in a category.
File Mine	www.filemine.com	You prospect File Mine for the files you want. You can select multiple files and download them at the same time or download individual files as you see them.

Site Name	URL	Description
Softseek	www.softseek.com	Organized by categories. Additionally, the newest releases, editor's picks, and top downloads are listed.
Jumbo! The Download Network	www.jumbo.com	With 250,000 titles, you're sure to find the program you want. In addition to downloading software, visit Jumbo to play games or Jumbo Lotto.
SquareOne Technology-Shareware Downloads	www.squareonetech.com/sharware.html	Only a handful of programs are available here. You can download individual programs or purchase a mega-CD that contains most of the programs for under $40.
Microsoft	www.microsoft.com/msdownload	Free software that can be used with Internet Explorer and other Microsoft products.
Netscape	home.netscape.com/download/su2.html	Software obtained here is designed for use in the Netscape Communicator suite.

The Danger of Computer Viruses

One of the biggest obstacles to downloading files from the Web is the threat of computer viruses. Unfortunately, a *computer virus* can wipe out your hard drive or destroy key files on your computer. Viruses are passed unknowingly every day. Sadly, viruses don't generate spontaneously, but are written to perform a malicious function. Because most viruses are invisible, you might not know your computer is infected until it's too late.

Although you can't stamp out the danger of computer viruses altogether, you can take steps to prevent infection. The first step

Computer viruses pose a real threat

A computer virus is a program designed to affect your computer by altering the way it works without your knowledge or permission. Viruses are transmitted on computer files. After an infected file is introduced inside your computer, the virus can spread from one file to another.

is to download computer files with care. Obtain files from reputable sites that advertise virus-free software. (However, keep in mind that most software vendors won't absolutely guarantee that their files are virus free.)

The second rule of prevention is to use common sense. If someone sends you an unsolicited file attached to an email message, delete it without opening it. Be careful about accepting a disk that contains a file copied from someone else's computer. (My sister inadvertently copied a virus that destroyed her hard drive when she copied a recipe for chocolate chip cookies from her neighbor.)

The surest way to prevent infection from computer viruses is to install virus protection on your computer. Many of the best anti-virus programs can be downloaded from the Internet on an evaluation basis, or purchased on CD-ROM. New viruses appear daily, so you'll need to update your virus protection program on a regular basis. Virus protection programs are not free; most times you'll pay between $50 and $100 for the full-blown version. Considering the investment of time and money you have in your computer, it's a small price to pay.

Some virus protection programs sit in your computer's memory, scanning all incoming files and watching your system for the symptoms of viruses. Others offer "on demand" file scanning, telling you when and where to check files. If a virus is found in a file, it's removed or disabled so it can't cause damage. With virus protection enabled, you'll be able to share files with your friends and colleagues without worry.

Table 6.2 shows a few of the best commercial virus protection programs.

TABLE 6.2   **The best virus protection programs**

Program Name	URL	Approx. Cost	Description
Norton Anti-Virus	www.symantec.com/ nav/fs_nav4-95nt.html	$65	NAV covers all possible sources of infection, including the Internet, floppy

Program Name	URL	Approx. Cost	Description
			disks, email attachments, shared files, and networks. Updates can be downloaded monthly.
Virus Scan Security Suite	`www.nai.com/ products/antivirus /vss.asp`	$79	The combination of McAfee's VirusScan anti-virus software and the new WebScanX product results in one of the strongest defenses you can install on your computer.
Dr. Solomon's Anti-Virus Toolkit	`www.drsolomon.com/ /products/avtk/ /index.cfm`	$75	Dr. Solomon's Anti-Virus is backed by the proven expertise of Dr. Solomon's Anti-Virus Research Lab, a large, experienced research and development team dedicated to providing anti-virus solutions.
Pc-cillin Anti-Virus	`www.antivirus.com`	$50	Uses exclusive technology to scan compressed files and email attachments for virus infection. Viruses can be eradicated with the Clean Wizard for step-by-step removal.

Downloading Software from the Web

Visiting a software site on the Web is like going to a candy store. So many different varieties and "flavors" of software exist from which you can pick that it's hard to decide what you want.

Understand what you're getting before you download and install new software. Before you download a program, make sure that you can answer the following questions affirmatively:

- Is the program designed to work with your operating system? If the description doesn't say that the program is designed for use in Windows 95 or 98, don't waste your time.

- Will you use the software? Sometimes a program that looks appealing turns out to be a mistake.

- If the program is an evaluation copy and expires after a set period—say two weeks or thirty days—will you have time to work with it? It doesn't make sense to install a program that will expire before you have time to try it out.

- If you're accessing the Internet from work or school, do you have permission to install a new program on the computer you're using? Many network administrators restrict the programs that can be installed on a user's computer. Check before you install a program on a computer that you don't own.

When you find a program that meets your needs, you click a link to download it and your browser handles the download. The duration of the download process is dependent on the size of the file, your computer, and the speed of your modem. Fortunately, you can continue browsing the Web or working with other programs installed in your computer while the download progresses.

After the download is completed, you need to install the program. Most programs need many files to run on your computer; the files are compressed into one file when you download the program. Sometimes, the decompression steps are built into the installation process and you don't need to do anything to decompress the files. However, many programs require that you manually decompress the file you downloaded before the installation process can proceed.

SEE ALSO

➤ *Review information about modem speeds on page 24.*

Downloading with Internet Explorer

Internet Explorer makes downloading programs a snap. When you click a link to a downloadable program, Internet Explorer enables you to make the following choices:

- **_Run_ or _Open_ this program from its current location.** When you select this option, Internet Explorer downloads the file and then looks for an application on your computer to run or open the file. For example, if the file is in compressed format, Internet Explorer looks through your installed software for a program that can decompress the file. If the file ends in .exe, Internet Explorer tells Windows to install it first and then run it.

  Choosing this option is the fastest way to install programs, although it might not be the safest option for your computer. Additionally, you won't have control over the folder in which the new program is installed.

- **_Save_ this file to disk.** Choose this option to save the file to a location that you specify on your computer. After the file is downloaded, you'll need to install it or open it. If you're using a virus-checking program, you can check the downloaded file for infection before you proceed.

SEE ALSO
➤ *You'll find information about digital certificates on page 324.*

Security Warning

When you tell Internet Explorer to run or open a file from its current location, a Security Warning dialog box might appear when the file has been downloaded. Usually, the alert is displayed if you've downloaded a program file. The warning lets you know that the program hasn't been digitally signed by the software publisher. In fact, most software publishers don't digitally sign their programs. Alternatively, the warning might inform you that the software manufacturer asserts that the software is safe, but tells you to install the software only if you trust the assertion. If you're sure that the software comes from a reliable source (such as a vendor like Microsoft), proceed with the process.

Get a new font from Microsoft

1. If you're using Internet Explorer, connect to the Internet and open the browser.

2. Type www.microsoft.com/msdownload in the **Address** box and press Enter. In a moment, the Download Free Microsoft Software page appears with links to downloadable programs arranged by category.

3. Scroll down the list and click a link to a program that interests you. In this example, we've chosen **TrueType Fonts on the Web-Windows** under the **Images and Interactive Media** section.

4. Scroll down the resulting page and click the link to download a font that looks interesting (in our example, we chose **Webdings for Windows 95 and Windows NT**).

5. The File Download dialog box appears, as shown in Figure 6.1. Because Microsoft is a reliable software publisher, you can click the option button next to **R̲un this program from its current location** and then click **OK**.

FIGURE 6.1

The File Download dialog box offers options for handling the file.

1 Click this option only if you're sure the publisher of the software is reliable

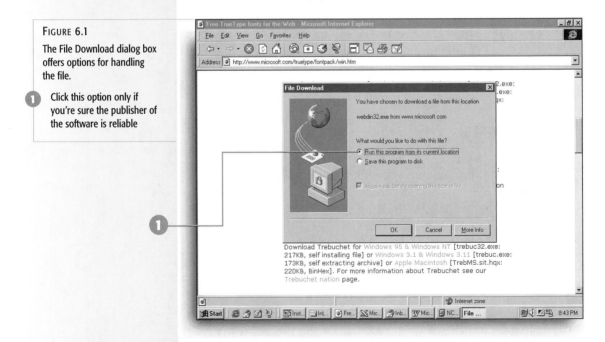

6. The File Download dialog box appears as the file is copied to your computer.

7. The Security Warning dialog box, illustrated in Figure 6.2, appears. Click **Yes** to continue.

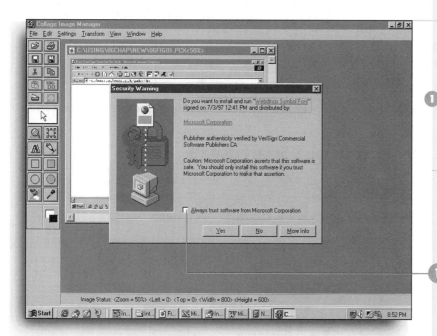

FIGURE 6.2

The Security Warning dialog box alerts you that the software might not be safe.

① Check this box if you want Internet Explorer to trust software from the publisher of the program you're downloading currently

8. Read the licensing agreement in the next dialog box that appears, pressing Page Down to see the entire agreement. When you're ready, click **Yes** to accept the agreement and continue.

9. Briefly, a dialog box appears as the Webdings font is installed. After the process finishes, a dialog box appears telling you that the installation is complete. Click **OK**.

Downloading Files with Navigator

Clicking a link to a downloadable file begins the process in Navigator. The type of file you've selected determines the action taken by Navigator. If the file belongs to a file type that Navigator recognizes and has seen before, such as a graphics file,

Follow the instructions

Depending on the file you choose, you might need to close and then reopen Internet Explorer or disconnect from the Internet and restart your computer. Follow the onscreen prompts when the file has been installed.

Navigator may load a previously installed *helper application* or *plug-in* so that you can view the file in the browser. If the file is an executable file (one that launches a program), Navigator displays the Save As dialog box and asks you to specify a folder location so that the file can be copied to your computer. You'll need to run the program later on.

Sometimes Navigator doesn't recognize the type of file you're downloading. In that case, you're presented with an Unknown File Type dialog box and given the option to save the file to disk. After the download is complete, you can work with the file, opening it with a compatible application or decompressing it.

Using Netscape's Smart Update

Netscape makes it easy to obtain the latest components or upgrades to existing programs in the Communicator suite. Smart Update takes you to the latest and greatest Netscape software.

You must already be a Communicator user to use the Smart Update feature. Connect to the Internet and open Navigator before you begin.

Extend the power of Netscape Communicator

1. Open the **Help** menu and choose **Software Updates** from within Navigator. The Smart Update page appears, as shown in Figure 6.3. Notice that the page is divided into numbered sections with the **Software Components** tab selected.

2. In the first section, click the **Your Software Profile** tab. In the Communicator Version section, the version of Communicator that's installed on your computer is displayed. Below the version is the Installed Components list. Make a note of the installed components and click the **Software Components** tab to return to the original view.

3. Scroll down the page to the list of Netscape Components and check the box next to a component you want to install.

4. Click the Down arrow in the second section and choose a download location from the list. The geographic location that's closest to you is your best bet.

Save it automatically

If you want to automatically save a file to disk, hold down the Shift key as you click the link. Navigator will prompt you to provide a folder location for the file and begin the download process.

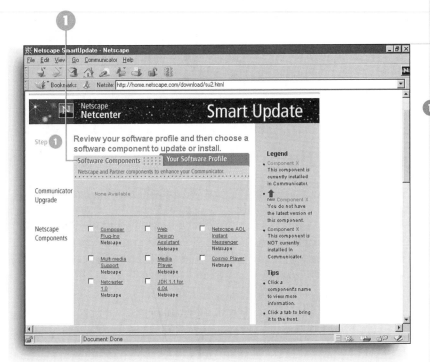

5. Move to the third section and click **Begin SmartUpdate**.

6. A new Navigator window appears, informing you of the progress of the download. When the file had been copied to your computer, another window appears, informing you that Netscape is setting up the files for the installation procedure.

7. (Optional) Depending on the component you've chosen, you might see a Java Security dialog box, advising you that Netscape Communications Company is requesting privileges to install software on your computer. Click **Grant** on this and any Java Security dialog boxes that appear during the installation process.

8. When prompted, click **Install** to install the component you've chosen. Netscape handles the installation process behind the scenes.

Every program is different

The download and installation procedure in Smart Update can vary from program to program. For example, you might be asked to exit and restart Communicator or told to restart your computer. To make sure that the program you're downloading will work correctly with Communicator, make sure you follow the instructions exactly as they're shown during the download and installation procedure.

9. A dialog box appears when the installation is complete. Follow the instructions in the box to exit and then restart Communicator. When Communicator is restarted, the new component you installed will be available for you to use.

SEE ALSO

➤ *You'll find information about downloading Netscape Communicator on page 53.*

Using WinZip

Later on, after you've downloaded a new program, you can use WinZip to decompress the files needed to install it. Many files build the decompression steps directly into the installation process. Navigate to the folder where you saved the program file If the file has an .exe extension, double-click it to begin the decompression/installation. (Generally speaking, files that use the *file extension* .exe are executable files and have the decompression routine built in.) If the filename ends in a .zip file extension, you've got a job for WinZip.

WinZip, a shareware product by Nico Mak Computing, is a compression utility that decompresses the compressed files you download from the Web. You'll be asked to register and pay a small fee (around $30) after you've tried the software for a while. WinZip can handle files in many formats, including .zip, .tar, and .gzip. If you're planning to download files from the Web, WinZip is an important addition to your computer.

Downloading WinZip from TUCOWS

1. When you're connected to the Internet with your browser open and on the screen, type `tucows.abac.com/tucows/` in the **Address** box and press Enter. The TUCOWS home page appears, as shown in Figure 6.4.

2. Click the link to Win 95/NT. The Windows 95 Software page appears, with links to 11 categories and more than 75 subcategories of software you can download.

3. Move down the page to the **General Tools** category and click the link to **Compression Utilities**.

4. The Compression Utilities for Windows 95 page appears. Press Ctrl+F to open the Find dialog box (see Figure 6.5). Type WinZip in the **Fi_nd what** text box and press Enter. The Find utility looks through the page and locates the first occurrence of WinZip.

Find it fast

The Find utility is a quick and easy way to pinpoint a word or phrase on a Web page. Access the Find utility with the key-board shortcut (Ctrl+F) or click the **Edit** menu and select **Find (on this page)** for Internet Explorer or **Find in Page** for Navigator. Using Find eliminates scrolling through a long or clut-tered page to locate the infor-mation you want.

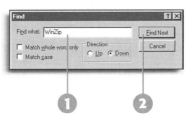

FIGURE 6.5

The Find dialog box in Internet Explorer allows you to search for something quickly.

1️⃣ Type the term you're looking for on the current page

2️⃣ Click **Find Next** to find the next occurrence

5. The Find dialog box remains onscreen so that you can search for the same term or a different one on the current page. Close the Find dialog box by clicking the Close (**X**) button on its title bar.

6. Information about WinZip, including the version number, release date, file name, and size, is displayed. Click the link to **Software Review** and read about WinZip. When you're done, click the Back button to return to the previous page.

7. Click the **Download** link next to the program title. (Even though the word is not underlined, you know it's a link because your mouse pointer takes the shape of a hand as it passes over the link.) Your browser contacts the download site. In a moment or two, the first step of the download begins. If you're using Navigator as your browser, skip down to step 9.

8. (Internet Explorer users only) The File Download dialog box appears. Jot down the name of the file, click the option button next to **S**ave this program to disk, and click **OK**.

9. The Save As dialog box appears with the name of the file displayed in the **File name** text box. Navigate to the folder where you want to save the file and click the **Save** button. A dialog box appears, showing the progress as the file is copied to your computer. Additionally, a **File Download** (Internet Explorer) or **Saving Location** (Navigator) button appears on the Windows taskbar. If the file you're copying is large, click the **Minimize** button and continue working with other applications on your computer, including your browser.

10. When the file has been copied from the Web to your computer, Internet Explorer users see a box, advising that the download is complete. Click **OK** to continue to close the File Download dialog box. Navigator users are not notified. No matter which browser you're using, the **File Download** or **Saving Location** button disappears from the Windows taskbar when the file download is finished.

Installing WinZip

1. Close all programs on your computer and navigate to the folder where you saved the downloaded file. If the folder is not on your Windows desktop, you'll need to use My Computer or Windows Explorer to get to the folder.

Track the percentage of completion

Even after you've minimized the File Download or Saving Location dialog box as you download a huge file, it's easy to track the progress of the transfer. Position your mouse pointer on the **Download** button on the Windows taskbar. In a moment, a ScreenTip appears, showing the percentage of completion.

Close the browser

The download process is separate from your browser. You can close your browser while you're downloading a file as long as you don't disconnect from the Internet. In fact, sometimes closing the browser frees up system resources and makes the download procedure go more quickly.

2. Double-click **Winzip95.exe**. A box similar to the one shown in Figure 6.6 appears. Click **Setup** to proceed.

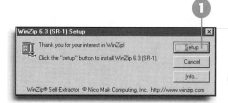

3. A dialog box appears, informing you of the proposed location of the files that will be installed. Click **OK**.

4. Files are copied briefly as the setup proceeds. When the basic installation is completed, the WinZip Setup dialog box is displayed on your screen. Read the information and click **Next**.

5. The next box to appear asks if you agree to the terms of the license agreement. Click **View License Agreement** to review the terms. When you're done reading, click **Close** on the License Agreement window and click **Yes** to continue.

6. The next box asks if you would like to start with the WinZip Classic or Wizard interface. You can choose either. However, if you're planning to use one folder to hold the files you download from the Web, click the option button next to **Start with the WinZip Wizard**. Then click **Next**.

7. In the next dialog box, you're asked if you want WinZip to search through your entire hard disk or perform a quick search to search for folders that contain files with a .zip extension so that the folders can be added to the list of **Favorite Zip Folders** (see Figure 6.7). Choose an option (either one is acceptable) and click **Next**.

8. WinZip searches through your hard drive and informs you how many folders were added to the list of **Favorite Zip Folders**. Click **Next** to continue.

FIGURE 6.7

WinZip searches for the folders that contain compressed files.

1   Choose the way you want WinZip to search

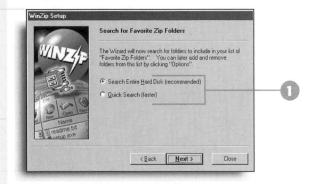

9. The WinZip setup is complete. Click **Next>** if you want to begin using WinZip right now. If you don't have files that needed to be "unzipped" (decompressed) just yet, click **Close**.

Using WinZip to decompress and install a file

1. Click the Windows **Start** menu and click the WinZip icon ▣ that was added to the top of your **Start** menu. If the icon is not visible, choose **Programs, WinZip**, and then **WinZip**.

2. If you haven't registered your copy of WinZip yet, you'll see a dialog box advising you that you're using WinZip for evaluation purposes. Click **I Agree**.

3. The WinZip Wizard dialog box appears. Click **Options** to confirm that the folder to which you downloaded the file appears on the **Favorite Zip Folders** list. If it doesn't, click **Add a folder to list** and choose the folder. When you're ready to move on, click **OK**.

Where's the file?

If the file you downloaded doesn't appear on the list, click the **Search** button. You'll be offered the option of letting WinZip search your hard drive for compressed files or you can choose to navigate to the specific folder in which you saved it.

4. Click **Next** to continue. The next dialog box to appear displays the compressed files in the folder(s) you added to the **Favorite Zip Folders** list.

5. Click the filename you downloaded from the list and click **Next.**

6. The WinZip Wizard-Install dialog box displays, telling you exactly how the program will handle your file (see Figure 6.8). Read the information and click **Next**.

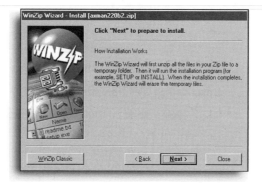

FIGURE 6.8
WinZip automates the installation for you.

7. When the files have been extracted, click **Install Now**.

8. The installation process for the program you're installing begins. Follow the onscreen prompts to install the program to your computer.

9. When the installation process is complete, click **Next** to work with another .zip file or click **Close** to exit WinZip. In either case, any temporary files are removed from your system. You're ready to work with your new program.

Using FTP to Download Files

The concept of FTP sites predates the World Wide Web. FTP sites are designed for the downloading of files and don't contain any of the text or graphics you're used to seeing on the Web. The structure of an FTP site is designed as a tree—similar to the files and folders inside your computer.

Although some FTP sites require the use of special FTP software, your browser can handle file transfers from most FTP sites. Both Internet Explorer and Navigator are designed to understand FTP protocols and work as an FTP client. Your browser displays the information on an FTP site as a column of links, with each link functioning as a file or a directory. You can download text and *binary files*.

File Transfer Protocol

FTP, short for File Transfer Protocol, is a way that files are transferred between computers. FTP sites use a hierarchical system of folders that looks similar to the view you see in Windows Explorer.

The URL of an FTP site begins with ftp://, signifying that the site uses the FTP protocol. Your browser makes it simple to visit an FTP site by entering the ftp:// characters for you when you enter the site's address in the **Address** bar.

Downloading files from the Fedworld FTP site

1. When you're connected to the Internet with your browser open and on the screen, type ftp.fedworld.gov/pub in the **Address** box and press Enter. The Fedworld Pub site appears with links to various publications produced by the U.S. government.

2. Scroll down the page and click the link to a folder that looks interesting. We've chosen the **misc** folder in our example. A new page of links to files appears, each displaying the date and time that the file was added (see Figure 6.9).

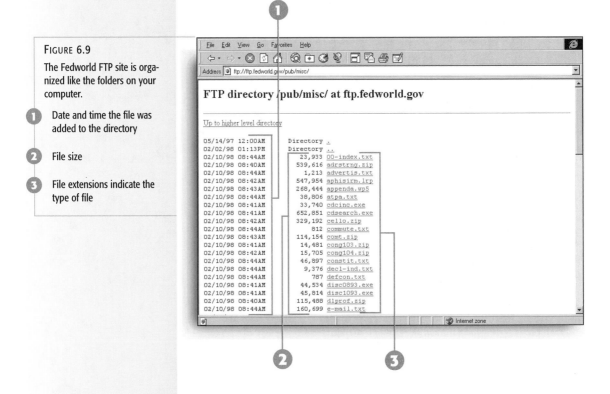

FIGURE 6.9

The Fedworld FTP site is organized like the folders on your computer.

1. Date and time the file was added to the directory

2. File size

3. File extensions indicate the type of file

3. Click the link to a file with the extension .txt to see the text of the file on your browser's screen. When you're done reading the text, click the Back button on your browser's toolbar to return to the **misc** page.

4. To move to another page in the FTP site, scroll to the top of the page and click the link to **Up to higher level directory**. When the main page appears, click the link to the new page you would like to view.

5. If you want to download a file, click its link. Depending on the file extension, you'll see the text or graphic on the screen or be presented with the option of saving the file to disk or opening it from Fedworld.

SEE ALSO

➤ *Review information about protocols on page 90.*

Telnet: An Internet Relic

In the days before the Web, a system called *Telnet* was used to connect one computer to other computers. Telnet works by making your computer a slave or *dumb terminal* of the computer to which you're attaching. The computer to which you're connected is in control during a Telnet session.

Telnet links on Web pages look like normal links. Your browser can access most Telnet links. Telnet is still used in some instances, but for the most part, few people need to use Telnet anymore. However, some government agencies, both local and federal, maintain Telnet sites. Some colleges and universities also have Telnet capabilities.

As the Web becomes more powerful, Telnet is quickly becoming a relic. Unless you're accessing the Internet from a college campus or computer lab, you might spend your whole life on the Web and never find a link or reference to a Telnet site. You're most likely to find Telnet links on Gopher menus, another Internet antique.

SEE ALSO

➤ *You can read about using Gopher on page 274.*

What Is a Plug-in?

Working with plug-ins

You download and install plug-ins like any other software program. Keep in mind that not all plug-ins are free. You might need to pay a fee or register your new program before you can use it.

Plug-ins are companion programs that work in tandem with your browser. Both Internet Explorer and Netscape Navigator have basic plug-ins that are included when the browser is installed. As you cruise the Web, your browser lets you know when you visit a page that requires a plug-in that isn't installed. After you install the plug-in, it blends seamlessly with your browser to bring you the special effects called for by the Web page you're visiting.

Table 6.3 displays the name and description of some of the most common plug-ins you might encounter as you visit pages on the Web.

TABLE 6.3   **Commonly used plug-ins**

Plug-In Name	Description
Shockwave	Delivers exciting multimedia effects to your browser.
Acrobat Reader	Enables files in .pdf format to be viewed. Many U.S. government agencies, such as the IRS, use this format. Additionally, onscreen documentation for programs is often stored in .pdf format.
QuickTime	Enables you to view movies and other multimedia effects built into some Web pages.
Live 3D	Turns your browser into a virtual reality program.

Working with Plug-ins in Navigator

When you visit a page that requires an additional program, Navigator informs you that you need a plug-in and identifies the plug-in needed. If you opt to get the plug-in, Navigator identifies the program you need and provides a list of the sites on the Web from which you can download it. You'll need to click the link to a download site and then follow the download and installation instructions shown to set up the program on your computer. In many cases, after the plug-in is installed, you must close and then restart Navigator and then reload the page you were trying to view.

Instead of downloading plug-ins on an as-needed basis, you can determine the plug-ins that are already installed and then visit Netscape's Plug-in Finder page to get the ones you want.

Obtaining new Navigator plug-ins

1. When Navigator is open on the screen, click the **Help** menu and choose **About Plug-ins**. The About Plug-ins page appears, showing the plug-ins that are currently installed with Navigator.

If you're a new Navigator user, you might see only the default plug-in, as shown in Figure 6.10. If you've been using Navigator for a while or you're upgrading from a previous version, your list of installed plug-ins might be longer.

Plug-in or helper application?

Programs that work in tandem with your browser can be plug-ins or helper applications. With a plug-in, the integration between the program and the browser is seamless; because the plug-in opens inside or inline in your browser, you aren't aware it's a separate program. Helper applications, on the other hand, are installed programs that your browser launches. For example, your browser might launch Microsoft Word to enable you to read a text file.

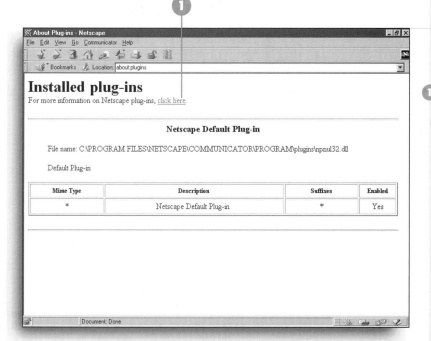

FIGURE 6.10
Only the default plug-in is installed.

❶ Move to the Inline Plug-ins page by clicking this link

2. Click the link to move to the Inline Plug-ins page. The plug-in programs on the next page are arranged by category.

3. Click the link to a category that matches your interests. For example, if you want to view Web pages that contain movies or sound clips, click the **Audio/Video** link (see Figure 6.11).

4. Scroll down the list, reading the descriptions of each of the plug-in programs. To see more information about a particular plug-in, click the link in the plug-in's title. Click the Back button on the Navigation toolbar to return to the Inline Plug-in page when you're finished.

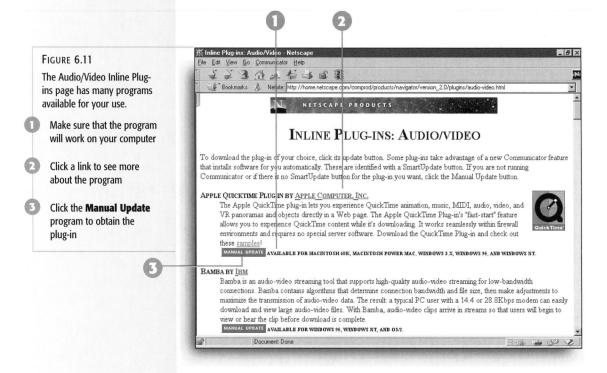

FIGURE 6.11

The Audio/Video Inline Plug-ins page has many programs available for your use.

1 Make sure that the program will work on your computer

2 Click a link to see more about the program

3 Click the **Manual Update** program to obtain the plug-in

5. If you find a plug-in you would like to install to work with Navigator, click the **Manual Update** link.

6. The next page contains information about the plug-in and download information. Follow the onscreen prompts to download the plug-in. When the download is complete, close all the open programs on your computer, including Navigator. Double-click the file to begin the installation procedure. (If the file is compressed, decompress it first with WinZip.)

7. (Optional) Repeat steps 3 through 6 to download and install additional plug-ins to work with Navigator.

Plug-ins, ActiveX, and Internet Explorer

Internet Explorer utilizes plug-ins to extend its capabilities. Like Navigator, Internet Explorer informs you that a plug-in is required when you click a link to a Web site that needs one. Some plug-ins, such as Shockwave at `www.macromedia.com/shockwave/download/`, have an AutoInstall feature that automates the download and installation procedure for you. Other times, you need to download plug-ins and install them.

ActiveX controls also extend Internet Explorer's capabilities. ActiveX is a powerful new technology, developed by Microsoft, that brings special effects to Web pages viewed in Internet Explorer. ActiveX controls might include live audio and video, banners, or windows within your Internet Explorer window.

When you encounter a page that uses an ActiveX control, you don't need to download or install anything to view the effects. Because ActiveX controls are so easy to use, many Web designers now add them to pages instead of using plug-ins. In many cases, ActiveX controls take the place of many plug-ins in Internet Explorer. In the future, even more ActiveX controls will be available.

Saving Graphics Files from Web Pages

Internet Explorer and Navigator make it easy to download images from Web pages. You can include the graphic in another document. Or, you can open it with a graphics program and modify the image.

Before you grab a graphic from a Web page, make sure that you have the permission of the owner of the page or the Webmaster. Copying one without permission amounts to Internet theft. Be very cautious when you're taking someone else's work; don't save the image if you're not sure that it's free and available.

Free clip art is available

If you want thousands of images that are free for the taking, search for **clip art** in Yahoo! You'll find a long list of links to sites that offer images for your use.

Saving a graphics image

1. When you're connected to the Internet, and the image you want to save is on the screen in your browser, position the mouse pointer in the image and right-click.

2. A shortcut menu appears. Internet Explorer users choose **Save Picture As**. If you're using Navigator, choose **Save Image As.**

3. The Save As dialog box appears with the name of the image displayed in the **File name** box. Navigate to the folder in which you want to save the image file and click **Save**.

   That's it! The image is saved to your computer.

SEE ALSO

➤ *You'll learn about graphics images on Web pages on page 430.*

III

Contacting the World with Email and Newsgroups

Sending and Receiving Email

An Overview of Email

Mail is often the highlight of your day. Even if you're dreading what the mailbox holds, you probably go through the letters, bills, and magazines before you get started with anything else. You toss out the junk mail, read the important letters, and set the other, less pressing mail aside to look at later. Mail plays an important role in the way people communicate.

Email is the Internet version of regular, or "snail," mail. You might already be familiar with email at your office or school. Most office and school mail systems work as an interoffice communication tool; you can send and receive messages from others connected with your organization. Internet email broadens this range. You can send or receive a message from an Internet mailbox, whether the person with whom you're corresponding is located across the street or across the world.

You don't need to be connected to the Internet for messages to be delivered to your electronic mailbox. Just as the letter carrier leaves your mail in your mailbox for you to pick up at your convenience, your electronic messages are waiting for you when it's convenient for you to retrieve them. They can be picked up whenever you're connected to the Internet. If you're like me, you can check for new email every hour. You can also wait and check it once a day, or whenever it's convenient for you.

Using email has many advantages over making a telephone call or sending a fax. Email is fast and inexpensive. You don't have to pay long-distance or connection fees. You never have to play "telephone tag" with someone because your message can be delivered and answered in a matter of minutes. Files such as letters, memos, and invoices can be attached to email messages. If you're sending the same message to more than one person, you can send the message to a group name once instead of sending it over and over to each person individually.

In this chapter we'll learn to send and receive email using the email programs that come with Internet Explorer and Netscape Communicator suites.

SEE ALSO

➤ *To learn more about sending email with other email programs, check out page 195.*

Understanding Email Addresses

Before you can send an email message, you need to know the email address of the recipient. Anyone who's connected to the Internet through an ISP or through a commercial online service such as America Online or CompuServe has an email address. You or co-workers might even have an Internet email address at your company or business. (Check with the network administrator if you're not sure.)

The following example is a standard email address:

`guinivere@camelot.com`

The first part of the address is the person's username and is already set up with the ISP. A username can be made up of any combination of letters and numbers. In the example, `Guinivere` is the username. The `@` sign is used as a separator between the name and second part of the address, which denotes the location. The third portion of the address, the part after the @ sign, shows the location of the mail server or domain name, which is `camelot.com` in our example.

Dealing with Spam

Spam is the Internet's version of junk mail. The subject of spam mail, the part of the message you see in your Inbox, is usually eye-catching. "Make $50,000 extra a year," offered one spam headline. Another asked, "Lonely? Call me now." If unsolicited advertising for goods and services shows up in your mailbox, you've been spammed. Usually you're invited to call a toll-free number to take advantage of the spammer's too-good-to-be true offer. Just like "snail" junk mail, the unsolicited offers and advertising are a nuisance. Valuable time and dollars are lost as the offending emails are sent, read, and deleted.

Check it out first

If you're connecting to the Internet from the office or school, check with your network administrator before you set up your own mail program or make changes to the one you're using. Many companies use a particular mail package and don't allow individual users to use another one.

Spammers get your email address from several sources. Some unscrupulous ISPs sell lists of their subscriber's addresses, although, fortunately, this practice is not common. More likely, your address was lifted from an email that you sent, probably to obtain information or request a free brochure. Another method spammers use to get email addresses is by the use of Web-Bots, electronic spiders that roam the Internet looking for email addresses on personal Web pages. Many spammers share their lists, so your address might be passed around several times. Or, your address might be obtained from postings you make to newsgroups.

To send the junk mail, spammers use sophisticated software that can send up to 250,000 emails at one time. Most spammers use a fake return address, so it is difficult to determine where the mail originated. Don't waste your time composing an angry reply to a spam message; it will probably be bounced back to you because the address is incorrect.

Spam mail is illegal and distracting. If you get spammed, forward the offending message to your ISP or network administrator. Fortunately, spam mail is starting to get the attention that it deserves. Recently, Juno Mail, a provider of free Internet email, took legal action against spammers that were falsifying return addresses to look like the messages had been sent from Juno accounts. New lawsuits against spammers are filed every day.

For the most part, spam mail is annoying, but harmless. However, spam mail may cost you money if you respond. One recent spam offer contained a toll-free number that was set to switch to a phone number overseas. The unsuspecting people who called were forced to pay thousands of dollars in long-distance charges. If you're tempted to respond to a spam offer, think carefully. After all, spam might be another word for scam.

SEE ALSO
➤ *You'll find all about Juno Mail on page 216.*

Different Email Protocols

When you send a letter or package through the regular postal service, your mail is routed to different locations and handled by several postal agents before it's delivered to the addressee. Electronic postal agents called *mail servers* handle email. The mail servers send, sort, and deliver email messages using special mail protocols.

Internet mail goes through *SMTP* (Simple Mail Transfer Protocol) gateways. Consider SMTP the official email language of the Internet because it processes messages sent from one email server to another. For example, your outgoing message is translated from Outlook Express or Messenger to SMTP, and sent over the Internet to your recipient's mail server. When it's received at the second SMTP gateway, the recipient's server, the message is translated again into the correct format, and then delivered to your recipient's mailbox.

POP3 and *IMAP* are protocols that are used only during the processing of incoming messages. A new message is first received at the incoming mail server and held there until you retrieve it. If your company or ISP uses POP3 (Post Office Protocol 3), your messages are deleted from the mail server as soon as you retrieve them. IMAP, short for Internet Message Access Protocol, is the latest standard protocol for receiving email messages from the mail server. If an IMAP server handles your incoming messages, you might have other options, such as viewing just the headings and the senders of mail messages before you decide to retrieve them.

Another recent development is the use of *LDAP*, a protocol that stores directories of email addresses in a standard format. Public LDAP directories are available all over the Internet. An LDAP directory on your company's server can contain the email addresses of all employees.

Comparing Outlook Express and Netscape Messenger Email Programs

Both Internet Explorer and Netscape Communicator come with full-featured email programs. Outlook Express and Netscape Messenger enable you to send and receive email messages. Both offer the capability to customize your mail to suit your personal needs.

Table 7.1 compares both Outlook Express and Messenger's use of common mail features.

TABLE 7.1   **Comparison of Outlook Express and Netscape Messenger**

Features	Outlook Express	Messenger
Send and receive messages	Yes	Yes
Store messages in folders	Yes	Yes
Create custom folders	Yes	Yes
Search through folders	Yes	Yes
Allow multiple mail accounts within one username or profile	Yes	No
Enable return receipts	No	Yes
Set up custom filters for incoming messages	Yes	Yes
Additional security features	Yes	Yes
HTML formatting in messages	Yes	Yes
Allow use of Address Book	Yes	Yes
Support for LDAP (Internet directories)	Yes	Yes
Spell checker	Yes	Yes
Insert personalized signature	Yes	Yes
Send address card with outgoing message	No	Yes
Read newsgroups	Yes	Yes, with Netscape Collabra

Looking at Outlook Express

Outlook Express gives you almost everything you could desire in an Internet email client program. In addition to the capability to send and receive messages, you get support for multiple accounts, security features, the option to filter incoming mail filters, and the capability to handle Internet newsgroup messages in addition to your personal email. Using a protocol called LDAP, Outlook Express also lets you quickly search Internet directory services right from within its address book.

Outlook Express is simple to use. When you first open Outlook Express, you see the Outlook Express window, as shown as in Figure 7.1. The Outlook Express window is your starting point for mail and contains icons to other mail functions. If you want to bypass this window and go directly to your Inbox the next time you open Outlook Express, uncheck the box next to **When starting, go directly to my Inbox folder**.

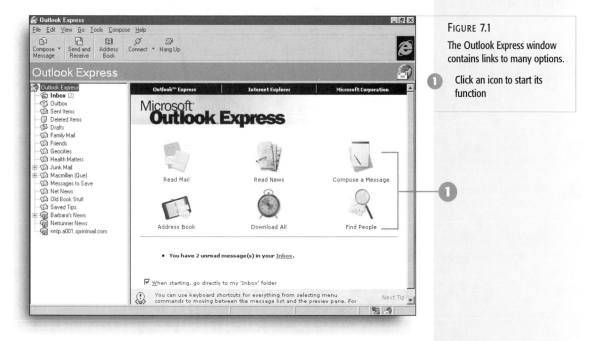

FIGURE 7.1

The Outlook Express window contains links to many options.

1 Click an icon to start its function

SEE ALSO

➤ *Detailed information about using frames is contained on page 107.*

The Outlook Express window provides all the tools you need for online communication. The page is arranged in frames (see Figure 7.2), each containing a separate aspect of the mail program. Across the top of the page is a toolbar with buttons for the most commonly used functions of the program. The frame to the left of the screen contains a list of the folders you use to store your messages. The top frame on the right contains a list of the message headers contained in the folder that's currently selected. The bottom frame contains the text of the message that's highlighted. If the message text is hard to read, you can double-click it to open the message in a separate, layered window.

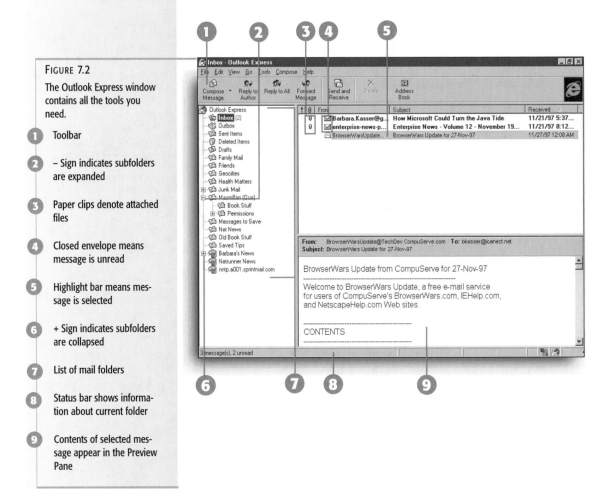

FIGURE 7.2

The Outlook Express window contains all the tools you need.

1 Toolbar

2 – Sign indicates subfolders are expanded

3 Paper clips denote attached files

4 Closed envelope means message is unread

5 Highlight bar means message is selected

6 + Sign indicates subfolders are collapsed

7 List of mail folders

8 Status bar shows information about current folder

9 Contents of selected message appear in the Preview Pane

The Inbox is where most of Outlook Express' action takes place. New messages are deposited in your Inbox when you click the **Send and Receive** button. When you click the **Compose Message** button, a New Message window appears, ready for you to type the new message. If you're sure that the mail recipient can receive mail with graphics formatting, click the down arrow next to **Compose Message** to select a message style from the list of stationery, as shown in Figure 7.3.

FIGURE 7.3
Creating a customized message is a snap.

Setting Your Email Preferences

Before you use Outlook Express, you must tell it a few things about you and your email preferences. After your preferences are set up, the program will refer to them each time it sends and receives mail. The first time you open Outlook Express, the Connection Wizard asks your email address, POP account name and password, names of the incoming and outgoing mail servers, and whether the incoming mail server uses POP3 or IMAP protocol. Unless you switch to another ISP or something else about your Internet account changes, you'll only have to work through these steps once. If you're not sure about any of the information, call your ISP before you configure your mail. However, you can always run the Connection Wizard again to change any of the information you've entered.

The Connection Wizard sets up Outlook Express mail

1. If it's not already open, open Outlook Express by clicking the Launch Outlook Express icon on the Quick Launch toolbar. Alternatively, click the **Start** button, choose **Programs**, and then select **Internet Explorer** and **Outlook Express**.

2. When Outlook Express appears on the screen for the first time, the Internet Connection Wizard appears to walk you through the setup process. Type your name in the **Display Name** text box and click **Next**.

3. In the next dialog box, type your email address in the **Email Address** text box (something like arthur@camelot.com) and click **Next**.

4. The third dialog box (see Figure 7.4) deals with email server names. Verify that the type of server listed in the box next to the words **My incoming mail server is a** is correct. If it's not, click the down arrow and choose the correct server type from the list.

Type the exact name provided by your ISP in both the **Incoming mail** and **Outgoing mail** text boxes. When you're ready to move along, click **Next**.

FIGURE 7.4

The name of the incoming and outgoing mail servers needs to be entered.

1 Type the names exactly as your ISP provided them.

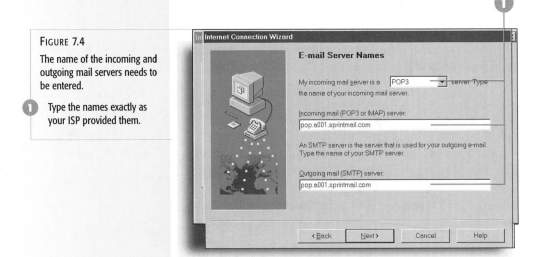

5. If your ISP indicated that you need to log on to the mail server with a special password, check the box next to **My mail server requires me to log on**. In the next dialog box that appears, type your mail account name and password. Click the **Secure Password Authentication** option box if your ISP requires SPA to log on and fill in the subsequent screen with the specific information provided by your ISP. Click **Next** to continue.

6. The next dialog box asks for a friendly name for the news account. Outlook Express supplies the name of the news server as a default. If you want to change the default name, click inside the **Internet mail account name** box and type a name you like (although it's not necessary). Click **Next** to continue.

7. The next dialog box asks you to choose a connection type:

    • If you connect to the Internet through an ISP and a modem, click the option button next to **Connect using my phone line**.

    • If you're connecting to the Internet through your company's local area network, click the option button next to **Connect using my local area network (LAN)**.

    • If you're planning to use Outlook Express when you're not already connected to the Internet, click the option button next to **I will establish my Internet connection manually**.

    Choose the option that applies to your connection and click **Next**.

8. The next dialog box asks for information about your dial-up connection.

    If you're planning to establish a new dial-up connection, click the option button next to **Create a new dial-up connection**. Additional Connection dialog boxes appear, asking you to fill in information such as the ISP's phone number, your name and password, and other information.

    If you already have a dial-up connection, the Internet Connection Wizard detects it and displays the name in the existing dial-up connection box. Click the option button next to **Use an existing dial-up connection** and select the connection (your ISP) from the list. (If you have multiple dial-up connections, make sure you select the one that connects to your ISP.)

After you've selected either a new or existing dial-up connection, click **Next**.

9. The final dialog box reads **Congratulations** and tells you that you have successfully entered all the information required to set up your account. Click **Finish**.

Adding Multiple Accounts

One of Outlook Express' unique features is the capability to set up multiple mail accounts. If more than one user is using your copy of Outlook Express, the program can check each person's mail and retrieve it at one time to the Inbox. (This feature is especially handy at my house because my husband, my son, and I all share one computer.)

To add multiple accounts, click the **Tools** menu from within Outlook Express and choose **Accounts**. The Internet Accounts dialog box appears. Click the **Add** button and choose **Mail** from the submenu. Complete each dialog box in the Connection Wizard, just as you did when you set up your first account. When you're done, the new account is added to the list.

You must set one of the multiple accounts as the default account; click the mail account name that corresponds with the ISP to which you're connected and then click **Set as Default**. (If you connect to another ISP later, select that mail account and click the **Set as Default** button.) Figure 7.5 shows the Internet Accounts dialog box with multiple accounts defined.

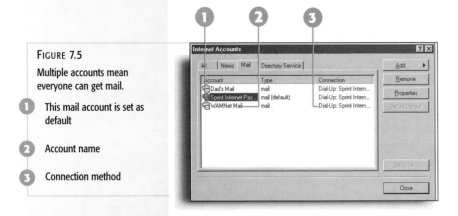

FIGURE 7.5

Multiple accounts mean everyone can get mail.

1 This mail account is set as default

2 Account name

3 Connection method

Looking at Netscape Messenger

Netscape Messenger is a full-featured email client program that handles all your messaging needs. Messenger stores both your mail and newsgroup folders in a set of hierarchical folders. Because Messenger is tightly integrated with Netscape Navigator, you can switch between the browser and mail program with ease. Messenger offers enhanced mail security and a Return Receipt option that lets you know when your outgoing message has been received. Because Messenger supports all mail protocols, your messages are sure to reach their recipients without becoming garbled.

Messenger is very intuitive and easy to use. Messenger opens to the Netscape Message Center, an area where your message folders are displayed. You're able to see the total number of messages stored in each folder, plus the number of read and unread messages (see Figure 7.6). Messenger creates six default folders, including **Inbox**, **Unsent Messages**, **Drafts**, **Samples**, **Sent** and **Trash**. You can add subfolders to the default folders or add them to your **Local Mail**.

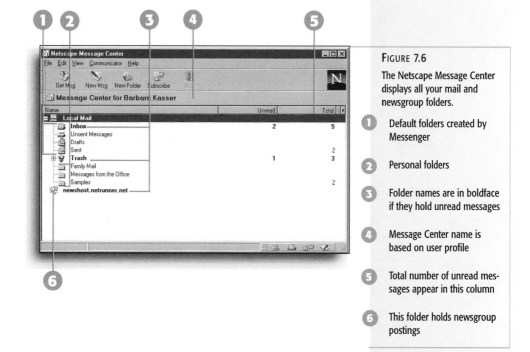

FIGURE 7.6

The Netscape Message Center displays all your mail and newsgroup folders.

1 Default folders created by Messenger

2 Personal folders

3 Folder names are in boldface if they hold unread messages

4 Message Center name is based on user profile

5 Total number of unread messages appear in this column

6 This folder holds newsgroup postings

The first time you use Messenger, you'll need to provide personal information to the Mail and Discussion Groups Setup Wizard. In the following step by step exercise, you set up Messenger mail for the first time.

Call your ISP if you don't know any of the information you're asked during the setup procedure. If you fill in the wrong information, you'll get errors instead of mail!

Using the Mail and Discussion Groups Wizard to set up Messenger

1. If it's not already open, launch Messenger by clicking the Windows **Start** button and sliding the mouse pointer to **Programs** and then Netscape Communicator and Netscape Messenger.

2. The first time you use Messenger, the Mail and Discussion Setup Wizard appears when you open the program. Read through the information displayed on the first screen and click **Next**.

3. The second dialog box asks you for several pieces of information about your outgoing mail. Type your name in the **Your name:** text box. Press Tab or click to the **Email address:** text box and type the email and the address provided by your ISP. (If you're not sure about what to type, follow the examples to the right of the text box.) Move to the **Outgoing mail (SMTP) server:** text box and type the name of your mail server. When all three boxes have been filled in, click **Next**.

4. The third dialog box to appear asks for information about your incoming mail server. Type your username in the **Mail server user name** text box (this name may be different from your full name) and the name of the mail server in the **Incoming Mail Server:** text box. Based on the type of server used by your ISP, click the option button next to either **POP3** or **IMAP**. When all the information is complete, click **Next**.

5. The final dialog box asks for information about your news server. If you know the news server name, fill it in now. If not, you can add the name of the news server when you work with Netscape Collabra. Click **Next**.

6. Click **Finish** to conclude the setup and get busy with
Messenger email.

SEE ALSO

➤ *You learn more about setting up Collabra on page 226.*

Later on, you can update any of the fields you entered by clicking the **Edit** menu and choosing **Preferences**. When the
Preferences dialog box appears, select **Mail and Groups** under
the **Categories** list on the left side of the screen and make the
changes to the appropriate subcategory, as shown in Figure 7.7.

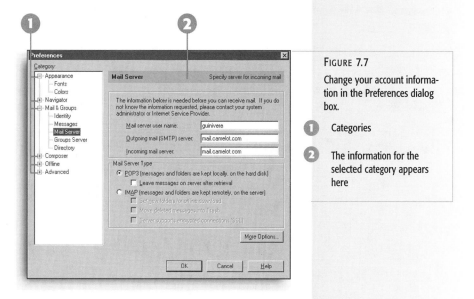

FIGURE 7.7

Change your account information in the Preferences dialog
box.

1 Categories

2 The information for the
selected category appears
here

Although your Message Center window displays information
about your mail folders, most times you'll want to view a specific
Message window for a particular folder like the Inbox. Unless
you set a mail filter, incoming messages automatically appear in
the Inbox folder. To move from the Message Center to your
Message List window (see Figure 7.8), click the **Communicator**
menu and choose **Messenger Mailbox**. (Alternatively, you can
click the Mailbox icon on the Component toolbar.)

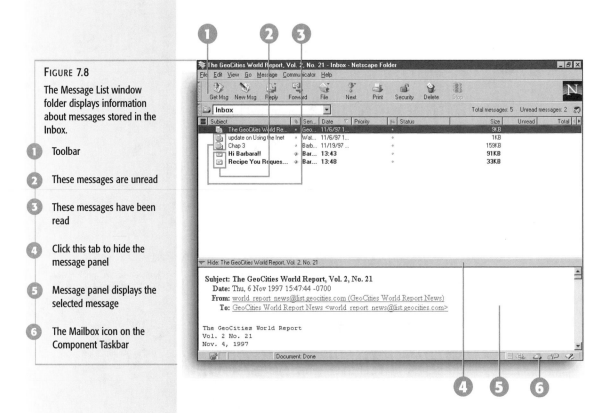

FIGURE 7.8

The Message List window folder displays information about messages stored in the Inbox.

1 Toolbar

2 These messages are unread

3 These messages have been read

4 Click this tab to hide the message panel

5 Message panel displays the selected message

6 The Mailbox icon on the Component Taskbar

Creating and Sending a Message

To complete the steps in this exercise, Outlook Express or Messenger needs to be open and active onscreen. If you're not connected to the Internet, you won't be able to send the message you create.

Composing and sending a message

1. Click the Compose Message (Outlook Express) or New Msg (Messenger) button on the toolbar. A new window appears for the new message.

2. Click in the **To:** text box and type the recipient's email address. If you would like to enter multiple addresses, press Enter after you type each address.

3. Click in the **Subject:** text box and type the subject of the message. If you leave the **Subject:** field blank, you'll be prompted to add a subject when the message is sent.

4. Click in the message area and type your message. The message area functions like a standard word processor, so only press Enter when you want to create a new paragraph.

5. When you're finished typing, read the text carefully. To make sure you haven't included an embarrassing typographical error, click the **Tools** menu and select the option to check your spelling.

6. If you want to send the message later, click the **File** menu and choose **Send Later**. The message is placed in the Outbox and will be sent later on. When you're ready to send the messages in your Outbox, make sure you're connected to the Internet:

- In Outlook Express, click the **Send and Receive** button on the toolbar.

- If you're using Messenger, click the **File** menu and choose **Send Now**.

8. To send the message now, click the Send button on the toolbar. The message is placed in the Outbox while the outgoing mail server is contacted to pick up the message and send it out. Delivery might take anywhere from a minute or so to a few hours.

Creating a Personal Signature File

A *signature file* is a great way to personalize outgoing email messages. Your "sig" might reflect your name, address, and email address, or it can contain a funny or philosophical message. Both Outlook Express and Messenger support the use of signature files, although each program uses a different method to create them. I'll explain how to create a signature file in both of the following email programs.

Did you get an error message?

If you typed a recipient's email address incorrectly (with even a letter out of place or a misplaced @ character), you'll receive a notice that the message couldn't be delivered.

Actually, signature files are an art form for many users, so expect funny and provocative sig files on many of the messages you receive. Some people take signature files to the extreme and include vulgarity or a crude message. Let good taste be your guide when you create your own sig.

Set up a signature file in Outlook Express

1. From within Outlook Express, click the **Tools** menu and choose **Stationery**. When the Stationery dialog box appears, make sure that the **Mail** tab is selected.

2. Click the **Signature** button to display the Signature dialog box, as displayed in Figure 7.9.

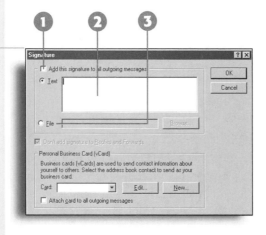

FIGURE 7.9

Create your own personal signature in the Signature dialog box.

1 Check this box to make your signature appear always

2 Click the Text option and type your signature here

3 Click the File option and choose a file from your computer

3. Click the option button next to **Text** and type your distinctive signature. Press Enter to advance to a new line.

4. If you've already created a file that contains the text you want to use, click the **File** option button and type the folder path and filename in the **File** text box. (You can use the **Browse** button to locate the file on your disk.)

5. Click the box next to **Add this signature to all outgoing messages** if you want the signature file to be included by default.

6. By default, the signature file is not included on message replies and message forwards. To change the default and include your signature on replies and forwards, uncheck the box.

7. Click OK when you've finished creating the signature file and setting options for its use. Then click OK to close the Stationery dialog box.

8. If you checked the option to attach your signature to all outgoing messages, your sig will automatically appear each time you send a message. If you didn't check the box, click the **Insert Signature** button whenever you want the signature to display.

Setting up your Messenger Sig

1. From within Messenger, click the Windows **Start** button, choose **Programs** and then **Accessories**. Select **Notepad** from the list of **Accessories**. The Windows Notepad program opens with the cursor flashing in the top, left corner of the screen.

2. Type your signature file, using no more than 72 characters per line. If you want more than a one line sig, press Enter after each line. When you're finished typing, click the **File** menu and choose **Save As**. The Save As dialog box appears.

3. Move to the folder in which you want to save the file. In the **File name** text box, type a name for the file and click **Save**. (If you can't think of a name, use my signature.)

4. The Save As dialog box closes and you're returned to Notepad. Close Notepad by clicking the **File** menu and choosing **Exit**.

5. Return to Messenger. If necessary, click the **Inbox** button on the Windows taskbar to make Messenger the active window.

6. From within Messenger, click the **Edit** menu and choose **Preferences**. When the Preferences dialog box appears, click the **Mail and Groups** category on the left side of the screen.

7. Click the **Identity** subcategory. Type the folder path and filename of the file you created in the **Signature File** text box, as demonstrated in Figure 7.10. Or, click **Choose** and navigate to the folder and filename.

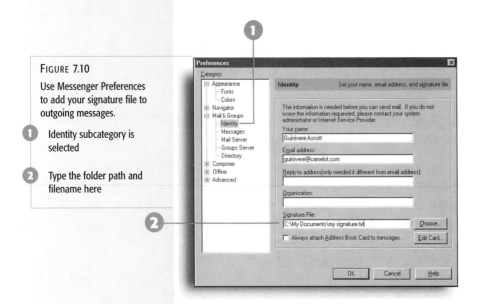

FIGURE 7.10

Use Messenger Preferences to add your signature file to outgoing messages.

1 Identity subcategory is selected

2 Type the folder path and filename here

8. Click OK to close the preferences dialog box and return to the Messenger screen. Your signature file will now be added to all your outgoing messages.

Reading a New Message

Whoever said something like, "It's better to give than receive," must have never used email! Sure, sending messages is fun, but receiving messages is twice the fun without any of the work. Of course, email messages in your Inbox can hold bad news, or requests for you to provide information. But no matter what the new messages hold, most everyone loves to see them in the Inbox.

To receive your mail in Outlook Express and Messenger, you need to be connected to the Internet. Click the appropriate button on the toolbar. (In Outlook Express, click **Send and Receive** and in Messenger click **Get Msg**). The mail program contacts your mail server and your new messages are delivered from the mail server to you. Depending on how your mail is set up, you may see a dialog box, like the one shown in Figure 7.11, that asks for your mail password. If so, type very carefully. Passwords are case-sensitive. Even if you type the password characters correctly, you won't get your mail if the case is wrong. Because the characters you type appear as asterisks on the screen for security reasons, you won't know if you've made an error.

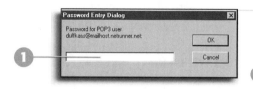

FIGURE 7.11

You may need to enter your mail password.

1 Type the password very carefully

When your mail is delivered, you'll see one line for each new message, which includes the header (subject line of the message), the name of the sender, and the date and time the message was sent. Closed envelope icons located at the left side of the message line denote new messages. Although both Outlook Express and Messenger provide preview areas below the list of messages, it's hard to read a long or important message when only a portion of the message is visible.

Double-click a message to open it in a separate window. You can drag the message window around the screen or maximize it, because the window is like any other in your Windows program. (If you look at the Windows taskbar, you'll see a button for the message window, as well as the mail program.) When you're finished reading the message, close it by clicking the Close button (the **X**) on the message window title bar.

Answering a Message

Some messages are self-contained and don't require any further action from you. Other times, you need to answer the message or forward it on to someone else for further handling. In Outlook Express and Messenger, replying to a message takes a few mouse clicks.

Replying to a message

1. Reply to a message by opening the message or selecting it in the **Inbox**.

2. In Outlook Express, click the **Reply** button on the toolbar if you want to reply to the person who sent the message or **Reply to All** if you want everyone who received the message to see your response.

In Messenger, click the **Reply** button and then choose either **Reply to Sender** or **Reply to Sender and All Recipients**.

The message opens with the recipient's name filled in the **To:** box and the subject of the original message proceeded by **Re:**

3. Type your reply and click **Send**. Your reply will be displayed above the text of the original message. Figure 7.12 demonstrates an example of a reply in Outlook Express.

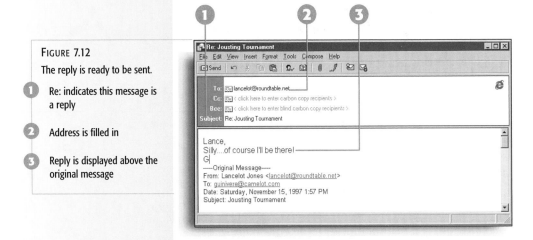

FIGURE 7.12

The reply is ready to be sent.

1 Re: indicates this message is a reply

2 Address is filled in

3 Reply is displayed above the original message

Print it fast

Want a hard copy of the message you're reading? Click the **Print** button while the message is open. The message will print at your default printer.

---

4. To forward a message, open or select the message first and then click the **Forward** button. The message opens with the subject of the original message preceded by **Fw:** (Outlook Express) or **Fwd:** (Messenger).

5. Type the email address of the person to whom you're forwarding the message in the **To:** text box. If desired, type a brief message and click **Send**.

Managing Your Email

Dealing with File Attachments

Files can be attached to email messages that you send and receive. Any file that resides on your computer can be attached to an Outlook Express or Messenger email message. In addition to standard text files such as memos, letters, and other business documents, you can use mail to send and receive graphics images and even sound or movie clips.

- If you want to attach a file to an outgoing message in Outlook Express, click the **Insert** menu on the New Message toolbar and choose **File Attachment**. When the Insert Attachment dialog box appears, click the **Browse** button and navigate to the folder that holds the file. Click the file you would like to attach and click **Attach**.

- In Messenger, as you're preparing your message, click the **File** menu and choose **Attach,** and then click **File** from the submenu. Type the folder location in the **File name** text box on the Enter file to attach dialog box and click **Open**.

Problems with Attaching Files

If the recipient doesn't have the same program on her computer that you used to create the file, the attachment might not be able to be opened. If the recipient has a similar program, the translation process might produce formatting or other serious errors.

Another problem occurs if the recipient's mail program doesn't have an automatic decoder to translate incoming file attachments. If this is the case, the attachment hasn't been translated properly; instead of the correct file, the recipient opens a file filled with strange, unreadable characters.

If you're sending a file attachment to a company or business, you need to find out in advance if file attachments are permitted. Some companies routinely strip attachments because they feel that attachments create an unnecessary security risk. Other companies permit attachments, but limit the file size. If you're attaching an important file, such as a business presentation, test it out before you actually send the real file. A few minutes of your time could save you a big headache later on.

Save yourself time and grief by checking with the recipient before you send an attachment. Find out if his mail program can accept attachments.

Files You Get Can Create Headaches

Files can also be attached to messages you receive. Alarm bells need to go off in your head when you see a file attachment. With the vast number of computer viruses floating out in cyber-space, you don't want to do anything to infect your computer. Be very careful; if the file attachment was unsolicited and you don't know the sender, don't open the file.

Even if you're sure of the sender, resist the temptation to open the attachment without checking it first. (My sister's computer was infected with a virus that came from a disk containing a recipe for chocolate chip cookies she'd gotten from her unsus-pecting neighbor. The virus wiped out both my sister's and the neighbor's hard drives.)

In both Outlook Express and Messenger, file attachments are shown below the text of the message. Each attachment is listed separately, with the name of the file displayed. When you're viewing a message with a file attached, perform the steps in the next exercise to save the file to your computer so you can check it first and then open it.

SEE ALSO

➤ *Read an in-depth explanation of computer viruses on page 149.*

Saving a file attached to an email message

1. Double-click the file attachment icon. Generally, the icon denotes the program used to create the icon. For example, a file created in Microsoft Word is shown with the same icon used to launch Word.

2. A warning dialog box appears; choose the option to save the file attachment to disk (see Figure 8.1).

FIGURE 8.1

The Open Attachment Warning dialog box message alerts you to potential danger.

  Choose the option to **Save it to disk**

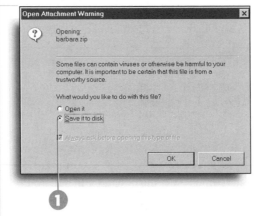

Play it safe!

Play it safe with files attached to mail messages. Never assume that because you know the sender, the file is not infected. Computer viruses happen on the computers of some of the nicest, most trusting individuals (as well as on computers of the malicious rats who design them in the first place). Take the extra time necessary to make sure you're not opening a damaged file.

3. When the regular Windows Save As dialog box appears, navigate to the folder in which you want to save the file and click **Save**. (If you don't know where to store the file, use the Saved from the Web folder we created in Chapter 4, "Moving on Through the Web.") If more than one file is attached to a message, repeat the procedure to save each one.

After the file is saved, use your virus checker to make sure the file is "clean." Only after you're sure that the file is not infected with a virus that could cause damage to your computer is it okay to open the file. Open the file by double-clicking it, or open it from within the program in which the file was created. (For example, if the file has a .doc extension, open it with Microsoft Word.)

Creating Entries in Your Address Book

It's mighty hard to remember everyone's email address. Even if you've got the name and mail server right, you might forget the exact syntax of the address, like the placement of the @ (at) or . (dot) characters. Make it easy on yourself and create an entry in your Address Book for each person with whom you correspond. After you've created some individual entries, you can combine the names into a group. You use the group like a master distribution list; for example, if you're sending the same email message to many recipients, why not send the message one time to all the names in the group?

Using the Outlook Express Address Book

1. Click the Address Book button on the Outlook Express toolbar.

2. When the Address Book window opens, click the New Contact button on the toolbar to display the Properties dialog box.

3. Enter the information for your new contact in the appropriate panel by selecting one of the six tabs shown at the top of the Properties dialog box. Table 8.1 shows the Tab name and the type of information about the contact you might want to include under each tab. You needn't fill in every field on each of the tabs. Enter only the data you need.

TABLE 8.1   New contact information

Tab Name	Data
Personal	Full name, nickname, and email address
Home	Home address and telephone number, URL of Web page, if any
Business	Business address and telephone numbers, job title, department name
Other	Personal notes about the contact
NetMeeting	Server name and other information used in Internet conferencing with Microsoft NetMeeting
Digital IDs	Digital IDs and associated email address for advanced security

4. Click the **Personal** tab and type the name and email address of the contact in the appropriate fields.

5. (Optional) Click any of the other tabs and enter applicable information about the contact.

6. Click **OK** to close the Properties dialog box when all the information about the contact is entered.

7. Repeat steps 1 through 5 to add more contacts to your Windows Address Book.

> **Create an automatic entry in your Address Book**
>
> From within Outlook Express, click **Tools** and choose **Options**. When the Options dialog box appears, select the **General** tab and check the box next to **Automatically put people I reply to in my Address Book**. Click **OK** to close the dialog box and return to Outlook Express.

Instead of sending out the same message to multiple recipients, why not create a distribution group? That way, you don't need to waste time sending the same message again and again.

Create a distribution group in Outlook Express

1. If the Address Book's not already open, click the Address Book button on the Outlook Express toolbar.

2. Click the **New Group** button on the Address Book toolbar. When the Properties dialog box appears, type a description for the group in the <u>**Group Name**</u> text box.

3. Click **Select Members** to display the Select Group Members dialog box. A list of all the contacts in your Address Book appears in a box on the left.

4. Select the name of the first person you want to add to the group and click the **Select** button. The name you chose now appears in the <u>**Members**</u> list on the right.

5. Repeat step 4 to add people to the distribution group. Alternatively, hold down the Ctrl key and click each name that you want to add to the group. When all the desired names appear highlighted, click **Select**.

6. When you're done adding names to the group, click **OK** to return to the Group Properties dialog box. Click **OK** to close the Group Properties dialog box and display the Windows Address Book. The name of the Distribution Group appears in bold type on the list of contact. The icon to the left of the group name displays several people, letting you know the entry is a group.

To send a message to the group, type the Group name in the **To:** box when you're composing a message. Outlook Express will send the message to each member of the group.

Using the Messenger Address Book

Messenger's Address Book makes it easy to keep track of all your mail contacts. Right-click a message on the Message List and choose **Add to Address Boo<u>k</u>** to place the sender's information in your Address Book. Select <u>**Sender**</u> if you want to add an entry for the person who sent you the message or **All** to add all the recipients if the message was sent to multiple addressees.

Or, create a manual entry following these steps:

Create an entry in the Messenger Address Book

1. Click the **Communicator** menu and select **Address Book** from within any open Communicator program. The Address Book opens in its own window.

2. Click the **New Card** button. The New Card dialog box appears.

3. The New Card dialog box is divided into three tabs: **Name**, **Contact**, and **Netscape Conference**. The first tab, **Name**, is open. Fill in the fields in the **Name** tab, pressing the Tab key to advance from field to field. An example of a completed **Name** tab is shown in Figure 8.2.

FIGURE 8.2

Fill in the fields you want.

1 The **Email Address** field must be filled in

4. If you want to store additional information, click the **Contact** tab and fill in any of the fields shown, including **Address**, **Home** and **Work Telephone**, and **Fax number**. (The third tab, **Netscape Conference**, is used for setting up Internet conferences with Netscape Conference; leave it blank for now.)

5. When all the information has been added to the card, click **OK**.

6. Repeat steps 2 through 5 to create additional Address Book cards.

7. Close the Address Book by clicking the **File** menu and choosing **Close** or clicking the Close button on the Address Book toolbar.

8. To use an Address Book entry when you're creating an email message, position your mouse pointer in the **To:** box and click the Address button on the toolbar. When the Address Book opens, double-click the name you want on the list. The list closes and the name is added to your message.

Make a distribution list to send one message to multiple recipients. Here's how:

SEE ALSO

➤ *You'll have a blast with Netscape Conference, page 409.*

Create a distribution list in Messenger

1. If the Address Book's not already open, click the **Communicator** menu and select **Address Book** from within any open Communicator program.

2. Click the New List button on the Address Book toolbar. When the Mailing List dialog box appears, type a descriptive name for the list in the **List Name** text box. If you want, type a nickname for the list and a brief description in the appropriate text boxes.

3. Tab to or click in the **Members Names** area and type the name of the first list member exactly as you entered it in the Address Book. As you type, Messenger completes the entry for you. Press Enter when the first name has been entered.

4. Repeat step 3 for each additional member you want to add to the list.

5. When you're done adding names to the list, click **OK**. The Mailing List dialog box disappears and you're returned to the Address Book. In addition to the entries for individuals,

an entry for the list is displayed. (Individual entries display email addresses; list entries do not.)

6. When you want to send an email message to the members of a Distribution List, position your mouse pointer in the **To:** box of the message you're composing and click the Address button on the toolbar. When the Address Book opens, double-click the List name you want. The Address Book closes, and the Distribution List name is added to your message.

Managing Your Mail Messages

When you first start using email, you probably won't get too many mail messages at one time. However, after you've established your cyber-identity and made a few online friends, your Inbox overflows with mail. With loads of messages stacked in your Inbox, you can't manage your mail efficiently. Stop the problem before it starts by devising a filing system for your mail messages.

The first rule to follow for your mail is to get rid of all messages that you don't need to keep. Unless you need to refer to a message later, delete it after you read it. Deleting a message is a snap. After you've double-clicked a message to open it, click the Delete button on the message toolbar when you've read the text. In both Outlook Express and Messenger, clicking the Delete button provides the added benefit of opening the next message on the message list.

Undoubtedly, some messages need to be retained. Rather than piling up in the Inbox, set up folders for the messages you plan to keep. Use your email Inbox like the Inbox at your office or your mailbox at home—deal with each new piece of mail as it comes in. Think of the Inbox as a starting place for the mail you receive.

How many folders should you create? Your filing system can be as elaborate or as simple as you choose. You can create folders and subfolders. If you're not sure, start with a few folders and see how it goes. You can create new folders, or delete existing ones, any time you're using mail.

Creating Mail Folders

Designing the structure of the filing system is the hard part; creating the folders is easy!

To begin, Outlook Express users should click **Outlook Express**, the first entry in the list of folders shown on the left side of the Outlook Express screen. If you're using Messenger, click the **Communicator** menu and choose **Message Center**.

Highlight the top folder (**Outlook Express** or **Local Mail**), click the right mouse button, and choose **New Folder** from the resulting submenu. Type a name for the new folder and click **OK**. The new folder you created appears in the list of folders.

Repeat the procedure to create as many folders as you would like. Remember, you can create a new mail folder any time. If you need to delete a mail folder, select it and then click the right mouse button. Choose **Delete** to remove the mail folder from the list (only after you've moved the messages you want to keep that were saved in the folder first).

Placing Messages in Mail Folders

Now that you've gone to the trouble to design a filing system, how about moving some of your messages into the folders you just created? Do it now. Mail has a way of building up.

Filing mail in Outlook Express

1. Click a message to select it. (The message appears highlighted.)
2. Without releasing the mouse button, drag the mouse pointer so that the tip of the arrow is positioned over the folder in which you want to place the message.
3. Release the mouse button and the message is transferred to the new folder.
4. To open a folder and display its contents, double-click the folder name.

Messenger users file email messages in a slightly different way:

Organizing mail in Messenger

1. Select the message you want to move and click the File
    button on the toolbar.

2. Click the desired folder from the resulting drop-down list of
    your mail folders. The message now is stored in the folder
    you selected.

3. (Optional) To move to your other folders from the
    Messenger Inbox, click the down arrow next to Inbox to dis-
    play a list of all the Messenger folders. Click the folder you
    want from the list. The new folder name is displayed in the
    box and the Message List shows the messages that are stored
    in that folder.

Using Third-Party Email Programs

Comparing third-party email programs

Downloading and configuring Eudora Light

Sending and receiving messages with Eudora Light

Looking at Juno Mail

In addition to the mail packages that come with the popular browsers, you can choose to use a mail program from a third-party company. Why would you do that? Well, there are a few reasons:

- For one thing, if you had your email already set up before you upgraded to the latest version of your browser, you probably don't want to switch now.

- Or, maybe you don't want to have to go through a transition period each time a new revision of the browser and companion programs is released.

- If you're using email at work, the computer professionals might have chosen a mail program package that's independent from a specific browser and will work with all the computers in the office or network.

Many people use third-party email programs. Although it's hard to get a handle on the actual number, many third-party software developers claim that users of their programs actually outnumber those using Outlook Express or Messenger. Table 9.1 provides a listing of some of the most popular email programs used by Internet users.

TABLE 9.1   Popular email programs on the Internet

Program Name	Description	Web Address
Eudora Pro	Powerful, full version mail program with support for IMAP, LDAP, and integrated address207 books and directories. Has superior capability to filter incoming messages. Easy to set up for multiple users. Eudora Pro has more than 15,000,000 users worldwide.	www.eudora.com
Eudora Light	Freeware version of Eudora Pro.	www.eudora.com
Email Connection	Simple to use and configure. Graphic interface is easy to understand.	www.connectsoft.com

Program Name	Description	Web Address
Pegasus	Needs minimal installation. Contains a glossary of common words to speed up typing. Provides enhanced support for Return Receipt and Delivery notices.	www.pegasus.usa. com/capable.html
Pronto Pro	Provides voice email. Enables users to set rules to file or forward incoming messages.	www.commtouch.com
Postman	Full featured email program with enhanced support for users who have more than one email account.	www.creativenet.net /postman/

Keep in mind that most of these programs are not freeware. You'll have to pay a small fee and register them to use the programs legally. Visit the home page of each program for more complete information. In this chapter, you'll learn about two of the most popular third-party free email programs, Eudora Light and Juno Mail. Each program is unique. Eudora Light is an email software program that you use to work with mail from your existing email account provided by your ISP. Juno Mail provides the necessary software as well as an account in which you get an email address—all free of charge!

Eudora Light

Eudora Light, designed by Qualcomm Software, is a freeware program that's easy to set up and use. Eudora Light can be set up in several languages, including French and Spanish. Eudora Light users can create nicknames for entries in the Address Book. Additionally, Eudora Light users can easily create a personal signature file and attach documents to email messages.

To run Eudora Light, you need a mail account with an ISP. You'll need the standard information for setup, including the names of your outgoing and incoming mail servers, your email address, and your username and password.

Installing and Configuring Eudora Light

In the following step by step exercises, you download Eudora Light and set it up on your computer. You must be connected to the Internet with your browser open and visible on the screen before you begin the steps in the first exercise.

Downloading Eudora Light from the Web

1. Type www.eudora.com in the Address box of your browser and press Enter. In a moment, the Qualcomm Eudora's Place page appears.

2. Read through the information on the page and click the link to Eudora Light. When the new page appears, read the information and click the link to Software and Documentation. Click the link to Download Eudora Light only, as shown in Figure 9.1.

3. If you're asked by your browser what to do when you begin downloading the file, choose the option to **S**ave it to disk and click **OK**.

4. Navigate to the folder in which you would like to store the file and click **S**ave. (Jot down the folder and filename because you'll need it later.) As the file is transferred to your computer, a dialog box similar to the one shown in Figure 9.2 informs you of the progress of the download.

After the file has been downloaded successfully, you need to install it. The next step by step exercise walks you through the procedure of setting up Eudora Light on your computer. Before you begin the steps, disconnect from the Internet. Additionally, close any programs, such as your Web browser, email program, or other software, before you begin.

SEE ALSO

➤ *For more information about downloading files, see page 149.*

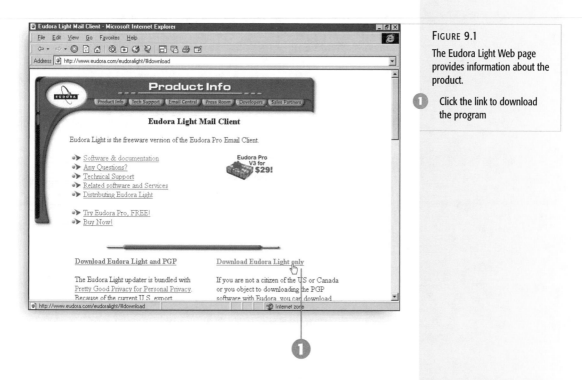

FIGURE 9.1

The Eudora Light Web page provides information about the product.

① Click the link to download the program

①

FIGURE 9.2

The File Download dialog box informs you of the status of the download.

Installing Eudora Light

1. Click the Windows **Start** button and choose **Run**. When the Run dialog box appears, type the folder path and filename (for example, `C:\WINDOWS\Desktop\Saved from the Web\eul305.exe`) in the Open text box and click **OK**. The Eudora Light installation program begins.

2. The first dialog box welcomes you to Eudora. Read the information in the box and click **Next**. Read the licensing information in the second dialog box and accept the terms by clicking **Yes**.

3. The third, fourth, and fifth dialog boxes ask you to confirm the default choices for installation options, program components, and destination location. Accept the program defaults by clicking **Next**.

4. As the files are copied to your computer, you'll see a meter that tracks the installation progress. When the installation is complete, a box appears letting you know the installation was successful.

5. Next, you'll be asked if you would like to view a readme file that contains information about the program. Click **Yes** to open the file in a Notepad window.

   Read through the file, pressing your Page Down key to move down through the text. When you're done, exit Notepad by clicking the **Close** button on the Notepad title bar.

That's all there is to it! Eudora Light is installed and ready for you to use.

Now you're ready to run Eudora Light for the first time. Before you can get busy with email, you'll need to answer a few questions to get the program set up. Follow the steps in the next step by step exercise to complete the setup process.

Setting up Eudora Light for the first time

1. Click the Windows Start button, select <u>P</u>rograms and choose the Eudora Light folder that's been added to your Start menu. To begin, click the Eudora Light program icon that looks like a mailbox.

2. (Optional) Depending on the programs that are already installed in your computer, you might be asked if you want to make Eudora the default mail client program. Click **Yes** unless you're installing Eudora Light as a backup program.

3. The Options dialog box appears, with the **Getting Started** Category selected. (Make sure you have all the information from your ISP about your account, incoming and outgoing server names, and whether your POP3 or IMAP protocols are used before you begin.)

Help is on the way

If you're not sure how to complete any of the fields during the setup, press F1. Eudora's context-sensitive Help program will recognize the field (by the position of the mouse pointer) and inform you what type of information needs to be filled in.

Complete each field on the Getting Started dialog box, as shown here:

- *POP Account.* Specifies the name of your account on the POP3 server of your ISP. For example, if your username is MerlinMag and the address of the POP3 server is `pop.a001.sprintmail.com`, you'll type `merlinmag@ pop.a001.sprintmail.com`.

- *Real name.* Specifies the name that will appear on your outgoing mail. For example, Merlin Magician.

- *Return address.* Specifies your email address if it's different from the POP Account already entered. If the address is different, type your email address, such as `merlinmag@sprintmail.com`.

- *Connection Method.* Your choices are **Winsock**, **Shell Account Access,** or **Offline**. If you're connecting to the Internet through an ISP, choose **Winsock**.

4. When you've entered the information click **Personal Info**, the second category. The information that appears here has been copied from the Getting Started screen.

5. Click the third category, called **Hosts**. The POP account information you entered appears in the POP Account box. Fill in the name of your outgoing mail server in the SMTP: box.

6. Although other configuration options are available, click **OK** to close the Options dialog box and start using Eudora.

SEE ALSO
➤ *Read all about email protocol on page 177.*

Using Eudora Light

Eudora Light is simple to use. The screen, shown in Figure 9.3, is crisp and easy to understand. To get acquainted with the program, move your mouse pointer across the toolbar buttons and read the pop-up screen tips to determine the function of each button. Eudora Light's menu bar, located at the top of the screen, contains many commands. Move your mouse pointer across each command and read the various options.

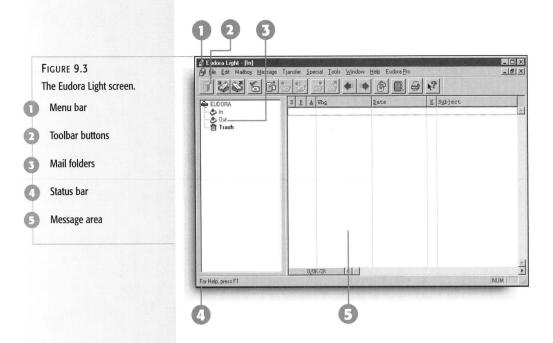

FIGURE 9.3

The Eudora Light screen.

1 Menu bar

2 Toolbar buttons

3 Mail folders

4 Status bar

5 Message area

Unless you know that you have some new mail waiting, why not practice with Eudora Light by sending a message to yourself or someone you know, following these steps:

Sending a message with Eudora Light

1. Click the New Mail button 📝 on the Eudora Light toolbar. A new message, called a Composition Window, appears on the screen.

2. Type the email address of the recipient in the **To:** line.

3. Tab to the **Subject:** line and type a few words to describe the context or purpose of the message.

4. (Optional) If you want to attach a file, tab to the Attached line and click the Attach File button 📎. Navigate to the folder in which the file is located and double-click the file to select it.

SEE ALSO

➤ *You'll find information on file attachments on page 196.*

5. Tab to the message body and type a brief message. An example of a message that's ready to be sent is shown in Figure 9.4.

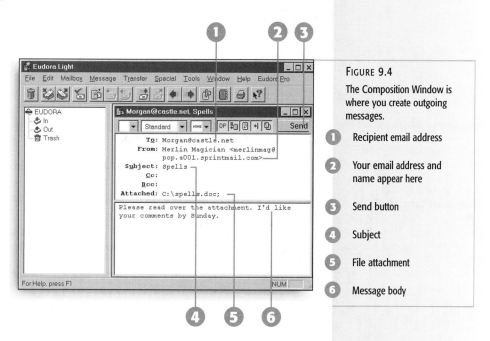

FIGURE 9.4

The Composition Window is where you create outgoing messages.

1 Recipient email address

2 Your email address and name appear here

3 Send button

4 Subject

5 File attachment

6 Message body

6. Click the Send button. Messages flash briefly as Eudora Light sends your message.

7. Click the Open Out mailbox button. Your sent message appears.

8. (Optional) Click the sent message and drag it to the Trash can located at the bottom of the In and Out mailbox folders. You can delete any message by dragging it to the Trash.

9. Click the Open In mailbox to return to the Inbox.

10. Click the Check Mail button. Various messages appear as Eudora Light contacts your email server and checks for new mail. If new messages are downloaded to the Inbox, a chime trills (if your computer can play sounds) and the New Mail dialog box, shown in Figure 9.5, proclaims that you have new mail. Click **OK**.

Take out the trash

Deleted messages remain in the Trash until you empty it. Click the **Special** menu and choose **Empty Trash** to clear all the messages. Perform this step with caution; after you empty the Trash, its contents are gone forever.

FIGURE **9.5**

The New Mail dialog box is a welcome sight.

11. Read a new message by double-clicking the header information (the sender, date, and subject).

Answering is easy

Reply or forward a message when it's open by clicking the **Message** menu. Choose from one of the menu options, such as **Reply**, **Reply to All**, **Forward**, and **Redirect**.

Free Mail on the Internet

If you're not in a position to set up an account with an ISP, and you don't have access to email from your workplace or school, you can send and receive electronic mail across the Internet. A service called Juno provides free email accounts. To use Juno, all you need is a computer running Windows and a modem (9600 kps).

Juno is the fastest growing service on the Internet. From April 1996, the date of Juno's appearance on the Internet scene, to the end of 1997, the free service attracted more than 3 million subscribers. In fact, officials at Juno claim that a new Juno account is created every three seconds.

Juno is easy to use and displays a point and click screen that makes it easy for beginners and experienced email users to move around. The program offers many customizable features, including the following:

- A spell checker
- A personal Address Book
- The capability to create mailing lists
- The capability to set your own colors and fonts
- Mail folders for storing your mail messages

In addition, you can set up Juno accounts for multiple users if several people use the same computer. One of Juno's best features is that you can select your username. Instead of a generic mail account name that has no meaning, you can use a name that makes sense. (For example: kingarthur@juno.com.)

All this for free? If you sign up with Juno, you don't pay anything for their email service. Juno is able to provide the service at no cost to you by running advertisements on the screen while the service is active. The advertisers actually support the cost of the email service. Ads, called banners, appear on the screen in the top right corner as you compose and read your email messages. While the Juno mail servers are contacted and mail is sent and received, showcase ads, which appear in a separate window, are visible. If one of the ads interests you, click it to view the advertiser's Web page. To use Juno, you need to set up the Juno software on your computer. In addition to running Windows, your computer should be equipped with a minimum of 4 MB of RAM, 15 MB of free space on your hard drive, and a VGA monitor. After the software is installed, you connect to Juno through one of their 400 local access numbers. You can't "surf" the World Wide Web through Juno because it's only designed as an email program (although you can click through to an advertiser's Web page). However, you can correspond with anyone who has an Internet email address. The service doesn't limit you to sending and receiving email with only other Juno members.

The Juno Web page, shown in Figure 9.6, provides information about the free email service and links to other information about Juno. The software can be obtained from the Juno page free of charge, or it can be mailed for a nominal charge. You can contact the folks at Juno at 800-654-JUNO for more information.

If you get stuck or need a little help, Juno offers some great technical support. Phone support is available at a per-minute charge. The Juno technical support team also provides email support for any problem you have with the service.

Juno is committed to providing the best email service to its subscribers. The workers at Juno feel that free email is important to the Internet community and take pride in their service. Juno recently filed suit against spammers who used forged Juno email addresses on unsolicited junk email. In the future, Juno plans to continue making the service attractive to new and existing users.

SEE ALSO

➤ *Read about spam on page 175.*

FIGURE 9.6

The Juno Web page provides links to information about its free service.

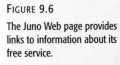
Click a link for details

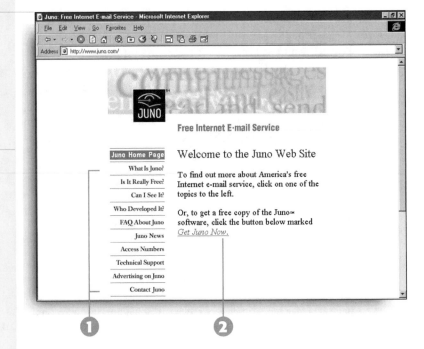
Click here to download the software

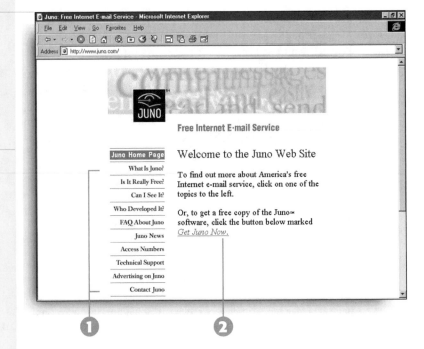

Joining a Newsgroup

Two types

Newsgroups can be moderated; in this case, submissions are automatically directed to a moderator, who edits or filters them and then posts the results. Most newsgroups are unmoderated; anyone can post anything. Discussions in unmoderated groups can get heated or raunchy.

What Are Newsgroups?

Can you imagine thousands upon thousands of people gathering every day to talk about everything under the sun? Such gatherings take place every day on the Internet. The discussions happen in *newsgroups*. From the Internet's earliest days, newsgroups have been a popular venue.

Most individual newsgroups discuss a particular topic, from a character's development in a soap opera, to reported Elvis sightings, to the meaning of life. The forum of a newsgroup can be likened to a virtual bulletin board—someone posts a question or comment to the board, and answers or related comments are placed underneath the original communication. The original posting and related articles make up a *thread*. Each newsgroup is made up of a collection of threaded articles, which look very similar to email messages.

To find groups and participate in discussions that interest you, you need a program called a *newsreader*. Microsoft Outlook Express, part of the Internet Explorer suite, works like a newsreader, as does Netscape Communicator's Collabra. Or, you can use an independent newsreader that is available free of charge, such as Free Agent, distributed by Forte Software.

You can jump into your newsgroups anytime with your newsreader. When you find groups that look especially interesting, you *subscribe* to have the newest postings automatically downloaded to your computer. Unlike when you subscribe to a news service or a magazine, your name isn't put on a master list when you subscribe to a newsgroup. Subscribing to a newsgroup tells your newsreader to get the latest postings for you. Depending on your newsreader, you can look for newsgroups and read and reply to the postings without becoming a member of the discussion group. Either way, it's best to hang back and read the postings of any new group for a while, called *lurking*, before you become an active participant.

Most of the Internet groups are part of a system called *Usenet*, short for user's network. Usenet has been around for more than 15 years. Usenet discussion groups talk about everything from soup to nuts—general topics, like current events or history, or very specific topics, like the exchange of low-fat recipes.

Also, your ISP might sponsor some newsgroups that are limited to use by subscribers and talk about technical support issues or connectivity issues. For example, my ISP has a Members Only newsgroup where subscribers talk about local issues, news, and restaurants. And, if your company or school has an intranet, newsgroups might exist that deal with inside topics or issues. Only the people who have access to a corporate or school Intranet can read and reply to its newsgroups.

SEE ALSO
➤ Read about Internet history on page 469.

Practicing Basic Netiquette

A system of rules and manners, called *netiquette*, governs everyone's conduct in a newsgroup. Visit the Netiquette home page at `http://home.netscape.com/menu/netet/news2.html#netiquette` for more information on the ins and outs of Usenet behavior (see Figure 10.1).

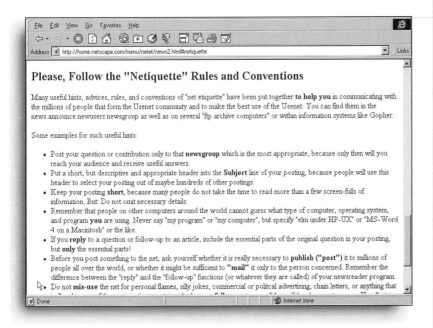

FIGURE 10.1

The Netiquette page provides good advice for new newsgroup users.

If you don't have time to learn all the rules of netiquette, make sure you follow the basic ones:

- Don't type your postings in all uppercase letters. UPPER-CASE LETTERS ARE THE NEWSGROUP (AND EMAIL) EQUIVALENT OF SHOUTING.

- Keep your postings short and to the point. Some news-groups receive hundreds of postings daily. Reading through a long, rambling posting makes people upset.

- Make sure your subject matches the body of your posting. Because people selectively choose the postings they want to read based on the subjects, you'll make people angry if your posting promises to be about one topic but discusses another.

- If you're answering someone else's posting, don't type something like I agree or I second the motion without referencing the original statement. Most people don't remember what they had for lunch yesterday, and they certainly won't remember what comment you're answering.

- If you're replying to a posting and you change the topic a bit, change the **Re:** on the subject line to **Tan:**, short for Tangent.

- Post appropriate messages to newsgroups. For example, don't post a message about a tofu recipe to a current events newsgroup. (I accidentally did this and got very nasty responses.)

Newsgroup etiquette isn't very different from the way that you expect to be treated by your colleagues and associates. If you treat your fellow discussion group members with courtesy and common sense, you won't step on any toes.

Deciphering Newsgroup Names

Newsgroup names are structured, and might seem like a secret code when you first see them. After you crack the code, the names are easy to understand. Like a URL, the names are hier-archical and each portion of a newsgroup name is separated by periods. The first portion of the name reflects the category of the newsgroup. The second portion shows the topic. Subsequent words break down the topic into subtopics. So, the newsgroup name `alt.music.byrds` translates into an alternative group that discusses music by the old sixties group, The Byrds.

Table 10.1 shows the most common Usenet groups and provides a brief description and a group name example.

TABLE 10.1   Common Usenet groups

Name	Description	Example
alt	Alternative subjects, ranging from the serious (computers and psychology) to the bizarre and unconventional (occult and alternative lifestyles)	`alt.fan.actors`
biz	Business subjects, including advertisements and solicitations	`biz.books.technical`
comp	Computer-related subjects	`comp.infosystems.` `www.misc`
k12	Educational topics relating to elementary and secondary education	`k12.ed.math`
misc	Miscellaneous topics like jobs, items for sale, and so on	`misc.forsale.` `comcomputer`
news	Information about newsgroups themselves	`news.announce.` `newusers`
rec	Recreational topics such as hobbies, sports, the arts, movies, and television	`rec.arts.tv`
sci	A vast variety of scientific topics including comets and cloning	`sci.bio.evolution`
soc	Discussions center around topics containing a social nature	`soc.history.what-if`
talk	Controversial topics that lead to debate and heated discussions	`talk.religion.course` `-miracles`

In addition to the names shown in the table, you might find several other group names. Groups that begin with "de" are discussions held in German, whereas Japanese discussion groups start with "fj." Corporations also maintain newsgroups. UPI offers a fee-based set of current events newsgroups that begin with "clari" (paid for by your ISP). As you look through the groups on the Internet, you'll find even more names.

SEE ALSO

➤ *You'll find everything you need to know about the structure of URLs on page 90.*

Getting Started with News

You need to set up your newsreader program before you can become active in newsgroups. You might have already filled in this information when you installed your browser suite. If not, you'll need to know the following information to be able to create and respond to newsgroup postings:

■ The name of the *Network News Transfer Protocol* (NNTP) server that your Internet service provider uses for news

■ Your email address

■ The logon name, authentication code, and password you need to access the news server

You'll need the information for the third item only if your ISP requires it. If you're not sure about your ISP's logon procedure to the news server, or any other piece of required information, call your ISP and confirm what you need to know before you start setting up your newsreader.

Setting Up Outlook Express to Read News

If you're an Internet Explorer user, you're already familiar with using Outlook Express as your email client program. Outlook Express doubles as a newsreader as well as a great way to send and receive email. When you first set up Outlook Express, you used the Internet Connection Wizard to set up mail, and you might have already entered all the information needed to use Outlook Express as a newsreader. If not, the Internet Connection Wizard will walk you through the steps you need to enter the world of newsgroups. Unless you switch to another

ISP, or something else about your Internet account changes, you'll only have to enter the information once.

To access the Internet Connection Wizard, open the **Tools** menu and choose **Accounts**. When the Internet Accounts dialog box appears, click the **Add** button and select **News** from the submenu. Fill in the information requested in each dialog box, clicking **Next** to advance to each box. (An example of the Internet News Server Name dialog box of the Connection Wizard is displayed in Figure 10.2.) The final dialog box reads Congratulations and tells you that you have successfully entered all the information required to set up your account. Click **Finish**.

FIGURE 10.2

The name of the mail server needs to be entered to access the newsgroups.

1 Type the name exactly as your ISP provided it

2 Check this box if your ISP requires a separate logon

The first time you set up a news account, Outlook Express asks if you would like to download the newsgroups from the news server you added. Click **Yes**. The Downloading Newsgroups dialog box appears and records the progress of the total number of groups downloaded. When the download is completed, the Downloading Newsgroups dialog box closes and the list of newsgroups from your news server appears in the Newsgroups dialog box.

If you ever need to change information about your news account, open the Outlook Express **Tools** menu and select **Accounts**. After the Internet Accounts dialog box appears, click

Setting up multiple news accounts

As with mail, you can have multiple news accounts if you have more than one service provider. If you need to set up additional news accounts, bring up the Internet Connection Wizard and type the applicable information about the other account in the dialog boxes. You'll need to run the Internet Connection Wizard for each separate account.

More than Netscape Navigator

To use Collabra, the Communicator suite of programs must be installed on your computer. If you've only installed Netscape Navigator, connect to the Internet, open Navigator and visit the Netscape home page at `home.netscape.com`. Click the **Software** link to access Netscape SmartUpdate. Follow the posted instructions to download and install Collabra, Messenger and any other programs in the suite.

the **News** tab and select the account for which you want to make the changes. When the account name appears highlighted, click **Properties** and make the necessary corrections.

SEE ALSO
➤ *For information on using the Internet Connection Wizard, reread pages 181-183.*

Setting Up Netscape Collabra

Collabra is the program in the Netscape Communicator suite that handles newsgroups. Collabra refers to newsgroups as "discussion groups" but, actually, both terms mean the same thing. Because Collabra shares many of its features with Netscape Messenger, you'll feel right at home when you use it. In fact, you might have already entered the necessary information to use Collabra when you configured Messenger for your email. Both Messenger and Collabra use the Netscape Message Center; you read and reply to newsgroup postings the same way you handle your mail messages. If you want, you can store newsgroup postings in the same folders as you store your mail.

Configuring Collabra

1. Click the Windows **Start** button, choose **Programs**, **Netscape Communicator**, and then **Netscape Collabra**. Collabra opens, displaying the Netscape Message Center, as displayed in Figure 10.3. Notice that the news folder is highlighted. (This folder is simply a placeholder for your news folders and won't actually retrieve any newsgroups.)

2. Open the **Edit** menu and select **Preferences**. The Preferences dialog box appears, with a list of categories displayed on the left side. If a **+** sign appears next to the Mail and Groups category, open the subcategory list by clicking the **+**. (The **+** sign changes to a **-** and all the Mail and Groups subcategories appear.)

3. Click the Groups Server subcategory on the left to display the Groups Server sheet.

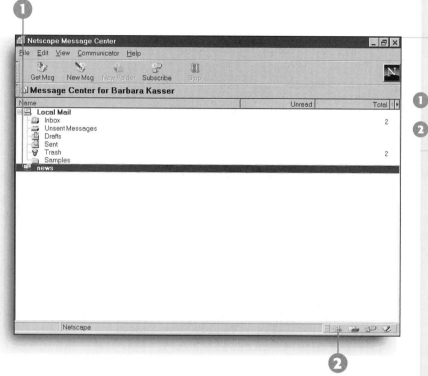

FIGURE 10.3
Open Collabra to display the
Netscape Message Center.

1 News folder is highlighted

2 Docked Component Taskbar

4. Click inside the **Discussion groups (news) server** text box
and replace the text that's displayed with the server name
provided by your ISP, as illustrated in Figure 10.4.

5. (Optional) If you have a good reason for changing the
default, click the **Choose** button and select a different folder
to store your discussion group messages.

6. When you're done, click **OK** to return to the Message
Center. A folder for the news server you entered is displayed
below the news folder.

7. Click the new folder once to select it. Open the **File** menu
and choose **Subscribe to Discussion Groups**. The
Communicator: Subscribe to Discussion Groups dialog box
appears on your screen.

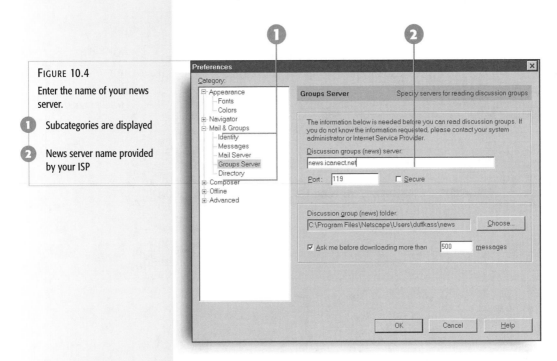

FIGURE 10.4

Enter the name of your news server.

1 Subcategories are displayed

2 News server name provided by your ISP

Be patient

With thousands and thousands of discussion groups, it might take a few minutes for the group list to appear on your computer. If you're not sure if anything is happening, watch the status indicator at the bottom of the dialog box.

8. The first time you click the **Subscribe to Discussions** button after you've set up a news account, Collabra contacts your news server to download the listing of available discussion groups (newsgroups) to your computer. The status indicator located at the bottom of the dialog box tracks the percentage of completion as the list of groups is being downloaded, as displayed in Figure 10.5. When the list is complete, group names appear in the box and the status indicator displays Document:Done.

SEE ALSO
➤ *For information on using Netscape Messenger as your mail program, review pages 185-187.*

Locating and Subscribing to the Right Group

Unless you're already aware of a specific newsgroup to which you want to subscribe, you probably want to peruse the list of group names and search for a group that best matches your interests. When you've picked out one or more groups that talk about topics that interest you, you're ready to become a member of the group. Don't worry; subscribing to a newsgroup doesn't represent a major commitment on your part.

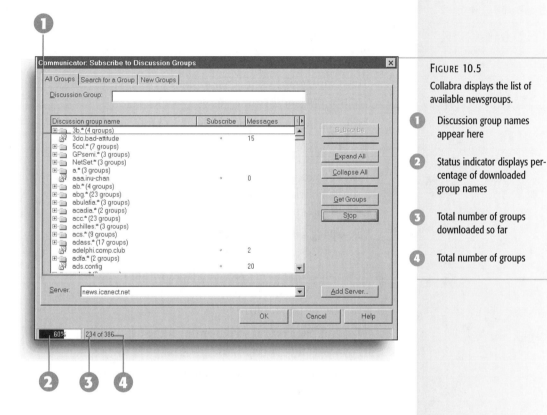

FIGURE 10.5

Collabra displays the list of available newsgroups.

1. Discussion group names appear here

2. Status indicator displays percentage of downloaded group names

3. Total number of groups downloaded so far

4. Total number of groups

You subscribe to the newsgroups in whose discussions you regularly want to participate. Subscribing to a newsgroup is a lot like joining a discussion group at your local public library or community center. As part of the group, you can comment on the discussions and even receive recognition or accolades from the other members of the group.

Because the discussion takes place over the Internet, you don't need to attend special meetings or pay dues to be a group member. In fact, because your subscriptions are tracked only by your ISP, the other members of the group won't know you've joined unless you tell them. Because your interests, tastes, and available time change, you can subscribe and *unsubscribe* to as many newsgroups as you want.

Visiting Newsgroups with Outlook Express

Outlook Express makes it easy to work with all the newsgroups. You can read the postings of a group, or you can subscribe and become a member of the group. In the following step by step exercise, you find a group that's right for you and subscribe. Make sure you're connected to the Internet with Outlook Express open and visible on the screen.

After you subscribe to a newsgroup, Outlook Express displays a subfolder for the group in your news server folder in the Outlook Express Folder list pane. When you're connected to the Internet and using Outlook Express, click the news server folder and then click the specific newsgroup subfolder to read that newsgroup's postings.

Subscribing with Outlook Express

1. If the Newsgroup dialog box isn't open and visible on the screen, open the **Go** menu from within Outlook Express and select **News**. Then, click the News groups button on the Newsgroup toolbar.

2. Drag the vertical scrollbar down the list of newsgroup names and descriptions.

3. When you see a newsgroup that interests you, click the group name to select it.

4. If you want to find groups that discuss a specific topic, click inside the text box beneath **Display newsgroups which contain** and type the word or phrase for which you're looking. Notice that as you begin typing, the list of newsgroup names changes to match the letters you've typed. Check the box next to **Also search descriptions** to broaden your search.

    When you're done typing, the list is shortened and displays only the groups that match the words you typed. The title of the first group on the list appears highlighted. If you see an interesting group, click the group name to select it.

5. To find different groups, click inside the text box again and type new keywords. To display the entire list, clear the contents of the box.

It's not up to you

Your ISP makes the decision about which newsgroups are available to you. Depending on the newsgroups to which your ISP subscribes, you might not be able to see all the groups on the Internet.

6. If you haven't already selected a newsgroup name, click a name from the list that appears on the screen. If you're sure you want to subscribe to the group, click the **Subscribe** button and skip step 7. If you would like to look over the postings before you subscribe, click the **Go to** button, as shown in Figure 10.6. The Newsgroups dialog box closes, and the postings of the group you selected are displayed in Outlook Express, very similarly to the way that your email messages appear.

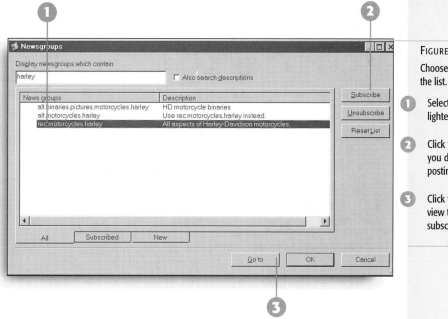

FIGURE 10.6

Choose a group name from the list.

1. Selected group appears highlighted

2. Click the **Subscribe** button if you don't want to view the postings first

3. Click the **Go to** button to view the postings before you subscribe

If the newsgroup you selected is active, with lots of postings, it might take a few minutes for the messages to download. However, the next time you view that newsgroup, the postings will appear much faster because Outlook Express will download only the messages not previously downloaded.

7. Subscribe to a group whose postings appear on the screen by opening the **Tools** menu and selecting **Subscribe to this newsgroup**. The dialog box closes and the newsgroup name appears beneath the news server name in the folder pane.

No postings appear

If you don't see any postings, the group isn't active and doesn't have any messages. Repeat the steps to select another group.

Read and Reply to Newsgroup Postings in Outlook Express

Like mail, the headers of newsgroup postings appear in Outlook Express. Headers contain the subject, sender, date and time, and size of the posting. When you click a header, the actual message is displayed in the Preview pane below.

Reading and replying to postings

1. Click a message header with a closed envelope icon next to it. The text of the message is displayed in the Preview pane and the closed envelope icon changes to a letter icon to signify that the message has been read.

2. Double-click a header to display it in its own message window. (If a posting is long, opening it in a separate window makes it easier to read.)

3. Click the Close button at the top right corner of the message window to close the posting.

4. A **+** sign to the left of a header signifies that the message header is the most current posting in a thread, or series of messages about the same topic and based on the same original posting. Click the **+** sign to expand the thread and display the other messages below the one that's showing now.

   When a thread is expanded, the **+** sign changes to a **-** sign. Click the **-** sign to collapse the thread.

5. Postings that you've read won't appear the next time you view the postings of the group. To mark an individual posting that you don't want to read so it won't display the next time you open the newsgroup, right-click the header and choose **Mark as Read** on the pop-up menu, as shown in Figure 10.7.

6. If the posting is one of a thread that you don't choose to read, choose **Mark Thread as Read** on the pop-up menu.

7. Reply to the posting you're reading by clicking the **Reply to Group** button on the Newsgroup toolbar. When the message window opens with the text of the original posting displayed, type your response and click the **Post** button. Shortly, your posting will appear as part of the thread.

Too many at once

If you're overwhelmed by the number of postings and don't have the time to read all of them, open the **Edit** menu and choose **Mark All as Read**. The next time you open the newsgroup, those postings won't appear. You might want to do this after you've been on a trip or if you've been too busy to check out the postings for a while.

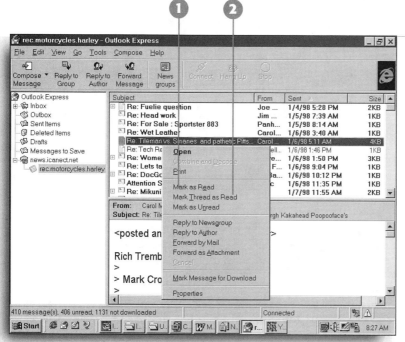

FIGURE 10.7
Mark a posting as read from the pop-up menu.

1 Click **Mark as Read** to prevent the header from appearing the next time you view the newsgroup postings

2 Click **Mark Thread as Read** to cancel all the postings in the thread

If you want to reply personally to the author of the posting without having your reply appear on the newsgroup's postings, click the **Reply to Author** button, type your response, and click **Send**.

8. Because Outlook Express is configured to handle both mail and news, you can forward a posting from a newsgroup to an individual. While you're viewing a newsgroup posting, click the **Forward Message** button. The message window opens with both the text and the header information of the original posting displayed in the message body. The subject of the original message appears, preceded by **FW:** and the sub.

9. Create a new posting by clicking the **Compose Message** button. The New Message window appears, very similar to the one you see when you're creating an email message.

Notice that the name of the newsgroup is already filled in the **Newsgroups:** portion of the message. When you're done typing your message, click the **Post** button to send it to the group.

10. If Outlook Express doesn't detect action from you for a while, the program shifts into Offline mode. If you attempt to read or reply to a posting, you'll receive an error message stating that you're not connected. Check your Internet connection; if you're still connected to the Internet, click the **Connect** button for Outlook Express to re-establish the connection to the newsgroup server.

11. Any time you want to view the latest messages that have been posted to the newsgroup, open the **Tools** menu and select **Download this newsgroup**. When the Download Newsgroup dialog box appears, first check the box next to **Get the following items** and then click the option button next to **News headers**, **New messages (headers and bodies)**, or **All messages (headers and bodies)**. Click **OK** to close the dialog box and retrieve the postings.

12. To return to the list of newsgroups, click the **Newsgroups** button.

SEE ALSO

➤ *For instructions on composing new mail messages, refer to page 188.*

Subscribing to Discussion Groups in Collabra

Collabra arranges the list of available discussion groups in a logical order. The master list of group names is organized in a hierarchical structure with the group categories arranged in alphabetical order. If a category contains subcategories, the number of subcategory groups is displayed next to the category name. Along with the number, a **+** sign next to a category name lets you know that the category is collapsed. (A **-** sign indicates that the subcategories are expanded; you'll see the subcategory names on the screen.) Click the **+** sign to display the subcategories.

In some categories, the subcategories drill down through several layers. For example, to view the discussion group name alt.animals.feline.snowleopards, you'd need to first open the alt category and then the animals and feline subcategories, as shown in Figure 10.8.

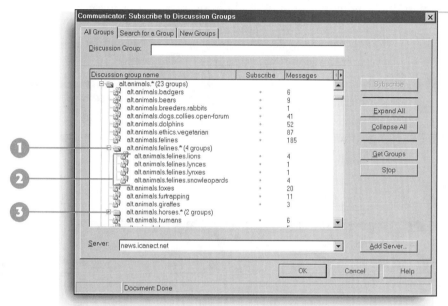

FIGURE 10.8

Collabra arranges the groups into subcategories.

1 - sign indicates subcategory is expanded

2 Groups in the subcategory

3 The subgroups are not visible because the category is collapsed

In the next step-by-step exercise, you use Collabra to find and subscribe to a newsgroup. For Collabra to find the master list of newsgroups, you must be connected to the Internet with Collabra open.

Finding and subscribing to newsgroups with Collabra

1. If the Communicator: Subscribe to Discussion Groups dialog box is not displayed on your screen, open the **File** menu and choose **Subscribe to Discussion Groups**. When the Communicator: Subscribe to Discussion Groups dialog box is visible, note the three tabs at the top: **All Groups**, **Search for a Group**, and **New Groups**.

2. Click the **All Group** tab to display the master list. Scroll down through the list. If you want to expand a category to see the subgroups underneath it, click the **+** sign.

3. When you find an interesting group name, click it to select it.

4. If you don't want to look through categories and subcategories, click the **Search for a Group** tab and type a keyword in the **Search for** text box.

5. In a moment, the search results are displayed. If you're not interested in any of the displayed groups, or no groups are found, type a new keyword and click **Search** again. If a group looks promising, select it.

6. When you've found a group to which you want to subscribe, click the **Subscribe** button. As displayed in Figure 10.9, a check mark appears in the **Subscribe** column. Click **OK** to close the Communicator: Subscribe to Discussion Groups dialog box. You're returned to the Message Center.

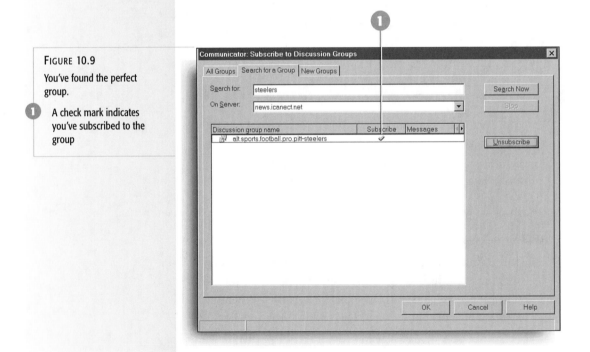

FIGURE 10.9
You've found the perfect group.

1 A check mark indicates you've subscribed to the group

7. In the area next to the name of your news server, the group name to which you subscribed is shown. Double-click the group name to view the postings. If the group has more than

500 postings, the dialog box shown in Figure 10.10 appears. Choose whether to **D**ownload all headers or **D**own**l**oad **500 headers** and then click the **Download** button. In a few moments, the message headers are displayed.

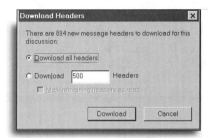

FIGURE 10.10

The dialog box indicates that the group has more than 500 postings.

Working with Newsgroup Postings in Collabra

Discussion group posting headers appear in a Collabra window with the name of the discussion group displayed across the top. Unread postings display the header information in boldface text. When the message has been read, the boldface is removed. A pushpin icon indicates that the posting is part of a thread.

A small triangle that's pointing upward appears at the bottom of the posting's window, as shown in Figure 10.11. Click the triangle if you want to read the discussion group postings in the same window as the message headers. The triangle disappears, and the window displays the message headers and the text of the message that's selected (see Figure 10.12).

Reading and replying to postings in Collabra

1. Click any header to read the text of the posting. To open the posting in its own window, double-click the header. When you're done with the posting, close it by clicking the Close button to the right of the posting window's title bar.

2. A pushpin icon and a **+** sign to the left of a header signify that the message header is the most recent posting in a thread of related messages. Click the **+** sign to display the other messages below the one that's currently displayed.

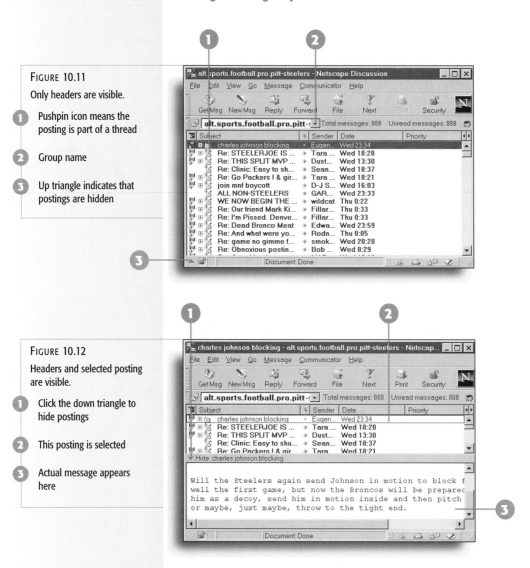

FIGURE 10.11

Only headers are visible.

1 Pushpin icon means the posting is part of a thread

2 Group name

3 Up triangle indicates that postings are hidden

FIGURE 10.12

Headers and selected posting are visible.

1 Click the down triangle to hide postings

2 This posting is selected

3 Actual message appears here

3. Only unread postings will appear the next time you access the discussion group. If you don't want to read a particular posting, select it and click the **Mark** button. The following options are available:

- *As **Read***. The posting won't appear the next time you view the newsgroup.

- *__Thread__ Read*. The entire thread (the current message and all related messages) won't appear the next time the newsgroup is accessed.

- *__All__ Read*. All the headers will be marked as read and won't appear again.

- *By __Date__*. If you choose this option, you'll be asked to provide a date for marking messages as read. Postings with dates prior to the date you enter won't appear again.

- *For __Later__*. All the postings will appear again.

4. Reply to the posting you're reading by clicking the **Reply** button on the toolbar. A drop-down menu appears with the following options: **Reply to Sender**, **Reply to Sender and all Recipients**, **Reply to Group**, or **Reply to Sender and Group**.

    When the message window opens with the text of the original posting displayed, the recipients that appear in the **To** box will be based on the reply option you selected. Type your reply and click **Send**.

5. Forward a posting from a newsgroup to an individual who is not a current recipient by clicking the **Forward** button. The message window opens with the subject of the original message appears in brackets and preceded by **FW**. Although the original message is not displayed on the screen, it will be displayed when the recipient opens it. If desired, type a message of your own to go along with the posting you're forwarding.

6. Create a new posting by clicking the **New Msg** button. A new message window appears with the name of the group typed in as the recipient. Type your posting and click **Send**.

7. Download the latest postings to your discussion group by clicking the **Get Msg** button. Collabra contacts your news server and places the latest ones at the top of your list of postings.

SEE ALSO

➤ *For instructions on composing new mail messages with Netscape Messenger, refer to page 188.*

Open it first

Before you can unsubscribe to a newsgroup in Outlook Express or Collabra, the program must be open and on the screen. Additionally, you must be connected to the Internet.

Unsubscribing to Discussion Groups

You're never locked into a newsgroup. You can unsubscribe any time you decide you no longer want to read the postings of the group. If you change your mind down the road, you can always subscribe again—without any penalty or fear of reprisals.

In Outlook Express, click the news server folder in the Folder list pane. The folder opens and the names of all the newsgroups to which you're subscribed appear. Right-click the group from which you want to unsubscribe. Choose **Unsubscribe from this group** from the resulting pop-up menu.

If you use Collabra as your newsreader, it's a breeze to unsubscribe from a discussion group. First, move to the Message Center by opening the **Communicator** menu and choosing **Messenger Mailbox**. (You can go to the Message Center from any program in the Communicator suite.) Right-click the group from which you want to unsubscribe and choose **Remove Discussion Group** from the pop-up menu. The group disappears from your list.

Liven Up Your Postings

As you read newsgroup postings, you encounter text that, at first glance, appears like typographical errors. In fact, these "typos" are not errors at all, but abbreviations for commonly used phrases and sayings. Table 10.2 describes the most commonly used abbreviations used both in newsgroup postings and email.

TABLE 10.2   Common abbreviations used in newsgroups

Abbreviation	What It Means
BBL	Be back later
BRB	Be right back
CYA	See 'ya
GMTA	Great minds think alike
HHIS	Hanging head in shame

Abbreviation	What It Means
IMHO	In my humble opinion
IRL	In real life
L8R	Later
LOL	Laughing out loud
LMSO	Laughing my socks off
OIC	Oh, I see
ROTFL	Rolling on the floor laughing

Using Other Newsreaders

Although both Microsoft and Netscape have worked hard to make Outlook Express and Collabra good newsreader programs, you can use several other newsreader programs. If you really get involved with posting and subscribing to newsgroups, you might find that a dedicated program works best. Table 10.3 provides more information about some of these newsreaders.

TABLE 10.3   **Dedicated newsreader programs**

Program Name	Company	Find More Information At	Cost	Comments
Agent	Forte	`http://www.forteinc.com`	$29.00	Considered the best newsreader by many users. Features include full email integration, the capability to set up special folders, and enhanced search for special postings.
Free Agent	Forte	`http://www.forteinc.com/forte`	Free-ware	Not quite as many features as Agent, but an excellent, full-

continues…

TABLE 10.3   **Continued**

Program Name	Company	Find More Information At	Cost	Comments
				featured program. Contains an easy-to-use interface.
News Ferret	FerretSoft	`http://www.webferret.com`	$13.95	Enables users to search and retrieve Usenet news articles for a topic of interest, without having to access each news-group separately.
NewsMonger	Tech Smith Corporation	`http://www.techsmith.com`	$39.95	Supports multiple searches, search scheduling, and email notification when new articles matching your criteria are discovered.
NewsXPress	Ken Ng	`http://cws.icorp.net/3 32news-xnews.html`	Free-ware	Offers user customization and great filtering and sorting capabilities.

SEE ALSO

➤ *For more information on downloading software, see page 146.*

Tracking Postings with Deja News

With so many available newsgroups and so many postings, it's impossible to keep track of everything that's discussed. Fortunately, you can obtain postings on just about anything by using Deja News on the World Wide Web. The Deja News site at www.dejanews.com contains archives of most postings on the Internet (see Figure 10.13).

FIGURE 10.13

Deja News maintains archives of most newsgroup postings.

❶ Choose one of these options to find a posting or newsgroup

Deja News offers several search tools for finding the postings you want to see:

- *Quick Search*. Offers a simple search. Type your keywords into the **Find** text box and click the **Find** button. Don't worry about capitalizing words because the search isn't case sensitive.

- *Power Search*. Provides more complex search capabilities. Structure your query with Boolean logic, using the terms AND, NOT, or NEAR, for example. Additionally, specify which archive is to be searched and how the keywords should be matched. For further control, specify how many and in what format the results should appear.

- *Search Filter.* Enables you to refine your searches by filtering on any message field. You can tell Deja News to look through the Group, Author, and Subject dates and specify a date range for the posting.

The alt group isn't indexed

Deja News doesn't display an index of the alt groups. However, if you enter an alt group name like `alt.animals`, Deja News will show all the related groups.

- *Interest Finder.* A quick way to find newsgroups. Type the topic for which you're looking into the **Find** text box and click **Find**.

- *Browse Groups.* Shows you the newsgroups arranged by category. If you've got an idea of a group name, type it into the **Browse** text box and click **Browse**. Otherwise, click the top level group name (for example, **comp**, **rec**, or **sci**) and click through the links of corresponding group names.

- *Post Messages.* Enables you to post non-commercial messages to any newsgroup. If this is your first time using the Deja News posting service, take a moment and register (for free) by clicking the **register for easy posting** link. Otherwise, you'll need to send a confirmation email for every posting you send.

In addition to these options, Deja News also features arrangements of newsgroups by categories and a technical support section for computer-related questions. You can also visit Deja News' Cool Stuff section to access online resources, Deja News Classifieds, and Yellow Pages search.

SEE ALSO

➤ *Bone up on search techniques on page 124.*

PART

IV

Turning to the Internet for Information

The Internet for Kids

Finding Web sites designed just for kids

Keeping children Net safe

Taking a break with some games

What's on the Internet for Kids?

It's hard to keep kids off of the Internet! Even the littlest tots enjoy visiting Web pages designed just for them. The Internet makes it easy for children to reach out to other kids, play games, and learn new facts. Global boundaries don't exist on the Internet; online, your children have the whole world at their fingertips. With the help and guidance of parents and teachers, the Internet can be a safe and entertaining place for kids to visit.

Kids can choose from sites that offer a range of activities from playing games to sharing original poetry and compositions. Many sites offer help with schoolwork. Children can chat with one another in real-time conversations, post messages to bulletin boards, and exchange email with cyber-pals.

Of course, one of the Internet's greatest strengths, its tremendous size, can also make it a scary place to send our children. The sheer volume of information and content on the Internet enables a child to accidentally (or intentionally) visit a site that contains objectionable words or content. Parents and teachers need to supervise their children's Internet experiences and make sure that the kids are practicing "safe-surf" techniques.

Kids-only pages

More and more young people are creating their own Web pages. Many Web communities, like GeoCities (`www.geocities.com`), have areas set aside for individual Web pages designed by children.

Yahooligans! Is a Great Place to Start

Yahooligans! is a wonderful Web navigational guide for kids. The service contains a searchable index of Web sites designed for children ages 7 through 12. Like its adult counterpart, Yahoo!, the Yahooligans! home page (see Figure 11.1) contains both a search area and a launch pad to several categories, such as **Entertainment**, **Arts**, and **Recreation**. From the home page, you can click links to new and cool sites for kids, or join Club Yahooligans!

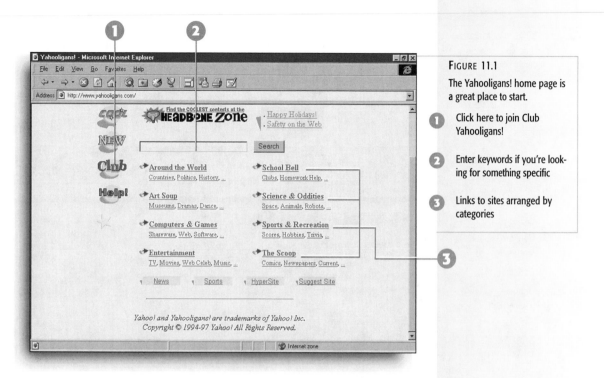

FIGURE 11.1

The Yahooligans! home page is a great place to start.

1 Click here to join Club Yahooligans!

2 Enter keywords if you're looking for something specific

3 Links to sites arranged by categories

Using Yahooligans! as a home base for kids offers some great advantages. Lots of time and resources have been invested by the folks at Yahooligans! to research the Web sites listed in the index. Because the sites are listed hierarchically, under defined categories, it's easy for children to click through the sub-categories to find the sites they want. For example, locating Web pages devoted to a child's favorite television show can be accomplished with a few mouse clicks.

Finding information with Yahooligans!

1. If you're not already connected to the Internet, connect now and open your browser. When the start page appears, type www.yahooligans.com in the **Address** box and press Enter. In a moment the Yahooligans! home page appears.

2. Click the link to **Entertainment**. An index of entertainment-related categories appears.

Join the club

Club Yahooligans! is a special kids-only Internet club. Members receive a monthly email of cool sites, get early notification of contests and other offers, receive a Web newsletter, and get discounts on Yahooligans! merchandise. Best of all, it doesn't cost anything to join.

Learn the lingo

The numbers that appear next to each Yahooligans! category tell how many Web sites are listed in those categories. The word "New" next to a category title indicates that new sites within the category have been added recently.

3. Click the **Television** link. A new index page appears, displaying links to several television categories, such as TV show listings, actors and actresses, and networks. The categories followed by an @ sign let you know that the category is listed in multiple places within the Yahooligans! directory, as shown in Figure 11.2.

FIGURE 11.2

The Television index makes it easy to find a site about a TV-related topic.

1 The @ sign indicates that the heading can be found in other Yahooligans! categories

2 Links to subcategories pinpoint what you're looking for

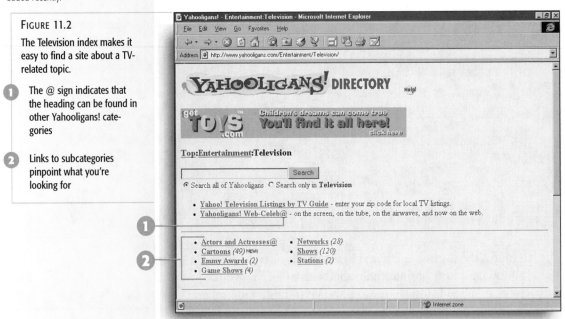

4. Scroll down the page and click the **Shows** category link.

5. When the index of sites about television shows appears, click a link to a site about a show you enjoy.

6. Review the new page that appears by clicking a link to a related site on the Web.

7. Click your browser's **Back** button as many times as necessary to move back to the Television page or to the Yahooligans! home page.

In addition to maintaining an index of sites that kids like, Yahooligans! provides links to the latest and greatest sites, news, and sports information. Table 11.1 shows the name of the link and where it takes you.

TABLE 11.1   **Links for kids on Yahooligans! home page**

Link	What You'll See
New	A description and link to the Web sites added to Yahooligans! in the past week.
Cool	Links to sites that might be entertaining, funny, wild, educational, or useful.
Suggest Site	Online form used to submit sites for inclusion in the Yahooligans! site index. The page title, URL, and a brief description are required.
Hypersite	An exciting site selected by Yahoo! The hypersite changes weekly.
News	Current events aimed at kids. Click a headline to display the full story.
Sports	An index of major sports, with links to teams, scores, statistics, and other related information.

SEE ALSO

➤ *For detailed information on how to search in Yahoo!, see page 134.*

➤ *For ways to cycle back through pages you've already viewed, see page 55 if you're a Navigator user or page 67 if you're an Internet Explorer user.*

Touring Cyberkids

Cyberkids at www.cyberkids.com emphasizes creativity and participation for children on the Internet. The Cyberkids site has been an Internet fixture for a long time. Started in November 1994, the site published original work from Mountain Lake Software Inc.'s First Annual Kids' International Writing and Art Contest. From there, the site mushroomed to include many other facets.

Cyberkids features thought-provoking pages and displays. The site changes often to stay current; for example, you might see a link to a review of a new movie or interviews with noteworthy celebrities. Cyberkids also encourages children to submit original artwork and music compositions to the site. Click the link to **Art Gallery** or **Young Composer** to see and hear what other kids are doing.

If your children are too old for Cyberkids, the related Cyberteens site at www.cyberteens.com has links to sites and Web attractions that are age appropriate for teenagers. Figure 11.3 shows the Cyberteens home page. Cyberteens encourages creativity and provides feedback from other teens.

FIGURE 11.3

The Cyberteens site is for teenagers.

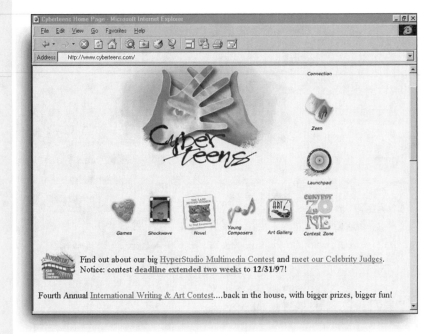

Cyberteens publishes an *e-zine* called *Zeen* that changes every few months. The magazine welcomes submissions from teenagers around the world. Featured in *Zeen* are original poetry, editorials, and original artwork, as well as links to sites set up by major teen advertisers.

Cyberteens Connection is a Cyberteens attraction that enables teens from all over the world to get together. You can access the Cyberteens Connection as a guest, but unless you register, you can't post to the site's message boards or participate in a real-time chat conversation at the Cosmic Café. In the following step-by-step exercise, you get connected at the Cyberteens Connection.

Connecting with other cyberteens

1. Type www.cyberteens.com in the **Address** box of your browser and press Enter. In a moment, the Cyberteens home page appears.

2. Click the link to **Connection**. If you've registered previously, type your name and password and click the **Login** button. If you're new, you can click **Guest Access** to read the messages on Cyberteens Connection.

   To register, click the **Register** button; when the New User Registration page appears, enter your name, password, and email address. Follow the onscreen instructions to complete the registration process.

3. The Cyberteens Connection Welcome Page is the starting page for both the real-time chat and the message boards. Click the link to **Cyberteens Chat**. Read the instructions on the page that appears and click the link to move to the **Cosmic Café**. (You need to have a Java-enabled browser, like Internet Explorer or Netscape.)

4. When the program is downloaded, a real-time chat conversation appears on the **Message Display** area, as shown in Figure 11.4. The participants' names are listed on the right side of the screen (your name appears in color). Type your comments in the message box and press Enter. Your messages appear in the **Message Display** area, along with other chatters' responses.

6. When you're done chatting, close the Chat window by clicking **File** and then **Close**. Click the link to **Cyberteens Connection** to view the other Cyberteen Connection options.

7. From the available discussion topics, click one that interests you. Each discussion group is organized in folders, which might have related subfolders. When you open a folder, the subject lines of the messages that have been posted are displayed.

Don't get impatient

The Cosmic Café is powered by different software from your browser program and opens in its own window. Depending on your computer hardware, it might take a few minutes for the Cosmic Café to appear on your computer screen.

SEE ALSO

➤ *Java is explained on page 19.*

➤ *You learn all about real-time chatting on page 377.*

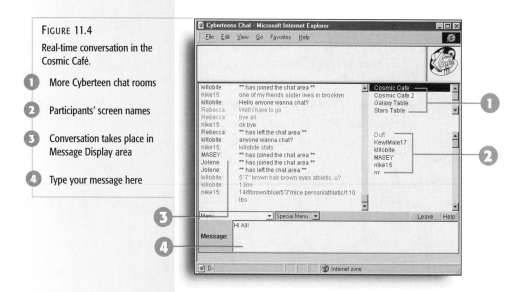

FIGURE 11.4

Real-time conversation in the Cosmic Café.

1 More Cyberteen chat rooms

2 Participants' screen names

3 Conversation takes place in Message Display area

4 Type your message here

Keeping Kids Net Safe

Keeping children *Net safe* is a prime concern for parents and educators. Web sites can contain violent, lewd, or lascivious language and pictures that are not suitable for viewing by children or young adults. News stories of unsuspecting children engaged in chat conversations or email with adults pretending to be children pop up with some regularity. Because of these problems, many adults are afraid to let children use the Internet.

Dangers for children on the Internet are similar to the dangers they face in everyday life. The same basic safety rules—not to speak to strangers or give out personal information—apply to the Internet as well as the mall or playground.

The following list of five rules should be discussed with kids before they use the Internet. Additionally, young children should never be left alone while they're online. If your children are older, use your judgment. If you're worried about sites that your children might be viewing on the Web when you're not supervising, let them know that you can and will track the sites they visit.

Internet commandments for kids

1. If you click a link or type a URL to a Web site that looks like it's for adults only, or contains pictures or material that's offensive, leave immediately! There are plenty of good "kid sites" on the Web.

2. If you receive email from someone you don't know, don't respond without checking with an adult.

3. Never give out your real last name, address, telephone number, login password, or other personal information to anyone on the Internet. If someone asks for information you know you're not supposed to give out, log off immediately and tell an adult.

4. If anyone uses nasty language or mentions things that make you uncomfortable, don't answer and log off immediately.

5. Never agree to meet with someone you met in a chat room or with whom you exchanged messages without asking permission from your parents first.

Lay the basic ground rules for Internet safety before your kids go online. Spend a little preparation time explaining the rules. Sit with older children during their online sessions for a while. Of course, if you're really worried, you can limit your child's access to sites by using a few different methods.

SEE ALSO
➤ *Review how to use your browser's History feature to track viewed Web sites on page 95.*

Screening Web Content

Several programs designed to filter undesirable Web pages from children's eyes are available on the Internet. Table 11.2 provides information about the four most popular Internet screening products. All the programs are designed for non-technical users and are relatively easy to install and set up. Each of the programs screen most types of Internet-related material, such as Web pages, chat sites, and FTP archives. Additionally, all the programs offer free, downloadable demo versions, so you can try them out before you buy.

TABLE 11.2   **Popular Internet-filtering software**

	Cyber Patrol	Cybersitter 97	Net Nanny	Surfwatch
Company, Contact Information	Microsystems Software 800-828-2608	Solid Oak Software 800-388-2761	Net Nanny Software 800-340-7177	Spyglass 888-667-9452
URL	www.cyberpatrol .com	www.solid oak.com	www.netnanny .com	www.surfwatch .com
Purchase Price	Approx. $30, including 3 months of updates	Approx. $40	Approx. $40	Approx. $50, including 1 month of updates
Monthly Update Fee	$30 per year	Free unlimited updates	Free, updated twice each month	$30 per year
Number of User Profiles	As many as 10 profiles	One profile; however, users pick "mature" or "adult" level	As many as 12 profiles	One profile
How it Works	Software works from two lists— CyberYES (40,000 plus sites good for kids) and more than 15,000 CyberNOT sites. Both are updated and maintained by staff, committees, teachers, and parents.	Blocks sites from database and uses context-sensitive filtering of phrases. Cybersitter staff members patrol the Web for sites to ban.	Uses database of GoodRats and BadRats. Also screens text for words added to a customizable list.	Staffers find and block sites with objectionable material containing sexually explicit material, violence, and hate, gambling, or information regarding drugs and alcohol. Users are encouraged to submit URLs of sites to be blocked.

Using RSACi Ratings with Internet Explorer

RSAC, short for the Recreational Software Advisory Council, is an independent, non-profit organization based in Washington, D.C., that helps parents and educators make informed decisions about Internet sites and software games. The section of RSAC that deals with rating Internet sites is called RSACi (for Internet). Their mission is twofold: to empower parents and educators to make appropriate choices as to what their children see and experience on the Web, while still protecting the rights of free speech of Internet participants. The RSACi home page and related pages such as the About RSACi page, shown in Figure 11.5, are great places to visit for information about the service.

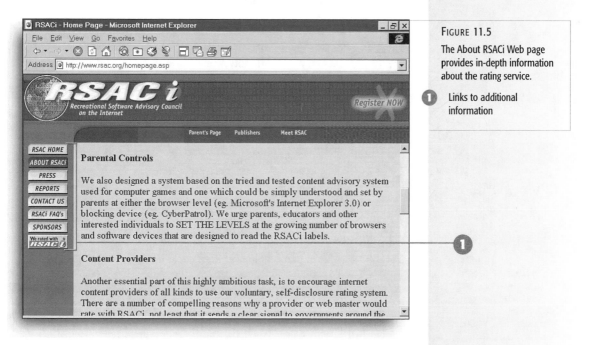

FIGURE 11.5

The About RSACi Web page provides in-depth information about the rating service.

1 Links to additional information

The system provides consumers with information about the level of sex, nudity, violence, and offensive language (vulgar or hate-motivated) that might be found at a Web site. Using a ratings system designed by the Platform for Internet Content Selection, or *PICS*, RSACi encourages Web designers to take a self-administered test to rate their sites, based on the information

Internet Explorer only

Currently, only the Internet Explorer browser makes direct use of RSAC ratings. The Internet Explorer Content Advisor manages the levels and other options provided by an adult.

found in Table 11.3. After a score is determined, a rating is assigned to the site and added to the list.

Parents or educators set the acceptable levels allowed for viewing in Internet Explorer by configuring a feature called the *Content Advisor*. Also customizable are the options to allow access to unrated sites and to enable a supervisor to enter a password to access blocked sites. The RSACi service can be enabled or disabled at any time by the parent or teacher who set the supervisory password.

TABLE 11.3   The RSACi rating system

	Violence Rating Description	Nudity Rating Description	Sex Rating Description	Language Rating Description
Level 4	Rape or wanton, gratuitous violence	Frontal nudity (qualifying as provocative display)	Explicit sexual acts or sex crimes	Crude, vulgar language or extreme hate speech
Level 3	Aggressive violence or death to humans	Frontal nudity	Non-explicit sexual acts	Strong language or hate speech
Level 2	Destruction of realistic objects	Partial nudity	Clothed sexual touching	Moderate expletives or profanity
Level 1	Injury to human being	Revealing attire	Passionate kissing	Mild expletives
Level 0	None of the above or sports related	None of the above	None of the above or innocent kissing; romance	None of the above

* Table used with permission of RSACi

In the following step-by-step exercise, you set up the Internet Explorer Content Advisor. At this time, Netscape Navigator does not offer a similar feature.

Configuring the Internet Explorer Content Advisor

1. From within the Internet Explorer browser, click the **V**iew menu and choose Internet **O**ptions. The Internet Options dialog box appears.

2. Click the **Content** tab located near the top of the dialog box. The **Content** tab is divided into three sections, **Content Advisor**, **Certificates**, and **Personal Information**.

3. Click the **E**nable button in the **Content Advisor** section. The dialog box appears.

4. Click in the **P**assword text box and type a password. Tab to the **C**onfirm Password text box and retype the password. Click **OK** to continue (see Figure 11.6).

FIGURE 11.6

A password is required to prevent children from turning off or changing the Content Advisor.

1 Password appears as asterisks

5. The Content Advisor dialog box appears with the **Ratings** tab selected, as shown in Figure 11.7. In the **C**ategory section, click the first key item, **Language**, and drag the **R**ating slider to the level you find acceptable. As you drag, the text in the **D**escription section changes to match the selected level.

6. Repeat step 5 for the other categories shown on the list.

7. When you've set rating levels for **Language**, **Nudity**, **Sex**, and **Violence**, click the **General** tab. In the **User Options** section, check the box next to **U**sers can see sites that have no ratings or **S**upervisor can type a password to allow users to view restricted content. You can check both boxes if you want.

   If you want to change the password you typed earlier, click the **C**hange Password button and follow the prompts shown on the resulting dialog box.

Save the password

It's a good idea to jot down both the password and the words "Content Advisor" on a sheet of paper and place it in a safe place. When you have a number of passwords, it's sometimes hard to remember which password matches which service.

FIGURE 11.7

Set rating levels to limit offensive content on the Internet.

1 Click a key to select the category

2 Drag the **Ratings** slider to set the level

3 The description explains the rating level

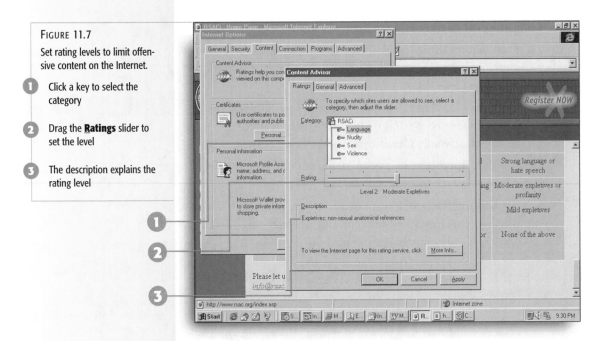

Think before you act

Because only a percentage of Web pages are RSACi-rated, you'll severely limit what sites can be accessed if you leave the box next to the **users can view unrated sites** option unchecked.

8. (Optional) If you've subscribed to a Web-content rating system, such as Cyber Patrol, click the **Advanced** tab and then click the **Rating Systems** button to choose the file provided by the system. (The rating system generally provides detailed instructions on how to proceed.)

9. Click **OK** to close the Content Advisor dialog box. An information box appears, letting you know that the Content Advisor has been installed.

10. Click **OK** to close the information box. When the Internet Options dialog box re-appears, click OK to close it and return to the Web page you were viewing previously.

When your child attempts to go to a rated site that contains material that matches the rating level you selected, a warning appears, advising that the site cannot be accessed. A box similar to the one shown in Figure 11.8 appears if you've opted not to let unrated pages appear.

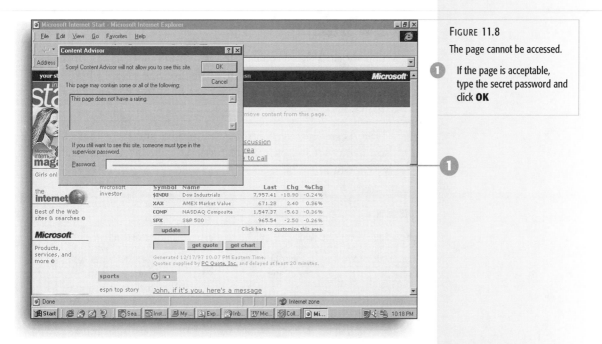

FIGURE 11.8

The page cannot be accessed.

1 If the page is acceptable, type the secret password and click **OK**

Experiment with the levels and categories in the Content Advisor until you find the combination that works best for your child. Keep in mind that if a site does not contain a RSACi rating, you won't be able to block it. However, if you choose to block all unrated sites, you'll severely limit the sites that appear on your computer.

You can change the levels you selected or disable the Content Advisor completely at any time. Click the **View** menu from within Internet Explorer and then choose **Internet Options**. Click the **Content** tab and then click the **Settings** button under the **Content Advisor** section. Make any changes to the categories or levels and click **OK**. Or, click **Disable** to remove the Content Advisor. Click **OK** to close the Internet Options dialog box.

Lasting changes

If you change a level within the Content Advisor or disable it completely, the changes will be in effect the next time you access the Internet. You need to select new changes to overwrite the ones you affected.

Have a Blast

The World Wide Web can be your child's playground. Special sites designed just for kids offer safe, exciting places where kids can take a break. Kids of all ages can find sites designed just for them.

Table 11.4 shows some great sites for kids and teens that offer some unusual and exciting features. Use the listed sites as a gateway for fun.

TABLE 11.4   Unusual sites for kids

Kid's Site	URL	Description
Berit's Best Sites for Kids	`db.cochran.com/li_toc:theoPage.db`	This site features links to rated sites with excellent descriptions. Many of the links point to unusual links that you won't see anywhere else.
Yuckiest Site on the Internet	`www.nj.com/yucky/index.html`	Although this site is actually designed as a resource for science facts, kids forget the site is educational! Meet people who eat cockroaches or who grow worms for fun.
Crayola	`www.crayola.com`	Visit a virtual museum or color an interactive card. The site changes often to match the season, so check back often.
Just for Kids	`scholastic.com/kids/index.htm`	Kids can visit the Magic School Bus, a Goosebumps page, or join the Baby Sitters Club at this site designed by *Scholastic Magazine*.

Kid's Site	URL	Description
Sports Illustrated for Kids	`pathfinder.com/SIFK`	Similar to the magazine of the same name, this site features sports with a kids' slant.
Solaria	`www.solariagames.com/`	Designed for older children or teens, this site features interactive games. Additionally, you'll find a Contests and a Chat area.
Teens (sites.com)	`www.sites.com/teens/`	Links to a variety of sites just for teens, including sites that contain movie reviews, advice on dating, and even a page for new teen drivers.

Game Sites for Kids

The World Wide Web can be your child's playground. Special game sites designed just for kids offer safe, exciting places where kids can take a break. The Happy Puppy Web site at `happypuppy.com`, shown in Figure 11.9, contains links to hundreds of sites from which you can download games and links to games that can be played online.

Internet games for kids (and adults) come in many varieties. The following list shows two of the most common types of games you'll encounter on the Web.

- *Single Player Games.* Designed to be downloaded to your computer or played online. The Official Lego Site at `www.lego.com` contains virtual Legos with which your kids can build. (Best of all, you'll never need to pick up the pieces!)

Just for girls

Visit Amber's Place at `www.davelash.com/amber/girlpage.html` for a special place on the Web for girls under age 12. The links lead to several non-commercial sites designed just for girls.

Every game is different

Pay careful attention to the instructions and hardware requirements on each game site. Some can be played directly from your browser, but others require you to download and install the game to your computer. Some games need extra hardware, such as a joystick or an accelerated graphics card. In a few cases, you'll need to register or pay a small fee. Make sure you know what you need before you try to play.

FIGURE 11.9

The fun begins on the Happy Puppy's Front Porch.

1 Link to hundreds of game-related sites

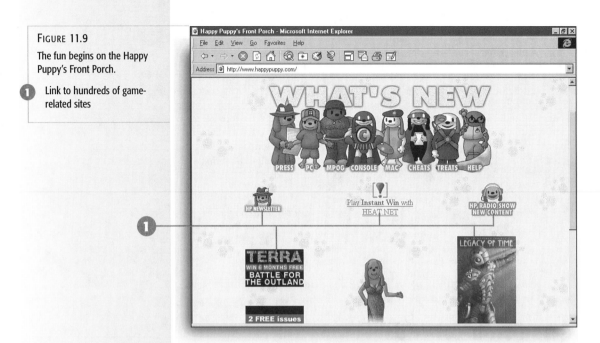

- *Interactive Web Games.* Played together by kids across the Internet. Some interactive games are violent or sexual in nature and not suitable for kids. Susie's Place at `www.primenet.com/~hodges/susplace.html` features some thought-provoking word games that older children will enjoy.

SEE ALSO

➤ *For details on downloading software, review page 146.*

Using the Internet as an Educational Resource

Finding homework help

Visiting the teacher's lounge

Touring Gopherspace

Earning a college degree online

Getting Help with Homework

Set up your query

Remember to set up your search query so that you find the most documents first. For example, if you're child needs information on how clouds affect weather, first use only the search term `clouds`. After you've viewed the resulting hits, narrow your query and search again, using a query such as `clouds+weather`. That way, you'll be sure you're getting the right documents.

If you quake every time your child needs help with homework, you can breathe a little easier now. Instead of rolling up your sleeves and trying to figure out a rough homework problem, turn to the Internet.

When you're looking for some homework assistance, start with your favorite search engine or navigational guide. Most of what you're looking for can be found with a simple search or two. If you want to harness the power of many search engines, use Metacrawler at `www.metacrawler.com`.

If you're more comfortable clicking links, return to Yahooligans!, the navigational guide for kids. You're already familiar with the Yahooligans! navigational guide and its parent site, Yahoo!. The Yahooligans! database holds thousands of documents, so it's unlikely you'll find exactly what you're looking for. Use the index to find a related site, and then keep working your way down through the links. Or, enter a query in the **Search** text box and click the **Search** button.

If you're looking for a very specific answer, visit Homework Help at `www.startribune.com/stonline/html/special/homework/`. The site is staffed by volunteer teachers and functions like a newsgroup. You post your question to a discussion group, and the answer is posted to the same group. Before you post your question, look through the questions that have already been answered. (It's quite possible another student had the same question first!) If you can't find the answer you're looking for, add your question to the discussion group. Make sure your question is clear and concise. In approximately one day, an answer to your question will appear in the discussion folder you selected.

Another great place for general homework help is a Web site called StudyWEB. Like Yahooligans!, the StudyWEB site contains categories. However, each category is sorted according to its approximate appropriate grade level, making the categories valuable tools for teachers looking for lesson plan and curriculum ideas. The information for each topic also advises about downloadable or printable images that might be used for visual aids in school reports or projects. The variety and depth of topics make StudyWEB a great ally in tackling homework problems.

A study session with StudyWEB

1. Connect to the Internet and open your browser.

2. Type www.studyweb.com/ in the **Address** box of your browser and press Enter. In a moment, the StudyWEB home page appears. Scroll down the page to familiarize yourself with StudyWEB's page, including the **Table of Contents**, **Search** box, and **Links**.

3. Click the link to a topic in which you're interested. We've chosen **Animals and Pets** in our example.

4. Scroll down the resulting page and click the link that further defines the topic you want (in our example, we chose **Pets— Companion Animals**, which opens a new page containing links to pages about many animals).

5. Click a link that interests you. If you click the link to **Cats**, the resulting page, shown in Figure 12.1, provides both links and detailed information about the information contained within the links.

6. Click a link on the page to a site about cats. View the site, clicking any other links that seem interesting.

7. When you're finished viewing the link to a site about cats, click the **StudyWEB** link in the top left corner of the page to return to the StudyWEB home page.

8. (Optional) If you think you might want to return to StudyWEB in the future, add it to your list of personal sites, following the instructions shown here:

FIGURE 12.1

StudyWEB links let you know what you'll find at each listed site.

1 StudyWEB link

2 This link has pictures that can be downloaded

3 Description of the link

4 Click here to view the linked site

5 The grade level for which the link is intended

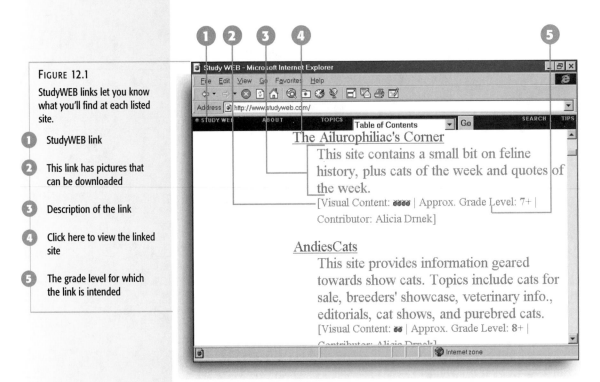

- If you're using Internet Explorer, click the **Favorites** menu and then choose **Add to Favorites**. When the Add to Favorites dialog box appears, check the box next to **No, just add the page to my favorites**, in response to the question as to whether you want to subscribe to the page and be notified whenever the page changes.

- Netscape Navigator users can set a bookmark with a quick keyboard shortcut by pressing Ctrl+D. Or, use the mouse by clicking the **Communicator** menu and selecting **Bookmarks**. When the **Bookmarks** menu appears, choose **Add Bookmark**.

SEE ALSO

➤ *To learn more about queries, read "Form Effective Queries" on page 136.*

➤ *For more about Yahooligans!, check out the section "Yahooligans!" on page 248.*

➤ *For detailed information about returning to your favorite sites, see page 101.*

Drop In to the Teacher's Lounge

Teachers, take heart! Pop into the Internet whenever your students push you to the limit. You can find lesson plans, classroom-ready materials, ideas for field trips and special projects, and even funny anecdotes shared by other teachers.

The CEARCH Virtual Classroom at `sunsite.unc.edu/cisco/schoolhouse.html` (shown in Figure 12.2) provides a comprehensive guide for teachers of all grades. (Students can go too.) The site offers a free service to educators, parents, and administrators (anyone involved in kindergarten through twelfth grade education) and includes everything from listings of schools with Web sites to lesson plans and a step-by-step guide to getting a school online. The site contains no advertising. CEARCH is one of the most popular resources for educators on the Web; approximately 150,000 people visit each month.

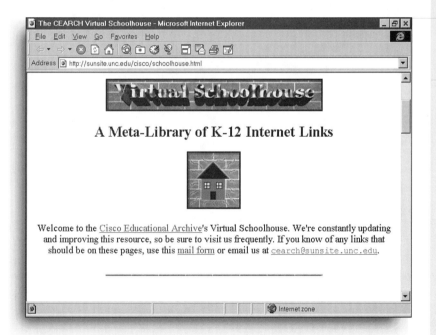

FIGURE 12.2
The Virtual Schoolhouse can be a teacher's best friend.

Call On Teacher Resources

Table 12.1 lists great Web sites for teachers. Use the following sites as an aid to getting great classroom materials and ideas, or simply as a way to take a break from the rigors of the day. One word of warning—because many of the sites shown contain links to other great sites, you'll probably spend longer than you intended!

TABLE 12.1   **Starting point for teachers**

Site Name	URL	Description
National Education Association	`www.nea.org`	Sponsored by America's oldest organization committed to public education, this site features articles on timely topics, such as how schools are faring with budget cuts and tips and tools for better schools.
ENC Online	`www.enc.org`	The Eisenhower National Clearing House (sponsored by the U.S. Department of Education) holds class materials, grant opportunities, and loads of curriculum resources.
K-12 Sources	`execpc.com/~dboals/` `k-12.html`	More than 500 links for teachers are offered here. Contains links to lesson plans, a wide variety of training materials, and health and safety issues.
Classroom Compass	`www.sedl.org/scimath/` `compass/cchp.html`	This site contains a collection of ideas, activities, and resources for

Site Name	URL	Description
		teachers interested in improving their instruction of science and mathematics. Interactive science or mathematics classrooms provide activities that illustrate abstract concepts.
AskERIC	http://ericir.syr.edu/	This site is a pilot project of the Educational Resources Information Center and the Department of Education. Its main purpose is as an Internet-based request service for teachers. Answers to questions about any topic in K-12 education are returned within 48 hours.
TeleEducation New Brunswick	teleeducation.nb.ca /lotw/	This Canadian site contains a structured tutorial to help teachers create an online learning resource. A French version of the site also exists.

Setting Up a Virtual Reference Desk

If you've ever written a term paper or thesis, you know how difficult it is to get everything right. When you've got everything together, the facts, direct quotations, and the correct wordings blend to elevate your work from average to excellent.

Reference sites abound on the Web. Although reference sites might not be the most exciting sites to visit, they do provide you with the tools you need to do a great job. Dictionaries, thesauruses, encyclopedias, and even Bartlett's quotations exist online.

Yahoo! has links to an entire section of some of the best reference sources on the Web. If you're not sure exactly what you're looking for, take advantage of all the legwork done by the researchers and indexers at Yahoo! to provide you with a variety of sites. Just go to the Yahoo! Web site at www.yahoo.com and click the **Reference** link (see Figure 12.3).

FIGURE 12.3

Yahoo! has a section of links devoted to online reference.

1 Category links

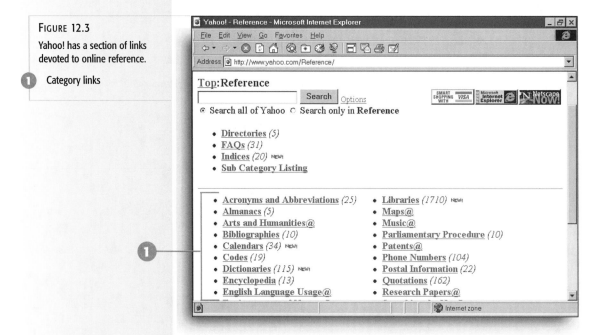

Click one of the category links to move down through the index. Or, if you know what you're looking for, type your search query in the text box and click **Search**.

A Reference Sampler

If you're the impatient type who can't stand to click links, or you just want to find some great reference sites fast, visit some of the sites listed here:

- One Look Dictionary at www.onelook.com contains an index of more than 208 dictionaries with more than 1 million words. Additionally, you can match words under different categories, including spelling and pronunciation.

- Roget's Internet Thesaurus at www.thesaurus.com enables you to find words that might be more suitable than the word you've chosen. As shown in Figure 12.4, type a word or phrase in the **Find** text box and click the **NOW** button. In a few moments, a list of entries that match your text appears as links. Click an entry link for a detailed look at its definition and usage.

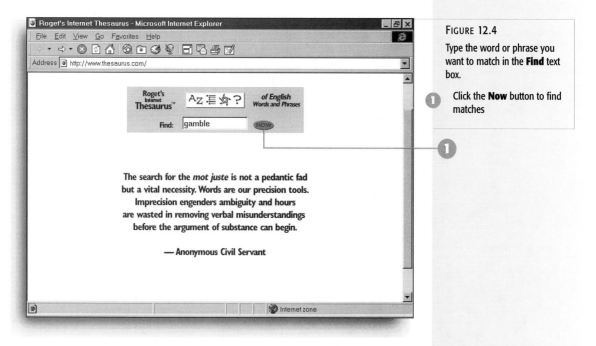

FIGURE 12.4

Type the word or phrase you want to match in the **Find** text box.

① Click the **Now** button to find matches

- Brittanica Online at www.eb.com is the online version of the legendary Encyclopedia Brittanica. For a fee that costs a lot less than buying the hardback edition, you can subscribe to this great service and get up-to-date articles and photos. If you want to try before you buy, a free trial subscription is offered.

- Bartlett's Quotations at www.cc.columbia.edu/acis/bartleby/bartlett/index.html is maintained by Columbia University. Click a link to one of the authors listed on the page or type the phrase for which you're looking in the text box and click **Search**. Either way, you'll find thousands of famous quotes.

Using Gopher

Why is it called Gopher?

Many people think that the term "Gopher" actually means "go for," which is what happens when you click a Gopher menu. Others claim that the name was used because the Gopher system was developed at the University of Minnesota, home of the Golden Gophers. Actually, the name evolved for both reasons.

Long before the World Wide Web, a system called *Gopher* connected universities, colleges, and government facilities all over the world. Even now, many online documents and books exist on Gopher servers across the Internet. The Gopher system is easy to use; because it's based on sets of related menus, you can make a series of menu choices until you find the information you want. Each time you make a menu selection, a *Gopher Server* is contacted to fulfill your request.

All the interconnected Gopher servers are collectively referred to as *Gopherspace*. Actually, using Gopher is a lot like using Yahoo!. (Of course, the major difference between Gopher and Yahoo! is that they look through different facets of the Internet.)

It's easy to use Gopher in both the Internet Explorer and Netscape Navigator browsers. Gopher sites are accessed by URLs that begin with gopher:// (see Figure 12.5) instead of the http:// that you're used to. The Gopher system generally contains documents that are text-based, although you might find sound or graphics files.

The Gopher still matters

Even though the Web has outdistanced Gopher as a major Web presence, many libraries, universities, and colleges maintain information on Gopher servers.

SEE ALSO

➤ *Review the structure of URLs in the section "The Address Is Everything" on page 90.*

How About Some Classics in Gopherspace?

Although more and more Gopher sites on the Internet are moving up to the Web, Gopherspace is still a great place to do scholastic research. Many libraries and colleges maintain Gopher sites. If you need to find the text of a classic novel or short story, you can probably find it at a Gopher site.

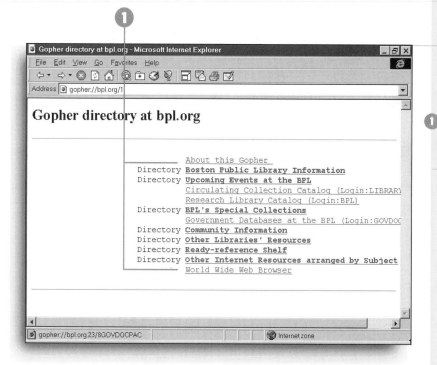

FIGURE 12.5

The URL in the **Address** box references the Gopher site of the Boston Public Library.

❶ Links to other related Gopher sites are arranged by directories

In the following step-by-step exercise, you visit a Gopher site called Alex and view online text versions of literature favorites.

Reading an online classic

1. Type `gopher://rsl.ox.ac.uk:70/11/lib-corn/hunter` in your browser's **Address** box and press Enter. Your browser processes the request and, accordingly, looks through Gopherspace. In a moment, the Gopher root at Alex appears.

2. Click the link to **Browse Alex**. A new page of links to several directories appears.

3. Click the link to **Browse by Author**. A list of directories containing alphabetical links appears.

4. Click the link to the directory named with the first letter of your favorite classical author's last name. A list of classic literature, arranged alphabetically by author, appears.

Looking at a directory

If you've used Windows Explorer or My Computer to look at the arrangement of files and folders on your computer, the Gopher root should look familiar. The "root," or top of the list, is like a tree trunk from which all other subdirectories branch. Click a link to a subdirectory to see both its associated files and subdirectories.

5. Scroll down the list and click a link to the text of your favorite literature. Because some of the files are quite large, it might take a while for the text to appear on your screen, as shown in Figure 12.6.

FIGURE 12.6

The text of *A Letter Concerning Toleration* by John Locke is contained here.

1 Small scroll box indicates the text spans several pages

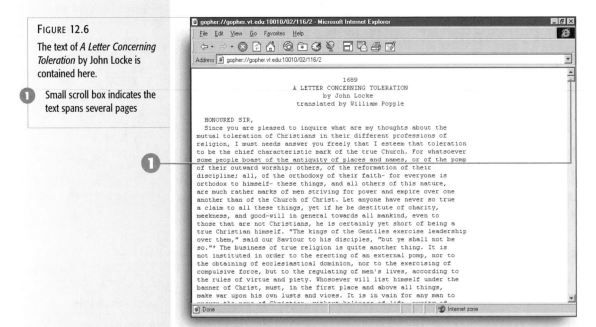

Just how long is it?

Use the size of the vertical scroll box (called a thumb) to gauge the length of any page displayed within your browser. The larger the thumb, the shorter the page. A tiny scroll box indicates that you're only viewing a small portion of the page; the actual size is quite lengthy.

6. (Optional) If your computer is attached to a printer, either directly or through a network connection, click the **Print** button on your browser toolbar. Be prepared for many sheets to print.

7. When you're finished looking at the text on the screen, click the **Back** button on your browser's toolbar to move back to the list of classics.

8. Click another classic on the list. If you're finished looking at classic literature for now, click the **Home** button on your browser toolbar to return to your Start page on the World Wide Web.

Getting Ready for College

College is a big step in the lives of many people. The Internet is waiting to assist college students of all ages and backgrounds. How? For one thing, you can do some serious test preparation for those infamous college entry exams. Or, you can get college credit for learning about the computer. If you're an older student holding down a job, you can attend an online college.

Online Counselors Help You Get Prepared

Say the words "College Boards" to a group of high school students and watch them turn green. The test scores seem to swing more weight than grade point averages or activity records for admittance to most colleges. Use the sites listed in Table 12.2 to get prepared for the tests and maybe even raise your scores a notch or two.

TABLE 12.2   Test prep made easy

Site Name	URL	Description
College Board Online	www.collegeboard.org	Provides test questions, online registration, and a calendar of test dates and locations; also features links to financial aid information and a college search.
The Princeton Review	www.review.com	Offers information on college admissions, courses, and test prep skills.
TESTPREP.COM	www.testprep.com	Designed by Stanford Testing Systems, Inc., this site contains a free SAT preparation course.

continues…

TABLE 12.2 **Continued**		
Site Name	**URL**	**Description**
Syndicate.com	`www.syndicate.com`	Students from middle school and up can visit this site for quizzes that help prepare them for PSAT(R), SAT(R), SSAT, GRE, or LSAT tests.
Kaplan Educational Center	`www.kaplan.com`	A comprehensive site that covers everything from online sample tests to financial aid and counseling.

Learning with Macmillan

Macmillan Computer Publishing, the folks who bring you this book and other exemplary publications about computer hardware and software, also provides an online learning center. From Internet topics to advanced programming, MCP's Online Learning facilities help you enrich your computer knowledge. The Online Learning Center, shown in Figure 12.7, offers two ways to learn:

- *eZone*. Offers courses, with college credit, on such topics as C++, HTML, Java and JavaScript, Office 97, Perl, Photoshop, VBScript, and Visual Basic.

- *Que Education and Training*. Publishes innovative teaching and learning materials for technology education and instruction in academic courses and corporate training.

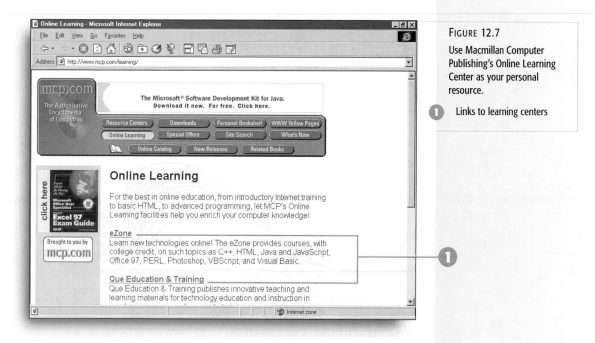

FIGURE 12.7

Use Macmillan Computer
Publishing's Online Learning
Center as your personal
resource.

1 Links to learning centers

Start Out as a Guest

Before you sign up as a member of the eZone, you're free to
look around. The eZone is set up so that you can review the
first chapter of each course. Evaluate the quality of the entire
course and look through the pages of the virtual class textbook.
Additionally, you're welcome to take the quizzes for the first
chapter. (However, your test scores won't be saved in the student
database if you're not registered.) You're free to visit the
Initiation pages to ask support questions and find out late-
breaking news.

The eZone has several zones to visit:

- *Learn Zone.* Shows a list of all the available courses and certificates, as well as how the interactive achievement programs work.

- *Mentor Zone.* Answers your questions.

- *Chill Zone.* Includes tools and resources that relate to your
  course.

- ***Initiate Zone.*** Provides a form to register for eZone classes, get support, or find out what's new.

- ***Catalogue and Pricing.*** Displays a description of the textbook used in the class, as well as the cost of the book and the class. (Most classes cost between $39 and $49, although a few are priced slightly higher.

You register and pay for the course and receive your textbook in the mail. When the book arrives, read through each chapter and, when you're ready, take a quiz on the subject material in the chapter. Your quiz results are stored in the Lesson grid. When you enter the Learn Zone, you can see how many chapters you have started, passed, or failed. As you pass the quizzes for each lesson, the chapter LED turns on and the chapter score, computed by averaging the lesson's quiz scores, is displayed. To receive access to download a Certificate of Completion, you must score a passing grade for each lesson in the course, as well as pass the midterms and final exams.

Visit Macmillan's eZone

1. Type www.mcp.com in the **Address** box of your browser and press Enter. In a moment, the Macmillan Computer Publishing home page appears.

2. Click the link to **Online Learning**. When the Online Learning page appears on the screen, read through the text to find out what's available. When you're done reading, click the **eZone** link.

3. The eZone page, shown in Figure 12.8, is divided into frames. When you click a link in the navigation frame, the content in the instruction frame changes. If you're uncomfortable working with frames, the page also contains a horizontal menu bar. Click the **Learn** icon in the left navigation frame, or click the **Learn** link on the horizontal menu bar.

4. Text boxes for your User ID and password appear in the instruction frame. Because you're visiting as a guest user, scroll down the page and click the word **guest** to continue.

Guest privileges are limited

Some eZone features, such as the ability to ask a question in the Mentor Zone, are available to registered users only. You'll find some links and menu features are dimmed out as you tour the eZone as a guest.

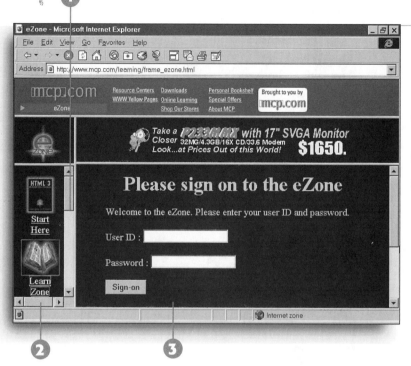

FIGURE 12.8

Use Macmillan Computer Publishing's Online Learning Center as your personal resource.

1 Drag a border to change the size of the frame

2 Navigation frame

3 Instruction frame

5. A page appears that shows the Courses and Certificate programs. Click a course subject you want to review.

6. The Chapter grid for the course you selected appears. Click the link to Chapter 1. (Because you're a guest, you can only view the contents of the first chapter.)

7. To read a lesson, click on the **Read** link for that lesson. To take a quiz, click on the **Quiz** link for that lesson. Normally, you should read through the lesson before taking the quiz. However, if you feel you know the subject material, take a quiz without further reading.

8. (Optional) Click the **Mentor** icon in the navigation frame or the **Mentor** link in the horizontal menu bar to read through the FAQ list about the course.

No grades now

When you take an online course, the grid on this page keeps track of your performance and the completion status for each lesson. At present, because you're a guest, all the LED status lights are grayed out and the scores are all marked N/A, for Not Available.

9. Click the **Initiate** icon in the left navigation frame, or click on the word Initiate in the horizontal menu bar.

Unlike the other areas in the eZone, the **Register**, **Support**, and **What's New** options in the Initiate Zone are universally available to both registered students and guests. To register for a course, click the **Register** icon and fill in the resulting onscreen form. Click the **Support** icon to get help with shipping, media, and billing problems. Click **What's New** to find out about the latest additions and deletions at the eZone, as well as previews of new courses.

SEE ALSO

➤ *To find out how to navigate through frames, review the information in "Dealing with Frames," on page 107.*

Earn a Cyberdegree

One of the latest ways to obtain a college degree is over the Internet. More than one million students now attend *cybercolleges*. Many four-year colleges and universities offer virtual college classrooms, in addition to their regular on-site classes. The number of cyberstudents grows with each school term.

Cybercolleges offer many advantages over their more traditional counterparts. Many cyberstudents hold down full-time jobs; taking online classes usually means that the students don't need to interrupt their careers to pursue higher education. Online education makes it possible for students to transcend their geographic locations. Students from all over the world can participate in degree programs at prestigious schools without leaving home.

The Internet plays a huge role in cybereducation. Assignments are transmitted via email. Students put together study groups that meet in Internet conferences, using software like Microsoft NetMeeting or Netscape Conference. Coursework and other classroom materials can be downloaded from the college's Web page (see Figure 12.9).

College degrees are earned

Don't confuse genuine cybercolleges with phony correspondence schools that offer to "sell" a degree to a student in exchange for money. A cybercollege degree is earned, rather than bought.

FIGURE 12.9
The University of Phoenix Online Campus home page has links to information about its many programs.

Tuition costs at cybercolleges vary. Generally, a premium for online participation is added to the per-credit cost. However, because you won't need to pay dormitory or athletic fees, you'll probably end up spending less on your cyberdegree.

Table 12.3 lists a dozen top cyberuniversities. If you don't see your favorite college on the list, call and ask if they're offering online classes. Many of the programs are new, so not all degrees are available in all disciplines.

TABLE 12.3   Top cyberuniversities

School Name	Physical Location	Phone	URL	Comments
California State University, Dominguez Hills	Carson, CA	(310) 243-2288	www.csudh.edu /dominguez online	B.A., B.S.N, M.B.A., M.A., and M.S. via computer, video-conferencing

continues…

TABLE 12.3   **Continued**

School Name	Physical Location	Phone	URL	Comments
Carnegie Mellon University	Pittsburgh, PA	(800) 850-4742	gsia.cmu.edu	M.B.A. and A.S. via computer, video-conferencing
City University	Bellevue, WA	(800) 426-5596	city.edu	A.S., B.A., M.B.A., M.P.A., and M.E. via computer
Indiana University System	Bloomington, IN	(800) 334-1011	www.indiana.edu.iub	A.G.S., A.S.L.S., B.G.S., and B.S.L.S. via computer, video-conferencing
Michigan State University	East Lansing, MI	(517) 353-1771	www.msu.edu	M.S. via computer, video-conferencing
Old Dominion University	Norfolk, VA	(800) 968-2638	www.odu.edu	B.S., M.S., and M.B.A. via tele-conferencing
University of Alaska Southeast at Sitka	Sitka, AK	(907) 747-6653	www.jun.alaska.edu	A.S., B.S., and M.P.A. via computer, tele-conferencing
University of Maryland University College	College Park, MD	(301) 985-7000	www.umuc.edu	B.A., B.S., and M.A. via computer, tele-conferencing
University of Phoenix University Online Campus	Phoenix, AZ	(800) 742-4742	www.uophx.edu/online	B.A., B.S., M.S., and M.B.A. via computer
Washington State University	Pullman, WA	(800) 222-4978	www.wsu/edu	B.A. via computer

Finding a New Career on the Internet

Designing the résumés you need in today's job market

Posting your résumé to an Internet résumé bank

Looking through job listings on the Web

Networking with newsgroups

Begin with a Résumé

The U.S. Department of Labor projects that you will change professions at least three times in your work life, by your own choice or because modern technology has made your job obsolete.

Switching careers is a thrilling challenge if you make the decision to do something more rewarding. Changing your career, or at least your job, is exciting if you're not happy with your present work situation. It's tougher to find a new position when you've been "downsized" or you're in a shrinking or dying profession.

A good résumé is the first thing you need to find a new job. A standard résumé lists your name, address, experience, and education. You probably have a résumé and think it's effective. If you set your résumé up like most people, it's designed to be folded into an envelope and sent through the mail. When it gets where it's going, there's a good chance that your résumé will never be viewed by the person who's doing the hiring.

Why? Because many companies now rely on electronic résumés, or *e-résumés* for short. An e-résumé is one that can be stored on a computer. Most companies bundle all the e-résumés into one giant database, so they can search for a particular keyword or qualifier. For example, if a company's looking for someone with experience in Environmental Health and Safety, it can extract the names of the qualified candidates from the hundreds of résumés they receive.

Your résumé can become electronic in a few ways:

- You send a paper copy of your résumé, and it's scanned into the computer system with the use of OCR software
- You email your résumé
- You post your résumé to the Internet

Keywords Pave the Way to Success

Part of the challenge of creating a great paper copy résumé is designing an artistic masterpiece. Finding the exact shade and thickness of the paper (with a matching envelope, of course), using the right fonts, and balancing the margins is almost as important as what the résumé says. After all, a paper résumé needs some visual excitement to make it stand out from all the others. Getting noticed is half the battle.

E-résumés, on the other hand, depend on content more than form. Because no one is going to judge the appearance of your e-résumé, you don't need to worry about the color or quality of the paper. Fonts and margins are also irrelevant.

Keywords are the most important part of your e-résumé. These special words describe your special talents, skills, and experience. Keywords are almost always nouns. If you've been taught to use action words, or verbs, on your résumé, you need to adjust your thinking.

Use keywords to describe:

- *Skills.* These might include problem-solving, network administration, or word processing.
- *Education.* Keywords in the Education section of your e-résumé might include the following: Bachelor of Arts, Philosophy, or High School Graduate.
- *Job titles.* Some good examples are Help Desk Specialist, Webmaster, or Sales Representative.

After a keyword search is performed on electronic résumés, the ones that contain the best matches or hits are sorted into job categories. If your résumé comes up with multiple hits, it can be placed in more than one job category. The more categories in which your résumé is placed, the better your chances are for finding the perfect job.

A Résumé for Every Circumstance

Consider maintaining your résumé in four ways. Because the job market is so competitive, why not have the capability of submitting your information in whatever format is required? Set up your résumé in the following formats:

- Traditional
- Scannable
- ASCII
- Web-ready (HTML)

The Traditional Version

Your traditional, hard-copy résumé is the first form you should keep on hand. If you've been looking for a new job for a while, you might have one ready. Your hard-copy résumé needs to list your name and contact information, experience, education, and skills. It's up to you whether you want to include a section discussing your objectives. Check your word processing program for built-in résumé templates if you need some help.

Unless you're applying for a job as an artist or a graphic designer, make sure the résumé looks elegant and businesslike. Fancy fonts, brightly colored text, and graphics images make you seem unprofessional. Limit yourself to one or two fonts, and don't use wildly colored paper or ink. Draw attention to the headings with text attributes, such as boldface and underlines.

If you're using networking strategies to find a new position, distribute your traditional résumé to as many people as you can. If you send it, use a matching envelope and a cover letter.

The Scannable Version

Look at the job listings in the paper or online Classified sections of most large town newspapers and you'll note that the word *scannable* appears. By using the scan method, a company can quickly enter and evaluate hundreds of applicants.

Scanning a résumé is similar to making a copy on a copy machine. After it's received, an operator feeds your résumé into a scanner that copies the image from the paper. Next, special *OCR* (Optical Character Recognition) software is used to turn the résumé image into text data.

To be effective, the scannable version of your résumé needs to be different from your traditional one. The old rules don't apply with this version. When you design your scannable résumé, think keywords, keywords, keywords. A résumé that's set up to be scanned needs to contain as many keywords as possible. Remember to use nouns—the more the better. List your job titles and areas of expertise. Try to look over your résumé and pick out the keywords. For example, if your résumé says something like "Supervised staff of three clerks," consider changing the phrase to "Clerical supervisor."

Because your scannable résumé is going to be fed into an electronic device, send it in a 9" by 12" envelope to avoid creases. Folds can pull the paper off track and make it difficult for the OCR software to read your text. If the paper is too heavy, like extra-thick bond, or too light, like onionskin, the scanner might have problems pulling it through. Use regular weight paper to ensure a good scan.

A clear, crisp font such as Arial or Helvetica will enable the OCR software to read the text. A font in the 10- to 14-point size works best; don't use tiny fonts. Never use a script font or one that's ornate or heavy. Borders or shading don't work on a scannable résumé because the OCR software will (unsuccessfully) try to convert the border characters to words.

The ASCII Version

Many job listings ask you to email your résumé. Email speeds your résumé to its destination in a matter of minutes. To make sure that the receiving computer can read it, send your résumé in *ASCII* text format.

ASCII is computerese for plain text format. Although ASCII documents aren't visually exciting, their great advantage is that any computer can read them. To ensure this compatibility, a document saved in ASCII doesn't contain any special fonts, or attributes like boldface, italics, or underlines. In fact, an ASCII document has no tabs or indents.

Like its scannable cousin, your ASCII résumé should contain noun keywords because it will probably be placed in a searchable

OCR software can't work miracles

Depending on the sophistication of the OCR software used, the accuracy of the resulting scanned document can range from very accurate to imprecise. Because you don't know which OCR program will be used to translate your résumé, make sure it's as crisp and simple as possible.

Creating the ASCII version

You can create an ASCII version of your résumé in most word processing programs, making sure that you haven't used fonts, attributes, or tabs. Save the file as a text file; your word processing program will assign it a .TXT file extension.

database. Make sure you proofread and spell-check your ASCII résumé carefully. Just because it's ASCII doesn't mean that typos won't stick out! Obviously, the color and grade of the paper don't matter because your ASCII résumé is completely electronic.

SEE ALSO

➤ *For more information on sending email, see Chapter 7, "Sending and Receiving Email."*

The Web-ready Version

If you really want to make a splash with your résumé, post it on the World Wide Web! Think of the impact your résumé might have on the computer screen of a prospective employer or recruiter. If you're looking for a computer-related position, your Web résumé proclaims that you're on the cutting edge of technology.

The World Wide Web is a multimedia paradise. In addition to links to relevant sites, you can add graphic images, like your photo, or sound or movie clips to your résumé. Use different background colors or font faces to create a visual feast for your viewers.

What's HTML, anyway?

Web pages are written in a special language called HTML, short for Hypertext Markup Language. HTML documents contain the formatting instructions for properly displaying the text and graphics on a Web page. When you view a Web page in your browser, the underlying HTML code is responsible for the page you see on the screen.

You can create your own Web résumé. Or, if you're unsure about how to set up an HTML document, contract with a *page designer*. Many Web design companies create résumés in HTML, the language in which Web pages are written. If you decide to pay someone, ask to see some of their previous designs and get references. Because the service can get expensive, find out in advance what you'll have to pay. Try to choose a designer who will place your page on the Web and maintain it as part of the service.

When you're ready to publish your résumé, contact your ISP or network administrator for instructions on the best way to proceed. If you're placing your résumé in a Web community such as Geocities (www.geocities.com) or Tripod (www.tripod.com), go to the community on the Web and make sure your page conforms to the community's standards. When your page is published to the Web, open your browser and visit the page. Have your family and associates visit the page, too. When you're sure that your Web résumé is ready for the scrutiny of a prospective employer, distribute your URL.

SEE ALSO
➤ *You'll learn all about HTML documents on page 433.*

Creating a Web Résumé with Netscape Templates

If you're using Netscape Communicator, you can create a Web
résumé in a few minutes, even if you don't know a bit of HTML.
Netscape understands that you want to jump into Web design
right away. Accordingly, their design team has done all the
preparation work for you by setting up page templates for many
types of Web pages. Use the Netscape résumé template as a
springboard for own creative Web résumé.

Using Netscape's résumé template

1. Connect to the Internet and open the Netscape browser.

2. Click **File** and choose **New**. When the submenu appears,
   select **Page from Template**.

3. When the New Page from Template dialog box appears,
   click **Netscape Templates**. A page on the Netscape site
   appears that displays instructions and information about the
   templates at the top and links to the templates as you scroll
   down the page, as shown in Figure 13.1.

4. Scroll down the page until the categories appear, and click
   the **Résumé** link. A sample résumé appears, along with
   instructions on the use of the template at the top of the
   page.

5. Click **File**, **Edit Page** to copy the template to your computer so that you can make changes to it. (When you first open
   the page, you're looking at the original version maintained
   by Netscape.) The page now appears in Netscape
   Composer.

6. If you haven't worked with Composer before, take a
   moment to familiarize yourself with the screen. Pass your
   mouse pointer over the buttons on the Composition and
   Formatting toolbars and read each ToolTip. Notice the title
   bar reads Composer, and that buttons for Navigator and
   Composer are displayed on your Windows taskbar.

Using Composer

Netscape Composer is the program in the Communicator
suite that enables you to create
great-looking Web pages. You'll
continue working with
Composer in Chapter 18,
"Creating Your Own Web Site."

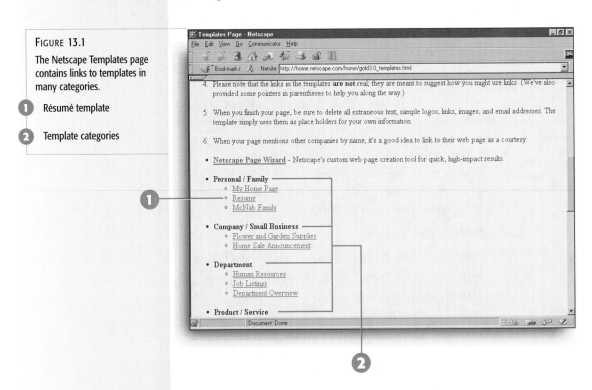

FIGURE 13.1

The Netscape Templates page contains links to templates in many categories.

1 Résumé template

2 Template categories

Adding your photo

If you have a scanner that can handle photos, you can scan your picture and add it to the résumé. Although there are many brands of scanners, the EasyPhoto Scanner by Storm Technologies is an inexpensive way to get started. You'll learn more about adding pictures to HTML documents in Chapter 18, "Creating Your Own Web Site."

7. Select the sample name of "Clea Barnett" and type your name. Your name now appears at the top of the page.

8. Click the sample photo so that it appears framed, and press Delete. The picture is removed from the résumé.

9. Select the word "Writer" and type your own job title or profession. If you want to make the typeface larger or smaller, highlight the text you want to change and click the Down arrow next to the current point size button on the Formatting toolbar and choose another size from the list, as illustrated in Figure 13.2. The list closes and the text appears in the size you selected. Press the Right arrow key to deselect the highlighted text.

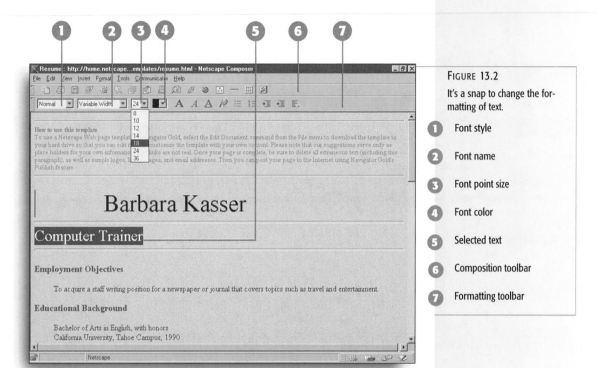

FIGURE 13.2

It's a snap to change the formatting of text.

1. Font style

2. Font name

3. Font point size

4. Font color

5. Selected text

6. Composition toolbar

7. Formatting toolbar

10. Highlight the sample text under the **Employment Objectives** section and type your own objective. Because Composer handles text similarly to your favorite word processing program, you don't need to press Enter at the end of each line. Instead, Composer wraps the text for you.

11. Move through the résumé, highlighting the sample text and replacing it with your own. If you want to add more information, such as additional lines under Educational Background, press Enter and type your information, just as you would on a word processing program.

12. Change the color of text by highlighting it first and then clicking the Down arrow next to the Font color button on the Formatting toolbar. Choose the desired color from the palette. Press the Right arrow key to deselect the text.

13. Change the alignment of text by selecting it first, and then click the Alignment button on the Formatting toolbar, as shown in Figure 13.3. Click the Left, Center, or Right button to move the highlighted text. Deselect the text by pressing the Right arrow key.

F<small>IGURE</small> 13.3

Change the alignment of the selected text.

1 Left alignment

2 Right alignment

3 Center alignment

4 Alignment button

14. Give your résumé some added pizzazz by changing the background color. Click **Format**, **Page Colors and Properties**. When the Page Properties dialog box appears, click the **Colors and Background** tab.

15. Click the **Background** button to open the color palette, as shown in Figure 13.4, and click a new background color. The palette closes and the color you selected appears in the sample. Uncheck the box next to **Use Image**. (The current gray, pebbly background on the résumé page is actually a graphic image, which overrides the color selection.) Click **OK** to close the Page Properties dialog box and return to the résumé in Composer.

16. Click the **Tools** menu and choose **Check Spelling**. Even if you can't see any apparent spelling mistakes, double-check for them now. If Composer encounters an unfamiliar word, such as your name or a real typing error, your options include replacing the selected word, ignoring it, or adding it to the Composer dictionary. When the spell checking is completed, read the résumé for grammar mistakes.

17. Press Ctrl+Home to move to the top of the page. Highlight the instructions about how to use the template and press Delete to remove them from the page.

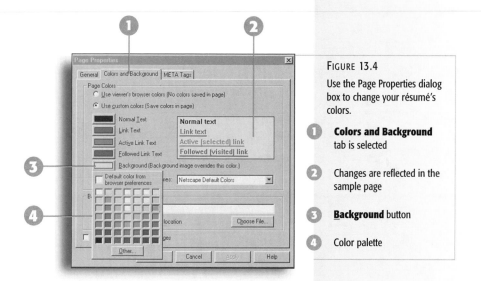

FIGURE 13.4
Use the Page Properties dialog
box to change your résumé's
colors.

1 **Colors and Background**
tab is selected

2 Changes are reflected in the
sample page

3 **Background** button

4 Color palette

18. Save the résumé by clicking **File**, **Save As**. When the Save
As dialog box appears, type a name for your résumé in the
File name: text box. Use one or two words strung together
with no spaces or punctuation. Also, make sure you add the
file extension .html to the name. If you want to change the
location of the file from the folder that's displayed, navigate
to the new folder or drive. Click **Save**. The Save As dialog
box closes and the filename you typed appears in the
Composer title bar.

19. Close Composer by clicking the Close button (the **X**) on the
Composer toolbar to return to Navigator.

20. (Optional) If you want to make additional changes later,
click the Windows **Start** button and select **Programs**,
Netscape Communicator and then select **Netscape
Composer**. When Composer opens, click **File**, **Open Page**
to open the Open File dialog box. Type the drive letter,
folder location, and filename (for example, `C:\My Documents\`
`MyRésumé.html`) in the location text box. Or, click **Choose
File** and navigate to the correct folder location. Either way,
when the correct filename appears in the box, click the
Open button.

Get Résumé Help Online

The Web has a number of sites that provide help with
e-résumés. Table 13.1 lists the Web addresses and information
about some of these sites.

TABLE 13.1   E-résumé sites on the Web

Web Address	Page Title	Comments
www.erésumés.com	Rebecca Smith's eRésumés and Resources	An online guide to preparing effective electronic résumés for a variety of online situations
www.umn.edu/ohr/ ecep/résumé/	Resumania On-Line	A site put together by the University of Minnesota to help you design an effective résumé by using tutorial-type exercises
www.provenrésumés .com	Proven Résumé Career Center	Site offers 23 free online résumé and job search workshops
www.resumix.com/ résumé/résumé_tips .html	Preparing Your Résumé	Comprehensive guide to putting together an electronic résumé

Posting Your Résumé to a Résumé Bank

If you're serious about using the Internet as a resource in finding
a job, post your e-résumé to several of the résumé banks that are
out on the Web. A *résumé bank* holds thousands of individual
résumés that can be looked at any time.

Posting your résumé to a Web résumé bank offers some definite
advantages. First of all, all prospective employers have access to
your résumé. In addition, because most résumé banks are free or
charge only a small fee, you won't need to make a substantial
investment to get worldwide exposure. If you decide to post your
résumé to a Web bank, consider letting your present employer
know you're looking for a new job. Think what might happen if
your boss comes across your résumé in a résumé bank, and plan

accordingly. After all, you don't want to do something that will cause you embarrassment, not to mention possible repercussions.

Do some research to determine which résumé banks meet your needs. Search for the term "résumé bank" on some of the major search engines and services, such as Infoseek, HotBot, and Yahoo!. Although there are many large résumé banks, you might have better results if you post your résumé on a bank that offers specialized jobs, such as positions in the Automotive field. To find a résumé bank that limits résumés to a particular field, narrow your search criteria. For example, the query résumé +"automotive job" finds links to Web sites that specialize in automotive positions.

URL	Résumé Bank Name	Fee for Posting	Résumé Format	Comments
www.careerexpo.com	Career Expo	Free	Complete highly structured online form with preset menu of choices	Site offers both public and private databases. Public contains all your information; private forwards interested employers to you.
www.careermosaic.com	Career Mosaic	Free	Complete online form or cut and paste ASCII text	Claims that the site is searched 40,000 times per day.
www.espan.com	E.span	Free	Fill in online résumé	Automated emailing of jobs that match candidate qualifications and profiles.
www.occ.com	Online Career Center	Free	HTML, email, or snail mail	Non-profit consortium of sponsoring employers. Only these sponsors have access to the résumé listings.
www.jobcenter.com	JobCenter Employment Service	Approx. $20	HTML or online form	Posts submitted résumés to Usenet jobs newsgroups. Matching jobs are emailed to you.
www.skillsearch.com	Skill Search	Approx. $139 first year	HTML or online form	Professional membership organization for individuals with varied experience in the workplace. Online application is used to request enrollment package that is sent by mail.

FIGURE 13.5

Major résumé banks on the Web.

SEE ALSO

➤ *Review how to search for information on the Web on page 122.*
➤ *Review more information on choosing the best wording for queries on page 136.*

Submitting Your Résumé

Submitting your résumé to a résumé bank is simple. Even if you're sure of the finished product, recheck your handiwork before anyone else sees it. (My good friend Kathy used the phrase "detial-oriented" on her e-résumé and was mortified when she received an email message from a national recruiter, advising her of the misspelled word.) Each résumé bank has different submission requirements; read them over carefully before you begin.

In addition to submission requirements, most résumé banks post detailed instructions about how to submit your résumé. (See Figure 13.6 for an example.) Because résumé banks really want your résumé, most of the time the instructions are clear and easy to follow. Take a few minutes and make sure you understand what you need to do.

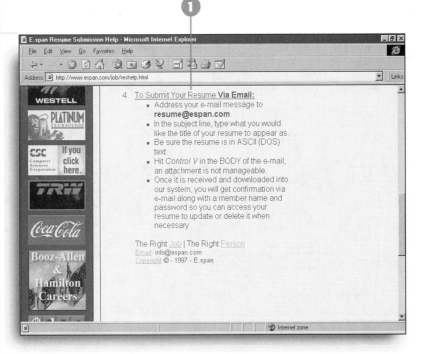

FIGURE 13.6

E.span offers clear, concise instructions on how to post your résumé to its site.

1 The Instruction frame tells you how to proceed

Some résumé banks ask you to email your résumé. If you're familiar with sending email, you might be tempted to attach the computer file containing your résumé to the email message. Don't! Instead of sending a file attachment, paste your résumé into the body of the email message.

If you're unsure how to manage cutting and pasting your résumé, let a little bit of Windows magic help you accomplish the task in short order. Make sure that the email message in which you'll send your résumé is open before you start the steps.

Copying your ASCII résumé into an email message

1. Open the file that contains your résumé and, if necessary, re-save it in ASCII format. Remember not to use fonts, attributes, or tabs.

2. Highlight all the text and click **Edit**, **Copy** or press Ctrl+C.)

3. Hold down the Alt key and press Tab. A box appears, showing the name of an open application on your computer. Without releasing the Alt key, cycle through the open applications on your computer by repeatedly pressing Tab. When you see the email message displayed in the box, release both the Alt and Tab keys. The email message is now displayed on your screen.

4. Position the insertion point at the top of the message body area and press Ctrl+V. Like magic, your résumé is pasted into the email message.

5. Look over the message to make sure that your résumé appears correctly. (If not, delete the text that you pasted by highlighting it and pressing Delete. Next, switch back to the open résumé file and repeat steps 2, 3, and 4.) Click the **Send** button when you're ready to post your résumé.

Fill-in forms are another way many résumé banks request your information. Because a fill-in-the-blank résumé format uses pre-defined fields, each résumé in the bank conforms to a common standard. Résumés submitted via a form are easy for an employer to look through and search.

Figure 13.7 demonstrates a fill-in online résumé form. Type the information in each field, pressing Tab to move from one field to another. If you want, you can copy and paste text from your ASCII résumé into the online form, or you can retype it in the appropriate boxes.

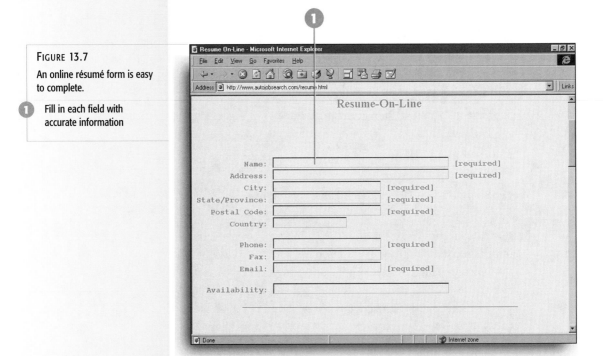

FIGURE 13.7

An online résumé form is easy to complete.

1. Fill in each field with accurate information

When all the fields are completed, take a second to review the information you filled in and make any necessary corrections. After all, employers can view your online résumé worldwide, so you need to make sure the information has been entered correctly. Click the **Submit** or **Send** button to transmit the information to the résumé bank.

Some résumé banks accept your résumé in HTML format. If you've created an HTML version of your résumé or had one designed by a professional Web designer, follow the résumé bank's instructions on the proper way to submit the HTML file. You may be asked to send it as an email attachment or on a disk, via snail mail.

SEE ALSO

➤ *For details on sending email, see Chapter 7, "Sending and Receiving Email."*

Searching for a Job Online

Online job listings exist in many places on the Web. Many local newspapers now post their Classified sections on the Web. Some newspapers even combine their Classified ads with other nearby towns, or offer links to other Help Wanted sections. If you don't know if your local newspaper has an online presence, call and ask.

Résumé banks are another great source for finding job listings. The same résumé banks to which you posted your résumé often offer job listings. Some job banks, such as E.span, perform the search for you and email you the listings that match your qualifications.

Looking at Online Listings

Many Web employment resource sites offer great job listings. In addition to job listings, you might find online job fairs and links to employer home pages. The listings are updated frequently, so don't be discouraged if you don't find the perfect job the first time you search. Successful job hunting is a matter of being in the right place at the right time, so plan to check back several times a week.

To find the right job listings, you need to enter keywords that match your qualifications and the type of job you hope to find (see Figure 13.8). Choose your keywords carefully. As a general rule, use specific words to describe the job for which you're looking. The database holds hundreds of job listings, and the more exacting your search, the more accurate your results.

Generally, the search results appear in a list, similar to the result list from a search engine or search service (see Figure 13.9). If one of the listings interests you, click the link to find out more about the position.

FIGURE 13.8

Keywords make the search go faster.

1 Enter job-specific keywords

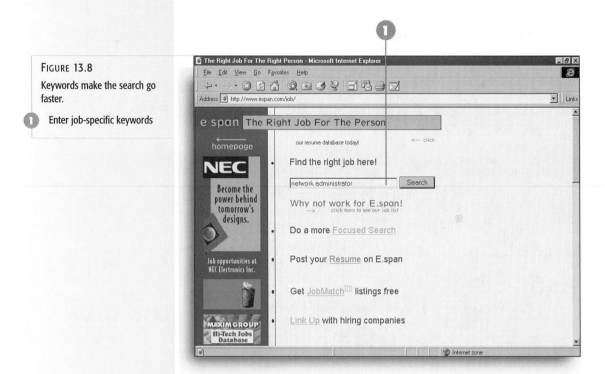

FIGURE 13.9

These positions matched the keywords.

1 Click a link to see information about the position

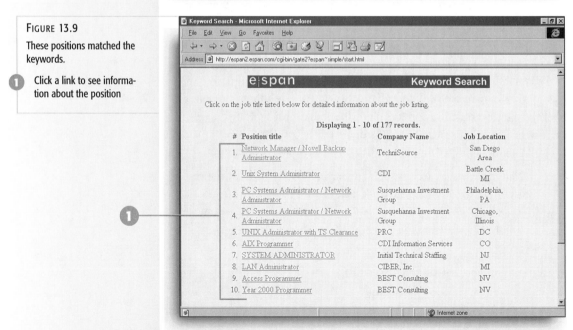

Read the job description and information. If the job looks good, follow the instructions shown to submit your e-résumé. If your first search doesn't produce the job listings for which you hoped, use additional keywords and search again.

Table 13.2 lists Web sites that you can visit to see job listings. Use the sites shown here in addition to the résumé banks listed in Table 13.2 to find your dream job.

TABLE 13.2   Popular Web job banks

URL	Job Bank Name	Comments
www.monster.com	Monster Board	Site offers listings for more than 50,000 jobs worldwide
www.jobweb.com	Job Web	Offers regional listings in the U.S. and Canada
www.americas employers.com	America's Employers	Listings contain more than 50,000 positions and 40,000 company profiles
www.intellimatch.com	Intellimatch	In addition to résumé posting and job listings, site features automated Job Agent to match job seekers with employers
www.careerpath.com	Career Path	Contains links to want ads listed in major U.S. newspapers; also offers résumé posting
careers.wsj.com	Wall Street Journal Interactive	Offers job listings, career news, and articles as well as additional job resources

Network with Newsgroups

Looking for a job can be a lonely proposition. It's hard to sit and wait for the phone to ring, or for an email to land in your Inbox. Newsgroups are great ways to meet and greet both employers and other job seekers on the Internet.

As you learned in Chapter 10, "Joining a Newsgroup," newsgroups are Internet discussion forums. Think of a newsgroup as a virtual bulletin board. Instead of sending a letter to individual

---

Start with a broad search

Make sure you're looking at all the jobs that match your interests and qualifications. Enter general keywords first, such as `network administrator`. After you view the results, narrow the field by adding a word or phrase to your keyword search, such as `Novell` or `Microsoft`.

Work for the Feds

Want to work for the U.S. Government? If you're considering becoming a civil servant, visit the site `www.usajobs.opm.gov/index.htm`. The site shows available Federal positions and enables you to apply online. *The U.S. Government's official site for jobs and employment information is provided by the United States Office of Personnel Management.*

members, messages are posted to the group, as shown in Figure 13.10. In turn, responses are posted to the group.

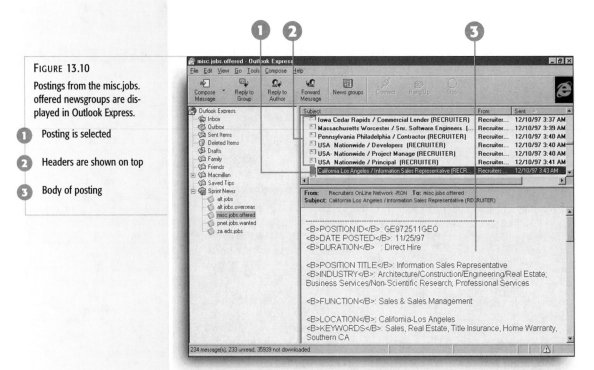

FIGURE 13.10

Postings from the misc.jobs. offered newsgroups are displayed in Outlook Express.

1 Posting is selected

2 Headers are shown on top

3 Body of posting

Newsgroups can be organizational in nature. For example, the group misc.job.résumé contains postings of résumés. Or, groups can be regional. The group houston.jobs.offered holds postings about jobs offered in the Houston, Texas area. Although there are more than 30,000 newsgroups, many ISPs don't carry all of them. If you hear of a group that isn't available to you, contact your ISP.

Table 13.3 lists some of the miscellaneous job-related news-groups.

TABLE 13.3   **Job-related newsgroups**

Group Name	Description
alt.jobs	Primarily technical jobs offered
alt.jobs.offered	Variety of available positions; positions offered outside the U.S.

Group Name	Description
alt.building.jobs	Constructions jobs offered
can.jobs	Canadian positions
can.jobs.gov	Canadian governmental jobs
fl.jobs.computers.misc	Computer-related positions in Florida
misc gov.us.topic.gov.jobs. offered	Miscellaneous U.S. Government positions
misc.jobs.contract	Contract jobs located in the U.S.
misc.jobs.offered	Global positions
misc.jobs.offered.entry	Entry-level positions throughout the U.S.
misc.jobs.resumes	Postings of résumés available for employers to view
pnet.jobs.wanted	People looking for jobs
vmsnet.employment	Workplace employment-related issues discussed; jobs looked for and offered
za.ads.jobs	Jobs sought and offered

Check out these and other newsgroups. Before you post to a newsgroup, check out the postings for a few days. *Lurking* enables you to get familiar with the tone of the group before you chime in.

As you read through a newsgroup's postings, you might notice that the same message appears in several groups. This practice, called *cross-posting*, enables someone like a recruiter or an employer to reach as many people as possible with one message. Keep track of the postings to which you respond. It would be embarrassing to accidentally send two résumés for the same open position that appeared in two newsgroups.

Use newsgroups as a valuable resource in your quest for the perfect position. You'll find a wealth of information. You might also find a group of great people, willing to help you find your dream job.

SEE ALSO

➤ *Learn all about newsgroups on page 220.*

Keep it light

Resist the temptation to slam your present or former employer in a newsgroup posting. Because you have no idea who might be reading your posting, you don't want to come across as nasty or vitriolic.

Buying on the Web

Finding your favorite cybermall

Understanding cookies

Making travel reservations on the Web

Looking at online consumer resources

Dealing with transaction security

Going to the Cybermall

Start your Web shopping trip at a *cybermall*. Instead of having to search for each store you want to visit, cybermalls enable you to find a collection of merchants in the same location. When you're through looking at one shop, you can use your browser's Back button to get back to the mall's home page.

Table 14.1 shows some of my favorite cybermalls on the Web. Use the malls shown here as a starting point—you're sure to find many more you like.

It looks different

Don't be surprised if the cybermall you browsed a while ago looks different since your last visit. The Web is ever-changing. Many Web malls are redesigned for ease of use or to attract new customers as e-commerce becomes more of a buying force.

TABLE 14.1   **Great places to shop**

Mall Name	URL	Order Method	Comments
Internet Plaza	internetplaza.net/	online, email, fax, or phone	More than 200 establishments are located under one cyberroof! The mall is broken down by streets, such as Fashion Boulevard and Gourmet Lane. The Internet Plaza features a Window shopping link that enables you to isolate specific products and services.
Web Warehouse	www.webwarehouse.com	online, email, fax, or phone	In addition to hip brands such as The Armani Exchange, you can buy insurance, tickets to events in your local area, and even look at real estate for sale.

Mall Name	URL	Order Method	Comments
			The site is easy to move through because it's arranged by a series of links.
Shops.Net	shops.net	online, email, fax, or phone	Although Shops.Net is just made up of links to other sites, you'll find big-name shops such as Levi Strauss, The Sharper Image, and Toys-R-Us mixed in with a broad variety of goods and services.
eMall	emall.com/	online, email, fax, or phone	Find mainly specialty gourmet and garden items at this small shopping site.
The Microsoft Plaza	www.eshop.com	online, email, and phone	A collection of the same stores you'll find at most upscale malls, including Godiva Chocolates, GAP, Sharper Image, and The Disney Store.
Brands4Less	www.brands4less.com	online	A giant collection of stores all featuring brand names. Some of the prices are very reasonable.

SEE ALSO

➤ *Review information about HotBot on page 126.*

Search for What You Want

Another great place to find Web merchants is right on the pages of your favorite search engines. Search engines such as HotBot and Infoseek have links to the Web sites of many of your favorite merchants.

You can also use your favorite search engine to set up a search query detailing what you want to find. It's likely that you'll locate a Web merchant who can provide what you're looking for without having to try too many times. Remember to start with a broad-based query and then narrow it down.

SEE ALSO

➤ *Review how to set up an effective search query on page 136.*

Understanding Cookies

Some Web shopping sites ask you to register before you can look at the available products and services. Later on, when you return to the site, the site recognizes you and might even send out a personal greeting. You might wonder how the Web server knows who you are.

Even if you don't register at a site, your browser passes information to some of the Web sites you visit. When you visit a page on the Web, that site can record a lot of information about you, including your name, your company name, your location, the type of computer you're using, your operating system, the type and version of your browser, and what Web pages you've looked at. This exchange of information is called a *cookie*.

Cookies are stored on the hard drive of your computer. Most of the time, cookies are used for innocent purposes. For example, if you customize your Microsoft Start page, the customization information is stored in a cookie. When you access the page, the cookie tells Microsoft what you've chosen to include on your page.

Other times, cookies might have a more sinister use. Even though you haven't granted permission, your movements on the Web might be tracked by the cookies your browser exchanges with Web servers. Some unscrupulous sites could build a database of your viewing habits and sell it to Web advertisers. If you're concerned about your privacy or don't want anyone to know what sites you've accessed, you can block the exchange of cookies.

Unfortunately, a browsing session without cookies has drawbacks. For one thing, you might not be able to access some of the sites you really like. If you've set up customization options in a starting page or another Web site, those special options won't be available.

Cookies are actually simple text files that are stored on the hard drive of your computer. Internet Explorer stores individual cookies in a folder generally called Cookies that's in your Windows directory or in your profile. If you're a heavy Web user or browse to many sites, the files inside that directory can occupy a lot of space on your hard drive. Navigator stores all the cookies in a file called cookies.txt that's stored in the same folder that holds other information about your user profile (generally c:\Program Files\Netscape\Users*your profile name*). You can delete the cookie folder or files, but your browser will automatically create a new one.

Managing Your Cookies

Should you worry about cookies? Many seasoned Web users say no. They reason that cookies are part of the necessary exchange of information on your Web excursion. Of course, most of these users are careful which sites they access and what information they provide. Other Web users take the opposite approach and take steps to deal with cookies as they're passed to and from their browser.

The Anonymizer Web page at www.anonymizer.com offers a service that can give you the capability to make sure that you're completely anonymous on the Web. The Anonymizer acts as an agent between you and the site you want to view. Instead of accessing the page from your browser, you provide the URL to the Anonymizer. In turn, the Anonymizer accesses the page and provides it you. You can use the service free of charge, but expect a delay as the page is accessed. For under $20 per quarter, the Anonymizer ensures that the page it accesses for you will appear with no discernible delay.

If you don't want to look at sites through a third party, but are concerned about cookies, you can change some of the settings in your browser. Internet Explorer and Navigator enable you to monitor when and where cookies are passed between your browser and a Web server.

Many users opt for their browser to let them know when cookies are being passed back and forth. The choice is yours. I think of cookies as a device like the caller ID that's attached to some telephones. I know that sometimes the pages I visit know information about me and therefore, I'm careful where I go and what information I submit to insecure sites. However, I understand that someone, somewhere might recognize who I am; my possible lack of anonymity is a small cost to pay for using the Internet.

Changing the way Internet Explorer handles cookies

1. From within Internet Explorer, click the **View** menu and select **Internet Options**. The Internet Options dialog box appears.

2. Click the **Advanced** tab.

3. Scroll down the Advanced options until you reach the section on Cookies. The following options are available:

- *Always accept cookies (the system default).* This means that Internet Explorer will send information about you whenever asked. Additionally, Internet Explorer will store information about your Web sessions.

- *Prompt before accepting cookies.* This means that whenever a Web server attempts to send you a cookie, you'll be notified via dialog box and can accept or reject it. You'll see the first few characters of the cookie (although sometimes the information is coded) before you make your decision.

It's a trade-off

If you opt to be notified each time your browser deals with cookies, you'll be kept busy choosing to accept or reject each one. This can get annoying. On the other hand, you'll know exactly what information is being transmitted between computers. Try it both ways before you decide.

• *Disable all cookie use.* This means that you won't be able to access many of the sites on the Web. You'll be anonymous as you go from site to site. However, any site that requires information from you, such as a page that provides a custom stock portfolio, won't be available to you.

4. Click the option button next to **Prompt before accepting cookies**, as illustrated in Figure 14.1, and click **OK**.

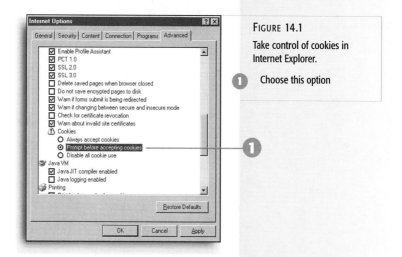

FIGURE 14.1

Take control of cookies in Internet Explorer.

① Choose this option

5. Connect to the Internet, open your browser, and visit some Web sites. As you move to a new Web page, you'll see a Security Alert dialog box advising you that a cookie is about to be passed.

When the Security Alert dialog box is on the screen, click **More Info** to display what information is contained in the cookie (see Figure 14.2).

6. Click **Yes** if you'll accept the cookie and **No** to reject it. If you click **No**, you'll still be able to access the site but the page might not display correctly.

FIGURE 14.2

Read what will be placed on
your computer.

1 Date the information will be
deleted

2 Coded information

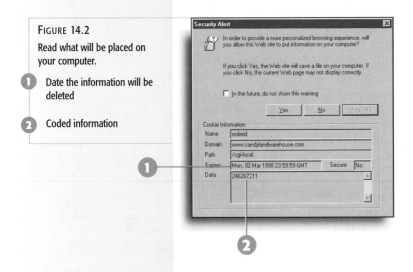

FIGURE 14.2

Read what will be placed on
your computer.

1 Date the information will be
deleted

2 Coded information

Setting cookie options in Navigator

1. From within Navigator, click the **Edit** menu and select
    Preferences. The Preferences dialog box appears with a list
    of Categories on the left side.

2. Click the **Advanced** category to display the options shown
    in Figure 14.3.

FIGURE 14.3

The **Advanced** tab enables
you to change how cookies
are handled.

1 Default choice is already
selected

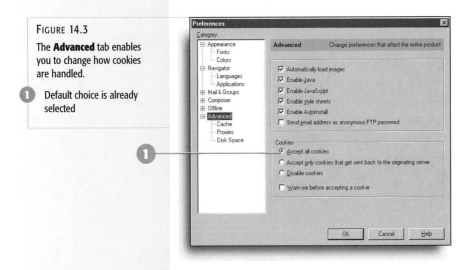

3. The following options are available:

   - *Accept all cookies.* The Navigator default, cookies will pass freely between your computer and Web servers.

   - *Accept only cookies that get sent back to the originating server.* Some cookies will get through.

   - *Disable cookies.* No information will pass between you and the Web server. Some Web pages may not be available and others might not display properly if you choose this option.

   - *Warn me before accepting a cookie.* Choose this option if you want to make a choice each time a cookie is about to be passed.

4. Click the option button next to **Accept only cookies that get sent back to the originating server** and check the option to **Warn me before accepting a cookie**. Click **OK** when you've made your selections, and close the Preferences dialog box.

5. Move around the Web, typing URLs and clicking links. When you attempt to access a site that requires the exchange of information via a cookie, you'll be offered the choice to accept the cookie, as shown in Figure 14.4. Click **OK** to accept the cookie or **Cancel** to reject it.

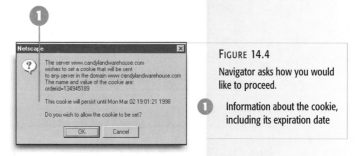

FIGURE 14.4

Navigator asks how you would like to proceed.

① Information about the cookie, including its expiration date

If you choose **Cancel**, the new page will appear but might not display correctly.

Going to an Online Department Store

If you're like me, you can't walk out of a department store without buying many more items than originally planned. A gadget or two always catches your eye or you see a gizmo you can't live without. You're sure to find the same is true at the online version of some of the popular discount department stores listed here:

- Target at www.targetstores.com has something for everyone. The site has links to several children's departments. If you're a new bride, sign up at the Club Wedd bridal registry. Sign up for a Target credit card with Target's secure online application. If you feel the need to walk the aisles and push a cart, you'll find a store locator at the site.

- Kmart.com at www.kmart.com is a fun place to visit. The site is designed for easy navigation (you'll never get hung up in frames). You can click a link to see the weekly sale circular. If you're a television commercial junkie, be sure and visit Kmart's Online Video Theatre to download the latest Kmart ads to your computer.

- Wal-Mart Online at www.wal-mart.com is almost as good as going to the store. The friendly Wal-Mart greeter stands on the home page to greet you. The site is set up as a navigational guide. You can click department links to move through the online store, or you can search for a product. As you move through the store, you're provided with a virtual shopping basket. At check out, you can review the items in your basket before you pay. The payment procedure is easy and secure.

SEE ALSO

➤ *If you need help downloading files, review page 151.*

Online Consumer Resources

Although online transactions generally work out satisfactorily, sometimes things go wrong. The item you purchased could arrive damaged or broken. The quality of the item might be a lot lower in reality than the way it appeared on the Web. Fortunately, a few online consumer resources exist to help you.

The WebWatchdog, located at www.webwatchdog.com, tracks Web businesses. Web merchants are encouraged to register and place a link back to WebWatchdog on their sites. Although not all legitimate merchants are registered with the WebWatchdog, use the registry to search for merchants about which you're unsure. You can search the database for a specific business or search by category to find a list of companies that provide specific goods or services. If a consumer has filed a valid complaint about a Web business, you'll find the company in the Webwatchdog dog house.

In addition to WebWatchdog, other services are waiting to help you. Table 14.2 shows some of the best consumer resources.

TABLE 14.2   Consumer resources on the Web

Name	URL	Comments
Better Business Bureau Online	www.bbbonline.org	The Better Business Bureau Online provides excellent service to online merchants and consumers. Visit the site to read articles on online commerce, learn how to avoid scams, and search for a company's rating.
National Fraud Information Center	www.fraud.org	Although the site lists all types of fraud, the Internet Fraud Watch is a major component. Links to pages such as Internet Tips, Credit Card Safety Online, and Online Travel Scams make the site a place to go before you buy.

continues...

TABLE 14.2   **Continued**

Name	URL	Comments
Internet Consumer Advocacy	www.consumers.com	The ICA is a new organization that has pledged to help consumers on the Web. Information and laws in each state are spelled out.
CyberCops	www.cybercops.com	CyberCops is organized like a neighborhood crimes watch and is made up of private citizens who police many aspects of the Web, including commerce. If you have a complaint against a Web merchant, CyberCops can probably help resolve it. You can read about disputes that have been resolved by CyberCops at their site.
NetCheck Commerce Bureau	www.netcheck.com	NetCheck is a private agency dedicated to the goals of assisting consumers on the Internet. NetCheck works to resolve disputes and complaints between consumer to company, company to company, and company to consumer.

Paying by Credit Card

Most of the purchases you make on the Web require payment by credit card. (It's rare to find a Web merchant who accepts COD terms.) Chances are, you're a little uncomfortable about providing your credit card information across the Internet. Many people don't take advantage of e-commerce because they share this concern.

Transaction security is the number one concern on every Web shopper's mind. Credit card fraud on the Internet is a frightening thought. Can some hacker see your credit card information and use it for criminal purposes? Although Internet credit card fraud can happen, you're more likely to have a problem if an unscrupulous restaurant server or salesclerk gets hold of your credit card and makes a copy of the card, or writes down the number and expiration date. (Think how long a server is out of sight with your card when you pay for dinner at a restaurant.)

Fortunately, technology has kept up with the need for transaction security. Several methods are used to ensure that the Web merchant with whom you've placed the order will be the only one to see your payment information. But you still need to remember that you can't be too careful. Don't order from an unknown Web merchant who has posted an offer that's too good to be true. You probably don't duck into back alleys and deal with shady merchants on your real buying trips, so don't order from the Web equivalents.

Transaction Security Measures

Transaction security is a serious matter. In fact, the future of e-commerce depends on the ability to assure buyers and sellers that transactions between both parties are private. Internet Explorer and Navigator support security protocols and work, often behind the scenes, to keep your transactions from the eyes of snoopers.

Many companies are working on new and improved Internet security measures. All the competition to develop better and better transaction security measures is good for the consumer. For example, Clay Pigeon Technologies, established in 1997, is developing a new technology called CyberTokens. Other companies are following suit.

The most common protocol used in transaction security is called *SSL*, for Secure Sockets Layer. SSL was developed by Netscape and has gone through a few upgrades to make it even more secure. Other protocols used are Secure Electronics Transaction, or SET, and Private Communications Technology, or PCT.

Read all about it

You can find a description of how SSL works in a page designed by Netscape. Visit the page at `search.netscape.com/assist/security/ssl/howitworks.html` for more information.

Cracking the code

A few years ago, two University of California-Berkeley students and a researcher in France simultaneously announced that they had cracked the code generated by Netscape. The Internet world was horrified. Since then, Netscape has taken steps to make it virtually impossible for anyone to decipher the code again.

Both use the basic SSL model and add even more features for enhanced security.

Deciphering Secure Socket Layers

Netscape first developed the Secure Sockets Layer to create an environment for secure Web transactions. SSL uses high-level technology to ensure that your transactions are secure. Let's briefly examine each of the elements that make up SSL.

Public Key Encryption

Your browser and a secure Web server exchange public keys. The *key* is actually the code used to scramble the information such as your credit card number and what you're ordering. As the information goes out across the Internet, only your browser and the Web server can read it. As an added security measure, the information can be unlocked with a private key when it reaches its destination.

The encoding and decoding is actually accomplished by the use of two random numbers. The first random number is the *public key* that's known by your browser and the secure server. The second random number is the *private key*, only known at one end of the transaction, or the other. Security is provided by the fact that the random numbers are very large. Because of the large number of possible combinations, it would be impossible to work through every one.

Digital Certificates

Digital certificates provide an added measure of security. When you send the public key, a digital ID goes along as well. The digital ID works like your driver's license and identifies you. Because digital certificates are used for extra security, you don't need one to shop on the Web. However, if you're doing a lot of online shopping, you can obtain your own digital certificate.

Authentication

The third portion of SSL is called *authentication* and checks to make sure that you are who your certificate says you are.

Authentication is handled behind the scenes when you transmit information in a message. Your computer creates a mathematically designed digest of the message called a *hash*. Each hash is unique. When the receiving computer receives your message, it runs the same hash function you used. If both hashes aren't identical, the message is rejected.

Viewing Secure Web Sites

Fortunately, most Web merchants take care of the advance work of making their sites secure. You don't need to do anything special to visit a secure site because all the work is done for you, behind the scenes. Internet Explorer and Navigator both provide visual clues to let you know you're accessing a secure site:

- *Warning dialog box.* If you click a link or type in the URL to a secure site, your browser displays a dialog box, similar to the one shown in Figure 14.5, to let you know that the site you're accessing is secure.

FIGURE 14.5

Internet Explorer informs you that the site is secure.

1   Check this box if you don't want to see this message again

---

Internet Explorer status bar

If you're an Internet Explorer user, you might have chosen not to display the status bar. If you can't see the status bar, click **View, Status Bar** to re-display it.

- *URL identification.* The URL in the Address box changes from `http://` to `https://`, as shown in Figure 14.6.
- *Security Padlock icon.* Internet Explorer and Navigator display a security icon, shaped like a padlock, on the status bar at the bottom of the page. When the icon looks like a closed padlock, you know the site is secure (see Figure 14.6). Navigator adds a visual clue by coloring in the padlock icon so that it stands out.

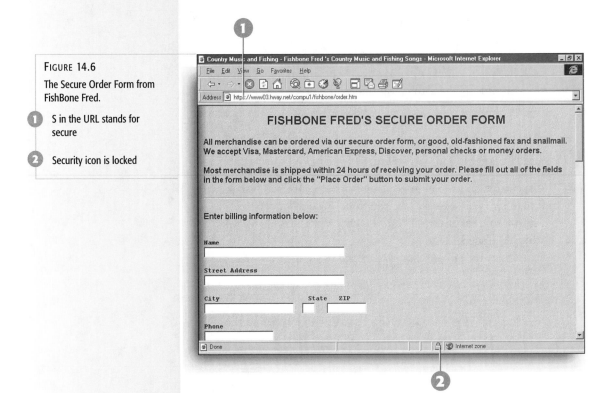

FIGURE 14.6

The Secure Order Form from FishBone Fred.

1 S in the URL stands for secure

2 Security icon is locked

For even more information about a secure document, you can double-click the closed padlock icon on the status bar. A window appears with categories of information about the security levels on the page. When you're finished reading the information, close the window to return to the secure page.

It's important to remember that not all Web merchants offer secure Web transactions. If you're worried about exchanging credit card information on a non-secure site, don't complete the transaction.

Making Travel Reservations

Instead of shopping for products and services, you can shop for your next vacation. So many sites on the Web are devoted to travel that you can act as your own travel agent. Many sites feature discounted prices to cruises, airfare, and hotels. And of course, planning your trip on the Web means that you can make your arrangements any time it's convenient for you.

The sites shown here are just a sample of what you can find.

- Internet Travel Mall at `www.thirdrock.com/itm` is a navigational guide to hundreds of travel-related links. You'll find links to airlines, cruises, motorcoach travel, and more. You can even find links to travel agencies in out of the way locations such as Belize or Antarctica.

- Travel Discounters at `www.traveldiscounters.com` can help you find the lowest airline fares available. The site also features monthly specials and tips for finding the lowest fares.

- Travelocity at `www.travelocity.com` is powered by SABRE, the reservation system used by many professional travel agents. You'll need to register with the service and call or fax your credit card information before you can purchase tickets. Travelocity provides sections for today's lowest fares and last minute deals.

- Preferred Cruises at `www.bargaincruising.com` takes the work out of planning your dream cruise. You fill out a brief form about your preferred destinations and accommodations and when you want to cruise. Within 24 hours, you'll have information on the best rates and cruise lines available for the time you specified.

Using Microsoft's Expedia Travel

The Microsoft Expedia.com site at `www.expedia.msn.com` is the premier travel site on the Web (see Figure 14.7). Collected in Expedia's pages is everything you'll need to plan the perfect vacation. You can visit the site on the Web or, if you're using Internet Explorer, you can add it to your active channels. The Expedia service is free. However, Expedia requires you to register to access their travel planning services. The registration is accomplished with a Registration Wizard that asks you to fill in some basic information about yourself. The information you submit is processed over a secure connection.

FIGURE 14.7

The Expedia.com home page starts your dream vacation.

1 First-time visitors need to register

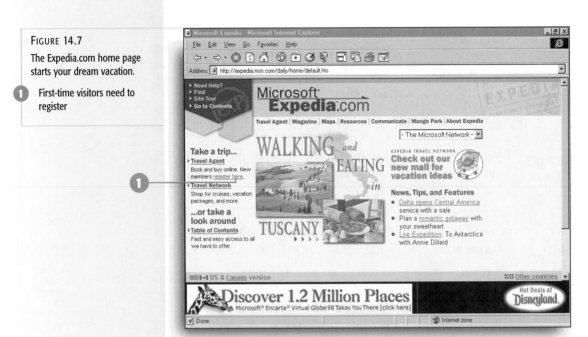

After you've registered with Expedia, you can use their **Reservations** service, look for a vacation package deal through **Destinations**, and register to win trips and other prizes at **e-Specials**. **Hot Deals,** updated every Friday, is a guide to late-breaking vacation discounts. If you need help with any of your travel plans, **Customer Service** is a quick click away. Using the secure payment system, you can even pay for your vacation online.

SEE ALSO

➤ *You'll find information on working with Microsoft Active Channels on page 334.*

Other Ways to Pay for Web Purchases

In addition to submitting your credit card information each time you make a purchase, you can choose another way to pay. If you're an Internet Explorer user, you can store your payment information in *Microsoft Wallet*, which we'll talk about in a moment. Some Web merchants now accept *digital cash*.

The concept of digital cash is simple—you transmit information to the merchant who then uses the information to get the real cash from your account. The use of digital cash has been slow to catch on. However, two companies are developing digital cash systems:

- *CyberCash.* Requires you to install special client "wallet" software onto your computer. When the software is installed, you open an account in a participating bank. Using the CyberCash software, you move money from your checking account into your CyberCash account. When you make a purchase with a merchant who uses the CyberCash system, the payment is made out of your CyberCash account. Because the merchant only sees your CyberCash account number, there's no danger that your real bank account or credit card numbers can be misused. Read more about the CyberCash system at www.cybercash.com.

- *DigiCash.* Works like a checking account. You make a deposit in a DigiCash bank and are given Ecash certificates that you use to purchase items on the Web. Ecash is completely untraceable, giving you privacy and confidentiality when you shop. Visit the DigiCash site at www.digicash.com for more information about the payment system.

Working with Microsoft Wallet

If you're shopping with a Web merchant who accepts Microsoft Wallet, you can send your information with a few mouse clicks. Microsoft Wallet offers a convenient and secure way to pay for your purchases on the Web. Your payment and address information is stored within the wallet. When you make a purchase, your payment information is sent from the Wallet. You don't need to retype the same information again and again. Your payment information is secured by password, so you don't need to worry that someone who uses your computer can access your confidential information.

Microsoft Wallet is set up with two sections, the Payment and Address Selectors. The Payment Selector enables you to choose how you'll pay for your purchase. The Address Selector automates the entry of your shipping and billing addresses.

Only some merchants accept Microsoft Wallet payments

Right now, not all Web merchants accept payments using Microsoft Wallet. However, more and more merchants are enabling Microsoft Wallet payments on their sites.

You can use the wallet whenever you want to pay by credit card for a purchase on the Web. Microsoft Wallet uses SSL security, so you can be sure that no one else can view your payment information. It also supports other payment methods, including industry-standard Secure Electronic Transaction (SET) as well as add-on payment methods, such as digital cash, and electronic checks.

Microsoft Wallet also includes a protected storage area in which private information is stored. Payment information contained in the Wallet protected storage is encrypted and can only be accessed by the owner of that specific information.

Setting up Microsoft Wallet

1. Connect to the Internet. From within Internet Explorer, click the **View** menu and select **Internet Options**. When the Internet Options dialog box appears, click the **Content** tab.

2. In the Personal Information section of the **Content** tab, click **Addresses**.

3. The Address Options dialog box appears, layered over the Internet Options dialog box. Click **Add** to add your address information.

4. The Add a New Address dialog box appears. Type the information in each box. Click the **Home** or **Business** button to specify the location of the address. Type a descriptive name in the **Display name** text box, if you don't like the name that's added for you. If you would like to use a name that you've entered in your email Address Book, click the **Address Book** button. (Figure 14.8 shows the box after it's been completed.) Click **OK** after you've checked over the information you typed.

5. The **Display name** appears in the Address Options dialog box. Click **Close** to return to the Internet Options dialog box.

Navigator users can use Microsoft Wallet, too

If you're a Navigator user, you can use Microsoft Wallet as a Navigator plug-in. Visit the Web page at `www.microsoft.com/ commerce/wallet/ local/naven.htm` for information on how to download and set up the wallet. (You'll find information about Navigator plug-ins in Chapter 6.)

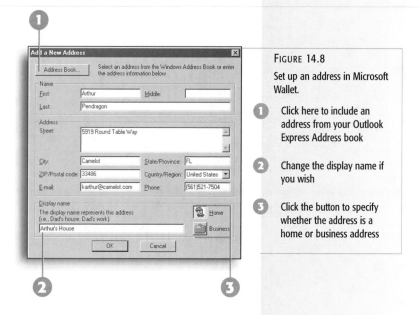

FIGURE 14.8

Set up an address in Microsoft Wallet.

1 Click here to include an address from your Outlook Express Address book

2 Change the display name if you wish

3 Click the button to specify whether the address is a home or business address

6. Now you need to enter your payment information. Get the credit cards you're going to use (or write down the type, name, number, and expiration date of each card) and click **Payments**. When the Payment Options dialog appears, click the **Add** button and choose the type of credit card—Visa Card, Master Card, or American Express.

7. The first box of the Add a New Credit Card Wizard appears, Read the information and click **Next**.

8. The Credit Card Information dialog box appears, as shown in Figure 14.9. Type your name, credit card number, and card expiration date exactly as they appear on the card. If you want, change the information on the Display name dialog box to something that's meaningful to you. When you're sure you've entered the credit card information correctly, click **Next**.

9. In the Credit Card Billing Address dialog box, choose the billing address from the ones you've already entered or click the **New address** button to add a new address. Click **Next** when you're done.

FIGURE 14.9

Select your credit card type from the list.

1 Click the card type that matches yours

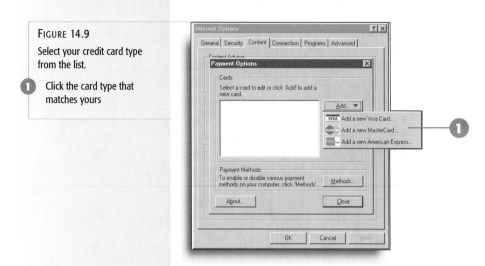

10. The Credit Card Password dialog box appears. This box is very important because it's the key to accessing your credit card information. Type a password you're sure you'll remember in the **Password** text box. Retype the password in the **Confirm password** text box. Click **Finish**.

11. If you want to add another credit card, repeat steps 6 through 10. After you've entered all your applicable credit card information, click **Close** to return to the Internet Options dialog box. Close the Internet Options dialog box by clicking **OK**. You're ready to go shopping with your Wallet.

Shopping with your Microsoft Wallet is a snap. Many retailers will accept the information you've entered in the Address Register of your Wallet when you register on their sites, so you don't have to type in your name, address, phone, and email id. Additionally, you'll see your Wallet when prompted for the address to which you want to ship the product while you're shopping. You'll also see the Wallet when asked to select your payment method.

Table 14.3 contains a list of a few of the Web merchants who support Microsoft Wallet. To see a longer list, visit the Microsoft Wallet—Shopping on the Web page at

www.microsoft.com/commerce/wallet/directory.htm#list

TABLE 14.3   Merchants who support Microsoft Wallet

Name	URL	Description
Bombay Company	www.bombayco.com	Classic and modern furniture and gifts
General Tool and Repair	www.gtr.com	Online superstore for brand name tools
Seidler's Jewelers	www.seidlers.com/sj/default.asp	Fine jewelry and gifts
Skymall	www.skymall.com	Selections from many well-known catalogues
Universal Studios	www.universalstudios.com	Clothing, music and props from the famous Hollywood studio

Getting News and Information on the Web

Learning about push technology

Subscribing to Web channels

News on the Web

Reading Web magazines

Finding people on the Web

Pushing Information to Your Computer

So far, the quality of your Web experience has been based on the searches you conduct and the links you click. You need to do the work to make your browsing worthwhile. Instead, imagine an automated delivery of information to your computer on topics you've requested. After the information is copied to your computer, you can view it at a convenient time.

The delivery of information to your computer is called *push technology*. Push offers an interesting alternative to users who pull the information they want to see. Generally, push providers, called *Webcasters*, organize information into channels to which users can subscribe. A *channel* is actually a Web site that's updated at intervals determined by the owner. When you view a channel, you might see a simple Web page, a high-tech animated page with lots of linked pages, or a live news feed.

After a channel has been updated, the new information is available to the subscriber. The channel is sent to subscribers who requested automatic updates. Alternatively, subscribers who set up manual updating can request new updates when it's convenient.

Differences Between Web Sites and Channels

Channels and Web sites share many common elements. Both provide information to you. Channels and Web sites usually contain links that jump you from one spot to another. Sometimes it's hard to know if you're looking at a Web site or a channel.

As a rule, the types of content that lend themselves to delivery through channels are different from the content contained in most Web sites. Channel content is usually time-intensive. You subscribe to a channel because you want the latest news, sports scores, stock prices, or other timely information. Instead of looking for it, the channel brings you what you want to know.

If you read the daily newspaper or watch the evening news, you're familiar with the concept of getting the latest information. Just like your morning paper or favorite newscaster, channels provide timely and relevant information, Internet style.

The Hidden Danger of Channels

Channel subscriptions can wreak havoc on the computers of unsuspecting users. To bring you updated content, graphics images, and special effects, many files must be copied to the hard drive of your computer. Those files can take up a lot of valuable hard drive space. The more channels to which you subscribe, the more files are copied. Even the roomiest hard drive can get squeezed after a while. A computer with a smaller hard drive can feel the pinch with only a few subscriptions.

Viewing a channel is memory intensive and uses valuable system resources. If other applications are open on your computer when you're looking at a channel's content, you might see a Windows message stating that your system is dangerously low on resources, or your system might hang. To prevent problems, close all open programs before you begin to view channels.

Channels, Channels, and More Channels

The concept of push technology isn't new. In fact, it's very closely modeled after the way you get information from radio and television. You can sit in front of your television set as the nightly news is "pushed" to your living room, or you can see the same information presented on your computer. Similar to radio and TV channels or stations, different Internet channels provide diverse information. Channels are generally sorted by topic.

Microsoft's Active Channels and Netscape Netcaster provide a wide range of channel topics, including News and Technology, Sports, Entertainment, and Business. Under each topic is a list of channels to which you can subscribe. Some channels are presented with graphics, movies, or other multimedia effects. In fact, viewing a channel is usually a cross between viewing a television show and a Web page. Many channels might seem familiar because content providers often maintain Web pages that are similar to their channels.

Table 15.1 shows some of the most popular Web channels and a brief description of the channel content.

TABLE 15.1 **Popular Internet channels**

Name	Microsoft Active Channel	Netscape Netcaster	Description
Disney Channel	Yes	Yes	Features great games for kids and valuable information for parents. You'll also get the latest information on your favorite Disney characters, products, and services.
TV Guide	Yes	Yes	TV listings are specific to your zip code, ensuring you'll know what and when you want to watch on TV.
People Online	Yes	No	An online version of the popular magazine. Read the latest celebrity news and human interest stories.
Quicken.com	Yes	Yes	Offers tools, resources, and expertise for making financial investments and financial choices.
CBS Sportsline	Yes	Yes	The latest news, scores, standings, and statistics for just about any sport you can imagine.
Mapquest	No	Yes	Create interactive maps and explore international travel destinations.
ZDNet	Yes	Yes	Find out what's happening in the computer world. Get product reviews, late breaking news, and free downloads.
MSNBC	Yes	No	Microsoft and NBC combine to bring late-breaking news with a thought-provoking style.

Using Microsoft's Active Channels

Internet Explorer includes push technology as an important way for you to get news and information from the Web. In fact, Microsoft is so committed to the future of push technology that they've developed a standard for channels called *Channel Definition Format*, or CDF for short.

You can preview any Microsoft Active Channel to sample its content. If you like the channel, you need to subscribe so that the updated content can be pushed to your computer. Subscriptions are free and can be canceled at any time.

As part of the subscription process, you set the interval at which the new material will be copied to your computer and specify how you want to be notified that new material is available for viewing. When you receive notification that new material is available, you can view it while you're connected to the Internet. Or, you can disconnect from the Internet and view the channel offline.

Viewing and subscribing to a Microsoft Active Channel

1. When you're connected to the Internet with Internet Explorer open and visible onscreen, click the Channels button on the Standard Buttons toolbar.

2. The Explorer Channel bar appears on the left side of the page. The Channel bar contains buttons for some pre-selected channels and channel topics.

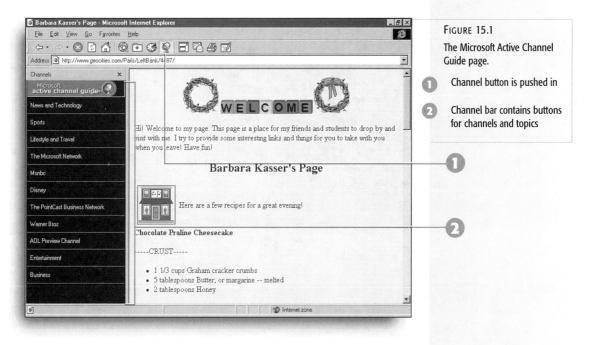

FIGURE 15.1

The Microsoft Active Channel Guide page.

1 Channel button is pushed in

2 Channel bar contains buttons for channels and topics

3. Slide the mouse pointer through the channel buttons. As the mouse passes over a channel, the text converts to the channel's icon. Click the Microsoft Channel Guide button on the Channel bar.

4. The Microsoft Active Channels Guide page appears to the right displaying a list of channel topics. To view a listing of the channels that are available under a topic, click the topic heading on the Microsoft Active Channels Guide page. If the topic has many available channels, such as Sports (see Figure 15.2), you'll only see seven channels listed at a time. Click the number buttons to display additional channels.

FIGURE 15.2

Many sports channels are available.

1. Search for additional channels

2. When you choose a channel from the Channel bar...

3. Click a number range to display more channels

4. ...its contents are displayed here

5. When you find the channel that has content you would like to view, click the channel name. In a moment or two, the opening page of the channel appears onscreen.

6. Click the **Add Active Channel** button. A dialog box may appear briefly on the screen, telling you that files are being copied to your computer. When the files have been copied, the Add Active Channel content dialog box, shown in Figure 15.3, appears onscreen. Choose one of the following options:

- *N*o, *just add it to my Channel Bar.* Instead of setting a subscription, you add a button to your Channel bar. Click the button to view the channel content when you're connected to the Internet.

- *Yes, but only tell me when updates occur.* If you choose this option, a button for the new channel appears on the Channel bar. When the content of the channel is updated, a gleam (red starburst) appears next to the channel name. You can also request to be notified of content changes by email.

- *Yes, notify me of updates and download the channel for offline viewing.* In addition to receiving notification when the channel content is updated, you can view the channel when you're not connected to the Internet.

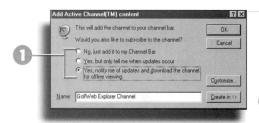

FIGURE 15.3

The Add Active Channel content dialog box lets you choose how the subscription is handled.

1 Choose one of the subscription options

7. A button for the channel you selected appears at the top of your Channel bar and the channel content appears on the screen. Look through the channel, clicking links to move through the pages.

8. Close the Channel bar by clicking its Close button (**X**).

Sounds and special effects

If your computer is equipped with speakers and a sound card, don't be surprised if you hear music or sounds (like the sound of a game-winning home run) while you're viewing a channel. Many channels feature stunning special effects.

Customizing a channel subscription

1. Repeat Steps 1 through 5 from the previous exercise to find an Active Channel to which you would like to subscribe.

2. Click the **Add Active Channel** button to display the Add Active Channel content dialog box.

3. By default the third option, **Yes, notify me of updates and download the channel for offline viewing** is selected. Click **Customize**.

4. The first dialog box of the Subscription Wizard appears. Click the option button next to **Download only the channel home page** if you're planning to view the channel while you're still connected to the Internet. Choose the option button next to **Download all content specified by the channel** if you're planning to view the channel content offline. When you're done, click **Next**.

5. The next dialog box informs you that you'll be notified by a red gleam next to the channel icon when the content has been updated. If you would like to receive additional notification, click the option button next to **Yes, send an e-mail message next to the following address** and verify that your email address is displayed correctly. (If it isn't, click the **Change Address** button and make the necessary changes.) Click **Next** to continue.

6. In the next dialog box you choose how the subscription should be updated. For an automatic update, click the option button next to **Scheduled**. The default schedule is the Publisher's recommended schedule, but you can change that by clicking the Down arrow next to the option that's currently chosen and select another update schedule from the list (see Figure 15.4). Click **Finish** when you're ready to move along.

7. The Add Active Channel content dialog box reappears on the screen. Click **OK** to close the dialog box. The new channel is added to the Channel bar.

8. Close the Channel bar by clicking its Close (**X**) button. The content of the new channel appears onscreen. View the new channel, clicking links to move around.

Automatic dialout

If you have a direct connection to the Internet, or you want to set up your computer to dial the Internet at a set time, say, 3:00 a.m., click the option button next to **Dial as needed if connected through a modem**. You'll need to specify a time and enable AutoDial in the Windows DialUp Networking panel. Of course, your computer will need to be running to enable the AutoDial procedure.

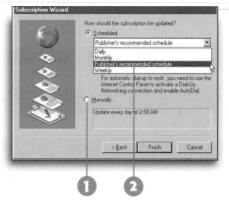

FIGURE 15.4

Select how often the channel content will be updated.

① Click here to schedule the update manually

② Choose an interval from the list

Viewing Updated Channel Content

Unless you specified automatic updates, you need to update your channel subscription so that the new information is copied to the hard drive of your computer. You can update each channel individually, or you can update all your channels at one time.

When you update your channels, Internet Explorer obtains the new material from the channel content provider. Each channel is updated based on the schedule you set when you subscribed. You need to be connected to the Internet to update your channel subscriptions.

Updating a channel and viewing new content

1. Open Internet Explorer, if it's not already open.

2. Click the **Favorites** menu and select **Update All Subscriptions**. The Downloading Subscriptions dialog box appears as files are transferred from the channel provider to the hard drive of your computer.

3. If you want to look at the new content while you're connected to the Internet, click the Channel button on the Standard Buttons toolbar. A gleam appears next to the channels with updated content.

4. Click a channel's button to view the new content. If the Channel bar is in your way, close it by clicking its Close (**X**) button.

Is it a link?

The links you encounter while viewing a channel might not appear like the links you're used to seeing. The screen might change color or a sound might play as the mouse passes over a link on a channel page. If something on a channel page looks like it might lead somewhere else (such as a picture of a celebrity or a flashing arrow, for example), try clicking it to see if it's a link.

5. If you want to look at the new content offline, disconnect from the Internet.

6. When you're no longer connected, open the **File** menu and choose **Work Offline**. A check mark appears to let you know that you've activated the offline mode.

7. Follow the instructions in Step 5 to view the new content. (If the Channel bar is not visible, click the Channels button on the Standard Buttons toolbar.) You need to have selected the option to download all the channel content to be able to see all the information offline.

8. When you've finished looking at channels in offline mode, select **File** and **Work Offline** to clear the check mark and deactivate the offline mode.

Deleting a Microsoft Active Channel

1. If you decide to delete a channel to which you are subscribed, click the Channels button on the Internet Explorer Standard buttons toolbar.

2. When the Explorer Channel bar appears, right click the channel you want to delete.

3. Choose **Delete** from the shortcut menu. The Confirm Folder Delete dialog box appears, asking if you're sure you want to remove the channel's folder. Click **Yes** to confirm the deletion.

4. The channel is removed from the Channel bar and updates are canceled. Although you might see the channel on the screen now, you won't be able to view its content the next time you open the Explorer Channel bar.

Using Netscape Netcaster

Netscape includes push technology in the Communicator suite with a component called Netcaster. The Netcaster program pushes information to your computer. You select the Web-based channels you want to download from a collection of topics and

---

Deactivate offline mode

Make sure to select **File, Work Offline** to deactivate the offline mode when you're finished working offline. If you forget, Internet Explorer will open in offline mode the next time you launch it and you won't be able to move around the Web.

then specify the interval at which the new content will be copied to your computer. Because the content is stored on your hard drive, you can view it anytime—even when you're not connected to the Internet.

Although you can view the channel content in the familiar Navigator browser window, you can view it in the new viewing window called a *webtop* instead. A webtop is a borderless Navigator window that might not contain the standard buttons or menus. Each channel designer can create custom navigational aides that fit on the webtop and tie in with the content of the channel.

Netcaster channels use standard Web design tools like HTML, Java, and JavaScript. Although this doesn't make much apparent difference to the people who view Netcaster channels, it does mean that a few things take place behind the scenes. The first time you open Netcaster, you might see a Java Security dialog box asking you to grant permission for Netcaster to proceed. (Depending on the other programs you're running and permissions you've granted, you might have already taken care of granting the necessary permission.) Actually, you needn't be concerned, even though the language in the dialog box might seem a bit intimidating. Because Netcaster needs to write to your hard disk, the Java security system asks you to grant it permission to do so. Before you click **Grant**, check the check box labeled **Remember this decision each time I start Communicator**.

Adding a Netcaster channel

1. Connect to the Internet and launch Netscape Navigator. When the Navigator browser is visible onscreen, click the **C**ommunicator menu and select **N**etcaster. Netcaster opens in a new window with the Netcaster Channel Finder located in a bar on the right side of the screen (see Figure 15.5). (If you're running only the Navigator browser, and didn't install the suite, click **W**indow, **N**etcaster.)

Constellation or Netcaster?

Before Netscape Communicator was released, Netscape's working name for the Netcaster portion of the suite was Constellation. If you hear someone talking about *Constellation*, they're actually talking about Netcaster.

Netcaster isn't installed

If you can't find Netcaster on the Communicator menu, you probably didn't install it when you set up Navigator. Click **Help**, **Software Updates** to go to Netscape's Smart Update and download Netcaster from the list of available programs. Follow the onscreen instructions for downloading and setting up Netcaster. In a short time, you'll be ready to begin using Netcaster.

FIGURE 15.5

The Netcaster Channel bar layers over your Navigator window.

1 Channel bars

2 Netcaster tab

3 Click the **More Channels** button to see a list of available channel topics

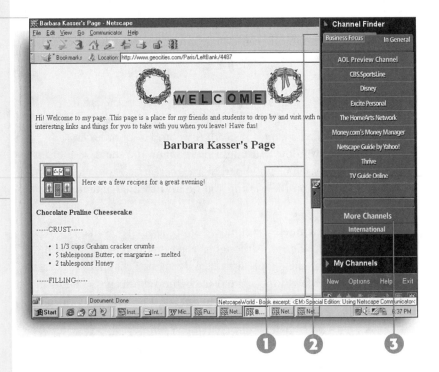

Netcaster Channel Finder stays on top

Whenever you launch Netcaster, it opens over any programs you have open, not just Navigator. If you switch to another program, the Netcaster Channel Finder will still be on top, making it hard to see the left side of the screen. Slide it out of the way and to the right by clicking the Netcaster tab. Click the tab again to view the Netcaster Channel Finder.

Want to see more channels?

If, at first, you don't see a channel you like on the Netcaster Channel Finder, click the **More Channels** button. In a few moments, a new page appears, displaying a list of channel topics across the top. Click a topic to see a list of available channels.

2. Click one of the channel bars. The Netscape Channel Finder expands and displays a graphic "card" for the channel you selected.

3. If the channel is active, both the **Add Channel** button and **Preview Channel** button appear at the bottom of card. Click the **Preview Channel** button to display a preview of the channel you selected in a new window. Most previews are animated and present some of the major features of the channel you selected. If you don't want to subscribe to the channel, click the **Cancel** button and repeat step 3 to find another channel.

4. Click the **Add Channel** button to subscribe to the channel. The channel appears in a new window.

5. Read the information on the screen and click **Continue**.

6. The Channel Properties dialog box appears with the **General** tab displayed, as shown in Figure 15.6. The check box next to **Update this channel or site every** is checked. If you want to select a different time interval to update the channel, click the Down arrow next to the time period that's currently shown in the box and choose another interval from the list.

FIGURE 15.6
The Channel Options dialog box helps you set your subscription.

1 Click this arrow to choose another update interval

7. (Optional) Click the **Cache** tab. The settings on the **Cache** tab are used to store the contents of the channel for offline browsing and reduce the amount of time needed to view the contents of the Channel. Change the numbers currently shown in the number of levels deep that will be downloaded or the maximum size of the information stored on your computer. (If you're planning to view the channel content offline, you might increase the number of levels.)

8. Click **OK** when you've made all your choices. The dialog box closes and the channel you added is added to the **My Channels** category.

Viewing a channel you've added

1. While you're connected to the Internet and Netcaster is open on the screen, click **My Channels** button on the Netcaster Channel Finder.

2. The **My Channels** button expands to show a list of the channels to which you've subscribed. Click the channel you want to view.

3. The channel opens on the screen. If the channel is displayed in webtop mode, as shown in Figure 15.7, you'll need to close or restore maximized programs to non-maximized size to see the channel.

4. View the channel content, moving around by clicking links.

FIGURE 15.7

The Lycos Channel appears as webtop.

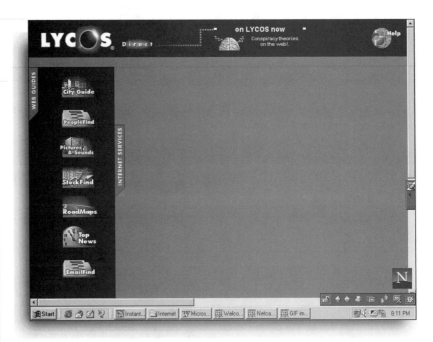

Viewing channel content offline

Keyboard shortcut to open Netcaster

If Netcaster is installed properly, you can display the Netcaster Channel bar with a quick keyboard shortcut. When you're in Navigator or any other program in the Communicator suite, press Ctrl+8 to open the Netcaster Channel bar.

1. Before you can view a channel's content offline, you need to make sure that you're viewing the latest update. If you're not already connected to the Internet, connect now. Open Netcaster from any Communicator program by clicking the **Communicator** window and choosing **Netcaster**. (If you're not running the full Communicator suite and are using Navigator only, click **Window**, and then **Netcaster**.)

2. Click **Options**. When the Options dialog box appears, click the channel you want to view.

3. Click **Update Now**. A gray and red scrolling line appears under the channel name on the Netcaster Channel bar as the latest content is downloaded to your computer. The **Change Update** button now reads **Stop Update**.

4. Click Close (**X**) to close the Options dialog box.

5. When the content has been downloaded to your computer, the red and gray scrolling line underneath the channel disappears. Disconnect from the Internet and click the channel name on the Netcaster Channel Finder.

6. The channel appears onscreen. Move around the channel, clicking links to move through the channel content. If a link refers to a site on the Web or a site that is deeper than the layers you specified when the channel was set up, you won't be able to view all the channel content.

7. Close the channel by clicking the Close (**X**) button when you're done looking at it.

SEE ALSO

➤ *Find out more about Java on page 19.*

Working with Webtops

Netcaster channels are presented to you in a new type of window, called a *webtop*. A webtop differs from the pages you view in Navigator. Most webtop pages are designed to create a replacement for your desktop. Instead of looking at Windows wallpaper, a webtop displaying updated information might remain in the background as you work.

Most webtops are designed to hide your Windows desktop. New programs that you open appear on top of the webtop, just as they would over the desktop. When you click a link on a webtop, you open a new, separate window. Think of a webtop as an anchor page or launching point from which you jump off to pertinent information.

By setting up the update interval to a short period of time when you set up the channel, a channel webtop can bring you up-to-date information. Many webtops allow you to customize the look and feel of the channel with custom menus or other personal preferences. Cookies are used to store the preferences you set so that they're available the next time you view a channel's webtop.

A webtop has two unique characteristics:

- The webtop appears in full screen view with no Navigator interface around it.

- The webtop is anchored to the desktop. Open programs will overlay the webtop; you cannot make it appear on top as the active window.

Some channels are designed to appear as webtops. If you're used to working with your Windows desktop, you might not like the way webtops make your computer look and act. No problem. If you don't like the way webtops cover your desktop, you can change the display of any channel designed to work as a webtop to a regular Navigator window.

Changing the display of a Netcaster channel

1. Open Netcaster and click the Options button on the Netcaster Channel bar. The Options dialog box appears with a list of all the channels to which you've subscribed.

2. Click the channel whose display you want to change. The channel name appears highlighted.

3. Click **Properties**. The Channel Properties dialog box appears.

4. Click the **Display** tab. Select one of the two display options: **Default Window** (to show the channel in a Navigator window) or **Webtop Mode**.

5. Click **OK** to close the Channel Properties dialog box, and then click **OK** to close the Options dialog box.

6. Reload the channel by selecting it from the My Channels list. The channel appears in the display mode you selected.

SEE ALSO
➤ *Review how cookies work on page 310.*

Deleting a Netcaster Channel

Things change. The channel that seemed so appealing when you subscribed might seem too overwhelming now. Or, maybe you don't have the time to look at all your subscriptions. For whatever reason, deleting a Netcaster channel is simple.

Deleting a Netcaster channel

1. When Netcaster is open, click **Options**. The Options dialog box appears displaying a list of the channels to which you've subscribed.

2. Click the name of the channel you want to remove from the list of the channels to which you've subscribed.

3. Click **Delete**. The JavaScript Application dialog box appears. Click **OK** to confirm the deletion. The channel name is removed from the list of channels.

4. Click Close (**X**) to close the Options dialog box. If you're done working with Netcaster, click **Exit**.

Looking at the Latest News

If you're working at your computer, you don't need to get up to find out what's happening in the world. Many Web pages display the updated news and weather. You can view the news on pages provided by television networks and national newspapers. In fact, it's possible that your hometown newspaper has an online version.

Table 15.2 shows a few of the Web's best sources for news.

TABLE 15.2 **Great sources for news on the Web**

Site Name	URL	Description
ABC News	abcnews.com	Updated headlines, news, and weather. Local news and audio clips are available.
CBS	www.cbs.com	Enter your zip code to get news, sports scores, and weather presented from your local CBS television affiliate's perspective.
MSNBC	www.msnbc.com	Microsoft and NBC team up to provide you with the latest news. Click the link to **Quick News** if you're in a hurry.

continues…

TABLE 15.2 **Continued**

Site Name	URL	Description
CNN Interactive	www.cnn.com	The news is broken into categories such as World, U.S., Local, Showbiz, and Books, making it easy to find what you want to know. You can also view the site in Spanish.
USA Today	www.usatoday.com	The online version of the popular newspaper is easy to read and move through. Click a headline to read the full story.
Wall Street Journal	www.wsj.com	The Wall Street Journal Interactive online packs as much financial clout as its print version. Subscriptions cost around $49 per year, but you can preview the site free of charge for two weeks before you decide to subscribe.
The New York Times	www.thenewyorktimes.com	The New York Times online is free, but you'll need to register first. The online version retains the look of the print version.
Washington Post	www.washingtonpost.com	For what's happening in Washington, the Washington Post can't be beat. Political stories and the paper's Style section are its strong points.
The Times	www.the-times.co.uk	How about the news from a British perspective? You'll find international news at this site, along with the latest cricket scores and standings.

If you use the Microsoft Start Page or the Netscape home page as the first page you see when you open your browser, you can see the latest news. Both Microsoft and Netscape feature links to the latest news headlines. Navigator also offers a feature called In-Box Direct. Navigator users can request daily emails on Today's News, as well as many other topics.

SEE ALSO

➤ *Review information about start pages on page 113.*

Reading an Online Magazine

If you count on magazines to keep you posted on the latest and greatest news, trends, and gossip, turn to the Web. You can choose between two distinct types of publications. You can look through an *e-zine* for an original, often bizarre or opinionated viewpoint. Or, you can turn to the online version of many popular magazines, called *Webzines*, found at newsstands.

In the early days of the Internet, many independent publications flourished. E-zines, as they're called, are not generally considered to be mainstream publications because they generally cater to small groups. E-zines contain their own flair and style and feature original articles. Many e-zines deal with topics and subject material that could be considered objectionable or downright crude. Other e-zines deal with "hot" topics, like politics and religion. Advertising and endorsements (unless they're for another e-zine) are rare.

With the explosion of the Web, Webzines burst onto the scene. Webzines are the online versions of many of the same magazines that you find at the newsstand. Webzines contain advertising. Most Webzines retain the look and feel of their printed counterparts. Webzines are commercial publications—most e-zines are not.

Whatever your tastes or preferences, you'll find an electronic publication that meets your needs. If you would like a list of links to many of the best e-zines on the Web, visit John Labovitz's page at `www.meer.net./~johnl/e-zine-list`. The page contains links to 1,770 e-zines. If your tastes are more mainstream, you'll probably be able to find the online version of your favorite newsstand magazine. Table 15.3 shows several popular Webzines and where to find them.

TABLE 15.3 **Popular online Webzines**

Name	URL
Ebony Online	ebonymag.com
Eating Well	www.eatingwell.com

continues…

TABLE 15.3 **Continued**	
Name	**URL**
Harper's Magazine	www.harpers.org
Car and Driver Magazine Online	www.caranddriver.com
Elle International	www.elle.com
Reader's Digest World	www.readersdigest.com
Soap Opera Digest	www.soapdigest.com
The National Enquirer	www.nationalenquirer.com

Searching for People

Searching for a phone number or a snail mail or email address can be a chore. Instead of fruitlessly calling Directory Assistance or looking through the small print of a telephone directory, turn to the Web. Several sophisticated sites help you locate information about the person for whom you're looking.

Most of the people-finding services on the Web work best if you're looking for a person in the United States. You can find information about a person by entering only a name. However, the more information you can provide, such as a city or state, helps to narrow down the list. People move all the time; the databases used by most of the services on the Web don't always reflect up-to-the-minute information, so you might find an old address or phone number instead of the newest one.

Table 15.4 lists some of the best sites on the Web used to find information about a person.

TABLE 15.4 **People-finding services on the Web**		
Name	**URL**	**Description**
Switchboard	www.switchboard.com	Contains listings for millions of personal and business phone numbers, as well as mailing addresses. You can also find Web sites and email addresses.

Name	URL	Description
Four11	www.four11.com	The service, which recently merged with Yahoo!, has separate listings for email addresses. Also found here are telephone numbers for individuals, Yellow Page listings, and AT&T toll-free numbers. You can also find links to email and mailing addresses for various celebrities.
Big Foot	www.bigfoot.com	Featuring an Advanced Directory Search, free personal email, and other "feetures," Big Foot is more like a community than a directory.
Internet Address Finder	www.iaf.com	Contains almost 7 million email addresses. Usersadd their listings to the database. The service is available in five languages other than English.
Who Where	www.whowhere.com	Use this site to find not only people, but apartments, cars, and jobs. Choose whether you want to find an email address or phone number and address.

Communicating in Real-time

Chatting on the Internet

What Is Chatting?

Chatting on the Internet is similar to sitting down at a large family gathering. Many different conversations occur at the same time in the same room. On the Internet, the conversation appears as text in a window on your screen instead of bantered about at the dining room table. Even though chat conversations are written, they still progress at a very rapid pace. Don't be surprised if you actually forget you're typing your conversation on your computer and not having a "real" discussion.

Chat rooms have a bad reputation. Many people think that a chat room is an area to avoid. Because chatting allows people to hide behind "nicks," slang for *nicknames*, participants can often be either rude or risqué. Don't let these boors discourage you. If you feel uncomfortable with the group in a particular chat room, just leave it and go to another room. As you chat on the Internet, you're sure to meet many great people who you'll wind up chatting with regularly!

If you're not interested in meeting new people, chatting can still be of great value to you. Many Internet users use chat as a free, convenient way to stay in touch with friends and family. In addition, many businesses are turning to chat programs for communicating both inside and outside of their organizations. Some companies use chat to stay in touch with clients, others as a means of providing technical support, and still others use it for in-house communications.

Chatting on the Web

Historically, a special standalone program had to be installed on your computer to enable you to chat. More recently, chat applications have been developed that enable you to enter a chat session from a Web page. Because you're already Web savvy, we'll begin by exploring Web-based chatting. Table 16.1 shows a few popular Web-based chat sites where you can have some great conversations.

TABLE 16.1   Web-based chat sites

Name of Site	URL	Comments
Ultimate TV's TV Chat	tvchat.ultimatetv.com	Conversations about popular television programs.
Spiritual Web Chat	www.spiritweb.org/ Spirit/chat.html	Conversations about spiritual or religious matters.
Yahoo Chat	chat.yahoo.com/	General chat with loads of "guest stars" and celebrity events.
Excite Chat	www.excite.com/channel/ chat/	Choose to chat by topic or peer group.

Visiting Talk City

Talk City is one of the most comprehensive Web chat sites on the Internet. Talk City has hundreds of different chat rooms available for you to enter. Some rooms are "hosted," which means that there are people available all the time to help with any problems or to enforce the rules (known as City Ordinances). Enforcement of the Ordinances ensures that the site is a fun and safe place for all visitors. In addition to special events and conferences, Talk City helps users to form "communities" for the continued sharing of information.

Because Talk City uses a Java-based program, you don't need to download any plug-ins or any extra software to chat. You simply go to Talk City, choose a chat room, and wait for the program to load.

SEE ALSO
➤ *Look back at page 19 for an explanation of Java.*

Chatting at Talk City

1. Type www.talkcity.com in the **Address** box of your browser and press Enter. The Talk City home page appears, as shown in Figure 16.1.

FIGURE 16.1

The Talk City home page is
filled with interesting
information.

1 Links to Talk City venues

FIGURE 16.1

The Talk City home page is
filled with interesting
information.

1 Links to Talk City venues

2. For information about Talk City, click the About Talk City
link at the top of the page. The information on the resulting
page is divided into short topics and provides the background of Talk City as well as the rules of the site. When
you're done reading, click the Back button on your browser's
toolbar to return to the Talk City home page.

3. Click the Chat link on the top of the page. The Enter Chat
page appears with a form for you to fill out.

4. Click in the **Nickname** box and type a nickname for yourself. The nickname you type is the name that other Talk
City participants will see. You can also fill in the **Real Name**
box below if you want your true identity to be available to
other participants.

5. Click the down arrow in the **Room** box and choose a chat
room to enter from the list. (Because this is your first time
chatting, you might want to scroll down and choose
New2TalkCity.) Make sure that the option button for **EZ
Talk Lite** in the Chat Method section is selected.

6. Click the **Enter Room** button. A new page appears with a large gray area in the center. The gray area is actually a Java script, loading the chat room.

The first time you visit a Talk City chat room, it might take a few minutes before you can enter a chat room. After you've visited Talk City, your connections will be faster because the information you entered in step 4 is already registered.

7. After the Java script has finished loading, a window appears in the center frame, as shown in Figure 16.2. A list of the participants, labeled Who's Here?, displays on the left side and the conversation appears on the right. A text box also appears in the bottom of the window in which you can type what you want to say.

Before entering into the ongoing discussion, watch the conversation for a while. This practice is known as "lurking."

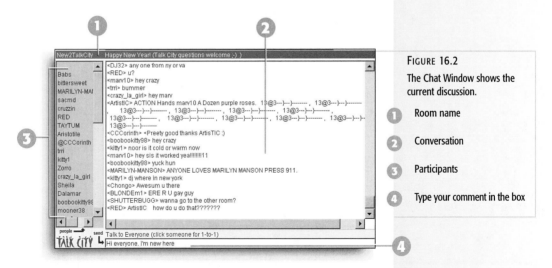

FIGURE 16.2

The Chat Window shows the current discussion.

① Room name

② Conversation

③ Participants

④ Type your comment in the box

8. Type a comment in the **Talk to Everyone** text box and press Enter. Your comment appears in the conversation next to your nickname (in brackets).

Make your own

As you become more experienced with Talk City, you can create your own chat rooms. Create a room by typing its name in the **Other Room** box and clicking the **Enter Room** button.

Cat got your tongue?

Many verbal, articulate people get tongue-tied when they first start chatting on the Internet. If you're feeling shy or awkward, let the participants in the room know that you're new.

9. Continue chatting as long as you want. Notice how quickly the conversation moves.

10. Click the **List Rooms** link on the bottom of the page. A new window appears that lists the chat rooms currently active in Talk City. Next to each room name is the room topic and the number of people currently chatting in the room.

11. Click the name of a room that sounds interesting to you.

12. Click back to the EZTalk window on your Windows taskbar. The New2TalkCity chat room is replaced with the one you just chose. (You'll know you're in the new room because the room name appears on the title bar and the conversation on the screen is different.) Continue chatting in the new room.

13. (Optional) If you want to chat privately with someone else in the room, click the person's nickname on the **Who's Here?** list. The line above the text box changes from "Talk to Everyone" to "1-to-1 with [the person you chose]." Whatever you type shows up only on the chosen person's screen. Click the blank slot at the top of the list to continue chatting with everyone in the room.

14. When you've finished chatting, click the **Done Chatting** link at the bottom of the window. The Talk City home page reappears.

Talk City has conferences and events to please everyone! Make sure you check out the Events Calendar link.

Talk City Options

If you just accepted the default settings when you entered the chat rooms in the previous exercise, you chatted using EZ Talk Lite. This version of the Talk City software is limited in its features, but loads relatively quickly. If you have a fast connection to the Internet and want more chat options, click the **EZ Talk Pro** option button in the Chat Method section of the form you use to enter the chat rooms.

With EZ Talk Pro, your comments appear in a different color from the rest of the conversation. Additionally, you can locate someone else in Talk City by nickname, and open a separate window for private conversations.

Spiffing Up Your Conversation

Chatters have developed a language of terms that are used in most typed conversations. Many of these terms are leftover phrases from the old days of CB radio. For example, the term "10-4" means "I'm signing off." Most chat terms are used interchangeably with the ones you use in newsgroups.

Emoticons, often called "smileys," are used in most chat conversations. Table 16.2 shows the most common emoticons and what they mean. Show that you're a chatting pro and use them in your own conversations.

TABLE 16.2   Common chat emoticons

Emoticon	What It Means
:)	Smile
;)	Winking smile
:(	Sad face
:P	Sticking out your tongue
:°~	Sticking our tongue and making a "raspberry"
:X	My lips are sealed or I'm tongue-tied
:D	Laughing out loud
:O	Yelling or astonished
:-{}	Blowing a kiss
\-o	Bored
:-c	Bummed out
(((((name)))))	Hug (cyber hug)

SEE ALSO

➤ *For the special terms used in newsgroups, see page 240.*

Internet Relay Chat

Although chatting on the Web is relatively new, special *IRC* programs, short for Internet Relay Chat, have been around for many years. These programs use the same client/server model that much of the rest of the Internet uses.

The *IRC servers* are computers connected to the Internet that host Internet Relay Chat connections. Users (chatters) connect to these servers by using special client software on their local computers. Like other Internet servers, IRC servers enable multiple users to be connected at once. However, IRC servers enable users to talk to each other.

Using Microsoft Chat

Microsoft Chat is one of the most exciting *standalone chat programs* that can be used on the Internet. Chat has some great features that set it apart from other standalone chat programs. Microsoft Chat works differently from most chat programs; in addition to viewing plain-text conversations, you can also view your conversations in comic strip form. In fact, many users use the term "Comic Chat" when they refer to Microsoft Chat.

Downloading and Installing Microsoft Chat

Microsoft Chat is one of the options available on a Full installation of Internet Explorer. However, even if you performed a Full Install, you might not have the latest and greatest version of Microsoft Chat. If you completed a Full Install, click the **Start** button and choose **Programs** from the **Start** menu. Slide your mouse pointer over to Internet Explorer and click the icon for Microsoft Chat. When the program opens, click the **Help** menu and select **About Microsoft Chat**. The version number of the program should read 2.1. If the version number shown is 2.0 or below, follow the steps to download and set up the latest version.

If you're using Netscape Communicator, or didn't do a full installation of Internet Explorer, you'll need to download Chat from Microsoft using the following steps. Make sure you're connected to the Internet, with your browser visible on the screen before you begin.

Getting set up with Microsoft Chat

1. Type www.microsoft.com/ie/chat in the **Address** box of your browser and press Enter. The Microsoft Chat home page appears.

2. Click the Download link at the top of the page and choose Microsoft Chat from the drop-down list, as shown in Figure 16.3.

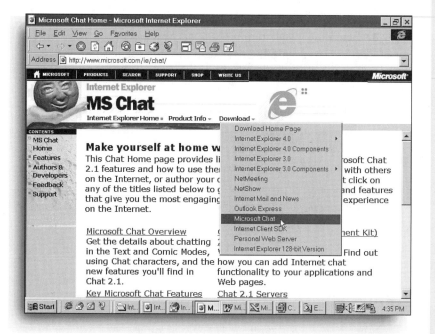

FIGURE 16.3
Choose Chat from the list of available downloads.

3. In a moment, the Microsoft Chat download page appears in its own frame. Scroll down to the **Select which version** section of the Download page and, if it's not already selected, choose the version of Chat for Windows 95 and NT. Click **Next** to continue.

4. When the next page appears, click the link for the file on the server closest to your geographic location.

5. The File Download dialog box appears. Make sure that the **Save this program to disk** option is selected and click **OK**. The Save As dialog box appears.

6. Choose the folder in which you want to save the file and make a note of the folder and filename. Click **Save** to begin the download process.

7. When the file has been copied to your computer, a box appears announcing that the download is complete. Click **OK** to close the box. Then, navigate to the folder where you saved the file and double-click it to begin the installation process.

8. Begin the installation by clicking **Yes** in response to whether you want to install Chat. Read through the resulting licensing agreement and click **Yes** to continue.

9. A dialog box appears, asking where you'd like to install the Chat files. Unless you have a specific reason to change the installation folder, click **OK** to select the default (C:\Program Files\Microsoft Chat). If a dialog box appears asking if you would like to create this folder, click **Yes**.

10. (Optional) If prompted, restart your computer to complete the installation process (but don't forget to disconnect from your ISP first).

SEE ALSO

➤ *For complete information on downloading files from the Web, see page 151.*

Chatting with Microsoft Chat

Now it's time for the fun part. You're ready to meet new friends and have fun with a great chat experience. Make sure you're connected to the Internet before you begin the exercise.

Using Microsoft Chat

1. Click the Start button, choose **Programs** and select Microsoft Chat. The Chat Connection dialog box appears, with four tabs across the top—**Connect**, **Personal Info**, **Character**, and **Background**. Although later on you can

Its own program

Microsoft Chat is a program separate from your browser and can be run on computers using either Netscape Navigator or Internet Explorer. When you open Microsoft Chat, a button for the Chat program appears on your Windows taskbar. In fact, you can switch between your browser and Chat (or any other open programs on your computer).

change the server and chat room listed next to the **Go to chat room** option button, for now don't make any changes.

2. Click the **Personal Info** tab to display the box shown in Figure 16.4.

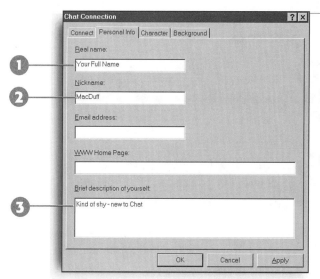

Chat Connection

Connect | Personal Info | Character | Background

① Real name:
Your Full Name

② Nickname:
MacDuff

Email address:

WWW Home Page:

③ Brief description of yourself:
Kind of shy - new to Chat

OK   Cancel   Apply

FIGURE 16.4

The Microsoft Chat Connection dialog box with the Personal Info tab displayed.

① Your full name is optional

② The Nickname box holds your "nick"

③ Information you type in the Personal description box is optional; don't give out too much personal data

3. Establish an identity for yourself by clicking in the **Nickname** box and typing a nickname. If you choose a nickname that someone else is using, you'll be prompted to type a different one. If you want the other chatters in the room to know more about you, you can complete any of the other fields.

4. Click the **Character** tab. From the list of available comic characters, click each name until you find a comic character that matches your identity, as shown in Figure 16.5. (Notice that each time you click a name in the **Character** pane, the comic character in the **Preview** Pane changes. When you've found a character you want to represent you, click **Apply**.

Not everyone is honest

Many people fill in pseudonyms, instead of their own real names. For example, Joan of Arc, Charles de Gaulle, and Marie Curie were listed as the real names of some chatters in a chat room I visited recently.

FIGURE 16.5

Choose a character that
matches your identity.

1 Character names

2 Preview of selected
character

3 Choose an expression from
the emotion wheel

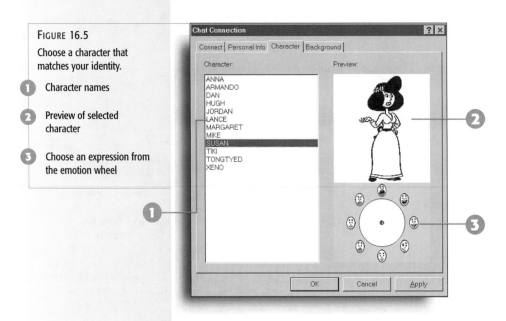

FIGURE 16.5

Choose a character that
matches your identity.

1 Character names

2 Preview of selected
character

3 Choose an expression from
the emotion wheel

5. Click the **Background** tab and choose the **Field**, **Pastoral**,
or **Room** background to serve as a backdrop for your Chat
conversation. When you've chosen the background you like,
click **Apply**. (Because other chatters choose their own backgrounds, only you will see the background you choose.)

6. Click **OK** to close the Chat Connection dialog box and
begin your conversation. In a moment, the connection to an
available chat room is established and the Message of the
Day appears. Read the information, and uncheck the **Show
this whenever connecting** option if you don't want to see
this message again. Click **OK** to close the Message box.

7. The chat screen appears, as shown in Figure 16.6. The chat
screen contains a member list, a conversation area, an area
that displays your current comic character, an "emotion
wheel" to change your character's facial expression, and a
place to type your comments.

FIGURE 16.6
Microsoft Chat program window.

FIGURE 16.6
Microsoft Chat program window.

① Conversation appears in comic strip panes

② Member List pane shows nicknames of people in the chat room

③ Your comic character

④ Emotion wheel

⑤ Compose pane—Type your comments here

⑥ Say

⑦ Think

⑧ Whisper

⑨ Perform an action

⑩ Play a sound

8. Hang back for a while and observe the ongoing conversation on the screen. People's words appear in bubbles above their character's pictures, just like in a comic strip.

9. When you're comfortable with the conversation, type Hi All! or another greeting of your choice and press Enter. Alternatively, click the **Say** button (the first button on the right of the **Compose** box). In a moment, following a brief *lag*, your character appears in the conversation area along with your comment. Because chatters are a vocal group, wait a moment and someone will probably respond to you.

10. Express emotions in Microsoft Chat by changing your character's facial expression. Click the facial expression that best matches your comment in the Emotion wheel at the right of the chat screen.

11. Type a message in the **Compose** box and press Enter. When your text appears in the conversation pane, your character appears with the emotion you chose.

12. If you meet someone with whom you want to have a private discussion, whisper to the character by first clicking on the individual's name in the **Member List Pane** and typing a message in the **Compose** box. Click the **Whisper** button (the third from the text box) to send your comments. Your message appears in a dashed bubble over your characters head. Only you and the person you whispered to can see your comments.

13. Chat automatically associates some words and phrases with particular facial expressions. For example, if someone in the room says something funny, type LOL (laughed out loud) and press Enter. Your character automatically appears to be laughing. Typing text followed by three exclamation points (!!!) makes your character appear on the screen screaming what you said (see Figure 16.7).

See and say

Responses to your comments appear on the screen in one of the comic panes as a bubble over the character that responded. If the person answering you begins a statement with your name, your character appears in the comic pane with the speaker, even if you haven't said anything.

Many ways to speak

In addition to "saying" something in a chat room, you can also think aloud, perform an action, whisper a private message to just one person, or send a sound.

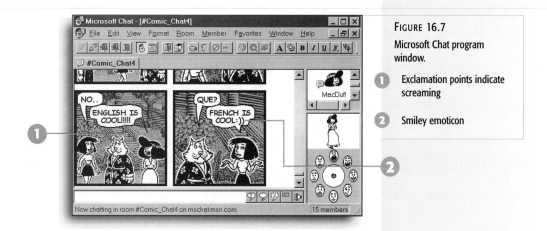

FIGURE 16.7

Microsoft Chat program window.

1. Exclamation points indicate screaming

2. Smiley emoticon

Let Your Fingers Fly with Keyboard Shortcuts

Instead of clicking buttons to portray thinking, whispering, performing actions, or playing sounds, you can use keyboard shortcuts. Table 16.3 lists the keyboard shortcuts for each type of communication.

TABLE 16.3   **Keyboard shortcuts in Microsoft Chat**

Effect	Keyboard Shortcut
Say	Ctrl+Y
Think	Ctrl+T
Whisper	Ctrl+W
Action	Ctrl+I

Moving Through Chat Rooms

Even the most sparkling conversations lose their punch after a while. If the conversation in your current chat room gets dull or offensive, Microsoft Chat makes it easy to move to another room. If you're good at carrying on two conversations at one time, you can enter a conversation in another Chat room while remaining in your current Chat room.

Want to check out another Chat room? Open the **Room** menu and select **Room List**. The Chat Room List dialog box opens. Click inside the **Display chat rooms that contain** text box and type the word or phrase you want to find in a room title. As you type, the list changes to accommodate the letters you've typed. Alternatively, scroll the list of rooms until you find one that looks interesting. Either way, when you find the room name you want to visit, click it one time (the room name will appear highlighted) and then click the **Go To** button.

The new room appears on the Chat screen in its own window. Tabs for each open Chat Room appear underneath the Chat toolbar. Although you can go to as many Chat rooms as you'd like, only one room can be the active room. Click the tab of the room in which you want to be active in the conversation.

Leaving a room is simple. Open the **Room** menu and choose **Leave Room**. Instantly, the room and its conversation disappears from the Chat screen. (If only leaving a real conversation could be so painless!)

If none of the available rooms looks appealing or you'd like to create your own room, you can set up your very own Chat room with a few simple mouse clicks.

Creating your own Chat room

1. Open the **Room** menu and choose **Create Room**. The Create Chat Room dialog box appears.

2. Click in the **Chat room name** text box and type the name of your new room. The name must be one word because spaces aren't allowed. (If you're feeling unimaginative, call it `myplace`.)

3. If you like, click in the **Topic** box and type in a room topic. For example, you can type `A nice place to drop by and talk`. Choose options for your new room by clicking the check boxes shown in Figure 16.8. Each of the available room options is described in Table 16.4. When you're done, click **OK**. You are now in your newly created Chat room.

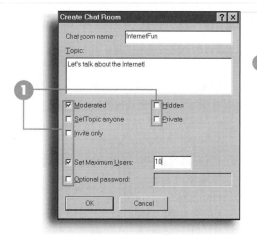

FIGURE **16.8**

Set up your own Chat room.

1 Check the box next to an option you want

TABLE 16.4   **Chat room options**

Option	What It Does
Moderated	In a moderated room, only a room host (operator) or someone designated by the host can speak. Others in the room are called spectators.
Hidden	Keeps the room off the Chat Room List. Someone who wants to enter the room must know its name. Creating hidden rooms is great if you want to set up private chat sessions for family, friends, or business. However, play it safe and don't discuss anything confidential.
SetTopic anyone	Permits anyone to change the room topic. Otherwise, only room hosts can set the topic.
Private	Specifies whether information about who is in the room is available to others outside the room.
Invite only	Allows only participants who have been invited to enter the room.
Set Maximum **U**sers	Sets an upper limit on the number of people in a room.
Optional password	Designates a password that a user must know to enter the room.

Customizing Microsoft Chat

With Microsoft Chat, you can allow people to know as much or as little about you as you like by creating a profile. Your profile can include your real name (or some other of your choosing), your email address, the URL of your home page, and a brief description of yourself (real, or otherwise). If you create a profile, other chatters can view your profile and find out about you.

Chat also enables you to control how your screen appears and how you appear to other chatters. You can change your cartoon character at anytime. You can change the background scene and number of comic panels that display in the comic strip version of the chat session on your computer. Alternatively, if you find the use of comic characters hard to follow, switch to plain text mode to see only the text portion of the on-screen conversation. Remember though, because chatters set up their own settings, the changes you make to all but your cartoon character won't be noticed by the other participants.

Set up Chat your way

1. Open the **View** menu and choose **Options**. The Microsoft Chat Options dialog box appears with six tabs across the top.

2. Click the **Personal Info** tab. A screen appears prompting you for information about yourself for your profile. The information you typed in when you opened Chat for the first time is displayed.

3. Fill in as much information about yourself as you want, clicking or pressing Tab to move from box to box. Your nickname is the only mandatory field that needs to be filled in. The optional fields include your real name, your email address, your home page, and a brief description of yourself. (You don't need to be totally truthful. I often use my dog's name instead of my own!) When you're done, click **Apply**.

4. Click the **Settings** tab. The screen is divided into four sections (see Figure 16.9). The first section, called **Connection**, enables you to choose the option **Don't send Microsoft Chat specific information**. Check this box if you're planning to chat with people who aren't using Microsoft Chat as their chat program.

Find out more about the other chatters

During a Chat conversation, view the profile of any chatter by right-clicking the name of the participant and choosing **Get Profile**. The chatter's profile is displayed in a comic strip in the **View** pane. If **Get Profile** is not available on the menu, it means that the chatter is using a different IRC program.

More characters are available

You can download additional Chat characters from the Microsoft Chat home page at www.microsoft.com/ ie/chat.

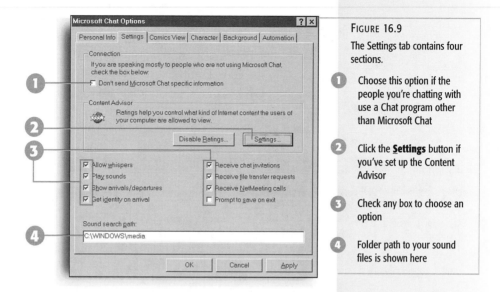

FIGURE 16.9

The Settings tab contains four sections.

1 Choose this option if the people you're chatting with use a Chat program other than Microsoft Chat

2 Click the **Settings** button if you've set up the Content Advisor

3 Check any box to choose an option

4 Folder path to your sound files is shown here

5. The **Content Advisor** is the second section. If you've set up the Content Advisor to block certain words or sites for your children and want to make changes, click the **Settings** button and make your changes on the Content Advisor dialog box. Click **OK** to return to the **Settings** tab when you're through. (Make changes here carefully because it's easy to accidentally block out all the available rooms!)

6. The third section contains check boxes for several options. By default, most of the boxes are already checked. Check or uncheck any of the options to your liking.

7. The fourth section points the way to the sound files installed on your computer. If your sound files are in a different location, click in the box and type the correct folder path.

8. Click **Apply** when you're done with the changes in the **Settings** tab.

9. Click the **Comics View** tab to change the layout of the comic strip. Click the down arrow in the **Page Layout** section of the box and choose **3 Panels Wide** from the drop-down list. When you return to chatting, your screen will display three panels across instead of the default two.

10. The Comic Sans font is normally used in Chat conversations. To change the font, click the **<u>C</u>hange Font** button
and choose from the fonts installed on your computer, as
shown in Figure 16.10. When you've selected a font, click
OK to close the Font dialog box and then click **Apply**.

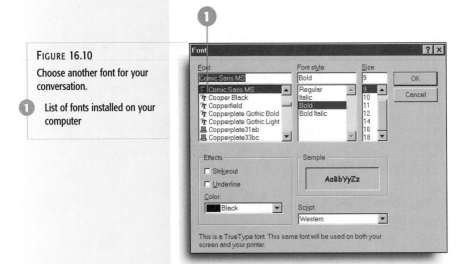

FIGURE 16.10
Choose another font for your
conversation.

1 List of fonts installed on your
computer

11. Click the **Character** tab to display the list of available comic
character names appears along with a preview window.
Choose a new character from the list and click **Apply**.

12. Change the background image for your comic screen by
clicking the **Background** tab. Three backgrounds are available for your use. Click the name of each background in the
list. A preview of each appears in the box.

13. Click your favorite background to select it, and click **Apply**.

14. Click the **Automation** tab. The first section of the tab displays an automatic greeting that can be sent to each new
participant who enters a room in which you're chatting.
Currently, the option is set to **<u>N</u>one**. Click the option
button next to **<u>S</u>aid** or **<u>W</u>hispered** to send the autogreeting.
The other settings shown here are somewhat advanced so,
for now, don't make any changes to the program defaults.

15. Click **OK** to close the Microsoft Chat Options dialog box and return to the conversation.

Chatting in comic strip form sets Microsoft Chat apart from other IRC programs and makes it fun and enjoyable. However, sometimes the comic strips can be a distraction. With only a limited number of characters to choose from and so many people chatting, conversations in well-attended rooms are confusing. Trying to keep track of which Lance character (the one with the paper bag over its head) is currently talking can distract you from the conversation.

If you find comic conversation confusing, you can switch to plain text mode. In plain text mode all messages typed by users appear as text only, without the comic characters. Regular conversation, thoughts, whispers, and actions each appear as different colors in text mode. Anything typed by a room host (operator) will appear in bold.

Change your conversation into text view by clicking **View** and then **Plain Text** on the menu bar. The screen changes from comic view to text view and the entire conversation is presented as text, as shown in Figure 16.11.

In plain text mode, communicate just like you did in comic mode. Speak by typing a comment in the **Compose** pane and clicking on the **Say** button. Or, type a comment and click the corresponding button to think, whisper, and perform an action. Notice that each type of message appears in a different color and is preceded by your nickname.

SEE ALSO

➤ *For complete information about setting up the Content Advisor to block sites for your children, page 255.*

mIRC for advanced users

If you're becoming a "chat-o-holic," you might find that programs like Microsoft Chat and other IRC programs don't supply the advanced features you'd like. A chat client called mIRC might be the next logical progression. The mIRC client program for chatting is not designed for beginners. mIRC programs are generally shareware programs and need to be downloaded and installed before you can use them. Most mIRC programs are not free. To get information and links for downloading mIRC, visit `mirc.stealth.net` on the Web.

FIGURE 16.11

A plain text conversation is easy to follow.

1 Participants list

2 Conversation

3 Compose pane

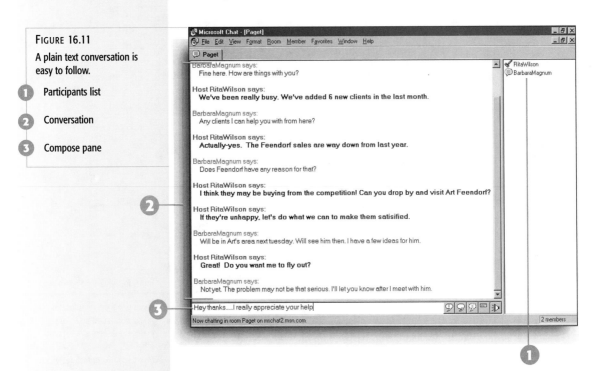

Conducting an Internet Conference

Installing and setting up Microsoft NetMeeting and Netscape Conference

Conducting an Internet conference

Using other tools during your conference

Looking at other conference programs

What Is Conferencing?

Just a few years ago, Internet conferencing seemed more like an item from a science fiction movie than a reality. The idea that people could sit at their computers and actually talk to one another through computer microphones and see each other with video equipment seemed far-fetched. However, Internet conferencing is not a space age dream; it's a real way that people can communicate.

In addition to conferencing software, some basic hardware is necessary to participate in a conference. If you want to have a voice-to-voice conversation, your computer needs the following hardware:

- *Sound card.* Preferably one with full-duplexing so that participants can talk at the same time.
- *Microphone.* Relatively inexpensive, your microphone works as your mouthpiece.
- *Speakers.* Amplifies your conferencee's responses. Better speakers (and a better sound card) help make the conversation clear.

You can also add live video shots of the conference participants. If you're going to be doing a lot of Internet conferencing, consider adding a *digital video camera* to your computer. Although these cameras are pricey, they bring live video directly to your computer. Some companies feel that the cost of a few digital video cameras is less than flying employees all over the world for face-to-face meetings.

Internet conferencing is a great way for business colleagues or friends to have real-time conversations over the Internet. In addition to live speech and video capabilities, most conferencing programs offer other tools, such as text-based chat and a whiteboard for graphics.

Conferencing might not be available

If you're connecting to the Internet from your office, school, or a public location like the library, you might not be able to use Internet conferencing software. Many network administrators don't allow the use of conferences because they can represent a security risk. Check with your network administrator before you set up your conferencing software.

How Conferencing Works

When you connect to a conference call, your computer is identified by its IP number. However, if you're like most folks, you use your modem to dial into your ISP, who assigns your computer a different IP number each time you connect. It's as if you were assigned a new telephone number every time you used the phone.

Fortunately, both Microsoft NetMeeting and Netscape Conference solve this problem by sending your name and email address to a *directory server* when you open the program. The directory servers maintain the current IP numbers of each user's computer, but display the name information. Instead of needing exact IP addresses, users who want to initiate a conference can find each other on the directory. When you close NetMeeting or Conference, your information is removed from the respective directory after a short period of time.

SEE ALSO

➤ Read about IP numbers on page 30.

Comparing NetMeeting and Conference

Both Microsoft and Netscape include conferencing programs in their browser suites. Table 17.1 displays the components of each program.

TABLE 17.1 Components of NetMeeting and Conference

Option Name	NetMeeting	Conference
Audio Conferencing	Yes	Yes
Video Conferencing	Yes	Yes
Text-based Chat	Yes	Yes
Whiteboard	Yes	Yes
Send and Receive Files	Yes	Yes
Collaborative Web Browsing	No	Yes
Application Sharing	Yes	No

Internet long distance

Conferencing is the equivalent of Internet long distance. Instead of using the telephone, a technology called *Internet telephony* sends voice transmissions between colleagues or friends over the Internet. Even with the newest version of this technology, called the H.323 standard, you might find that the transmission is not as crisp or fast as a telephone conversation. However, you'll never need to pay long-distance charges!

Getting Started with Microsoft NetMeeting

NetMeeting, version 2.0, is one of the programs available on a full installation of Internet Explorer. Since Internet Explorer was released, version 2.1 of NetMeeting has been made available for download. Many of the changes in the new version take place behind the scenes and haven't changed the basic way in which the program works.

However, some of the changes, such as the use of icons instead of tabs and an optional folder view of the available servers, make NetMeeting 2.1 easier to use. Additionally, some of the "under the hood" changes support new multimedia technologies that come with Windows 98.

Even if you've installed the version of NetMeeting that comes with Internet Explorer 4, take a few minutes to download the newest version. If you didn't perform a full install of Internet Explorer or you're using another browser, you'll need to download and set up the program to take advantage of Microsoft's conferencing tools. You'll find the newest version of NetMeeting at www.microsoft.com/netmeeting/.

Configuring NetMeeting

1. Click the Windows **Start** button, choose **Programs**, and select Microsoft NetMeeting. The first dialog box to appear lists the program's features. Read them over and click **Next**.

2. The second dialog box, shown in Figure 17.1, deals with directory servers. Make sure that the box next to **Log on to a directory server when NetMeeting starts** is checked. A default directory is shown in the text box below the question **What directory server would you like to use?**. Click the down arrow next to the directory that's shown and choose one that begins with the letters "ils," as shown in Figure 17.1. When you're done, click **Next**.

NetMeeting is free

Microsoft NetMeeting is available free to anyone. All that you need to use it is an Internet connection. If you're a Netscape user, you can download and install NetMeeting.

NetMeeting now uses ILS

Previous versions of NetMeeting used the ULS, or User Location Server. However, with the newest versions of NetMeeting, Microsoft uses the ILS, or Internet Locator Server.

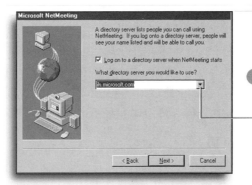

FIGURE 17.1

Set the directory server to which you'll log in.

1 Switch to an ILS server

3. The third dialog box asks for personal information. Keep in mind that whatever you enter on this screen will be displayed on the directory listing. Only the fields for **First name**, **Last name**, and **Email address** are mandatory. If you want to remain anonymous, type bogus information. When you're finished typing, click **Next**.

4. The fourth dialog box asks if you would like the information you provided in the last step to be categorized **For personal use**, **For business use**, or **For adults-only use**. (Both personal and business use are categorized as suitable for all ages.) Click the option button next to your selection and click **Next**.

5. Confirm the speed of your Internet connection: **14,400 bps modem**, **28,800 bps or higher modem**, **ISDN**, or **LAN (local area network)**. Check the option button that matches your connection and click **Next**.

6. The Audio Tuning Wizard takes over. In the next few dialog boxes, you'll answer questions about the sound card installed inside your computer and speak into your computer microphone.

The first dialog box of the Audio Tuning Wizard appears. Read the information in the box and click **Next**.

7. If prompted, confirm the information about your sound card and the playback volume of your speakers by clicking **Next** to move on to each new box.

Full or half duplex

Sound cards can be *half duplex* or *full duplex*. The Audio Tuning Wizard detects which type of sound card you're using and bases its questions accordingly.

Making adjustments with Audio Tuning Wizard

Later on, if the person on the other end has a problem hearing you, or you need to make other adjustments, you can always click the **NetMeeting Tools** menu and choose **Audio Tuning Wizard**. Go through the dialog boxes and make any necessary changes.

8. A dialog box appears that asks you to read a sentence into the microphone attached to your computer to verify your audio settings. Click the **Start Recording** button and record for up to 9 seconds. As you read, a meter tracks your progress. When you're done reading, click **Next**.

9. The final dialog box of the Audio Tuning Wizard advises that you've tuned your settings. Click **Finish** to close the Audio Tuning Wizard and launch NetMeeting.

SEE ALSO

➤ *See information about the buttons on the Outlook Express toolbar on page 179.*

➤ *If you're not sure how to download software, look back at page 151.*

➤ *Review information about modems on page 24.*

Microsoft Directory Server Woes

A directory server works like a telephone directory. The process of registering your information with a directory server is called connecting. After you're connected, or registered, other NetMeeting users (and some users of Internet conferencing software) can access the directory server and find your name on the list. From there, they can ask NetMeeting to call you and invite you to join a conference call. When you're not connected to a server, your name, or the pseudonym you used, won't appear in the directory listing. However, even if you're not connected to directory server, you're still a valid NetMeeting user.

When you open NetMeeting, the program attempts to connect to the directory server you specified during the setup procedure. Connecting might take a few minutes. So many people are using NetMeeting that you might see an error message advising that you were unable to connect to the specified server. The difference between connecting to a directory server and not connecting is that no one will be able to call you unless they know your IP number.

If you want to try to connect to another directory server, click **Call** and choose **Change my Information** to open the Options dialog box. Select the **Calling** tab. In the top section of the tab, labeled **Directory**, click the down arrow next to the server that's currently displayed in the **Server name** text box and choose another server from the list (see Figure 17.2). Click **OK** to close the Options dialog box and return to the NetMeeting screen. When NetMeeting asks if you would like to connect to the directory server you just selected, click **Yes**.

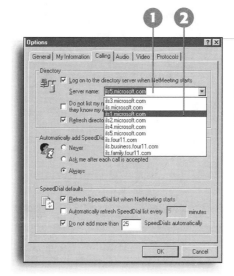

FIGURE 17.2

Select another directory server.

1   Server currently selected

2   Highlight another directory server from the list

Be patient! If you're connecting during peak hours, such as a weekend or during the evening hours, it could take several tries to get connected. Remember though, even if you're not connected to a directory server, you can still make calls. In fact, if someone knows your IP number, they can call you.

Looking at the NetMeeting Screen

Figure 17.3 shows the NetMeeting screen and explains the various program components.

FIGURE 17.3
The NetMeeting window.

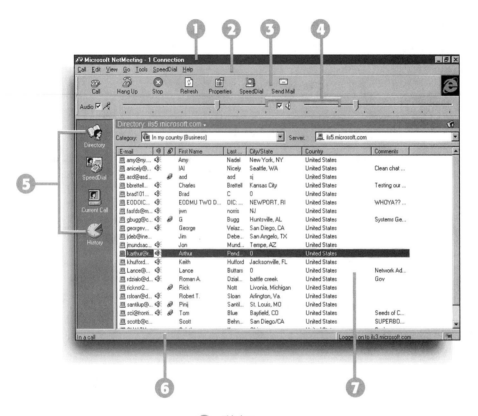

1. Title bar

2. Menu bar

3. Toolbar

4. Audio controls

5. Navigation icons

6. Status bar

7. List area

The following describes each element on the NetMeeting screen:

- *Title bar.* The title bar displays how many people, if any, are connected.

- *Menu bar.* Similar to other Windows programs, NetMeeting features a menu from which you can select all the commands.

- *Toolbar.* The NetMeeting toolbar enables you to access the most common commands.

- *Audio controls.* Adjust the speaker and microphone volume by dragging the slider.

- *Navigation icons.* The top icon indicates the current view. Based on the view that's selected, the list area changes.

- *List area.* Depending on which navigation icon is chosen, the list on the screen changes to one of the following four views:

  - **Directory** view displays the email address, name, city, state, country, and comments of the other people logged in to the directory server.

  - **SpeedDial** view shows the information for people for whom you've entered a speed dial entry.

  - **Current Call** view displays the names and connection information of the people currently connected.

  - **History** view shows the names and connection information of people you've called.

- *Status bar.* Displays messages about the current connection.

Placing a NetMeeting Call

After you open NetMeeting, you can call other people who are currently using NetMeeting. You can make a call in one of the following ways:

- *Directory Service.* Choose a name from the directory that's currently displayed or look over the names in another Microsoft directory

- *SpeedDial*. Select an entry from your list of previously entered names.
- *Internet Address*. If you know the IP address of the person you're calling, you can enter it directly. You don't even need to connect to a directory service.
- *History List*. Choose a name from the list of NetMeeting users you've called previously.

Making a NetMeeting call from the directory service

1. If you're not already connected to the Internet with NetMeeting open and connected to a directory server, do so now.

2. Scroll through the list of people connected to the directory service. If you want to look through the names of users connected to another server, click the down arrow next to the server name on the NetMeeting window and choose another server from the list, as illustrated in Figure 17.4. In a moment, the new names appear in the List view.

FIGURE 17.4

You can look through the names of people connected to other servers.

1 Select another server

3. When you find the name of someone you would like to contact, click the name and then click the **Call** button on the NetMeeting toolbar.

4. The New Call dialog box appears, displaying the name and email address of the person you're contacting. Click **Call**.

   As NetMeeting contacts the party you're calling, the hourglass appears on your screen and various messages regarding the connection are displayed in the status bar at the bottom of the NetMeeting window.

5. When your call has been accepted, the view automatically switches to Current Call list view, showing your name and the other participant(s) in the NetMeeting conference.

6. Speak slowly and clearly into your computer microphone. If necessary, adjust the audio and microphone settings with the slider bars under the NetMeeting toolbar, as shown in Figure 17.5.

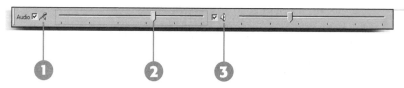

FIGURE 17.5

Adjust the microphone and speaker controls.

1 Microphone control

2 Drag the slider bar

3 Speaker control

7. Take a few minutes and enjoy the conversation.

8. Click the Directory icon to switch back to Directory List view. Make sure that the names of all the people who are connected to the server are displayed on the list; click the **Refresh** button.

9. If you change your mind as the call is being processed, click the **Stop** button to cancel it.

10. End your call by clicking the **HangUp** button on the NetMeeting toolbar.

Using Video During a Conference

Video adds excitement to your conference. If you and your conference members have digital video cameras attached to your

Two at a time

Although you can have up to 32 participants in a call at one time, only two of those participants can use the audio or video capabilities of the program at one time.

computers, the video pictures will be displayed in separate windows on the right side of the NetMeeting screen. (Although up to 32 people can participate in a NetMeeting call, only the first two have audio-visual connections.)

To send video, click on the **Play** button in the My Video window to send a video transmission. If more than two people are in the call, the person who's currently sending or receiving video and audio transmissions can give the audio-video portion to another call participant. If you're one of the people who are using the audio or video portion of the call, click the **Switch** button and choose the person to whom you want to give the audio-video capability. If the **Switch** button isn't visible, click the **Tools** menu and select **Switch Audio and Video** to display the list of names. Of course, when you switch the audio-video portion of the call, it's no longer active on your computer.

Answer a NetMeeting call

1. Nothing is easier than receiving a NetMeeting call. Connect to the Internet and open NetMeeting. When someone calls you, you hear a ringing phone sound and see a dialog box, like the one shown in Figure 17.6, at the lower-right corner of your screen, displaying the name of the person who's calling you.

Practice with a friend

If you have a friend or colleague who's also using NetMeeting, try to set up a time for both of you to practice sending and receiving NetMeeting calls. Otherwise, you'll have to wait for someone to call you.

FIGURE 17.6

Someone is calling you!

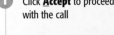 Click **Accept** to proceed with the call

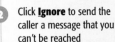 Click **Ignore** to send the caller a message that you can't be reached

2. If you want to participate in the call, click **Accept**. The call will proceed normally. If you don't want to accept the call, click **Ignore**.

3. If you don't want to accept more calls right now, set the **Do Not Disturb** option. Click **Call** and then **Do Not Disturb** to block new calls from coming through.

4. When you're ready to receive more calls, repeat step 3 to remove the **Do Not Disturb** option and allow calls.

Working with Netscape Conference

Conference is the component of the Netscape Communicator suite that handles Internet conferencing. Conference enables you to talk to people across the world with the same ease that you talk to people across the street. Conference is a great Internet conferencing program because you can have an Internet conference with people who are using Conference or other conferencing software, such as NetMeeting.

Although you can use Conference without audio equipment, you should have a sound card and speakers attached to your computer to take advantage of Conference's voice transmission capabilities. A digital video camera adds visual excitement to your conference.

Even though the Conference program is part of the Communicator suite, you might not have it installed on your computer. During the installation of both the Standard and Professional versions of Communicator, you might have decided not to set it up. Or, if you are running Navigator Stand Alone, Conference won't be installed.

If you're using either version of the Communicator suite or the Stand Alone version of Navigator, check to see if Conference is installed. Click the **Start** button and choose **Programs** then choose **Netscape Communicator** and look for **Conference** in the list of programs in the submenu. If Conference isn't installed, you'll need to download it from the Netscape site. The download process takes only a short while. If you found Conference in the list of Communicator programs that are installed on your computer, you're ready to jump into Internet conferencing. Otherwise, you'll need to download and install Conference before you can proceed.

Netscape users only

You must be using Netscape Communicator or Navigator Stand Alone to use Conference. However, the Navigator browser doesn't need to be open for you to place a Netscape Conference call.

SEE ALSO

➤ *For help on downloading and installing software with Netscape's Smart Update, read page 156.*

The Conference Assistant Keeps You Informed

The Conference Assistant is a sidekick program that places a telephone icon in the system tray whenever you open Conference. (The Conference Assistant is automatically installed at the same time you install Netscape Conference.) When Conference is open and ready to receive calls, the telephone icon 📞 shows two telephones that are not connected. When a call is active, the telephone icon in the system tray 📞 changes to two telephones connected by a cord. Position your mouse pointer in the Conference Assistant icons any time to find out more about Conference's status.

Using Conference for the first time

1. Connect to the Internet if you're not already connected. Click the **Start** button and choose **Programs**, then **Netscape Communicator**, and then **Netscape Conference**. The Welcome to Conference dialog box appears.

2. Read the information in the box and click **Next.**

3. The second box informs you that you'll need to know your name, email address, and how you connect to the Internet (for example, by your modem). If you know the information, click **Next.**

4. The next dialog box to appear is called Setting up Your Business Card. Type your name and email address (real or false) as shown in Figure 17.7. If you have a scanned photo or graphics image that you would like to display on your business card, type the folder path and filename in the **Photo** text box. When you're done, click **Next.**

5. The next dialog box, Setting Up Your Directory Preferences, enables you to set the directory in which your name will appear when you're using Conference. Unless you are planning to list your name in another directory server or the URL of a different phonebook, accept the defaults and click **Next.**

Your Business Card identifies you

Other Conference users can display your Business Card to find out more about you. If you don't want to display real information, you can type an alias and a phony email address. Remember, you can edit the information on your Business Card at any time.

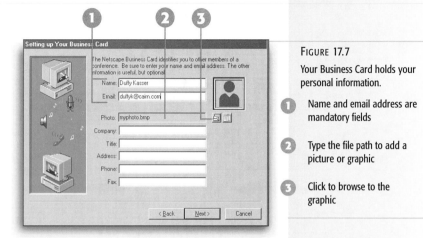

FIGURE 17.7

Your Business Card holds your personal information.

1 Name and email address are mandatory fields

2 Type the file path to add a picture or graphic

3 Click to browse to the graphic

6. In the Specify Your Network Type dialog box, click the option button next to the entry that most closely matches your connection and modem information. When you're done, click **Next**.

7. The next few dialog boxes deal with making sure that Conference is configured to get the optimal use of your computer hardware. The Detecting Your Sound Card dialog box displays information about the type of microphone and speakers detected by the Conference Setup Wizard. Unless you're sure that the information is not correct, click **Next** to continue. (Change the information by clicking the down arrow next to the hardware listing you would like to change and make a new selection from the list.)

8. The first of two Testing Your Audio Levels dialog boxes offers some advice about testing your audio equipment. If you don't want to make audio adjustments right now, click **Skip**.

If you decide to test your audio equipment, read the information and click **Next**. The second Testing Your Audio Levels dialog box contains three steps, you'll need to take to test your audio levels. Perform the steps, making any necessary adjustments. When you're ready to move along, click **Next**.

9. The Setup Complete dialog box congratulates you and lets you know that the Conference setup is complete. Click **Finish** to conclude the setup and launch Conference for the first time.

Viewing the Conferencing Screen

Figure 17.8 displays the Conference screen and details its components.

The following describes each element on the Netscape Conference screen:

- *Title bar.* The title bar displays the name of the program.
- *Menu bar.* Similar to other Windows programs, Conference features a menu from which you can select all the commands.
- *Toolbar.* The Conference toolbar contains buttons to open the Whiteboard, Chat, Collaborative Browsing, and File Exchange tools.
- *Email address text box.* An area in which you can type the email address of the person you want to call.
- *Dial/Hang Up button.* If a name appears in the **Email address** text box, the button becomes active and, depending on the status of your conference, toggles between **Dial** and **Hangup**.
- *Open Web Phonebook button.* Click this button to open the directory server you specified when you set up Conference.
- *Open Personal Address Book button.* Click this button to open your Personal Address Book that you set up with Messenger.
- *SpeedDial tab.* Click the tab to display up to six SpeedDial entries you've set up previously. The tab toggles between **Display** and **Hide**.
- *Audio controls.* Adjust the speaker and microphone volume by dragging the slider.
- *Status bar.* Displays messages about the current connection.
- *Video box.* If the person with whom you're conferencing has a digital video camera, the video feed appears here.

FIGURE 17.8
The Netscape Conference window.

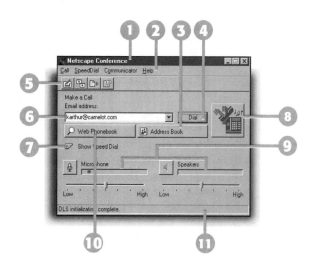

① Title bar	⑦ SpeedDial tab
② Menu bar	⑧ Video box
③ Open Personal Address Book button	⑨ Audio controls
④ Dial/Hangup button	⑩ Open Web Phonebook button
⑤ Toolbar	⑪ Status bar
⑥ Email address text box	

Initiating a Netscape conference

1. When you are connected to the Internet and Netscape
   Conference is open and visible on the screen, click the **Web
   Phonebook** button. If you haven't changed the directory in
   step 7 of the previous step-by-step exercise, the Four11 Net
   Phone Search page appears in Navigator, as illustrated in
   Figure 17.9.

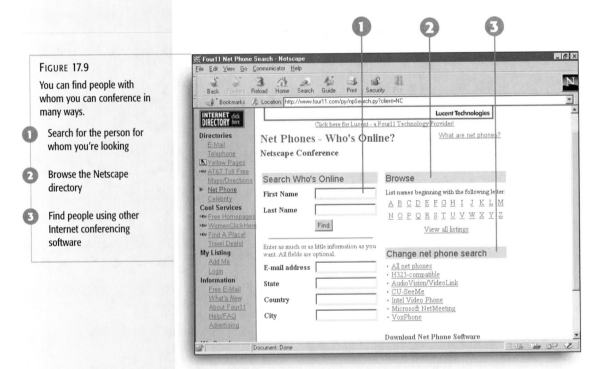

FIGURE 17.9

You can find people with
whom you can conference in
many ways.

❶ Search for the person for
whom you're looking

❷ Browse the Netscape
directory

❸ Find people using other
Internet conferencing
software

2. Choose the way in which you want to find someone:

   - **Search Who's Online** to look through all the names
     and addresses of people using Conference

   - **Browse** through a list of Conference users arranged
     alphabetically or letter by letter, or view all the listings

   - **Change net phone search** to look for users using
     other conferencing software

Unless you know the name of someone you want to find, click **View all listings** in the **Browse** section to display a listing of Conference users.

3. The first page of the Four11 Net Phone Search Results page appears, displaying a list of names and comments, if any, that were provided by the person (see Figure 17.10). If, as you scroll though the list, you're unable to find the name of a person with whom you would like to conference, click the **Next** link at the bottom of the page to move to the next page of listings. When you find the name of someone you would like to call, click the **call now** link on the same line as the name.

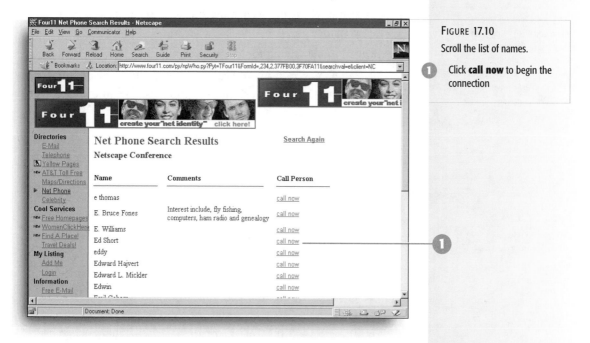

FIGURE 17.10

Scroll the list of names.

① Click **call now** to begin the connection

4. The Who's Online page appears, showing the name and email address of the person you selected. Netscape Conference has filled in the **Call With** text box. Click the **Call With** button.

5. The Conference program window reappears on the screen with the email address of the person you're calling displayed in the **Email** address box. As the call is dialed, a Pending

Invitation dialog box appears on the screen that shows the name of the person you're calling and the call status. Additionally, you might hear ringing as the call is dialed.

6. When your call has been accepted, the ringing stops and the Pending Invitation dialog box disappears. The icon in the Conference Attendant changes to two telephones connected by a cord.

7. Turn on the microphone by clicking the microphone icon on the Conference screen. (The microphone appears pressed in.) Say a few words clearly and slowly into the microphone.

8. Listen to the reply. Depending on your computer hardware, you might need to click the speaker icon again to hear the response.

9. Continue talking for as long as you want.

10. When you're ready to break the connection, click **Hang Up**. When prompted, confirm that you want to end the call. The **Hangup** button toggles back to a **Switch** button.

Accepting a conference call invitation

1. Make sure you're connected to the Internet and Conference is open on your computer.

2. If you want to switch to another application, such as Navigator, while you're waiting for a call, do so now.

3. When a call is placed to your computer, you hear a telephone ringer sound. The Call Invitation dialog box appears on your screen.

4. Click **Accept Call** if you want to talk. If not, click **Reject Call**.

5. If you accept the call, the Conference Attendant changes to the connected icon and the conference call begins.

Using Other Tools in Your Conference Call

Talking across the Internet is a great way to stay in touch. But why not extend the call with a few other tools? Both NetMeeting and Conference offer subprograms including:

Filter out noise

If a lot of background noise is around you, filter it out when you're not speaking. Each time you finish talking, click the microphone icon again to turn it off. Just remember to turn it on again when it's your turn to talk.

- *Text-based Chat.* Use Chat if someone doesn't have audio capabilities or if the voice transmission is crackly or hard to understand.

- *Whiteboard.* A graphics program that enables people connected in a conference to work collaboratively on a graphics file. The Whiteboard can be used for fun as a shared doodle pad or as a serious graphics application.

- *File Transfer.* People connected in a conference can transfer files from one computer to another.

Additionally, NetMeeting offers the capability for all the users in a NetMeeting call to share an application, such as Microsoft Word, that's physically located on the computer of one of the participants. Conference enables one of the call participants to lead the others on a tour of the Web.

Using Chat

1. While you're connected to a NetMeeting call, open the **Tools** menu and select **Chat**. If you're in a Netscape Conference call, click the Chat tool button. As soon as one person in a call opens the Chat program, the Chat subprogram opens on all the participants' screens. Notice that a button for Chat now appears on your Windows taskbar.

2. If you're using NetMeeting, type your comments in the **Message** text box and click the **Send** icon, located next to the **Message** text box. If you're using Conference, type your comments in the **Personal Note Pad** and click Ctrl+Enter. Your comment is displayed, preceded by your name. Responses to your comments appear underneath your original comment, shown with the name of the person who typed it.

3. (NetMeeting users only) If more than two people are participating in a NetMeeting call, you can direct your comments to a single participant. Click the down arrow next to the **Send to** text box and choose a name from the list. Your typed comments will appear only on that person's screen. Remember to change the **Send to** option back when you're ready to direct your conversation to the group.

Chat provides alternatives

Chat is a great supplement to a NetMeeting or Conference call. You might want to switch to Chat if the audio portion is garbled or full of static. If your participant doesn't have audio equipment or it's not working properly, switch over to Chat. Another reason for using Chat is to include everyone in the call if more than two users are connected in a NetMeeting call.

4. Change the appearance of the Chat conversation on your computer by clicking the Chat **Options** menu and selecting **Font.** When the Font dialog box opens choose a new font, font style, or size for the typed conversation.

5. Close Chat by clicking the Close box on the Chat window or open the **File** menu and choose **Exit** (NetMeeting) or **Close** (Conference).

(NetMeeting users are presented with the option of saving the current list of messages. If you don't want to save the messages, click **No.** If you would like to save the messages (typed conversation), click **Yes,** and when the Save As dialog box appears, navigate to the drive and folder where you would like them to be saved. Enter a name in the **File name** text box and click **Save.**)

Using the Whiteboard

1. While in a NetMeeting call, click the **Tools** menu and select **Whiteboard**. Open the Conference Whiteboard window by clicking the Whiteboard icon [img] on the Conference toolbar. The Whiteboard subprogram, which looks similar to the screen shown in Figure 17.11, opens in its own window on your screen and on the screens of the other participants in the call.

2. Select a drawing tool and practice drawing on the screen. Speak into your microphone and invite the other call participant to add some characters to your drawing. Your combined handiwork appears on the screen.

3. To enlarge the drawing on the screen in NetMeeting, click the Zoom tool, shown in Figure 17.11. You might need to reposition the scrollbars to see your drawing. Restore the drawing to its previous size by clicking the Zoom tool again.

Conference users can change the magnification of the document on the Whiteboard screen by clicking the **Tools** menu, choosing **Zoom,** and then selecting one of the levels of magnification shown on the submenu.

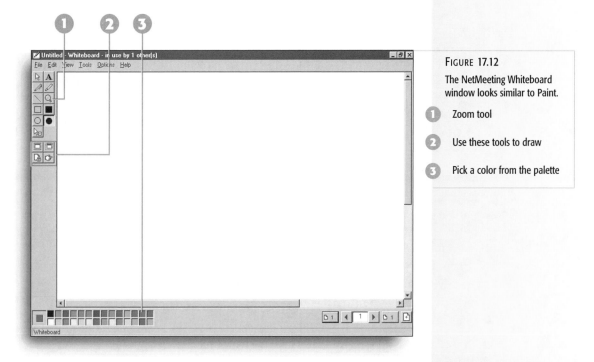

FIGURE 17.12

The NetMeeting Whiteboard window looks similar to Paint.

1 Zoom tool

2 Use these tools to draw

3 Pick a color from the palette

4. NetMeeting users can clear the screen by clicking **Edit** and then **Clear Page**. Answer **Yes** in response to the question of whether you want to clear the contents of the page.

Conference users can clear the screen by opening the **Edit** menu and then selecting **Clear Whiteboard**.

5. Close the Whiteboard window by clicking the Close button on the program's title bar. The Whiteboard disappears from the screen; the Whiteboard button is removed from the Windows taskbar.

Exchanging files in NetMeeting

1. To transfer a file, open the **Tools** menu, choose **File Transfer,** and then select **Send File**. The Select a File to Send dialog box appears.

2. Select the file you want to copy from your computer and click **Send** to start the file transfer. After the file has been copied successfully, a confirmation message is displayed.

More than fun

Although you can use the Whiteboard for fun, it can also be used as a serious collaborative graphics tool. Graphics that have been placed on the Windows Clipboard can be pasted into the Whiteboard and edited by a group of people.

3. If someone attempts to send you a file, you see a dialog box with the **Close**, **Open,** and **Delete** buttons across the bottom as the file transfer begins:

  - Choose **Close** to save the file on your computer in the C:\ProgramFiles\NetMeeting\Received Files folder.

  - Choose **Open** to launch the application (or a related one) in which the file was created and open the file.

  - Choose **Delete** to cancel the incoming transfer.

4. Open a file that's been transferred to your computer by opening the **Tools** menu and selecting **File Transfer** and then **Open Received Files Folder**. You see a list of all the files you've received. Double-click the file you want to open; provided you have the correct application on your computer, the file opens on your screen.

Sending and receiving files in Conference

1. While you're participating in a Conference call, click the File Exchange button ⬚ from the Conference toolbar. The Conference File Exchange dialog box appears.

  The dialog box is divided into two sections. The top half shows the files you're sending, and the bottom half displays the files you've been sent.

2. Click the **File** menu and choose **Add to Send List**. When the **Add File to Send List** dialog box appears, browse to the file on your computer, click the file to select it (the file will appear highlighted), and click **Open**. The complete folder path and filename are displayed in the **File(s)to Send** portion of the screen.

3. Repeat step 2 to add more files to the list.

4. Send the files by clicking the **Send** button or pressing Ctrl+Enter.

5. If your conference partner has sent you a file, the filename appears on the **File(s) received** portion of the screen. Click a filename, click **File**, and select **Save**. When the Save As dialog box appears, navigate to the folder where you want to

Be careful

Always be extra cautious about opening files that have been transferred to your computer. Open them only if you're sure what the file contains and you know the person who sent it to you. If someone you don't know tries to transfer an unsolicited file during a conference call, stop the transfer immediately. If you can't stop it, delete the file without opening it when the transfer is complete.

save the file and click **<u>S</u>ave**. After it's saved, the filename is removed from the **File(s) received** list.

6. Delete a file from the list without opening it by first selecting the file and then clicking **<u>F</u>ile** and choosing **<u>D</u>elete**.

7. Click **<u>F</u>ile** and then **<u>C</u>lose** to return to Conference when you're done transferring files.

Sharing applications in NetMeeting

1. Open the application and the documents you're going to share.

2. After you're involved in a NetMeeting call, open the **<u>T</u>ools** menu and select **<u>S</u>hare Application**. A submenu of all the applications currently open on your computer appears.

3. Chose the application from the list of programs running on your computer, and then click **OK** in the Microsoft NetMeeting dialog box that informs you that you'll be sharing files.

   The application then appears on the screen of every computer connected to the conference. Additionally, the words **In Control** appear in the **Sharing** section of the window on the line with your name.

4. Work with the application normally. The conference users can see the changes you make and discuss them with you.

5. To give conference users access to make changes to your document, click the **Collaborate** button on the NetMeeting toolbar. Read the information about sharing applications in the resulting dialog box and click **OK**. The **Collaborate** button toggles to a **Work Alone** button.

6. Make changes to the document, discussing them with your conference members. When someone else is in control of your application, the mouse pointer appears with the initials of the person in control, and you can follow their actions in the file.

7. If collaboration is enabled, take control of the file by double-clicking the program window.

Play it safe

Sharing an application on your computer is equal to giving someone the keys to your house. When you share an application, you're actually sharing your entire computer. Never open your computer to strangers. No matter with whom you're sharing an application, prevent someone from wandering around your computer by making sure that My Computer and Windows Explorer are closed before you begin.

8. End application sharing by closing the application you were sharing with other members of the conference.

SEE ALSO

➤ *For more information regarding the dangers associated with transferring files from computer to computer, see page 149.*

Using Conference's Collaborative Browsing Tool

The Collaborative Browsing tool enables one user to take control of Navigator on both his computer and that of the other conference member. That way, both conference members can take a shared tour of the Web. The Collaborative Browsing tool has a major drawback—pages that contain frames cannot be displayed. Because so many Web pages contain frames, you'll find your tour is limited.

If you want to lead a Collaborative Browsing session while you're in a conference, click the Collaborative Browsing button ▦. When the Collaborative Browsing dialog box appears, click **Start Browsing**. Conference opens Navigator on your computer (if it's not already open) and sends an invitation to your conference partner.

When the invitation is accepted, first check the **Control Browsers** box and then click **Sync Browsers**. Move around the Web by using your bookmarks, clicking links, or typing URLs in the **Location/Netsite** box. Whatever appears on your Navigator screen appears on the other computer. When you're done touring the Web, click **Stop Browsing**.

SEE ALSO

➤ *Review how to use Navigator bookmarks by looking at page 64.*

Connecting Fast with SpeedDial

Both NetMeeting and Conference enable you to set up SpeedDial entries. SpeedDial works like the speed dial buttons on some regular phones. When you want to call someone for an Internet conference, you click his name from your **SpeedDial** list instead of typing name, email, or IP information—or hunting for the person's entry in a directory server listing.

Using SpeedDial in NetMeeting

The names of the people who call you and whose calls you accept are automatically added to your SpeedDial entries. Click the **SpeedDial** icon located on the left side the NetMeeting window to display a list of names and to determine if they're logged on. If the icon isn't visible, click the **SpeedDial** button on the toolbar or open your **SpeedDial** list by clicking the **View** menu and choosing **SpeedDial**.

If the person you want to call is logged on, click the name once to select it and then click the **Call** button (see Figure 17.12). NetMeeting places the call for you in the regular manner.

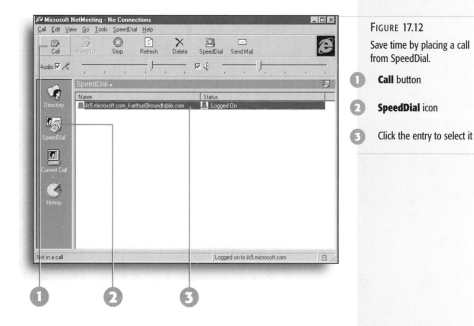

FIGURE 17.12

Save time by placing a call from SpeedDial.

1   **Call** button

2   **SpeedDial** icon

3   Click the entry to select it

You can create a SpeedDial manual entry, as well. However, you need to know the person's email address. Click the **Call** menu and choose **Create SpeedDial.** When the Add SpeedDial dialog box appears, type the person's address and choose the connection method (Directory Server or TCP/IP). Make sure that the option button next to **Add to SpeedDial List** is selected and click **OK**.

Using SpeedDial in Conference

Conference enables you to set up to six SpeedDial entries. If your SpeedDial entries aren't visible, display them by clicking the **Show SpeedDial** tab on the Conference window. When you're ready to make a call, just click the name of the person from the list of SpeedDial entries, as shown in Figure 17.13. Conference places the call for you. To hide your SpeedDial entries when you're not using them, click the **Hide SpeedDial** tab.

FIGURE 17.14

Conference SpeedDial entries automate the dial-up process.

1 **SpeedDial** tab toggles from **Display** to **Hide**

2 Entries that have been created

3 These entries are blank

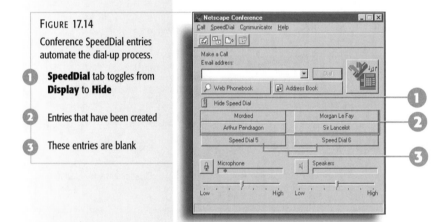

Creating a Conference SpeedDial entry

1. From within Netscape Conference, click **SpeedDial** from the menu bar and choose from **SpeedDial 1** through **SpeedDial 6**, and then choose **Edit**. The Speed Dial Edit dialog box appears.

2. Type the person's name and email address in the respective text boxes.

3. If the person you're calling has a permanent IP address, type it in the **Direct Address** text box.

4. When you're done typing, click **OK**.

5. Repeat steps 2 through 4 for each SpeedDial entry you create. You can set up to six entries.

6. Each time you create an entry in SpeedDial, the name of the person replaces the words **SpeedDial** and the entry number. To edit an entry, click the **SpeedDial** menu, select the entry, and choose **Edit**. Make your changes in the resulting Speed Dial Edit dialog box and click **OK**.

7. Delete a SpeedDial entry by clicking the **SpeedDial** menu, selecting the entry, and choosing **Clear**. The entry is deleted.

Other Conferencing Programs

Although NetMeeting and Conference are the most popular Internet conferencing programs, many people successfully set up conferences with other, less-known programs. Some of the programs are surprisingly powerful. If you're not happy with NetMeeting or Conference, or just want to try something else, consider using one of the following programs:

- *Tribal Voice PowWow* is a free program that enables up to nine users to communicate in real-time conversation across the Internet. In addition to conferencing, PowWow users can send and receive files and cruise the Web in a group. A version of PowWow called Kids PowWow is designed for use by children up to age 13 and alerts children when an adult attempts to reach them. You can read all about PowWow and download the program at www.tribal.com/ powwow.

- *CU-See Me* was developed by Cornell University in 1992. The program was one of the first Internet video-conferencing tools and has a devoted following among colleges and universities. CU-See Me has kept pace with the latest technology and has a new version for download. Visit the CU-See Me site at cu-seeme.cornell.edu.

- *VoxPhone* is another strong contender in the Internet conferencing arena. VoxPhone users can conference with as many as five people who are using other Internet conferencing users. VoxPhone is not free. Find out more about Voxware at www.voxware.com.

Putting Yourself on the Internet

Creating Your Own Web Site

What's a WYSIWYG HTML Editor?

Building your Web page with FrontPage Express

Creating a Web page with Netscape's Page Wizard and Composer

Publishing your Web site

Web Page Elements

Web pages are created using *Hypertext Markup Language*, usually called *HTML*. HTML isn't a language that you can speak. Instead, it consists of tags that tell your Web browser how to display text, images, links, and other aspects of a Web page. At first glance, HTML code might be intimidating. Relax! Many *WYSIWYG* (What you see is what you get) programs enable you to design Web pages without forcing you to learn about how to write HTML. In fact, if you're using Internet Explorer or Netscape Communicator, you probably already have a Web design program on your computer.

Although Web pages can take many forms, most Web pages contain common elements. Table 18.1 lists some of those elements and explains what they do.

TABLE 18.1 Common elements on a Web page

Table Element	Function
Page title	Appears in the browser title bar. Many search engines index pages based on the words in the page title.
Headings	Break the page into sections, which adds organization and visual interest. Headings range from size 6, the smallest, to size 1, the largest.
Text	The text on a Web page is the "meat" because generally it provides the information.
Graphics	Pictures tell a story. Graphics images on the page need to be added separately. Some designers add graphics images to the background of a page.
Lists	Web pages lend themselves to list format. By using lists, information can be presented in a clear, concise manner. Lists generally appear with bullets or numbers before each point.
Hyperlinks	*Hyperlinks* on a Web page provide jumps to other locations. Each link is actually made up of two parts. The anchor, which is the portion you click, is usually text but can be a graphic. The URL portion shows the location to which the user moves when the anchor is clicked.
Contact information	Most pages display the name and email address of the page owner.

In addition to the elements shown in the table, the use of frames, tables, multimedia files, and Javascript are common.

SEE ALSO

➤ *You can review how to navigate through frames on page 107 and navigate through Web tables on page 113.*

WYSIWYG Editors Do the Work

Unless you're an accomplished HTML writer, creating pages in HTML can get frustrating. For one thing, you probably don't know all the codes and tags you need to make a Web page appear just the way you want it.

Fortunately, several WYSIWYG HTML editor programs take the guesswork out of Web page creation. All you need to do is type the text and add graphic images and maybe some multimedia effects. As you edit the page and move things around, the changes are automatically shown on the screen. During this time, your HTML editor is working in the background to generate all the necessary code.

Several good WYSIWYG programs are available. Fortunately, if you're using either the Internet Explorer or Netscape Communicator suite, you probably already have one installed on your computer.

Look at the code

Anytime you're viewing a Web page in your browser, you can view the HTML source code. In Internet Explorer, click **View**, and then select **Source**. Navigator users click **View**, and then **Page Source**. Your browser launches another window that contains the HTML code. Close the browser window when you're finished viewing its code to return to the page you were viewing previously.

Introducing Microsoft FrontPage Express

Microsoft's FrontPage Express is a great Web page design program provided with the Internet Explorer suite. FrontPage Express is a scaled-down version of Microsoft's full-blown, commercial HTML editor called FrontPage. FrontPage Express makes it easy to build some very exciting Web pages without prior HTML experience.

FrontPage Express can help you create a simple page or one with some flair. You can add fonts, tables, Java applets, and sounds. A page designed in FrontPage Express can rival one created with a more expensive, harder-to-use WYSIWYG HTML editor.

Building your first Web page

1. Click the **Start** button, choose **Programs**, select **Internet Explorer,** and then **FrontPage Express.** FrontPage Express opens with a blank page, as shown in Figure 18.1.

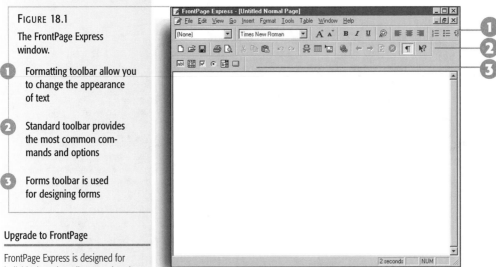

FIGURE 18.1

The FrontPage Express window.

1 Formatting toolbar allow you to change the appearance of text

2 Standard toolbar provides the most common commands and options

3 Forms toolbar is used for designing forms

Upgrade to FrontPage

FrontPage Express is designed for individuals and small companies. If you want to add some really snazzy effects, or you're planning on hosting your own page, consider upgrading to Microsoft FrontPage.

Can't find the program?

If you can't find FrontPage Express on your Windows **Start** menu, or the program doesn't open correctly, you'll need to install it again. If you installed Internet Explorer from a CD, insert the CD in your CD-ROM drive and follow the instructions to install Internet Explorer add-on components. Or, visit the Internet Explorer Products Download page at www.microsoft.com/ie/download and click the link to go to the 4.0 Add-ons page. Follow the instructions to download and install the program.

2. Click the **File** menu and choose **New.** The New Page dialog box appears.

3. Select **Personal Home Page Wizard** and click **OK**. The Personal Home Page Wizard dialog box appears, as shown in Figure 18.2. Several categories of information are already chosen for your page.

4. Select the types of information you want to include on your page and click **Next.** The next dialog box asks for a Page URL and a Page Title. (Uncheck one of the default boxes if you don't want its category to appear on your page.)

5. Click in the **Page URL** text box and type index.html as the name of the file you're creating.

   Click inside the **Page Title** text box and type the title that you want to be displayed on the browser's title bar when someone accesses you page. When you're done, click **Next**.

FIGURE 18.2

The Personal Home Page Wizard.

❶   Checked boxes show the type of information that will be included on your page

6. The next set of dialog boxes ask questions based on the options you chose in step 4. Fill in the information (as listed below) and click **Next** to advance from box to box.

- *Employee Information.* Enables you to select options to display your **Job Title**, **Key Responsibilities**, **Department or workgroup**, **Manager**, and **Direct reports**.

- *Current Projects.* Click in the **Current Project** text box and type a few things you're working on, pressing Enter after each one. Select a presentation style **Bullet list**, **Numbered list**, or **Definition list**.

- *Hot List: Interesting Web Sites.* Choose how to display the list of sites you like. You can display them as a **Bullet list**, **Numbered list**, **Definition list,** or **Import from Web page**. If you select **Import from Web page**, type the page's URL in the **File** text box.

- *Biographical Information.* Select from **Academic**, **Professional, or Personal** format.

- *Personal Interests.* Type a few of your interests and choose how you want them to be displayed (see Figure 18.3).

- *Contact Information.* You can include as much contact information as you want. Check the box next to **Postal Address**, **E-mail address**, **URL address**, **Office phone**, **FAX number,** and **Home phone** and type the information in the text box.

Index is the first page

Web sites can consist of many pages. Many Web servers display a file called index.html as the first, or home page, of the site.

Alter your selection

It's no problem to add or delete sections on your Web page. Click the **Back** button as many times as necessary to return to the first box of the Wizard and check or uncheck the boxes next to the sections you want to include or remove. When you're done, click **Next** to move through the Wizard.

Add Hot Links

Even if you're not sure you want to include links to other Web sites on your page, be sure and check the box next to **Hot List: Interesting Web Sites**. You'll learn how to work with links in FrontPage Express later in this chapter.

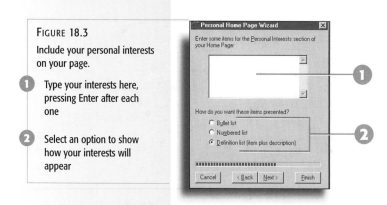

FIGURE 18.3

Include your personal interests on your page.

1 Type your interests here, pressing Enter after each one

2 Select an option to show how your interests will appear

- *Com**m**ents and Suggestions.* People who visit your page will be able to tell you what they think of it. Unless you're planning to publish your Web page with the Microsoft Internet Information Server, choose the **Use Link, send e-mail to this address** option and type your email address in the text box.

7. When you've completed the boxes that ask for information on the sections you selected, a new dialog box appears showing your sections and asking in what order you would like them organized. To move an item, click it and then click **Up** or **Down**. When the list is organized properly, click **Next.**

8. That's all you need for now! Click **Finish** for FrontPage Express to build the page, as illustrated in Figure 18.4.

Now that you've created your page, take a moment to save it. If you don't save it before you make changes, you won't be able to return to the page's current shell format. Worse, you run the risk of losing all your work if you exit from Windows without saving the page. Saving takes only a few seconds and preserves your hard work.

Saving your new Web page

1. With the page you created on the screen, click the FrontPage Express **File** menu and choose **Save**. The Save As dialog box appears.

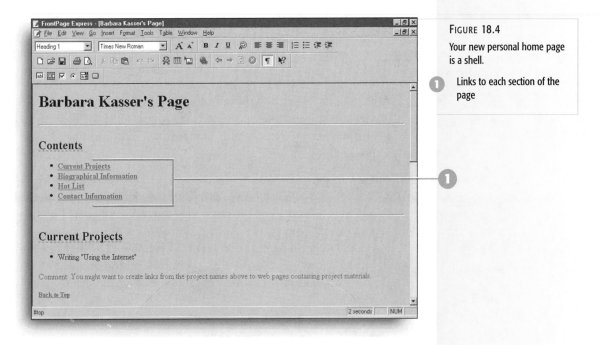

FIGURE 18.4

Your new personal home page is a shell.

① Links to each section of the page

2. By default, the FrontPage Express defaults to saving your page onto a Web server. Change the default and save the page to the hard drive of your computer by clicking the **As File** button.

3. The standard Windows Save As dialog box appears. Navigate to the folder where you want to save the file. Click in the **File name** text box and type the same name that you assigned the file in Step 6 of the previous step-by-step exercise. (You probably named the file index.html.) It's not necessary to type the file extension .html because it will be automatically assigned.

4. Click **Save**. Now you're ready to make changes to your page.

SEE ALSO

➤ *You'll find information on Java applets on page 19.*

Editing Your FrontPage Express Web Page

Not done yet

Don't close the page just yet. In the next few Step by Step exercises, you transform your page from a shell to a masterpiece!

Basically, you created a shell when you set up your personal Web page with the Wizard. Now it's time to fill in the blanks and enter some information on the sections you selected. Before you begin, you need to understand a few basics about FrontPage Express.

First, working in FrontPage Express is a lot like working in your favorite word processing program. For example, as you reach the end of a line, FrontPage Express wraps the text to the next line, so you needn't press Enter. Adding formatting options like bold, italic, and underline to existing text is accomplished by highlighting the text and clicking the appropriate button on the Formatting toolbar. Most other Windows editing commands work as well.

Paragraph Styles Are Important

Keep in mind that the text you enter is always part of a paragraph style. Table 18.2 displays the name of the available styles and provides information about each one.

TABLE 18.2   FrontPage Express paragraph styles

Style Name	What It Does
Normal	Used for entering regular text without text attributes.
Address	Used to create the name and email address of the owner of the page. The Address style is generally seen at the bottom of a page.
Bulleted List	Creates a list of items, with each item preceded by a bullet character. When the Bulleted List style is selected, pressing Enter adds another bullet to the list.
Defined Term	Items controlled by the Defined Term style appear lined up against the left margin.
Definition	Used in conjunction with the Defined Term style, items using this style are formatted with an indent.

Style Name	What It Does
Directory List	When the Directory List style is selected, the resulting text appears to be formatted like a Bulleted List. However, both Internet Explorer and Navigator display text formatted with the Directory List style differently. Play it safe and use Bulleted List instead.
Formatted	Recognizes multiple blank spaces inserted with the keyboard Spacebar. (Normal HTML code won't use more than one space between characters.)
Headings 1–6	The higher the number, the larger the font and darker the text.
Menu List	Like Directory List style, choosing Menu List formats text like the Bulleted List style. Don't use this style because it is handled differently by browsers; use Bulleted List instead.
Numbered List	When this item is selected, each line is preceded by a number.

If you want to select a style before you type text, click the down arrow on the Change Style button on the Formatting toolbar and choose the style you want. To change the style of existing text, highlight the text and then choose the style you want from the list of available styles.

Formatting and editing text

1. The page you created and then saved should be on the screen now. (If you accidentally closed the page, click the **File** menu from within FrontPage Express, and choose **Open**. When the Open File dialog box appears, click in the **From File** text box and click **Browse** to move to the folder where you saved the page. Select the file and click **Open**.)

2. The page title appears at the top of the page. Select the title and click the Center button on the Formatting toolbar. The title, still highlighted, appears centered on the page.

3. Click the Increase Text Size button once to make the text bigger.

Beware of fancy fonts

Even though you might be tempted to use some of the more dramatic fonts you have installed on your computer, restrict your choices to common fonts such as Arial, Times New Roman, or Courier. A page that looks great on your computer won't display properly on another computer unless the same font is installed. By choosing a standard font, you'll be sure that your page always appears correctly—no matter who's looking at it.

Replace placeholders

If you included a section for biographical information or another section for which you need to input your own personal data, you'll see some words that hold the space open. For example, instead of a calendar date, you might see the word "Date." Replace all the placeholders with real information.

4. Click the down arrow next to the Change Font button, and choose another font from the list. You'll be able to choose a font that's installed on your computer.

5. Click the Text Color button ![icon]. When the Color dialog box appears, click a new color for the text and click **OK**. Make sure that you don't choose the same color for your background, because this will render the text invisible. (The text won't appear in the new color until you deselect it.)

6. Deselect the text by pressing the right arrow key.

7. Move down through your page and select some text you want to change. When the text appears highlighted, type the new text.

8. Continue replacing text by repeating step 7.

9. Add text anywhere on the page. Click on the spot where you want the text to begin and start typing. Because FrontPage Express is a WYSIWYG editor, the text you add appears exactly as it will when you view the page in your browser.

10. To change the bland background, click **Format** and then **Background**. The Page properties dialog box appears with the **Background** tab selected, as shown in Figure 18.5.

11. Click the down arrow next to the **Background** that's currently selected and choose a color from the list. Don't choose the color that's the same as your text. Click **OK** to close the Properties dialog box and see the new color on your page.

12. Save the page by clicking **File** and then **Save**.

Adding a Link to Another Web Site

If you included a section for Hot Links on your Personal Web Page, FrontPage Express added sample links that you can modify. You need to point these links to your favorite Web sites. Before you begin, make a note of a URL or two that you want to add.

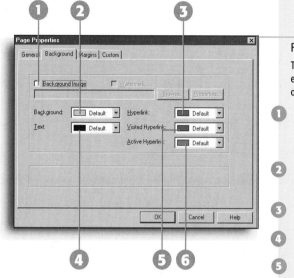

FIGURE 18.5

The Page Properties dialog box enables you to change the look of your page.

1 Check this box to insert an image file for the background

2 Changes the background color

3 Changes the color of links

4 Changes the color of the text

5 Changes the color of links you've visited

6 Changes the color of the link that's being clicked

A hyperlink is actually made up of two parts. The first part, called the *anchor*, is the text that appears in the Web page.

Adding working links

1. Scroll down the page to the Hot List section. Highlight the first sample link (**Sample Site 1**) and type the text you want to use as the anchor. As you begin typing, the highlighted text is replaced by the characters you type.

2. Select the anchor text you just typed and click the Create or Edit Hyperlink button 🔗 on the Standard toolbar. The Create Hyperlink window appears with the World Wide Web tab chosen, as shown in Figure 18.6.

4. Make sure that the **Hyperlink Type** reads **http:**. If it doesn't, click the down arrow and choose **http://** from the list. Highlight the sample URL that appears in the **URL** text box and type another URL. (If you can't think of one, use www.geocities.com/Paris/LeftBank/4487, the address of my Geocities page). Check your typing to make sure you didn't make a typing mistake and click **OK**. The link appears on your page.

Other protocols

A hyperlink doesn't need to point to a Web page. In addition to the http protocol you selected, you can point a link to other Web protocols, including a file, *FTP, Gopher,* https, mailto, news, *Telnet,* and wais.

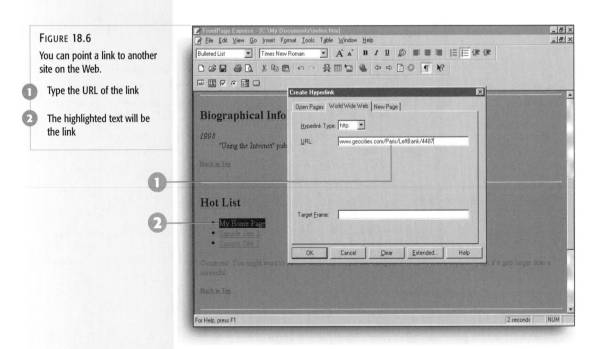

5. (Optional) Use an existing hyperlink on a page displayed in Internet Explorer to create a quick link. Open Internet Explorer (you need to be connected to the Internet) and move to the page that contains the link that you want to use. Click that link and drag it into the FrontPage Express window. When the mouse pointer is positioned where you want the link to appear, release the mouse button. The link appears in your page, along with its anchor.

6. When you've added a few links, test them before you publish your page. If you're not already connected, connect to the Internet. Position the mouse pointer over the link and view the URL of the link in the status bar.

7. Edit a link by selecting the anchor and clicking the Create or Edit Hyperlink button on the Standard toolbar. When the Edit Hyperlink dialog box appears, make your changes and click **OK**.

FrontPage Express Bug

At the time this book was written, FrontPage Express contained a program *bug*. Many Internet Explorer users reported errors when trying to edit a Web page by clicking the **Edit** button on the Standard toolbar. Additionally, FrontPage Express was unable to execute a **Follow Hyperlink** command. Instead of the expected Web page, an error message appeared, similar to the one shown in Figure 18.7, saying that FrontPage Express was unable to open the location.

FIGURE 18.7

An error occurs when FrontPage Express tries to open a Web page.

The folks at Microsoft recognize the problem and have posted two work-around solutions. If you see a message like the one in Figure 18.7, visit the Microsoft support site at support. microsoft.com/support/kb/articles/q174/9/74.asp and follow the instructions. Hopefully this problem will be resolved in the near future.

Creating a Page with Netscape Composer

Netscape Composer is the component of the Communicator suite that enables you to create great looking Web pages. Composer is a wonderful WYSIWYG editor. You can create a Web page from scratch, or you can take the easy route and visit Netscape's Web site to access the Page Wizard or Netscape templates. If you use a wizard or template, you can make editing changes later on in Composer.

Composer provides in-depth support for basic HTML elements, such as links, images, and tables. The editing screen looks a lot like Navigator's browsing window, with a similar menu structure and two toolbars. The Composition toolbar is used to add

Composer isn't installed

If you can't find Composer on your Windows **Start** menu, or you're sure you didn't install it, you can download Composer from the Netscape site in only a few minutes. Go to the Netscape home page at home.netscape.com and click the link to **SmartUpdate**. Follow the onscreen prompts to download and set up Composer or any other program in the Netscape Communicator suite.

standard HTML features, and the Formatting toolbar takes care of character and paragraph formatting. Composer works best when it's used to design a few individual pages or a small site. Composer doesn't offer support for frames or forms.

Composer offers the following features to make your Web page creation easier:

- Supports rich formatting, including fonts, styles, paragraph alignment, and bulleted and numbered lists
- Includes built-in spelling checker
- Supports drag-and-drop images, links, and Java applets
- Includes Page Wizard and page templates
- Enables easy table creation and editing

Working with Netscape's Wizards and Templates

Creating a page with the Netscape Page Wizard or Templates is fast and easy. Best of all, you can create a dynamite-looking page without needing to know anything about HTML. Because you'll be visiting the Netscape Web site when you set up your page using the Wizard or Templates, you need to be connected to the Internet.

Begin your page with the Netscape Page Wizard

1. Open Navigator. Click the **File** menu, choose **New,** and then select **Page From Wizard**. Navigator appears on the screen and the Netscape Page Wizard page loads one frame of a three-framed page.

2. Scroll down the Page Wizard page and read the instructions. When you're ready to begin creating your page, click the **Start** button. The **Instructions** frame displays instructions for building your page while a preview of the page you're building appears in the right (**Preview**) frame.

3. Click the **give your page a title** link in the Instructions frame. The **Choices** text box appears in the **Choices** frame, located across the bottom of the page, as illustrated in Figure 18.8.

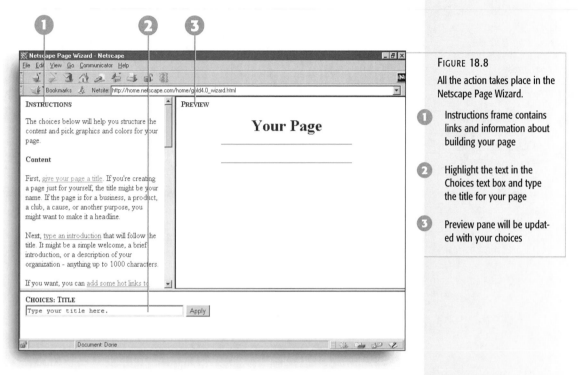

FIGURE 18.8

All the action takes place in the Netscape Page Wizard.

1 Instructions frame contains links and information about building your page

2 Highlight the text in the Choices text box and type the title for your page

3 Preview pane will be updated with your choices

4. Highlight the text in the **Choices** text box and type your page title. When you're done typing, click the **Apply** button. Your title now appears in the **Preview** pane.

5. Click the **type an introduction** link. A new text box appears in the **Choices** pane. Highlight the text that appears in the box and type a brief introduction to your page. When you're done, click the **Apply** button. Your Introduction text is added to your new page in the **Preview** pane.

6. Add a favorite link or two to your new page by scrolling down in the **Instructions** pane and clicking the **add some hot links to other Web pages** link (see Figure 18.9). Two new text boxes appear in the **Choices** pane.

Skip a category

Click the links and type text only for the sections you want on your page. If you don't want to include a section, such as an introduction or a conclusion, skip the link on the list in the Instructions frame.

FIGURE 18.9

A link to the Macmillan Computer Publishing site is being created.

1 The URL of the link

2 The link title is typed here

3 Click this button to delete links

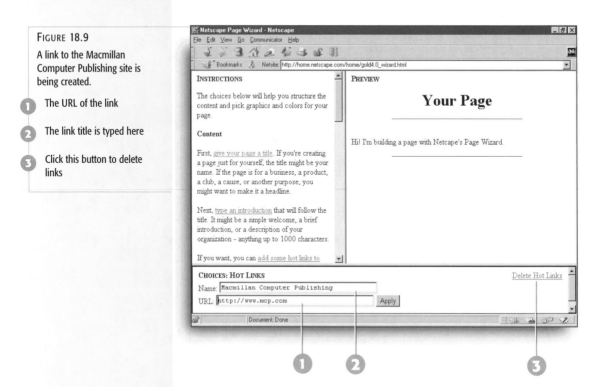

Don't want links?

You're not locked into adding links to your page. If you change your mind after you've added them, click the **Delete Hot Links** link to quickly remove them.

7. Highlight the text in the **Name:** text box and type the name of a favorite page. Next, highlight the text in the **URL:** text box and type the URL for the favorite page. (My Geocities page is at http://www.geocities.com/Paris/LeftBank/4487.) When you're done, click the **Apply** button. Your link appears in the Preview pane.

8. Repeat steps 6 and 7 for each link you want to add.

9. Add some conclusion text to your page by scrolling down in the **Instructions** pane and clicking the **type a paragraph of text to serve as a conclusion** link. When the conclusion text box appears in the **Choices** pane, highlight the text and type your conclusion text, taking care not to get long-winded and type something over 1,000 characters long. Click the **Apply** button when you're done to move your conclusion text to the **Preview** pane.

10. People can give you feedback if you add an email link to yourself. Click the **add an email link** link. When the email link box appears in the **Choices** pane, highlight the sample text and type your email address. Click **Apply**. An email link is added to the page, but you might need to scroll down in the **Preview** pane to see it.

11. Look over your page in the **Preview** pane. If you want to change anything you've added so far, click the link in the **Instructions** frame to the section you want to change. The text box that contains the text you typed for that section appears. Make the changes you want to the text in the box and click **Apply** to update the text in the **Preview** pane.

Dressing up your page with the Page Wizard

1. The page you created in the last step-by-step is visible on the screen. Scroll down the **Instructions** frame to the **Looks** section.

2. Choose one of the preset Netscape color schemes by scrolling down in the **Instructions** pane and clicking the **a preset color combination...** link. A sample of 18 color schemes appears in the **Choices** pane, as shown in Figure 18.10.

3. Click one of the color schemes that you like, and see how it looks in the **Preview** pane. If you want, try a few of the color combinations and choose the one you like best.

4. (Optional) If you would rather add your own touch to the color scheme, do so by clicking the links below the link to the preset color combinations. One at a time, click the links to **background color**, **background pattern**, **text color**, **link color**, and **visited link color**, and choose a color from the palette displayed in the **Choices** frame.

5. Click the **choose a bullet style** link and pick the style of bullet you want to use to set off the lists on your page from the **Choices** frame. You'll be able to pick from simple bullets to animated squares.

FIGURE 18.10

Preset color combinations make your page look professional.

1 Click one of these color combinations

2 The color scheme changes in the **Preview** pane

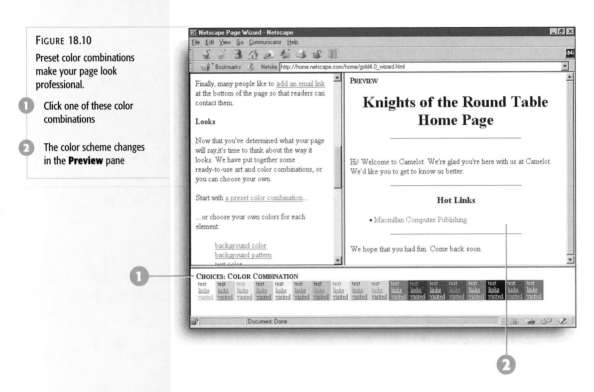

6. Choose a custom separator bar, or horizontal line, by clicking the **choose a horizontal rule style** link. Eighteen line styles appear in the **Choices** pane. Scroll through and click the one you like.

7. You're done! Look at the completed page in the **Preview** pane and make any corrections now.

Saving the page to your computer

1. Even though you might not be aware of it, all the work you've done so far is up on the Netscape Web site. Before you go on, you need to save the page to your computer. Scroll down the **Instruction** pane and click the **Build** button. Your new page appears in a Navigator window, as shown in Figure 18.11.

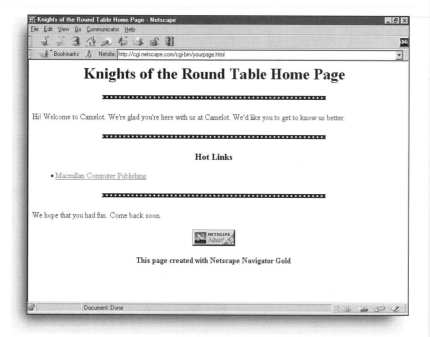

FIGURE 18.11
The completed page appears in Navigator.

2. Click the Navigator **File** menu and select **Edit Page**. The page now appears in Netscape Composer.

3. Save the page to your computer by clicking **File,** and then **Save**. When the Save As dialog box appears, navigate to the location where you want to save the page. The filename `yourpage.html` appears as the default name of the page. To change the default name, click in the **File name** text box and replace the default name with whatever you would like. Click **Save**.

Using some neat link tricks in Composer

1. Don't quit quite yet! First, add a link to a site on the Web that you've set as a bookmark. Click the **Communicator** menu and select **Bookmarks** and then **Edit Bookmarks.** The Bookmarks window layers over Composer.

2. Click a bookmark that you would like to use as a link and drag it onto the Composer window. As you drag, your mouse pointer displays a small box attached to the tip (see

Edit the page in Composer

Because Navigator and Composer look so similar, it's easy to forget which program you're using. Pages are edited in Composer and then previewed in Navigator.

Figure 18.12). When the pointer is located on the position you want the link to appear on the page in Composer, release the mouse button.

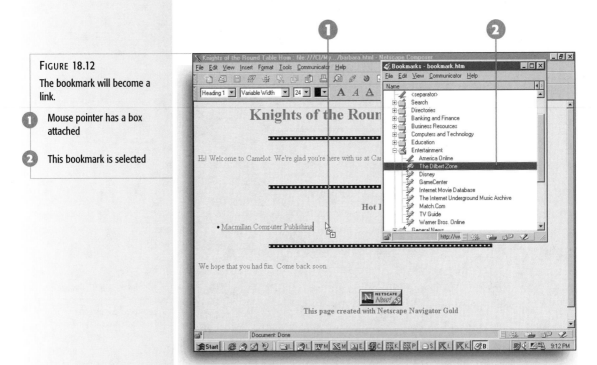

3. Repeat step 2 to copy additional bookmarks to use as links. When you're done, close the Bookmarks window by clicking the Close box on its title bar.

4. Some Web pages get quite lengthy. Make it easy for your viewers to get from the bottom to the top of your page with a mouse click. Press Ctrl+Home to move to the top of the page. When the insertion point is flashing at the top left corner of the page, click the Insert Target button ⬡ on the Composition toolbar. Type Top in the resulting **Target Properties** text box. A target icon appears.

5. Press Ctrl+End to move to the bottom of the page. Press the Enter key to move the insertion point to a blank and click the Insert Link button ⬡. The Character Properties

dialog box appears with the **Link** tab selected. The tab is divided into two sections.

6. In the first section, **Link source**, click inside the **Enter text to display for new link** text box and type Return to top.

Move down to the second section, titled **Link to**. First, click the option button next to **Current page** and click **Top** in the **Select a named target in current page** text box. **#Top** appears in the **Link to a page location or a local file** text box, as displayed in Figure 18.13.

Composer distorts the graphics

Remember that you're working in Composer, not Navigator. The Netscape icon that was automatically inserted into your page might look distorted or squashed. Don't worry; it'll look fine when you view it in Navigator.

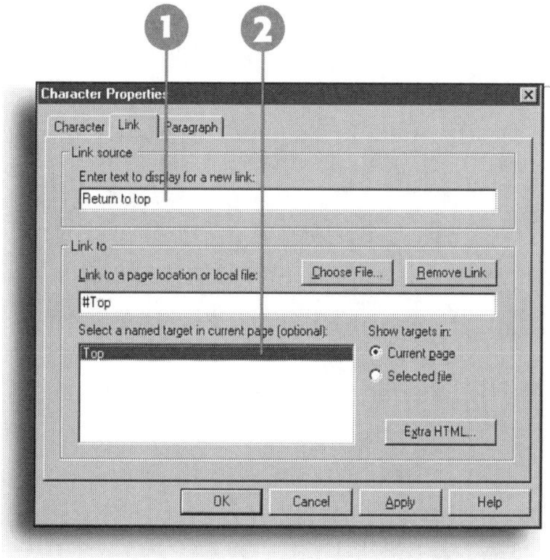

FIGURE 18.13

You control what happens when someone clicks a link on your page.

1 Type the text for the link

2 The target shows the location to which the link leads

7. Click **OK**. The Character Properties dialog box closes and you're returned to the Composer screen. The words Return to top appear at the end of the page.

8. Test your links by previewing your page in Navigator. Click the Preview in Navigator button. If you're informed you need to save the changes to the file before you can preview it, click **Yes** to save the file.

9. The page appears in Navigator. Click each of your links to make sure that they're working properly. If not, switch back to Composer. Highlight a non-working link and then click the Insert Link button. When the Character Properties dialog box appears, correct the error and click **OK**.

10. Remove a link on your page in Composer by highlighting it and selecting **Edit**, and then **Delete**. The link disappears from the page.

SEE ALSO

➤ *Review how to set and work with Navigator Bookmarks on page 64.*

➤ *You might have already created a résumé with the Netscape résumé template on page 286.*

Pictures Tell a Story

Graphics images add appeal to most Web pages. Pictures draw the eyes of your viewers and catch their interest. Adding a few graphics to a personal Web page is a sure way to make certain that people stay and read your information when they land on your page.

Only two types of images are commonly used on Web pages—*GIF* (Graphic Interchange Format) and *JPEG* (Joint Photographic Experts Group) files. Both of these file types work well on Web pages because they offer good compression ratios. Compression is important on the Web because the smaller the image file size, the faster it will download and appear on your viewer's browser screen. (Don't you hate waiting while a picture slowly unfolds before your eyes?)

Getting Images for Your Page

Images for your Web page can be obtained in many ways. One great way is to design them yourself. If you're the artistic type, you can use one of the many available computer graphics programs, such as Adobe Photoshop or Corel Graphics, to create your own images.

Another way to obtain images for your Web pages is to create them with a scanner or digital camera. In fact, the images created with a scanner or digital camera can be used in other electronic documents created with the latest versions of other computer software, such as Microsoft Word.

Scanners take a picture of the image and then convert the image to a graphics file. You can scan photographs, artwork, or even text documents. The most popular scanners come in two styles—flatbed and sheet feeder. A flatbed scanner looks like a desktop copy machine. A sheet-fed scanner takes up less space than a flatbed model. Some sheet-feeder scanners are small enough to sit behind your computer keyboard, making them handy to use as you work. Most scanners are easy to set up and install. Additionally, the price of scanners has dropped significantly in the past few years, making them affordable to most computer users.

If you're going to need a good number of photographs for your Web pages, consider purchasing a digital camera. Digital cameras bypass the paper stage because they store the images on your computer instead of negatives. You take photographs with a digital camera like you would with your regular camera. The resulting pictures must be downloaded to your computer with a serial cable that's part of the initial camera equipment. The images can be used on Web pages or other electronic documents. Digital cameras involve cutting-edge technology. Although the price of the cameras has decreased in the past year or so, they are still expensive. Additionally, your computer needs a large hard drive and lots of RAM to work efficiently with the images.

In addition to creating, scanning, or photographing your own graphics, plenty of other sources are available that can supply you with images others have designed. You can purchase clip art packages that contain thousands of uncopyrighted images for your use, or you can find images the fun and easy way—on the Web!

Thousands of images are available on the Web free of charge. In fact, many Web sites are devoted strictly to the task of providing you with these images. Run a quick search for *clipart* in Yahoo! or your favorite search engine to find many sources of great images for your page.

Table 18.3 lists some excellent places to begin exploring Web clip art.

EasyPhoto makes scanning a breeze

If you're serious about scanning, Storm Technolgies makes a line of inexpensive scanners that work great. Take a look at their line of scanners and related products at www. easyphoto.com.

TABLE 18.3 **Great clip art for free**

Title	Address	Description
Clipart Directory	www.clipart.com	A listing of clip art sites
Andy's Art Attack	www.andyart.com	A great source for free, original artwork and graphic design tips
Barry's Clipart	www.barrysclipart.com	Thousands of clip art Server images you can use
The Clipart Connection	www.clipart connection.com	Another large collection of free graphics connection
The Mousepad	www.vikimouse.com	A neat collection of graphics drawn by a mouse

SEE ALSO

➤ For information on using Yahoo!, turn to page 134.

Inserting an Image in Your Web Page

Both FrontPage Express and Composer make inserting an image a snap. Both programs support drag and drop. If your image is open in one program like Corel Photoshop or a shareware program like Paint Shop Pro, and FrontPage Express or Composer is also open, you can click the image you want to use and drag it into your Web page. Or, you can insert an image that's stored on the hard drive of your computer by using the FrontPage Express or Composer menu.

Inserting an image on your page

1. Open FrontPage Express or Composer and open your Web page file.

2. Click the **Insert** menu and choose **Image**.

3. Type the folder path and file location of the image in the resulting **From File** text box (FrontPage Express) or the **Image Location** text box (Composer), and click **OK**.

   The graphic is inserted into your Web page document, placed with the program default size and layout options.

Publishing Your Page

Now that you've created a page, you need to get it posted where people can see it. Unfortunately, no standard exists for publishing your page. Most Web hosting sites offer different instructions for getting your page online. Fortunately, many Web hosts are designed to be user-friendly and provide detailed instructions for getting your page online.

Contact your ISP and find out if your contract includes free personal space. If so, find out from your ISP what you need to do to upload the page. You might need to use special FTP software. Another option for a Web home for your page might be a Web community. These communities are springing up all over the Web. You can post your page in a "neighborhood" free of charge and have fun with your virtual neighbors. Two great examples of Web communities are Geocities at www.geocities.com and Tripod at www.tripod.com. (I've been a resident of Geocities for years, and I've become great friends with several other Geocities dwellers.) Both Geocities and Tripod offer easy upload directions for placing your pages on their servers.

SEE ALSO
➤ *See information about posting pages to the Web on page 438.*

Other Commercial HTML Editors

Although FrontPage Express and Composer offer a great way to create Web pages, both programs have limitations. After you've practiced a little, consider moving up to an HTML editor that offers more features than either of the two browser suite components. Table 18.4 lists other HTML editors you might want to try. Most of them are shareware, so you'll have a chance to try them out before you buy.

SEE ALSO
➤ *Learn about shareware on page 146.*

Know the filename

Although the instructions for posting your page vary from Web host to host, make sure you know the filename and folder location of the page and graphics files (if any) before you begin. You'll save yourself time and grief if you know where the page and all the images are stored.

Run your own Web server

If you have a permanent connection to the Internet and you're willing to leave your computer running 24 hours a day, you can take advantage of Microsoft's Personal Web Server and run your own Web server. Available free from Microsoft (http://www.microsoft.com/ie/ie40/features/pws.htm), Personal Web Server enables you to host your own Web pages.

TABLE 18.4   A sampling of commercial HTML editors

Program Name	URL	Cost	Comments
Microsoft FrontPage 98	www.microsoft.com/frontpage	$99	The best WYSIWYG HTML editor on the market. With an Office 97 look and feel, FrontPage creates simple pages as well as complex sites with ease. Editor provides WYSIWYG editing, built-in spell checking, easy creation of links and clickable images, forms creation, image type conversion, and more.
CoolCat 4.0	www.anawave.com	$100	Billed as the ultimate WYSIWYG editor, CoolCat can help you create virtually anything that you've seen on the Web. CoolCat also includes features such as Web site management, auto-uploading, Web site optimization, and much, much more.
Coffee Cup	www.coffeecup.com	$30	Shareware product, that comes with its own internal browser. Additionally, a Design Gallery of Images (many animated) to choose from, plus Javascripts and support for Active X technology. The Table Wizard reduces complicated table creation to a few mouse clicks.
Hot Dog 4.5	www.sausage.com	$100	Created in Australia and widely proclaimed by the Internet community, Hot Dog is the choice of many corporate Web designers. The program is easy to use and enables

Program Name	URL	Cost	Comments
			you to create great looking pages with no experience. Although Hot Dog is slightly more expensive than some of the other available HTML editors, the makers give away loads of software with it.
Home Site	www.allaire.com	$79	HomeSite features an intuitive WYSIWYN ("what you see is what you need") interface, and an extensive set of HTML and page-management tools. You'll be able to create pages quickly and preview your pages in HomeSite's built-in browser.
Web Weaver 97	www.mcwebsoft.com	$30	Web Weaver is an easy and comprehensive, feature-rich HTML editor. Tutorials and wizards step you through Web page creation, making you an HTML expert in no time! The program features colored HTML code for easier editing; wizards for advanced HTML elements such as frames, tables, and forms; easy-to-use tool bars; context-sensitive help; link verification and more!

Setting Up a Small Business on the Web

Posting your company site on the Web

Attracting customers and clients to your site

Using a virtual office

Backing up important data through the Internet

Do You Need a Web Site?

In today's economic climate, more and more workers are moving away from large corporations and traditional nine-to-five jobs to work in their own small, sometimes home-based businesses. These businesses, called *SOHO businesses* (short for small office, home office), have a silent partner in the Internet. First, a small business can set up a Web site to advertise and sell products and services. In some ways, Web sites are the great equalizers of business—large and small companies can have equally impressive sites.

The World Wide Web is a great place to advertise your products or services. Web sites provide universal exposure at a lower cost than more traditional advertising such as magazine or newspaper spreads or television and radio commercials. However, company Web sites aren't the sure-fire moneymakers some people believe them to be.

Before you jump on the Web bandwagon and post your company's site, consider whether the Web is an appropriate place for your business. The design, marketing, and maintenance of a Web site can take a good deal of time, effort, and money. Consider the following points before you decide to post a Web site:

1. Is your product or service unique in some way? If not, are you selling it for a lower price than the competition?

2. Does your product or service appeal to people outside of your immediate market area?

3. Would your sales benefit by advertising to customers around the country or the world?

4. Can you effectively deliver your product or service nationally or internationally?

If the answer to any of the above four questions is yes, a Web site might be a great addition to your business. If you answered yes to more than one of the questions, a Web site should figure into your short-range plans.

If you answered no to all four questions, don't dismiss the thought of a Web site. Many local businesses use their Web sites as a way to provide information to their local customers, or as a means of building name recognition.

Whether you decide to post a Web site to sell a product or service, provide information, build name recognition, or just for fun, make sure that your site is designed correctly. As with most other forms of advertising, a poorly designed Web site can make your business look silly or incompetent.

Call in an Expert

From your experiences in the last chapter, you've learned some Web site-building basics. Unfortunately, if what you learned in Chapter 18 is the limit of your knowledge of Web page design, it's probably not a good idea for you to be the chief designer in charge of setting up your first company Web site. (However, you probably know enough to be able to modify your site after it's designed.) Consider obtaining the services of a professional Web site designer to present your company to the world.

Web site design companies come in a variety of shapes and sizes ranging from one-person shops to major advertising agencies. Evaluate a few companies before deciding who will build your Web site. The following is information that Web design companies should supply to you:

- Ask the designer for the URLs of other Web sites the company has created. Use these other sites as references to see if you like the designer's style.

- Get client references from the designer. When you speak with clients, find out how helpful the designer was in making suggestions to improve the site. Also, if the designer helped with the site marketing, how successful were the marketing efforts? Because Web site advertising is new to you, you will need to rely somewhat on the designer.

- Make sure the designer explains exactly what you are paying for before any work begins. Find out if the work includes all the graphic design (or whether you need to supply artwork), as well as domain name registration and Web hosting. Will the designer be assisting in the marketing of the Web site, or is an additional charge? What's the price for updates? You'll need to know what's included in each designer's proposal to make a smart decision.

Finding a good Web site designer can be accomplished in several ways. One easy way is to do a search on the Web. Check into your favorite search engine or navigational guide and search for web designer. Most Web designers' sites will also contain links to samples of their work.

If you want to work with a local designer, look through your phone directory. (My local phone book lists more than 40 Web site designers.) Another excellent way to find a Web site designer is to find Web sites you like, and then see who designed them. Many Web pages include a link back to the company that created them. If not, just send a message to the owner of the site you like, asking for some contact information.

Your Name as Your Web Identity

Choosing your domain name is an important decision—it's how you'll be identified on the Web. Your domain name is a major component of your overall Web site advertising campaign. Therefore, choose a domain name that is close to, if not the same as, your business name. Alternatively, choose a domain name that's catchy or easy to remember.

Registering your name is the next step. An organization called InterNIC handles the registration and makes sure that each name is unique. For the top-level portion of your domain name (the ending three letters), you'll probably want a name that ends in .COM or .ORG

All over the world

International domains, such as .jp (Japan) or .il (Israel), are registered at specific international domain name registries.

Second level domain names are the names just before the final portion of the name, as in www.*yourname*.com. The second level is where you put your company name, or something easy to remember. For example, The Optical Studio, which bonds prescription lenses to scuba masks, uses the name www.seefish.com.

Using a name other than the name of your own company is sometimes preferable if, as in the case of The Optical Studio, the name makes the Web site easier to remember.

SEE ALSO

➤ *For detailed information on domain names, review page 90.*

Obtaining a Domain Name

After you've chosen a few potential names for your site, you need to find out if any of them are available. You can research domain names in several places. Search for a place on the Web, or, visit the ReignYourDomain site at www.reignyourdomain.org. The site was put together as a public service by a Web designer named Deborah Levitt of As Was (www.aswas.com).

Using ReignYourDomain's Domain Name Search Feature

1. Type www.reignyourdomain.org in the Address box of your browser and press Enter. The ReignYourDomain Web site appears, as shown in Figure 19.1.

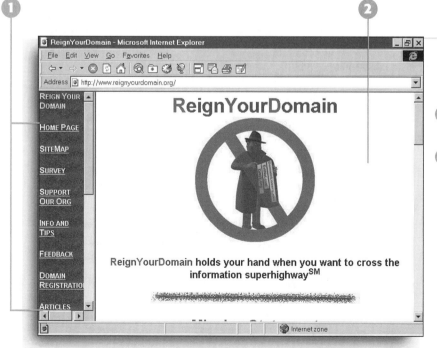

FIGURE 19.1

Check out your domain name and register it at the ReignYourDomain site.

1 Choose a link for more information

2 Main frame displays the selected link

2. Click the Domain Registration link in the navigation frame. When the Register Your Own Domains page appears, use the scrollbar in the main frame (on the right side) to scroll to the searches link.

3. Click the **Searches** link. When the Search page appears, read through the text for specific instructions on performing a search of the InterNIC database of domain names.

4. Scroll down to the search box and click in the **Search InterNIC** text box. For practice, type the name of a domain that is already in existence. The name should include the top- and second-level domains, but not the www (as in candylandwarehouse.com). Click the **Search InterNIC** button.

5. When the InterNIC results page appears, scroll through the page and view the registration information about the domain name you typed.

Use the information

Registration information can be a valuable business tool. Feel free to look up InterNIC registration information about any domain name on the Web.

6. Now that you have a feel for how the process works, click the **Back** button on your browser to go back to the search page. Enter the name you would like to use for your domain (for example, mycompany.com) in the text box and click the **Search InterNIC** button. Don't enter www in front of the name you type.

The results page tells you if your domain name is available. If not, click the **Back** button and try your search again with a different name.

SEE ALSO

➤ *Find some assistance about navigating through frames on page 107.*

Register Your Name

After you've determined that the name you chose is available, you must register the name before you can use it. Don't wait too long; someone else might register the name while you're deliberating! Your Web designer or Web hosting company can register the domain name for you. (If you let someone else register your name, make sure that they're trustworthy and experienced. Some scam artists promise to register the domain name, but disappear after they take your money.)

If you would like to register your domain yourself, you can get help with the process by returning to ReignYourDomain and clicking on the **Domain Registration** link. Follow the instructions on the resulting page to complete the process. If you decide to register the domain yourself, you'll need the name of the Web server that's hosting your site as well as its IP address. Obtain the relevant information from your Web hosting company.

Finding a Host for Your Site

Having a Web site designer and a domain name is like having an interior decorator and name for a retail store—it's a great start, but useless without a location. The computer files that make up your site need to be stored on a Web server. Instead of spending tens of thousands of dollars purchasing your own Web server, you can rent space on someone else's server for a nominal fee.

Check with your ISP first to find out if they'll host your business site. Most likely, the service won't be free. Most Web space that's included with your monthly dial-up service is usually limited to personal Web pages, and doesn't include the use of your own domain name. However, your ISP might offer hosting services for businesses. Next, use your favorite search engine or navigational guide or look in your local phone book to find companies that specialize in *Web hosting*.

Make your decision on who will house your pages based on who offers the best service. Table 19.1 shows some of the common services offered by a Web host.

TABLE 19.1   **Important Web hosting features**

Service	What You Get
Data storage	All your text, graphics, and special effects such as sound or videos can add up to a considerable amount of space. Make sure that you know how much space you can use before you sign up; additional space can be expensive.
Data served	Each time someone accesses your Web site, the server sends information (text, graphics, sound files, and so on) back to the user. The larger and more popular your site is, the more data that the server sends out (serves). Find out if your site has limits on the amount of information it can send out.
Accurate statistics	Many Web hosts furnish statistics about the number of hits, the dates and times, and even the domain from which your site was accessed.
Email forwarding	Email forwarding is a great tool. Your site contains an email link that sends mail to your Web host. The mail is automatically forwarded to an email address you specify.
Connections to the Internet	Make sure your Web host has a direct or high-speed Internet connection. Also make sure that if the connection goes down, for any reason, an alternative plan is in place. (Otherwise, your site will be inaccessible until the problem is fixed.)

When you start your business on the Web, use a Web host that offers different plans. As your Web business grows, you can move into more detailed plans that meet your growing needs. See Figure 19.2 for an example of such a Web-hosting company, RapidSite at www.rapidsite.net/plan_matrix.html.

If finding a Web hosting company sounds like a daunting chore, don't sweat it. Most likely, your Web site designer has a suggestion or two for you. (Many Web designers have working relationships with hosting companies.) Another source for information on Web hosting companies are the Web sites that rate hosting companies, such as The Ultimate Web Host List at www.webhostlist.com. The Ultimate Web Host List ranks the top 25 Web hosting companies each month and posts a list of them, as shown in Figure 19.3.

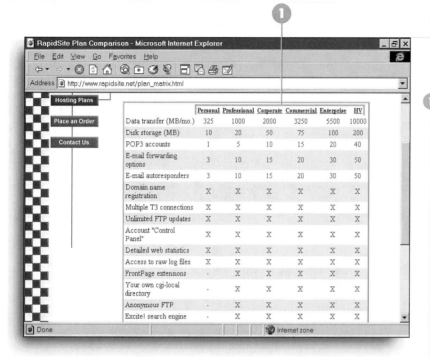

FIGURE 19.2
RapidSite offers a variety of
Web-hosting plans.

1 Each plan offers different
features

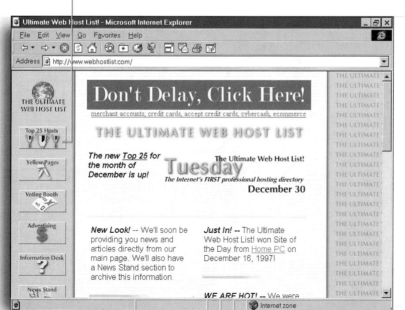

FIGURE 19.3
The Ultimate Web Host List is a
valuable resource.

1 Click the link to see the top
25 Web hosts

Marketing Your Web Site

After you've registered your domain name and posted your Web site, your company is headed for success on the Web. However, unless you're content to wait for someone to stumble across your site, you need to consider some marketing techniques. The world needs to know your site is on the Web before they can see it and gain insight into your company and find out what you offer.

As with traditional advertising, the more heavily you market the site, the better your results will be. Follow some tried and true marketing tactics to get your message out to the people who need to see your site.

Tell the Search Engines You Exist

One of the most important aspects of marketing your Web site is its inclusion in the databases of Web search engines and navigational guides. Even if you do an extensive amount of additional advertising, many of the visitors to your site will arrive via search engines. Instead of waiting for an electronic spider to catalogue your Web site, submit your site to as many search engines as possible.

When someone searches for a word or phrase related to your business, you want your site to show up as high on the results list as possible. Because each search engine catalogs Web sites differently, there isn't a magic formula for rating a top hit with all of them. Improve your chances of appearing in a result list by following some simple rules:

Are you ready?

Don't jump the gun! Before you submit your site to any search engines, make sure that your site is ready for public scrutiny.

1. Make sure that each page of your site has a title. The title is embedded in the HTML of the page and appears in the title bar of the browser when the page is viewed. Titles are important because they are displayed in the result list. In addition, some search engines use the words in the title to help categorize Web pages.

2. Make sure that the most important keywords for each page are included in the body of the page. For example, if your company sells cleaning supplies, make sure that those exact words (**cleaning supplies**) appear in the text.

After your site is ready, visit your favorite search engines and follow the instructions to submit your URL. However, with the ever-increasing number of search engines, it might be impractical to submit your site to each one individually. Some Web promotion companies use specialized methods that assist you in submitting your site to many engines and navigational guides.

The Web Promotion Spider at `www.cyberhammer.com` is one such service designed to distribute your Web site to many areas of the Web. Table 19.2 shows other popular services that submit your Web site to many search engines at one time.

TABLE 19.2   **Popular Web submission services**

Site Name	URL	Comments
Web Site Promotion	`cybermontana.com /Spider/spider.htm`	For approximately $10, CyberMontanta will register your site with 425 search engines and navigational guides.
Acclaim Web Services	`www.acclaimweb.com`	Choose from several packages, each with its own price structure, to register your site and guarantee its exposure.
Quickie Home Page Registration Services	`www.visitorinfo.com /services/reg.htm`	Site offers links to several major registration services on the Web.
Submit-It	`www.submitit.com`	Offers both a limited free service and a fee-based service for submitting your site to search engines and navigational guides.

Using the Submit It! free submission service

1. Type www.submit-it.com in the **Address** box of your browser and press Enter. The Submit-It home page appears.

2. Click the **Submit It! Free** link in the middle of the page. When the Submit It! Free page appears, scroll down the page to the Submit It! Free submission form, as shown in Figure 19.4.

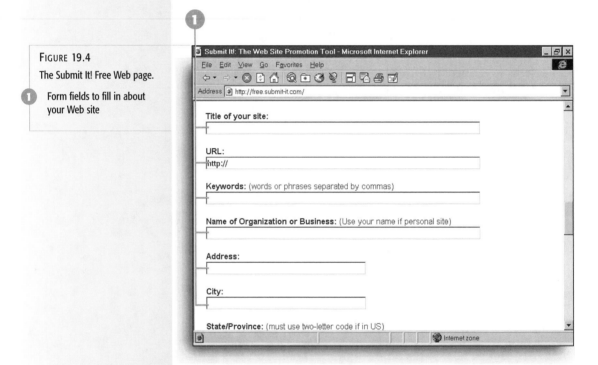

3. Click or press Tab to advance to each of the form fields and complete the information about your Web site. Although you don't need to fill in each field, try to provide as much information as you can.

4. After filling in each of the fields click the **OK, move on the submitting area** button. The Submit It! Free Submitting Area page appears with a verification of all the information you typed in.

5. Verify that the information you typed is correct and scroll
down the page to the list of individual search engines. Each
section of the list contains the name of a search engine, a
description of the engine, and a button to **Submit It!**, as
shown in Figure 19.5.

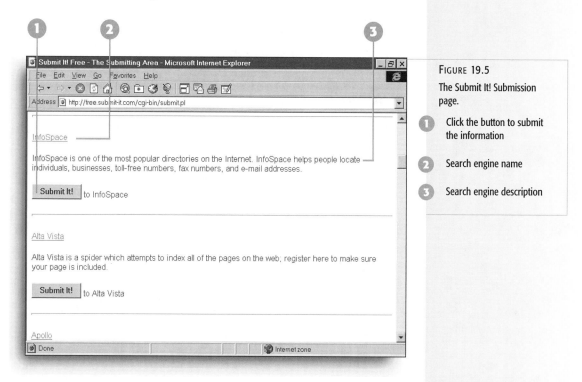

FIGURE 19.5
The Submit It! Submission
page.

1 Click the button to submit
the information

2 Search engine name

3 Search engine description

6. Read the description of each search engine. Click the
Submit It! button to include your page on the search
engines you want. For each engine you choose, a page listing the results of your submission to that search engine
appears.

7. Click the **Back** button to return to the Submission page and
submit your information to another search engine.

8. Repeat steps 6 and 7 until you've selected all the search
engines that you want to list your Web site.

SEE ALSO
➤ *For details on search engines, see page 122.*

Keep 'Em Coming Back

The most successful Web sites are the ones people return to again and again. Make sure your site is interesting and informative. Add links to other sites of interest and include general information about your own area of business. For example, the Crystal Collection site at www.crystalcollection.com not only sells art glass, but contains information about how the glass is made. As a means of providing information and driving traffic to its site, a computer training company called Computer Coach at www.computercoach.com has links to various Web resources on its home page.

In addition to offering information, provide some kind of entertainment on your site. If you include something fun on your Web site, such as music or a special graphic, people will come to see it and will tell their friends! Because everyone loves something for nothing, offer something for free. The Candy Land Warehouse attracts many new viewers at its contest site, as shown in Figure 19.6.

FIGURE 19.6

The Candy Land Warehouse hooks many new viewers with a drawing for free candy.

1 Fields inform the site owners of who's browsing the site

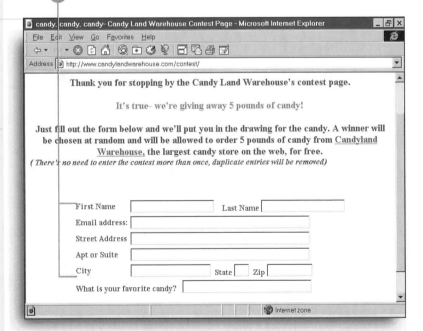

Using the Internet as a Business Tool

Until recently, small businesses had a choice to make—invest significant time and money in computer hardware and software to be able to compete with their larger counterparts, or go without some wonderful technology that would greatly enhance their business. The Internet has made it possible for small businesses to gain access to technology and services that were not easily available or affordable before.

Some of the services that business can now use via the Internet include enhanced communication services, networking, and data backup, all without the time and expense of a specialized computer department.

One of the most compelling reasons for any business to use the Internet is the ease of communication it offers. Services available on the Internet enable businesses to communicate within the company as well as with clients and customers. For example, small businesses can communicate in the following ways:

- Email
- Discussion groups
- Chatting
- Internet Conferencing

Using these communication tools makes the business world smaller and your business more competitive.

Using Email to Communicate

Email is one of the most powerful communication tools for your business. Customers can send you email messages any time, rather than trying to get in touch with you during regular business hours. If you work with clients in another time zone or sell your products internationally, email simplifies your communication. Additionally, clients don't need to spend long (expensive) minutes on hold, waiting for your telephone operators to take the call.

Email is also a great way to keep in touch with your staff. Email messages can take the place of hard-copy corporate memos for many of the items about which you need to talk to your employees. If either you or your employees travel, email is even more valuable.

In the past, using email on the road meant having to carry a laptop computer and possibly making a long-distance call or having to configure someone else's computer to receive your mail. *Browser-based email* enables you to pick up your email from a Web site. You can use any computer connected to the Internet that's running a current browser; simply type the URL of the site and enter your username and email password. Many ISPs currently feature browser-based email. If your ISP doesn't feature browser-based mail, the Web has a number of free services available that enable access to email. In particular, check out MailExite (`mail.excite.com`) and Hotmail (`www.hotmail.com`).

Talking Across the Internet

Getting all your employees together and talking out problems and key issues is helpful for you and your staff. However, if your small business has employees scattered in different locations, meeting face-to-face might be impractical. Instead, use the Internet to get together:

- *Web-based bulletin boards.* With a bulletin board, someone can post a message, and then anyone can reply to the message at a later time. Bulletin boards are also an excellent way for coworkers to share information about joint projects. Setting up a Web-based bulletin board requires some advanced knowledge, so you'll need to call your Web designer for help.

- *Real-Time Talk.* Sometimes your business communications require real-time discussions. (If you've worked through the chapters in this book, you're already familiar with the Internet tools you need!) Both chat and conference programs can be used to facilitate real-time discussions between coworkers or the company and its clients.

Your ISP might have a license for a chat program that you can use without incurring additional charges. A number of Web chat programs are available, with varying features, options, and prices. Parachat (`www.parachat.com`) is a free program that's easy

---

Safety drawbacks

Security issues can be a drawback to using browser-based email. If you're working with sensitive information or competitor information, you might not want to use someone else's computer or a computer in a public place, like a cyber-café.

to set up at your site. Typically, free chat programs require minimal work to implement, but are the least flexible in their options. Most free programs contain advertising or banners for other products and services.

By using services such as Sprint's Internet Conference Center at `www.sprintconf.com`, you can save time and money on your telephone conference calls. The Internet Conference Center enables you to hold a conference call with up to eight participants without the assistance of an operator. After you've set up an account with Sprint (which you do on their Web site), you can log in whenever you want and choose a list of participants from a personal phone book, or enter new ones. The service dials all the numbers for you. The other participants don't even need to have Internet access—they just talk on the phone.

SEE ALSO

➤ *If you need a refresher about chatting, see page 355.For detailed information about setting up a conference call, see page 377.*

Using the Internet as Your Own Local Area Network

The setup and maintenance of a *LAN*, or local area network, can eat up valuable time and money. Linking computers is even more difficult if your business has multiple locations. Instead, set up a cost-effective alternative called a *virtual LAN*. With a virtual LAN, you have access to all the basic features of a regular local area network—email, file sharing, remote access, and group scheduling—for a fraction of the cost. Virtual LANS typically cost between $10 and $50 per month per user.

A virtual LAN enables you to set up an online "office" for yourself on the Internet. Selected others can access your office. Depending on the virtual LAN software you select, people who have access to your office can check if you're online, leave you a message, chat with you, send you email, or share computer files. You can choose to allow a visitor to see what's on your computer screen and grant permission to share your keyboard or mouse.

A number of companies currently offer virtual office software. Two of the most popular are

- *Netscape Virtual Office.* (home.netscape.com/netcenter/vo) Designed by Netscape Corporation and Concentric Network Corporation.
- *Netopia Virtual Office.* (www.netopia.com/software/nvo) A comprehensive package set up by Farallon Communications.

Because information on a virtual LAN travels over the Internet, the connection can be somewhat slower than a regular LAN. All the users of your virtual office need to have a computer and Internet connection.

Backing Up Your Data to the Internet

It happened to me!

While writing this book, MY hard drive crashed! Within 24 hours after my frantic phone call, I received a CD that held all my computer files and Windows Registry from my online backup service.

Data loss should be a major concern for small businesses. If all the company data is stored on one computer, what happens if something happens to that computer? Until recently the process of backing up data involved purchasing and installing a tape drive and making sure that a number of blank tapes were on hand. Even with the necessary hardware, many office managers forget to run the backup or, worse, don't know how to do it. In most offices the backup tapes are stored in the same building as the computer, so in the event of catastrophe (such as a fire) the backup tape would be lost along with the computer!

The Internet offers an economical way to ensure that your company's data is backed up. Connect with an online backup service and take a great load off your shoulders. An *online backup service* connects to your computer at pre-specified intervals and makes a backup copy of your data onto the service's computer. If the unthinkable happens—your computer is damaged or the data is accidentally erased—you can retrieve your data from the service.

Online backup services, such as @Backup shown in Figure 19.7, are easy to use.

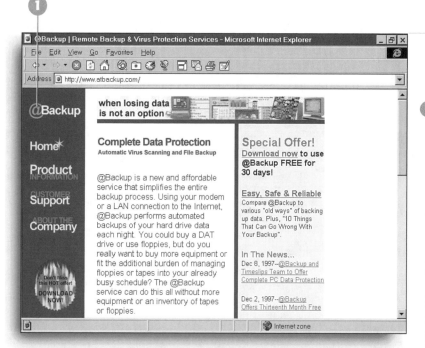

FIGURE 19.7

The @Backup home page provides information about the service.

1 Click a link to get a free 30 day trial

You download and install the software on your computer, indicate which folders to copy and schedule the service, and the program takes care of the rest. Some online backup services offer additional features to ensure the safety of your data and your computer. Table 19.3 lists some popular online backup services.

TABLE 19.3 **Online backup services**

Service	URL	Key Features
@Backup	www.atbackup.com	Offers data encryption and virus checking; stores the past 30 days of data separately.
DataSaver	www.datasaver.com	Backs up files that have been modified since the last backup. After files are copied, they are transferred to a tape and stored in a vault for safekeeping.

continues…

TABLE 19.3   **Continued**

Service	URL	Key Features
Atrieva	www.atrieva.com	Easy to use; offers 24 hour phone support.
Connected Online Backup	www.connected.com	Can get expensive if large amounts of data are uploaded and retrieved.
Safeguard Interactive Backup	www.sgii.com	Calculates backup size and upload time.

Most online backup services let you specify the media on which you receive your backed-up files. For example, you can ask for a tape or CD. Additionally, most services can provide your files to you within 24 hours.

SEE ALSO

➤ *For information on downloading and installing software, review page 151.*

PART

VII

Glossary and Appendixes

Glossary

Active Desktop   A feature of Internet Explorer 4 that controls the appearance and feel of your Windows desktop. Additionally, the Active Desktop integrates the Internet Explorer browser with the desktop.

ASCII format   A format for electronic files that uses only text and doesn't allow you to use text attributes or graphics images.

authentication   A process that occurs behind the scenes during an SSL transaction that makes sure your identity matches the one shown in your digital certificate.

Autosearch   A special browser feature that enables you to type a simple search query directly into the Address box.

binary files   Files that are stored in computer code so that the computer can understand them quickly. Program files and zipped files are examples of binary files.

bookmark   A site that's recorded within Navigator so that you can return to it quickly. Navigator provides a list of bookmarks to which you can add sites you want to revisit.

browser   A program used to navigate the World Wide Web. The browser controls the look of the Web documents and provides tools that enable you to move from one Internet location to another. Internet Explorer and Netscape Navigator are Web browsers.

browser-based email   A way to send and receive email using a Web page instead of a standard email program.

bug   A problem or error in a program that's typically discovered after the program has been released commercially.

cache   The area on your hard drive where temporary information is stored. Web pages you've viewed are stored in your browser's cache.

channel   A Web site that's updated with new information. The updated information is sent to users who have subscribed to the channel.

Channel Definition Format   Microsoft developed CDF as a standard format to be used by all Internet channel content providers. Netscape does not require CDF format.

compressed   A term that describes a file that has been compacted for reducing the time needed to copy it or to save space on the hard drive of your computer. Files that you download from the Internet are often compressed. See also **decompressed**.

computer microphone   A hardware device that plugs into the sound card of your computer and enables you to literally talk over the Internet.

computer virus   A computer virus is a malicious program that hides inside another file or boot sector of your computer. When you use the file, the virus can harm your computer by destroying data and making your system inoperable.

Content Advisor   An Internet Explorer feature that enables parents and other adult "supervisors" to limit children's access to sites on the Internet.

cookie   The exchange of information between your browser and the site you're visiting. A cookie can contain your name, your company name, your location, the type of computer you're using, your operating system, the type and version of your browser, and the Web pages at which you've looked. Cookies are stored on the hard drive of your computer.

crawler   An electronic tool that searches through the Web and adds new Web sites to a database or index. Crawlers are sometimes called electronic spiders, worms, or robots.

cross-posting   The practice of posting the same message simultaneously to a number of newsgroups. See **spam**.

cybercolleges   Universities and colleges that offer online college level classes.

cybermall   A Web site that contains an online collection of merchants.

decompressed   Files that are compressed in size to reduce transmission time or hard drive space on your computer must be inflated before they can be used. Programs like WinZip are designed to decompress files that you copy from the Internet. See also **compressed**.

digital cash   Similar to the principle of a checking account—you submit information to a merchant who uses that information to get cash from your account.

digital certificates   A personal certificate that identifies you or the vendor during secure business transactions. Because digital certificates add an extra layer of security, they are not required for most Web transactions.

digital video camera   A camera that records pictures on computer disks, as opposed to standard photographic techniques.

directory server   A listing of people who are available to participate in an Internet conference.

domain A set of network addresses that are organized in levels. The top level identifies geographic or purpose commonality (for example, the nation that the domain covers such as "ca" or a category such as "com"). The second level identifies a unique place within the top-level domain. Lower levels of domain may also be used.

domain name Also known as the host name, the domain name is a unique identification for a Web site. Each computer on the Web has a domain name that distinguishes it from the others.

dot Pronounced *dot*, the period character that separates portions of a URL, newsgroup name, or email address. The dot character also separates portions of domain names and IP addresses.

download To copy a file from another computer (usually a server on the Web) to your computer.

drivers Software that sets up some hardware that's connected to your computer. Printer drivers, for example, are needed by your computer so that it can successfully "talk" to the attached printer when you send a Web page or other document to print.

dumb terminal A computer that's attached to a server and can only run programs through that server. When you attach to a Telnet server, for example, you can only use the keyboard and monitor because the program on the server is in control.

email A system in which users can send and receive messages through their computers. Users have their own "mailboxes" that store messages sent by other users. When you sign up with an ISP, you're provided with an email address.

emoticons Combinations of ASCII text, such as letters, punctuation, or symbols used to express emotions during Internet communications.

e-résumé An electronic copy of a résumé that's designed to be stored on a computer.

extranet An intranet to which access has been granted to users outside the company. Many companies grant customers access to selected pages on their intranets.

e-zine An online publication that usually contains original, sometimes offbeat, or unusual content. Most e-zines are not commercial and don't contain advertising.

Favorites A list of marked sites in Internet Explorer to which you can return quickly.

file extension The suffix that follows a computer filename. The file extension generally identifies the file type. For example, most executable files (the ones that run programs) carry an .exe file extension.

firewall   A program, usually an Internet gateway server, that protects an intranet from users from other networks. Firewalls can also limit the Internet sites accessible to users who are accessing the Internet from their company's connection.

frames   A browser feature that enables a user to split a Web page into separate, scrollable windows.

freenet   A system that provides free, public access to the Internet. Freenets are often sponsored or supported by local library systems. Although they don't usually offer all the tools provided by an ISP, freenets give email services and limited access to the World Wide Web.

freeware   Software programs that you can download and use free of charge.

FTP   Short for File Transfer Protocol, a set of rules, or protocol, that controls the transfer of files between computers. Files can be transferred by other Internet protocols, including http://.

GIF file   Pronounced *jiff file* or *giff file*, it's a graphics file that's used in many Web pages. GIF (short for Graphics Interchange Format) was developed by CompuServe. GIF files are great for storing graphics information with a limited range of colors while maintaining a small file size.

Gopher   An older Internet program that is based on a hierarchy of menus and sub-menus.

Gopher Server   The physical server that holds the file or document you request from a Gopher menu.

Gopherspace   The collection of all the inter-connected GOPHER servers in the world.

GUI   Pronounced *gooey*, this is a graphical user interface that enables you to easily interact with a computer via pictures and menu-driven options for performing tasks. Typically, you use your mouse or other pointing device to make choices in a GUI program.

hash   A mathematically designed digest of a message that's sent during the authentication process of a secure Web transaction. Each hash is unique. When the receiving computer receives your message, it runs the same hash function you used. If both hashes aren't identical, the message is rejected. See also **authentication**.

helper application   A program that's installed on your computer and works with your browser. Other than the programs that come with the browser, helper applications are usually run in a separate window (unlike plug-in applications which are integrated with the main browser program). See also **plug-in**.

hit   A successful match in a search tool's database search. See also **search query**.

home page   The first page of a Web site. It usually serves as an index or table of contents for the rest of the site.

HTML   The set of "markup" symbols or codes placed in a file that's designed for display on a Web browser program. Pages you see on the Web are written in HTML.

hyperlink   A word, picture, or other element that you click to move from one Internet location to another. Hyperlinks, usually called *links*, can help you jump to a different location on the same Web page or to a different site.

Hypertext Markup Language (HTML) The set of "markup" symbols or codes placed in a file that's designed for display on a Web browser program. Pages you see on the Web are written in HTML.

IMAP   Short for Internet Message Access Protocol. IMAP is the most current standard protocol for receiving email messages from the mail server. It provides options such as viewing only the header or storing the messages you've read on the mail server.

Internet Architecture Board   A subgroup of Internet Engineering Task Force, the IAB is responsible for setting and overseeing Internet standards. Visit the IAB at www.iab.org/iab on the Web.

Internet Engineering Task Force Called the IETF for short, this organization is made up of network designers, operators, vendors, and researchers. The group is concerned with the evolution of the Internet architecture and the continued smooth operation of the Internet. Visit the IETF at www.ietf.org on the Web.

Internet service provider   Often called an ISP; the company that provides individuals and other companies access to the Internet.

Internet Society   Known as the ISOC, a non-profit, non-governmental organization located in Reston, VA that brings users of the Internet community together. Visit the ISOC at www.isoc.org on the Web.

Internet telephony   The use of the Internet, rather than the traditional telephone company infrastructure and rate structure, to exchange spoken or other telephone information.

InterNIC   The InterNIC, found at www.internic.net, is responsible for registration of domain names, support services, and online publications that summarize recent happenings of interest to Internet users.

intranet   A company's private internal Web site that lets only the people inside that company exchange and access information. An intranet usually looks much like any other site on the World Wide Web.

IP address   The unique number that's assigned to each computer that's connected to the Internet. IP addresses are written as a series of four numbers, separated by periods.

IRC   An Internet system for chatting that involves a set of rules and conventions and client/server software.

IRC network A collection of IRC servers that are banded together (connected) and share chat rooms and individual chatters.

IRC server A computer on the Internet that houses chat rooms.

JPEG file Prounounced *jay-peg*, this file type is used for storing graphics files that contain a full range of colors and is commonly used on Web pages. JPEG is an acronym for Joint Photographics Expert Group.

key In a secure business transaction, the key is actually the code used to scramble and unscramble information such as your credit card number as it's sent over the Internet and received by the merchant.

keywords Words that highlight or describe. In a search query, the keywords are what you're looking for. In an e-résumé, keywords are the nouns that highlight your special talents, skills, and experience.

lag A noticeable delay between the time you type something and when someone else reads it. Additionally, if you have an extremely slow computer or Internet connection, it can be the time between when you type characters and when they appear onscreen.

LAN Short for local area network, a group of computers that are connected, usually at a company, school, or government branch.

LDAP An email protocol that stores and retrieves directory information. Generally, LDAP enables you to search through Internet directories from your Personal Address Book.

link See **hyperlink**.

link anchor The part of a hyperlink that causes the mouse arrow to take the shape of a hand. See also **hyperlink**.

lurking Hanging back and reading the postings of a newsgroup without replying or submitting new postings.

mail servers Electronic postal agents that send, sort, and deliver email messages using special mail protocols.

meta-engine A powerful search tool that looks through multiple search tools to match your search query.

Microsoft Wallet A feature in Internet Explorer that stores your credit card number and other personal information. If you buy from a site that accepts Microsoft Wallet, you don't need to re-type your personal information.

modem Short for MOdulator-DEModulator. A device that translates computer information into sound, and then sends or receives those sounds over telephone lines.

Name resolution The behind-the-scenes process that converts text addresses, such as an email address or URL, to numbered IP addresses. For example, the URL www.mcp.com needs to be translated to IP numbers for your browser to access the site and display it on your computer screen.

Net safe   Keeping away from snoopers, strangers, or violent, lewd, or lascivious Web sites. The term is generally used in conjunction with children.

Net split   A communications break between IRC servers, giving the appearance that everyone's left the chat room.

netiquette   The conventions of politeness expected by Internet users. Although netiquette technically covers the use of the Internet, it's most often referred to in conjunction with newsgroups.

Network News Transfer Protocol   Often called NNTP, the server your Internet service provider uses for news.

newsgroups   Themed Internet bulletin boards for users who share a common interest. Messages are posted to a newsgroup and can be read and replied to by all members of the group.

newsreader   A special software program that enables you to read and reply to Internet newsgroup postings. Both the Internet Explorer and Netscape Communicator suites feature newsreaders. If neither of these suit you, you can choose from a number of third-party newsreader programs.

nickname   A name you use in chat programs instead of your real name.

OCR software   Computer programs that are designed to convert scanned graphics images into text documents.

online backup service   A service that enables you to have data from your hard drive backed up on another, remote computer via the Internet.

page designer   A professional company or individual who designs Web pages for a fee.

patch   A software program designed to correct problems or errors in an existing program or extend the power of the initial program. For example, a patch for Internet Explorer was designed to correct security errors in the original release of the program.

PICS   Platform for Internet Content Selection. A group of people from all walks of life who screens Internet sites and rates the content.

plug-in   A program that is linked to your browser and extends its capability. Plug-ins usually open in the same window as your browser.

POP3   Short for Post Office Protocol 3, the POP3 protocol deals with the way incoming messages are handled on the mail server. After you read a message that's been stored on a POP3 server, the message is deleted from the server (although it can be stored on your computer).

private key   Used in secure business transactions, the private key is a random number that's known by one party or the other—the merchant or the browser.

profile   A file used by your browser to hold all your personal settings and preferences. Individual profiles are especially helpful if more than one person is using the same browser program on a single computer.

Protocol type The rules that computers follow to store and transfer data over the Internet. HTTP:// is the most common protocol, but you might see GOPHER:// or FTP://.

public key Used in secure business transactions, the public key is a random number that's known only by your browser and the merchant.

push technology A technology that delivers information to your computer at preselected times. You can read the information while your computer is still connected to the Internet or you can disconnect and read it later.

résumé bank A Web site that stores electronic résumés. Prospective employers look through résumé banks to select candidates for positions within their companies.

RSAC Short for Recreational Software Advisory Council, this independent, non-profit organization based in Washington, D.C., uses a content advisory system to help parents and educators rate Web sites that may be viewed by children.

scannable A document that's ready to be fed through an electronic device. After a document is scanned, the resulting image file is read by an OCR program and converted to text. See also **OCR software**.

ScreenTip A pop-up explanation of a toolbar button's function that appears when the mouse pointer passes over the button.

search query A keyword or phrase used by the Internet search tool to find matching documents on the Web.

shareware Computer programs you can use free of charge on an evaluation basis, and then pay for if you decide to continue using them.

signature file A file that's attached to outgoing email messages and newsgroup posting. Called a *sig*, a signature file can contain address information, a funny or philosophical comment, or a picture drawn with text characters.

SMTP Short for Simple Mail Transfer Protocol, SMTP is the protocol that processes outgoing email messages.

SOHO business Small office or home office business.

source code The underlying HTML code that instructs your browser to display a Web page.

spam Unsolicited junk email you receive via the Internet.

Sprint Internet Passport The nationwide Internet access service provided by Sprint.

SSL An acronym for Secure Sockets Layer, SSL was developed by Netscape to provide security to buyers and sellers during an online transaction.

standalone chat programs Independent programs that enable you to participate in real-time communication with others on the Internet.

subscribe   The action of adding a newsgroup name to your regular newsgroup list so the newest postings are downloaded to your computer.

TCP/IP   An acronym for Transmission Control Protocol/Internet Protocol, TCP/IP is the preferred way for data to be transferred over the Internet. The sending computer places the data in packets and then sends the packets out. The receiving computer removes the data from the packets and reassembles the data into its original form.

Telnet   A system that enables you to connect to a server and run programs as if you were sitting at its keyboard.

thread   The original posting and collection of related responses in a Usenet newsgroup.

unsubscribe   Removing the name of a newsgroup from your regular newsgroup list. When you unsubscribe to a group, you no longer receive its postings.

upload   The act of submitting a file, in which the receiving computer is not the one originating the transfer.

URL   Pronounced either *you-are-el* or *earl*, the Uniform Resource Locator is the address of a file or other resource you access on the Internet.

Usenet   The collection of more than 32,000 Internet discussion groups that post messages to Internet newsgroups. Your ISP might not carry all the Usenet newsgroups.

virtual LAN   A method of networking remote users via the Internet instead of using a typical local area network.

virus   A computer virus is a malicious program that hides inside another file or the boot sector of your computer. When you use the file, the virus can cause harm to your computer by destroying data and making your system inoperable.

Web-based chat   Web pages that contain chat rooms you can enter and use to communicate with others.

Web hosting   A company that provides space and services for housing Web sites.

Web site   Related collection of Web files that include a beginning file called a home page.

Webcasters   The programs or content providers that deliver the information automatically to your computer. See also **push technology**.

Webring   A group of Web sites that are linked so that you can visit each site, one after the other, eventually returning to the first Web site.

webtop   A window used by Netscape that overlays your regular Windows desktop and contains channel content.

Webzine   The online version of a commercial magazine.

WYSIWYG   Pronounced *wiz-ee-wig*, the letters stand for what you see is what you get. WYSIWYG Web page design programs show you what the end result will look like as the page is created.

Background Information About the Internet

An Internet History Lesson

The amazing thing about the Internet is how quickly it has exploded into our daily lives. When you think about the history of flight, the Wright brothers in Kitty Hawk, North Carolina in the early 1900s probably comes to mind. The history of the automobile goes back even further. Unlike these, the history of the Internet began back in the 1960s. However, it's only been since the early '90s that the Internet has evolved into what we see today.

In its infancy, the Internet was created to carry governmental and military information in case of an atomic blast. Fortunately, the nuclear "event" never materialized. But the fledgling information system surpassed its developer's wildest dreams.

In 1957, the Soviets put a satellite called Sputnik into orbit. The launch surprised the world and shocked the American scientific community. President Dwight D. Eisenhower hurriedly put together a team of the brightest scientific minds in America. The resulting organization, run by the Department of Defense and called the Advanced Research Projects Agency, or ARPA, worked to protect American defense information from a nuclear explosion.

Sputnik and the subsequent Cold War caused a real panic among the U.S military. Nuclear attacks on American cities suddenly seemed possible. One of ARPA's missions was to create a

Storing bits of data in packets

RAND Corporation came up with a revolutionary system that enabled computers to talk to one another. Their idea was to break up large computer transmissions into several smaller pieces. These pieces, called packets, would be sent out through a network of telephone lines connecting numerous computers. The pieces would be reassembled into the original transmission after they arrived at their destination.

Using packets was an ingenious way to transport data. Each packet would begin at some specified source node, and end at a specified destination node. The packets would be able to make their way through the maze of the network of phone lines on an individual basis. If the first destination node was blown to bits, the packet would continue on to another node on the network. Because all the computers on the network were equal to each other, it didn't really matter where the final transmission was reassembled.

network of linked computers that each stored security data and could be accessed by Defense personnel from many locations. In the event of a nuclear strike, the network would still be able to function even if some of the computers were damaged.

The Birth of ARPAnet

In the mid-'60s a test network was assembled. At the same time, the United States government began to take a look at the impact computers could have on the private sectors of education and business. The Pentagon funded ARPA to produce a network of "super-computers" (primitive by today's standards) that would be linked and could easily communicate with one another.

The autumn of 1969 saw the first super-computer installed at UCLA in Los Angeles. Three months later, four computers, called nodes, were linked together on the network, which was nicknamed ARPAnet, after its founders. In 1971, the ARPAnet had 15 nodes, and by 1972, more than 30 more. By connecting to the ARPAnet, researchers and scientists could share one another's computer facilities.

One of the biggest advances of the ARPAnet project was the development of a common language that computers connected to the network could use to talk with one another. This language, called TCP/IP (Transmission Control Protocol/ Internet Protocol) network protocol, became the standard protocol for the ARPAnet. Because all the ARPAnet's computers used TCP/IP to communicate, the details of each node's brand and type were unimportant.

Bigger and Better

Because it was so easy to use TCP/IP, more and more computers joined ARPAnet. In addition to ARPAnet, other, smaller computer networks appeared. In turn, many of these smaller networks linked themselves to ARPAnet. Individuals or companies who did not adhere to ARPAnet's tight standards ran many of the smaller networks. Instead of exchanging information about scientific research and military secrets, the information some-times took a more folksy, conversational tone.

The nodes on the network were often used for the exchange of ideas and gossip. News and personal messages were commonly transmitted to users thousands of miles apart. The ARPAnet became a social haven as well as a scientific one. Mailing lists, a type of broadcasting technique in which one message could be sent automatically to large numbers of network subscribers, sprang up. The most popular mailing list was called SF-LOVERS and contained postings about science fiction.

In 1983, the military portion of ARPAnet splintered off and became MILnet. Without any military influence, ARPAnet grew rapidly. No membership restrictions existed; anyone with a computer, a phone line, and a simple knowledge of TCP/IP could connect. However, because computers were mostly found in colleges and universities, most of the growth took place in the educational sector. Instead of being known as the ARPAnet network, the collection of linked computers was dubbed the "Internet," short for inter-network.

The National Science Foundation Steps In

The '80s brought some key changes to the Internet. In 1984, the National Science Foundation set up a network. The NSFnet provided some great technological advances, including faster and more powerful super-computers to store information. The NSFnet upgraded and expanded every two years after its found-ing. In addition to the NSFnet, the National Institutes of Health, NASA, and the Department of Energy each set up and maintained their own networks.

The NSF decided to link five super-computing centers together to make research easier to complete. Although the NSF tried to enlist ARPAnet's help for the project, ARPAnet was unable to contribute assistance. Instead, the NSF built their own network based on standards set by ARPAnet. After the new network was built, the NSF linked colleges and universities in one region, and then linked each of the regional networks to the super-computing network. In a short time, the heavy network "traffic" generated by all the computers using the new network slowed the response time to a crawl.

As soon as they realized that the new network was too slow, the NSF commissioned an agreement with Merit Corporation, an outside consortium of Michigan educational institutions, to upgrade the physical system. Additionally, Merit Corporation was asked to maintain the administration for the NSFnet. The NSF network soon became the fastest and most reliable network on the Internet. Merit asked for permission to include commercial traffic on the Internet. Although the NSF disagreed at first, after much deliberation they agreed to allow commercial traffic.

In 1989, the funding for ARPAnet expired and the ARPAnet network disappeared. Few people noticed. Almost the entire Internet community had moved to the network run by the NSF.

The Name Game

From the early days of the Internet, keeping track of the aliases of each of the computers connected to a network was a problem. With so many networks and so many computers accessing the networks, the problem of tracking which computer was which rapidly escalated into a nightmare. For example, as far back as the early 1970s, a computer that was called PITT at one location might be called PITT-U at another and PITT-37 at another. Although it was clear that a list of distinct names needed to be maintained, no one would agree what the list should contain and who should control it. Different Internet factions suggested different types of lists—each getting a more hostile response.

Finally, after the bickering became intolerable, the Network Information Center (NIC) stepped in to take control. NIC announced that each site could determine the names of their computers, also called hosts. NIC would step in only if a duplicate name was requested. The warring Internet factions agreed to a truce, and NIC began its involvement in the registration of host names. In fact, NIC still is an active participant in registering Internet names.

The first naming system that NIC developed was labor-intensive and low tech. All the information for each host name was maintained in a file called hosts.txt. Each time a change was made to the file, all the users were expected to obtain and install the updated version on each of their systems. After a short while it was apparent that the name system needed to be revamped.

The earliest plans for the present day Domain Name System appeared in 1981. After several revisions, the plan to use top-level domain names that identified the specific network to which the host belonged was implemented in 1984. So, for example, PITT became PITT.ARPA. Now, two host computers that were part of different networks could have the same "first" name. Considering that a little more than 1,000 host computers existed, using a standard naming convention simplified the process of finding the host computer to which to connect.

Pretty soon, it became apparent that the naming system needed to be tweaked. A major change was instituted. Instead of using the network names such as ARPA or NASA, the names were divided into more basic varieties. Most computer names were assigned on the basis of six Internet "domains": edu, gov, mil, org, net, and com. Edu, gov, and mil represented educational institutions, government sites, and military installations. Names that ended in "org" meant that the host computer belonged to a non-profit organization. Net in a domain name indicated the host was a gateway between networks. The most common domain name, "com," stood for a commercial institution.

The History of Browsers

Only real "techies" were able to access the Internet early on. Users needed to type commands from an onscreen command prompt and interpret what appeared back on their screens. All the information appeared in text format; no colors, pictures, or sounds livened up the display.

The World Wide Web changed all that. The advent of the Web made it easy to get around. Instead of typing a series of commands to move from one Web location to another, users could click a hyperlink to jump from page to page. A Web browser (technically known as a client) is a software package you use to view information from the Internet. A browser program, such as Internet Explorer or Netscape Navigator, acts as the go-between for your computer and the Web. Although such programs have only existed for a short time, they have an interesting history.

Tim Berners-Lee and his colleagues at the CERN European Laboratory for Particle Physics conceived the first Web browser. In 1993, a new browsing program called Mosaic was introduced by the NCSA (National Center for SuperComputing Applications) at the University of Illinois. The inventor of Mosaic was a 22-year-old student named Mark Andreessen. Unlike the old CERN browser, the new client program (Mosaic) featured a graphical user interface. Instead of a plain background and a box in which to type text, Mosaic featured buttons to which users could point and click on to move around.

Mosaic was an instant success. In fact, using Mosaic was so simple that thousands of new users used it to visit the Web. Soon after the introduction of Mosaic, Cello, another GUI browser, appeared. In 1994, most users visited the Web with either Mosaic or Cello. When Windows 95 was introduced, Cello quickly disappeared from the market. Another browser called Winweb came and went around the same time period. In fact, a few scant years later, few people know that Cello or Winweb ever existed. Although Mosaic is still available, its popularity has declined rapidly.

Mark Andreessen and his friends left the NCSA and started Netscape Communications Corporation. In short order, their new browser stunned the Internet community. Netscape introduced a list of new Web browser features, including added support for displaying graphic images, advanced security for Web-based business transactions, the capability to open more than one Web site at a time, and much, much more.

Additionally, Netscape featured mail and news client programs along with its Web browser. Netscape was free for educational and non-commercial use; other users could download and preview it free of charge for an indefinite time. In a short time, Netscape became the undisputed star of the Web browser world.

Microsoft Corporation got into the browser market with the introduction of Internet Explorer. The first version of Internet Explorer caused few ripples in Netscape's pond. The Microsoft browser had only basic features and caused general protection fault errors on many computers. However, over a very short time, Microsoft introduced upgrades to the original Internet Explorer program that made it almost as powerful as Netscape. At one point, the war between the two browsers was so intense that upgrades to each program were introduced within a week of each other. Microsoft was quick to point out that Internet Explorer was completely free with no strings attached. The gap in popularity between the two programs narrowed.

In 1997, Netscape introduced Netscape Communicator and Microsoft introduced Internet Explorer 4. Both packages are rich with new and exciting features and offer much more than basic Web browsing. Although Netscape still holds the lead in popularity, Microsoft has made serious inroads on the quest to becoming the number one browser. Both rival companies have promised even bigger and better features in the near future.

Employer Sites from A to Z

B

If you are really serious about looking for a new career, why not visit some companies on the Web? You save valuable time and shoe leather. Additionally, with a Web visit, you never need to hear "No thanks" or other platitudes.

The companies shown here make up a cross-section of employers who display employment information on their Web pages. Most of the companies are large and might have an office or branch near your home. The advantage to visiting a company's employment or career page is that it generally offers up-to-the-minute opportunities. By the time an ad for the available position appears in the Classified section of the newspaper, some Web-ready soul (like you) might have snagged the job.

If you don't see the company for which you want to work in this appendix, search for that company's URL and visit the site. The job market is volatile; positions open and are filled quickly. A position that was open when this book was written might not be available today.

The following listings are broken down by the following:

- The name of the company
- The URL of the company's employment page or job listing
- A brief description of the typical employment opportunities offered by the company

AT&T

www.att.com/hr/

AT&T has jobs available in many of their divisions, including AT&T Business Multimedia Services, AT&T Information Solutions, and AT&T Wireless. Positions range from sales and marketing jobs, to administrative positions in Human Resources, Accounting, and Finance.

Bristol-Myers Squibb Company

www.bms.com/employ/

Bristol-Myers Squibb Company, a diversified worldwide health and personal care company, has many opportunities, including positions in chemical research and account executives. The site provides information on employee corporate benefits.

Club Med

www.cooljobs.com/clubmed

Club Med manages resorts in many countries and operates tours and cruises. Advertised positions include Resort Administration, Arts and Crafts, Maintenance, and Retail Sales. The site is available in French or English.

DuPont

www.dupont.com/careers/

DuPont, a research and technology company, produces chemicals, polymers, and fibers. Their career site features an ever-changing list of available positions, including jobs that range from technical and scientific to sales associates.

Electronic Arts

www.ea.com/companyinfo/jobs.html

Electronic Arts develops, publishes, and distributes software products and entertainment systems. The site features a search engine to help you search for the right position. (Remember keywords!) Positions include both technical and administrative jobs.

Fujitsu

ext.fujitsu.com/employment/empl.asp

Fujitsu offers employment opportunities all around the world in the field of Information Technology. With operations in more than 100 countries worldwide, the Fujitsu Group seeks people who want to working the fields of technology and business in computing, telecommunications, electronic devices, software, and services.

Greyhound Lines Inc.

www.greyhound.com/jobs.html

Greyhound Lines Inc. is a large intercity bus company. Available positions include Driver Operations, Customer Service Representatives, and Information Technology professionals.

Hewlett-Packard

www.jobs.hp.com/

The Hewlett-Packard site is a comprehensive site that enables you to search for jobs in Canada, the U.S., Europe, Latin America, and Asia Pacific. Hewlett Packard aggressively recruits employees and offers pages for job search and recruiting events.

Intel

www.intel.com/intel/oppty/

If you've heard of a Pentium computer chip, you've heard of Intel. The site provides links to Intel's Hot Jobs, in addition to links to Intel recruiting events and college programs. Job categories include technical positions such as Integrated Circuit Engineering and Manufacturing as well as positions in Marketing and Sales.

JCPenney

www.jcpenney.com/careers/woo/caropps.htm

JCPenney offers you many opportunities to build a rewarding career. The site features available jobs in the Sales and Catalog departments as well as other financial departments.

Komag, Incorporated

www.komag.com/career/career.html

Komag, one of Silicon Valley's largest employers, is a supplier of thin-film media for computer hard drives. Click one of Komag's locations on the world map at their site to view that region's opportunities. Komag's available positions are primarily technical, although clerical and administrative jobs are posted at the site as well.

Lowe's Companies, Inc.

content030e.advantis.com/frames/empopps/findex.htm

Lowe's, a prominent building materials/specialty retailer, plans to have 600 stores open by the year 2000. Positions are available at the General Office as well as at the retail store level.

Microsoft Corporation

www.microsoft.com/jobs/default.asp

If you're using Windows, you know something about Microsoft Corporation. Microsoft actively recruits recent MBA graduates and has available positions in both technical and non-technical areas. The Microsoft career site offers a link to a calendar of dates, places, and times that Microsoft will be recruiting locally.

Nabisco

www.nabisco.com

Start your visit to Nabisco at their Main Street page. Click the link to **Town Hall** and then find employment possibilities by clicking the **Job Opportunities** link. Because Nabisco is a global company producing packaged food, you can pick from available positions in the Headquarters, Data Center, or Bakeries and Field divisions.

Oracle Corporation

www.oracle.com

Oracle produces software for managing information and has more than 14,000 employees worldwide. Begin at the Oracle home page and click the link to **Jobs Online**. When the Jobs Online page appears, click the flag of the country in which you would like to work. Available positions exist in more than 15 employment categories and cover both technical and non-technical positions.

Procter and Gamble

www.pg.com/docCareers/career_ops/

Procter and Gamble sells more than 300 brands in over 140 countries. They offer entry-level career advice and internships. Or, you can search for and apply for one of their worldwide positions.

Quantum Corporation

www.quantum.com/hr/hr.html

Quantum makes computer storage products. Their Employment Opportunities page contains links to pages for College Relations, Current Job Openings, and Benefits, in addition to a page with instructions for applying for a job at Quantum. Choose a Quantum location to view the available positions. Jobs cover a wide range of areas, including positions in finance, administration, marketing, and sales.

Rubbermaid Incorporated

www.rubbermaid.com/corp/careers/rj2main.htm

Rubbermaid, a manufacturer and marketer of consumer products, lists career opportunities at their corporate headquarters in Wooster, Ohio and several other divisions. Positions run the gamut from Auditor to a Technical Facilitator.

Sears

www.sears.com/company/hr/jobpost.htm

Sears, a major retailer, offers positions in Automotive, Information Systems, Mall Management, Store Support, and Staff Support. Additionally, Sears' College Relations Department features a National Management Training program, designed to teach college students many aspects of the retailing business.

Tribune

www.tribune.com/employment/

The jobs listed on the Tribune Opportunities page include jobs located in Chicago, Orlando, and other Tribune sites. The Tribune is a provider of information and entertainment, and its jobs reflect the company's diversity. Available positions include jobs in journalism, accounting and payroll, and sales. Other jobs require expertise or experience in computer technology.

Unisys

www.corp.unisys.com/unisys/jobs.nsf

Unisys is a leader in the information management industry. View available positions broken down by geographic location or search for a job title. Most positions at Unisys are technically oriented and require experience or education in the computer industry.

Vanguard

www.vanguard.com/cgi-bin/Employ

Vanguard is a large company, dealing in mutual funds. Available openings are listed by geographic location and then broken down further into categories such as Customer Service and Management/Executive.

Wal-Mart

careers.wal-mart.com/

The Wal-Mart career site, called Careers@Wal-Mart, features information about the company and links to positions in its Retail Division and Information Systems departments. Also included on the page is a link to Wal-Mart's College Recruiting page.

Xicor

www.xicor.com/

Xicor is pioneering the application of field-alterable technologies in new markets such as linear and microcontroller peripherals. To get to the Career Opportunity frame, click the link on the menu at the left side of the main page. Although most of the positions require technical expertise, jobs like Material Specialist Stores that require mailroom and shipping and handling experience appear from time to time.

Yahoo! Inc.

www.yahoo.com/docs/hr

Yahoo! Inc. is an Internet media company with an intuitive, up-to-date and efficient guide to the Internet. Yahoo! calls their employees "Yahoo!s." Their Employment Opportunities page lists positions in technical areas, such as Engineering and Graphic Arts, and non-technical areas such as Sales. Also included are positions for Surfing Yahoo!s, people who review Web sites for inclusion into Yahoo's giant Internet index.

ZAC Catalogues

www.zaccatalog.com/jobs.htm

ZAC, based in Clearwater, Florida, is one of the leading direct sellers of software development tools. The positions on ZAC's site reflect the company's immediate hiring needs and can range from Customer Service Specialist to Director of Marketing.

Shopper's Guide

E-commerce is changing the way we shop. Visit the sites listed here to find a wide variety of goods and services.

The listings are broken down first by category, and then by the following:

- The name of the company
- The URL
- A brief description of how the site is organized or what you can expect to find

Apparel

L.L. Bean

www.llbean.com

L.L. Bean offers more than 600 of its most popular products on a Web site that's easy to navigate. The merchandise is divided into clearly defined categories and is accompanied by photographs and descriptions. If you don't want to order online, you can request a snail mail catalog.

Lands' End

www.landsend.com

The Lands' End site is more like a community than a store. In addition to providing clothing, shoes, and luggage, you can arrange a vacation or tour through the online travel service. Sign up to receive a monthly Lands' End newsletter or visit Dodgeville, Lands' End's online community. Kids can enter a poetry contest and compete for prizes for themselves and their school.

Fredericks of Hollyweb

www.viamall.com/fredholly

The famous lingerie catalog of Frederick's of Hollywood makes online sizzle. You can find lingerie, shoes, wigs, and gifts at this hot site. There's even a special plus-size collection of fashions.

Eddie Bauer

www.ebauer.com

Shop EB, Eddie Bauer's online catalog, is one of the best shopping sites on the Web. If you plan to shop at the site again, register for EB Exclusive, which stores your personal information such as important gift-giving dates. Or, set up email reminders of important dates.

Bedding and Bath Accessories

Pacific Coast

www.pacificcoast.com

Pacific Coast features natural, allergy-free, down pillows and comforters. After a hard day on the Internet, you can fall asleep in comfort and style with products from this site. Shop securely in Pacific Coast's online store, or find a retail store near you that carries their products.

Chadder & Co.

www.pncl.co.uk/chadder

How about luxurious bathroom fittings from one of England's suppliers of fine bathrooms? The prices are in British currency and don't include tax, duties, or shipping costs. Still, it's fun to look at the pictures of elegant fixtures and imagine them in your dream house.

Books

Amazon.com

www.amazon.com

A trip to Amazon.com, the leading online bookseller, can take hours. Books at this site are usually discounted. Search the site by author, title, or subject for any book in the extensive catalog. Amazon offers great personalization features for repeat customers. Book prices are discounted.

Macmillan Computer Publishing

www.mcp.com

The Macmillan online bookstore features more than 2,000 books and software products from some of the best names in the business: Adobe, Borland, Lycos, Netscape, New Riders, Que, Sams, Ziff-Davis Press, and others. You can use the search function to search for the right computing book. Visit the Software Super-Store for products designed to help you use your computer.

Barnes and Noble

www.barnesandnoble.com

A visit to the Barnes and Noble site is more than a trip to a book store. You can participate in a literary forum, read live online interviews, or search their extensive catalog. Barnes and Noble's

Personalized Book Recommendations suggest books just for you, based on your answers to a brief questionnaire.

Bargain Book Warehouse

`store.bargainbookwarehouse.com/`

You'll find savings up to 80% on all kinds of popular fiction and non-fiction books, both in and out of print. The site is designed for easy navigation. Although the catalog of available books is not as extensive as either Amazon or Barnes and Noble, you're likely to find the book you want.

Cars

Microsoft CarPoint

`carpoint.msn.com`

Although you might not want to buy a car online, you can do all the preliminary shopping at Microsoft CarPoint. CarPoint's Surround Video feature enables you to explore the interiors of most of the cars on the market. You can also use the CarPoint loan calculator to find out if you can afford the car you want.

Online Auto

`www.onlineauto.com`

If you've got an idea of the model and make of the car you would like to buy, visit Online Auto to confirm your choices. Online Auto features links to car dealers which can be sorted by state or vehicle. Online Auto also features free used car ads.

Computers

Computer Discount Warehouse

`www.cdw.com`

A no-frills site for the serious computer shopper. The Search, Browse, and Compose features help you find the best deal. If you want to be notified of special deals, sign up for the Buyer's Edge newsletter. Reviews and tips on the latest and greatest equipment are maintained on the site, so you can read about a product before you buy.

CompUSA

www.compusa.com

The computer superstore scores an online hit. Products are accompanied by detailed descriptions, so you're sure you're getting exactly what you want. While you're at the site, you can enter a trivia contest. A children's department has its own outer-space design. PC Modem, the online computer expert, answers any technical questions you might have.

Insight

www.insight.com

Hardware, software, and online technical support are packed into this great site. You can find daily specials on the latest and greatest computer equipment. Click a link to visit the Hard Drive-in Theatre for help picking the right hard drive for your computer. For amusement, visit the Insight Cybertainment center.

Entertainment

Reel

www.reel.com

Reel is the largest video store on the Web. With more than 35,000 videos for rent and 80,000 for sale, you're sure to find a movie you want to see. Searching for movies with Reel's advanced search tools is almost more fun than seeing the movie itself. For something different, sign up for Reel's virtual classes in film theory at their online Cinema U.

@Tower

www.towerrecords.com

The Tower Records online music store is one of the Web's hot spots. In addition to a great collection of CDs, you'll find special promotions and giveaways. If you need to search the catalog of CD titles, the Quick Search feature makes it easy to find just what you want.

Music Boulevard

www.musicblvd.com

Visiting this site of more than 185,000 CDs and tapes is almost like watching MTV. Listen to selected tracks before you buy. The site is organized into seven departments. Browse through all of them and look at the collection of cover art.

Food

NetGrocer

www.netgrocer.com

Shop with NetGrocer and receive your groceries by Federal Express the next day. NetGrocer, the first online grocery store, is a site to take seriously. A cash register keeps a running tab of your purchases as you add things to your virtual shopping basket. Items are sorted by 14 categories, including brand name, price, calories, and fat content.

Candy Land Warehouse

www.candylandwarehouse.com

Like hard candy? Many varieties are available at this online confectionery, including low calorie and sugarless flavors. The prices are better than you'll find locally. Enter the contest to win free candy.

Wilderness Coffee House

www.wilderness-coffee.com

The Web version of a famous Minnesota coffee store is designed so well that you'll swear you can smell coffee brewing when you visit the site. The prices of all items are clearly marked. You'll also learn the origin and history of the coffee beans. For online orders, the beans are roasted every Wednesday to ensure that you'll get fresh coffee.

Flowers

Virtual Florist

www.virtualflorist.com

Send beautiful bouquets anywhere from this Canadian-based florist. Or, as an added twist, send a floral image with a personalized greeting free of charge. Virtual Florist sends an email to the recipient, with a special URL. The virtual bouquets are easy to send and everyone loves getting one.

1-800-Flowers

www.1800flowers.com

With more than 150 floral arrangements and gifts to look through, it's easy to send someone a special gift. Read the online magazine, called Fresh Thoughts, for tips on caring for your flowers, the proper type of arrangement to send for a specific reason, and even the appropriate message to write on the card. If you want 1-800-Flowers to help you out, sign up for the Gift Reminder Service that alerts you five days before you need to send a bouquet.

Pets

The Dog House Online Emporium

www.thedogbakery.com

This site features gourmet foods for dogs. Treat your pet to a special goodie from the Gourmet Pet Bakery. Or buy your pooch some special beef taffy or a basted turkey foot. There's even a section to buy yourself a cute, non-edible gift.

Aardvark Pet

www.aardvarkpet.com

Featured as a site with gifts for pets and the people who love them, you're sure to find something for your favorite two or four-footed friend at Aardvark. The inventory is extensive and fun. In addition to the standard cat and dog supplies, you can find reasonably priced supplies for hamsters, and birds. The Gifts for People section includes apparel, software, jewelry, and toys.

Sewing and Needlework

Sarah Howard Stone Online Sewing Catalog

www.sarahhowardstone.com

This site has something for anyone who enjoys sewing at Sarah Howard Stone. Choose from patterns, notions, fabrics, ribbons, and lace. You can even buy gifts and jewelry from the site. Visit the gallery to see finished projects.

Vermillion Stitchery

www.vsccs.com

This site is a counted-cross stitcher's dream. Charts with all different types of designs are available at this site. You can even send away for a free flower chart, which changes monthly.

Crafts Galore

www.craftsgalore.com

With a catalog of more than 19,000 craft items, Crafts Galore has everything for the Webcrafter. The site is designed with buttons and lots of cute touches. You'll feel like you're visiting with old friends when you tour the site.

Toys

FAO Schwarz

www.faoschwarz.com

The ultimate online toy store has products for kids and adults. The site features challenging contests and great giveaways, as well as the best collection of toys in the world. You can shop at the site or send for a catalog.

Toytropolis

www.toytropolis.com

Toytropolis sells upscale toys at reasonable prices. Many of the toys featured at the site are award-winning classics from around the world. You'll find toys from Brio and Playmobil along with Japanese Tamagotchis. If you can't find an item at Toytropolis, you can ask them to locate it for you.

Index

Q